BEAUTY AND ♦ THE BEAST OF PARADISE LOST

3

KAORI YUKI

Synopsis

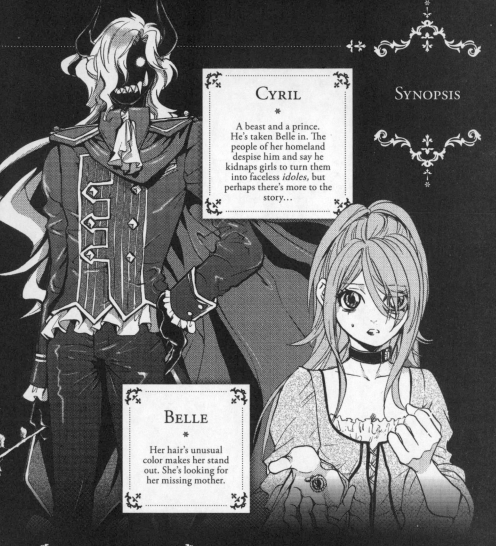

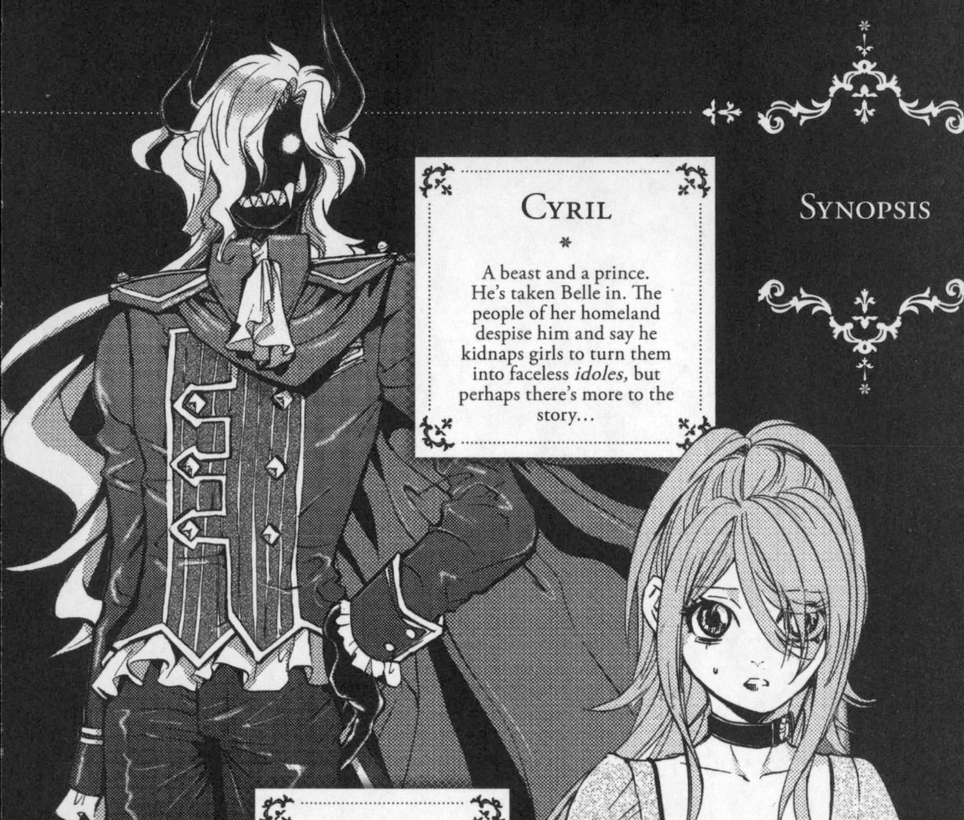
Cyril
A beast and a prince. He's taken Belle in. The people of her homeland despise him and say he kidnaps girls to turn them into faceless *idoles,* but perhaps there's more to the story…
Belle
Her hair's unusual color makes her stand out. She's looking for her missing mother.

The Story Thus Far

When Belle went out in search of her lost mother, she nearly died. However, Cyril saved her and made her his seamstress. Now she lives with him and his servants in his castle Eglantier, a refuge from the world that would persecute them for the monstrous forms of la Médium's curse. As she comes to know Cyril better, Belle finds herself falling in love with him. She then discovers he has a fiancée, also named Belle, who has been trapped in an eternal slumber. Now, Cyril has set out for his homeland of Issus at la Médium's invitation, and Belle is following not far behind. She soon encounters someone she believes to be her mother…but it is, in truth, none other than la Médium herself!

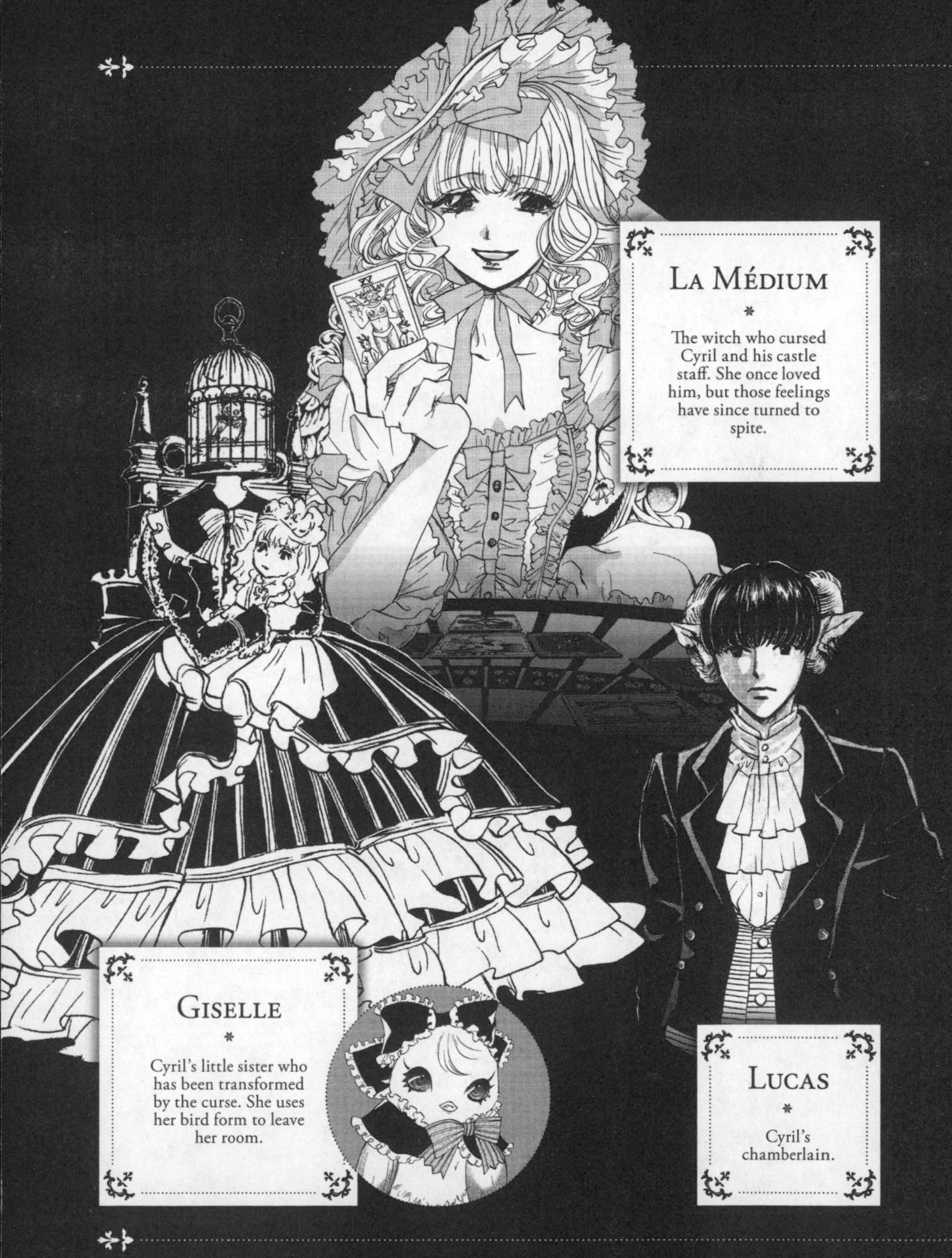

La Médium
The witch who cursed Cyril and his castle staff. She once loved him, but those feelings have since turned to spite.
Giselle
Cyril's little sister who has been transformed by the curse. She uses her bird form to leave her room.
Lucas
Cyril's chamberlain.

La belle et la bête
du paradis perdu

Table des matières

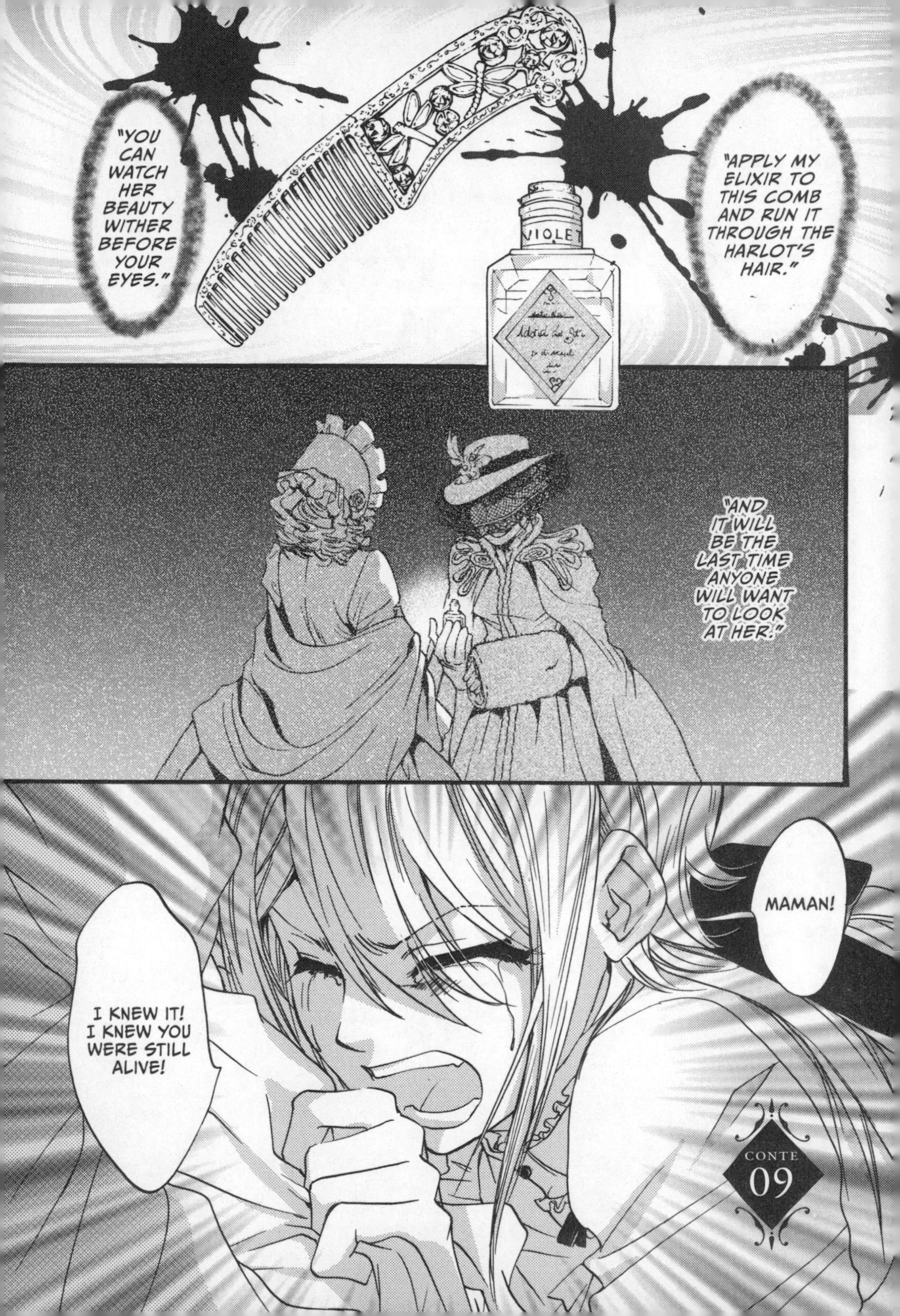
"APPLY MY ELIXIR TO THIS COMB AND RUN IT THROUGH THE HARLOT'S HAIR."
VIOLET
"YOU CAN WATCH HER BEAUTY WITHER BEFORE YOUR EYES."
"AND IT WILL BE THE LAST TIME ANYONE WILL WANT TO LOOK AT HER."
MAMAN!
I KNEW IT! I KNEW YOU WERE STILL ALIVE!
CONTE
09

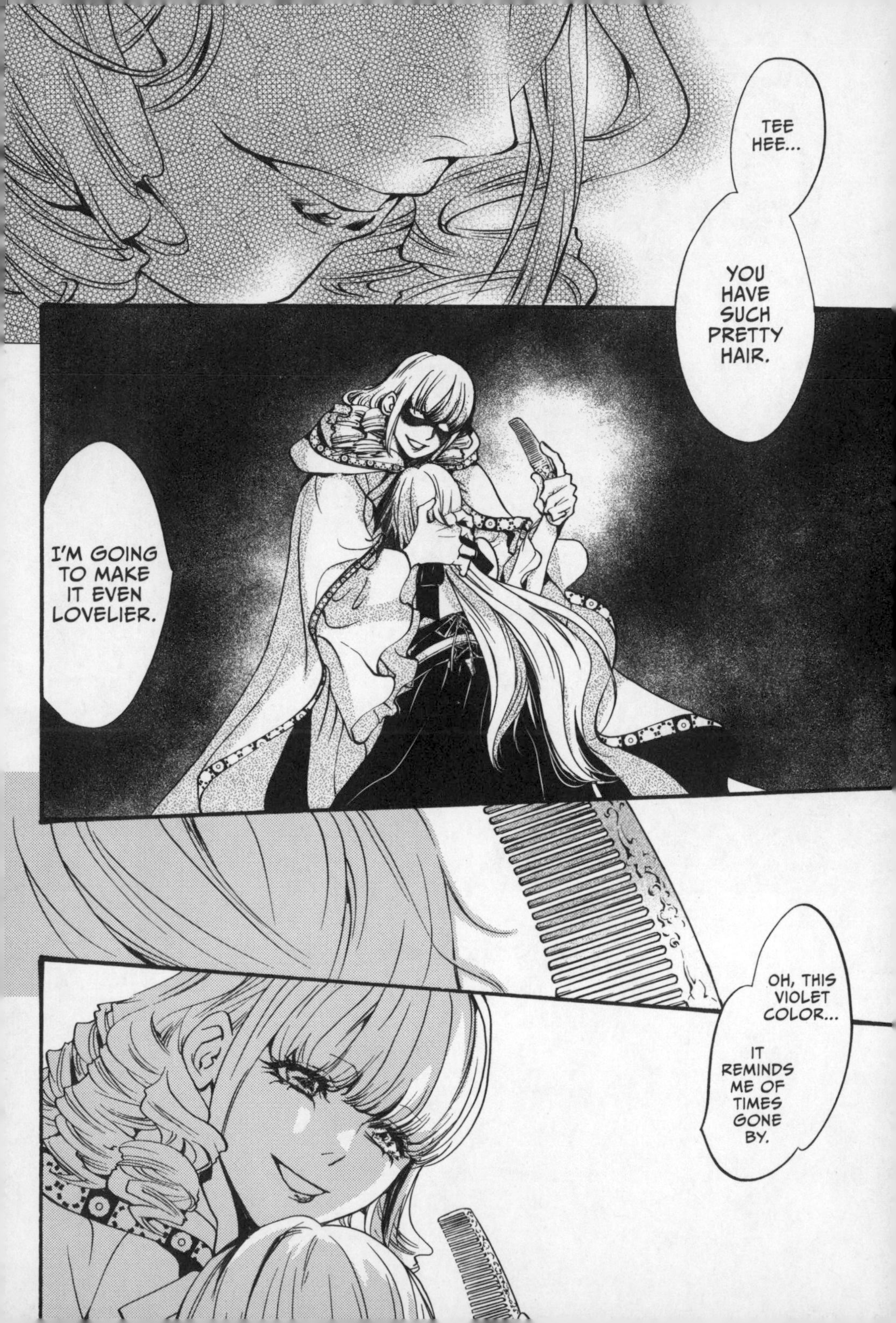
TEE HEE...
YOU HAVE SUCH PRETTY HAIR.
I'M GOING TO MAKE IT EVEN LOVELIER.
OH, THIS VIOLET COLOR...
IT REMINDS ME OF TIMES GONE BY.

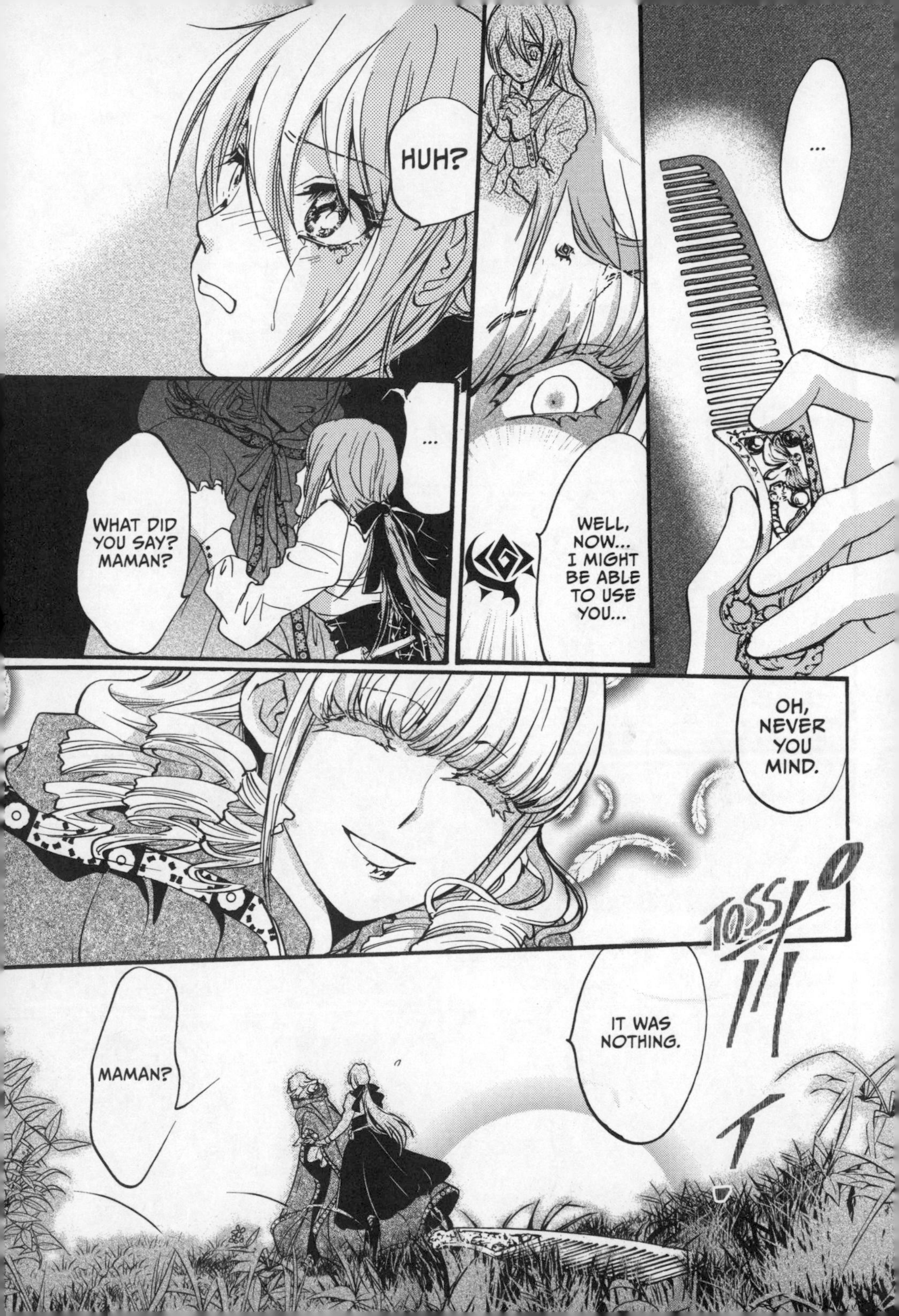
...
HUH?
WELL, NOW... I MIGHT BE ABLE TO USE YOU...
...
WHAT DID YOU SAY? MAMAN?
OH, NEVER YOU MIND.
TOSS
IT WAS NOTHING.
MAMAN?

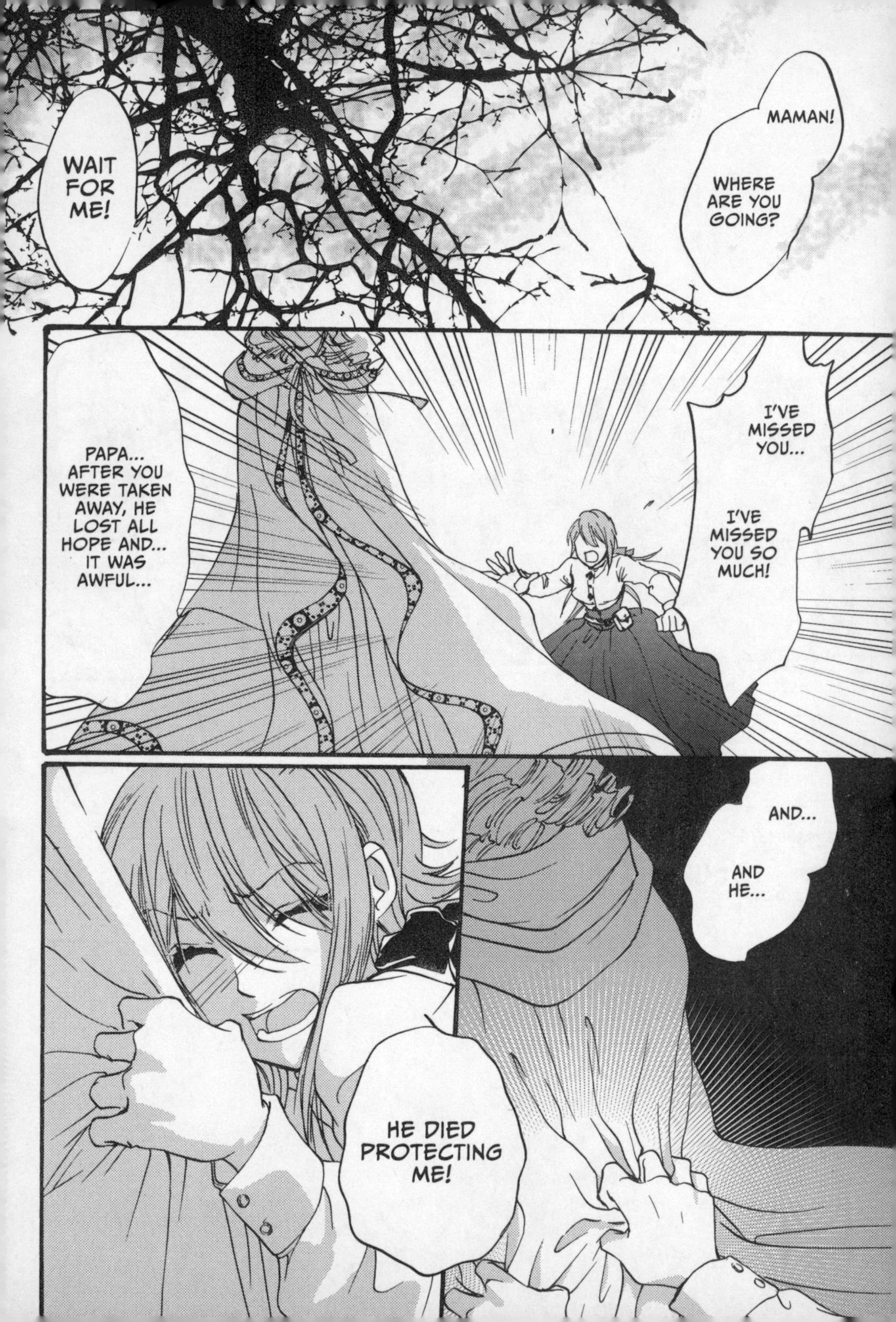
MAMAN!
WHERE ARE YOU GOING?
WAIT FOR ME!
I'VE MISSED YOU...
I'VE MISSED YOU SO MUCH!
PAPA... AFTER YOU WERE TAKEN AWAY, HE LOST ALL HOPE AND... IT WAS AWFUL...
AND...
AND HE...
HE DIED PROTECTING ME!

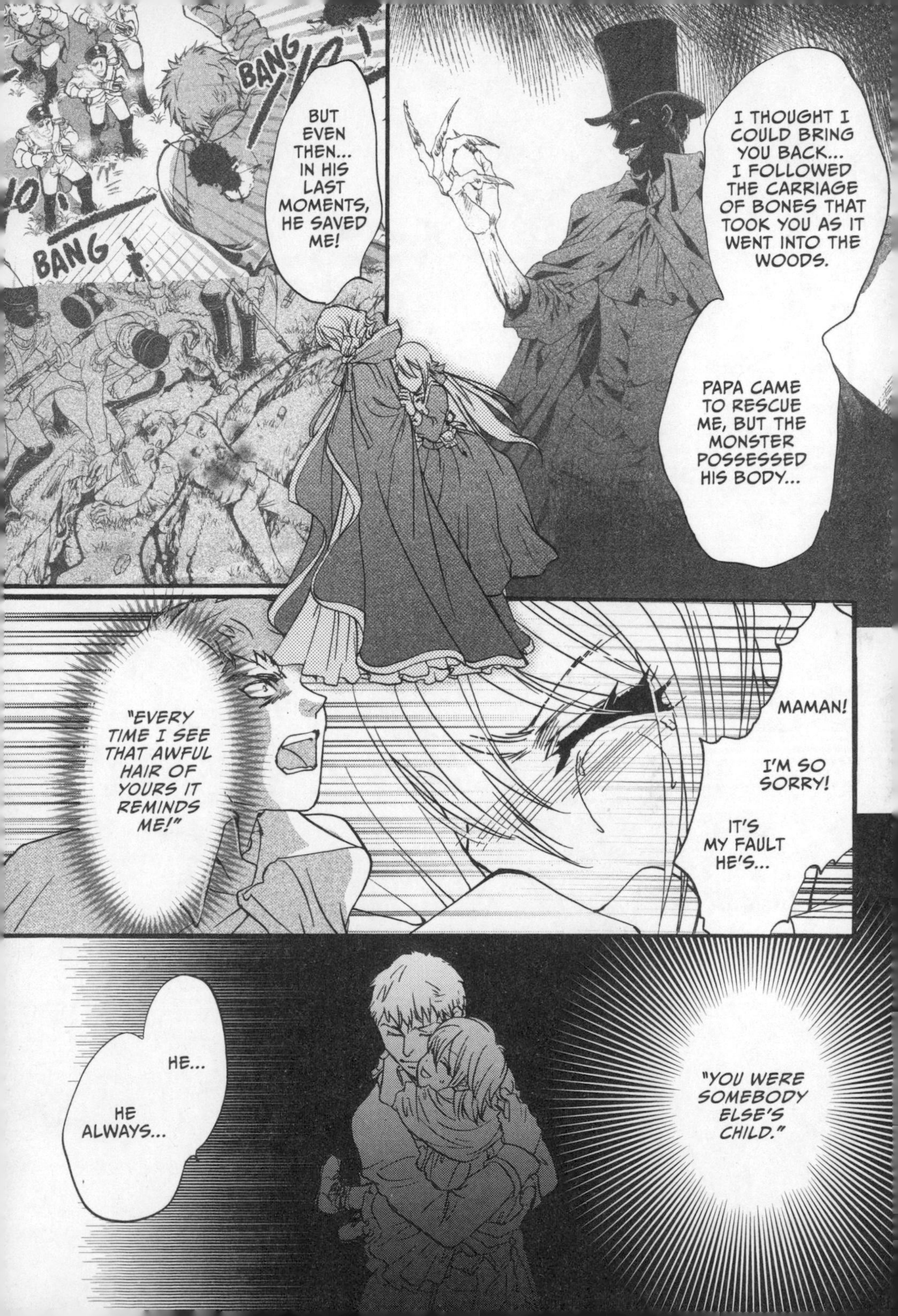
I THOUGHT I COULD BRING YOU BACK... I FOLLOWED THE CARRIAGE OF BONES THAT TOOK YOU AS IT WENT INTO THE WOODS.
PAPA CAME TO RESCUE ME, BUT THE MONSTER POSSESSED HIS BODY...
BANG
BUT EVEN THEN... IN HIS LAST MOMENTS, HE SAVED ME!
BANG
MAMAN!
I'M SO SORRY!
IT'S MY FAULT HE'S...
"EVERY TIME I SEE THAT AWFUL HAIR OF YOURS IT REMINDS ME!"
"YOU WERE SOMEBODY ELSE'S CHILD."
HE...
HE ALWAYS...

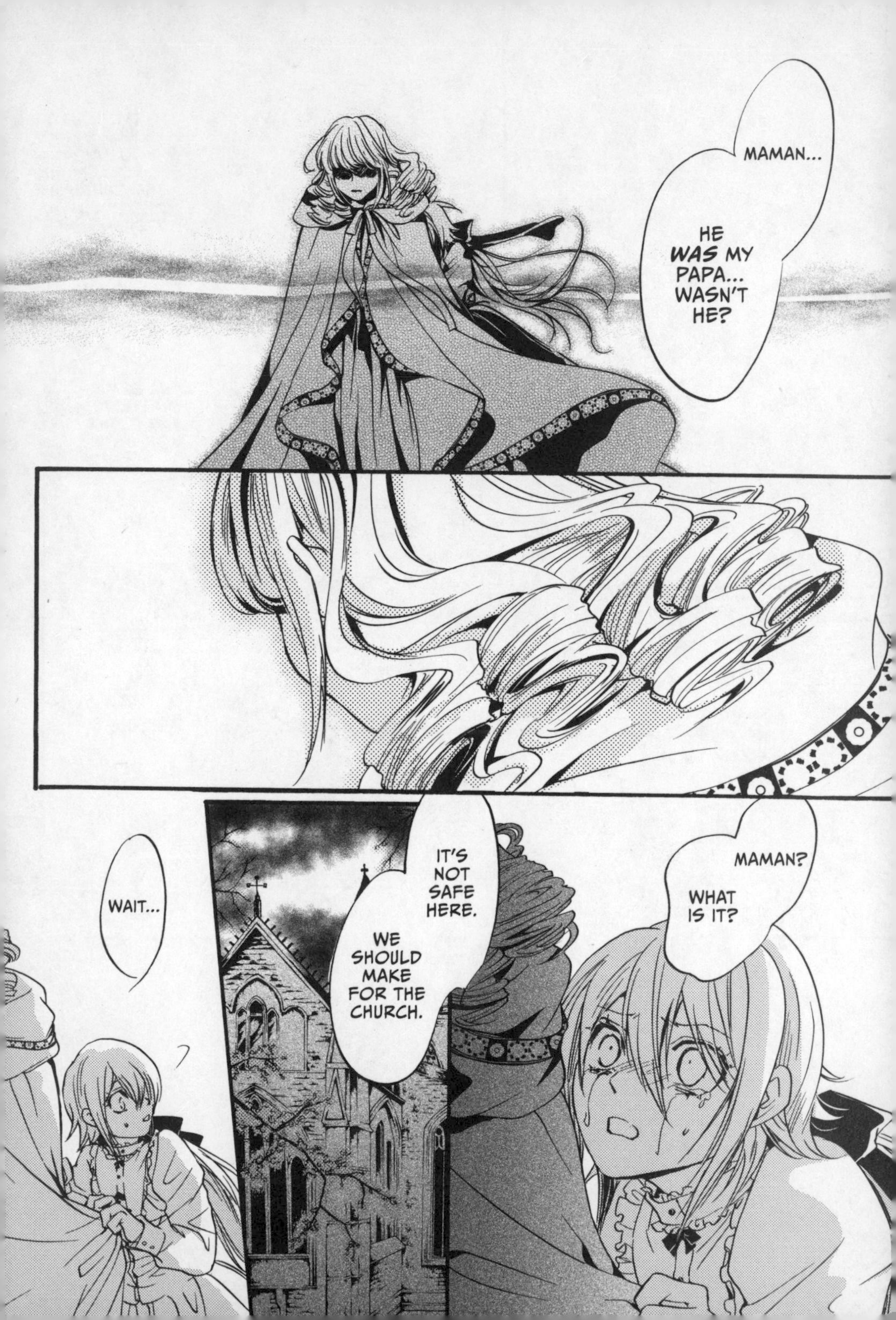
MAMAN...
HE *WAS* MY PAPA... WASN'T HE?
MAMAN?
WHAT IS IT?
IT'S NOT SAFE HERE.
WE SHOULD MAKE FOR THE CHURCH.
WAIT...

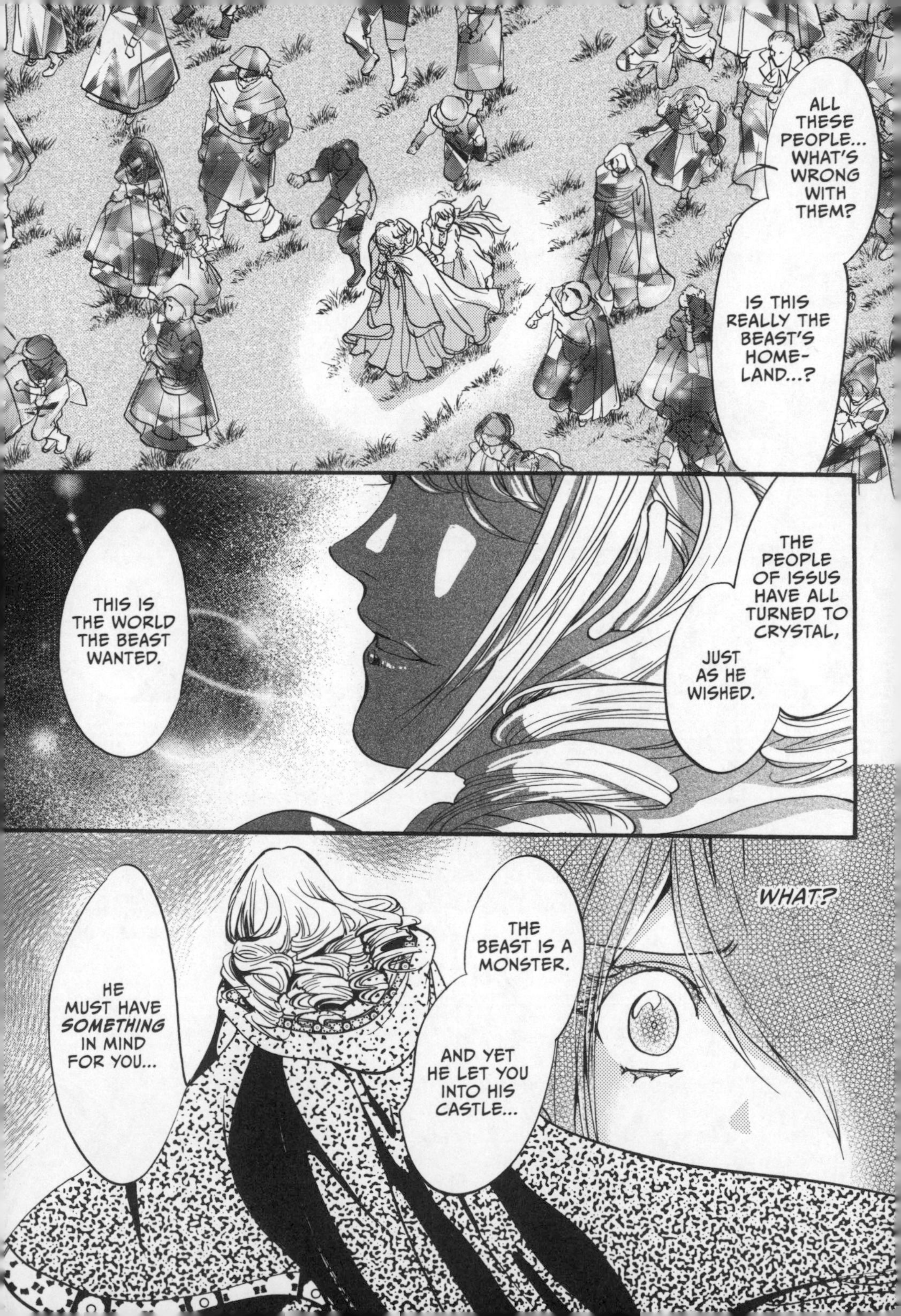
ALL THESE PEOPLE... WHAT'S WRONG WITH THEM?
IS THIS REALLY THE BEAST'S HOME-LAND...?
THE PEOPLE OF ISSUS HAVE ALL TURNED TO CRYSTAL,
JUST AS HE WISHED.
THIS IS THE WORLD THE BEAST WANTED.
WHAT?
THE BEAST IS A MONSTER.
AND YET HE LET YOU INTO HIS CASTLE...
HE MUST HAVE *SOMETHING* IN MIND FOR YOU...

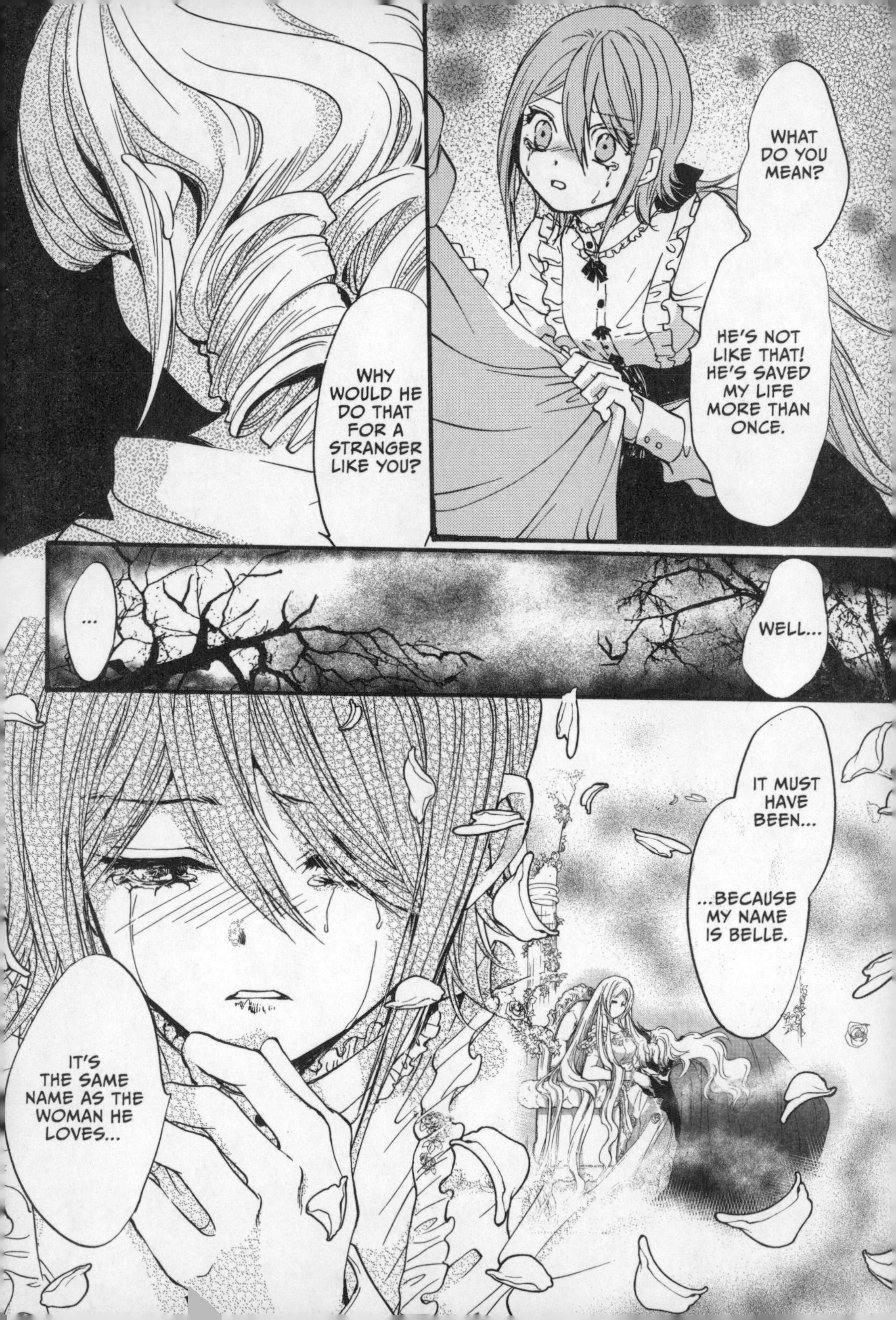
WHAT DO YOU MEAN?
HE'S NOT LIKE THAT! HE'S SAVED MY LIFE MORE THAN ONCE.
WHY WOULD HE DO THAT FOR A STRANGER LIKE YOU?
WELL...
...
IT MUST HAVE BEEN...
...BECAUSE MY NAME IS BELLE.
IT'S THE SAME NAME AS THE WOMAN HE LOVES...

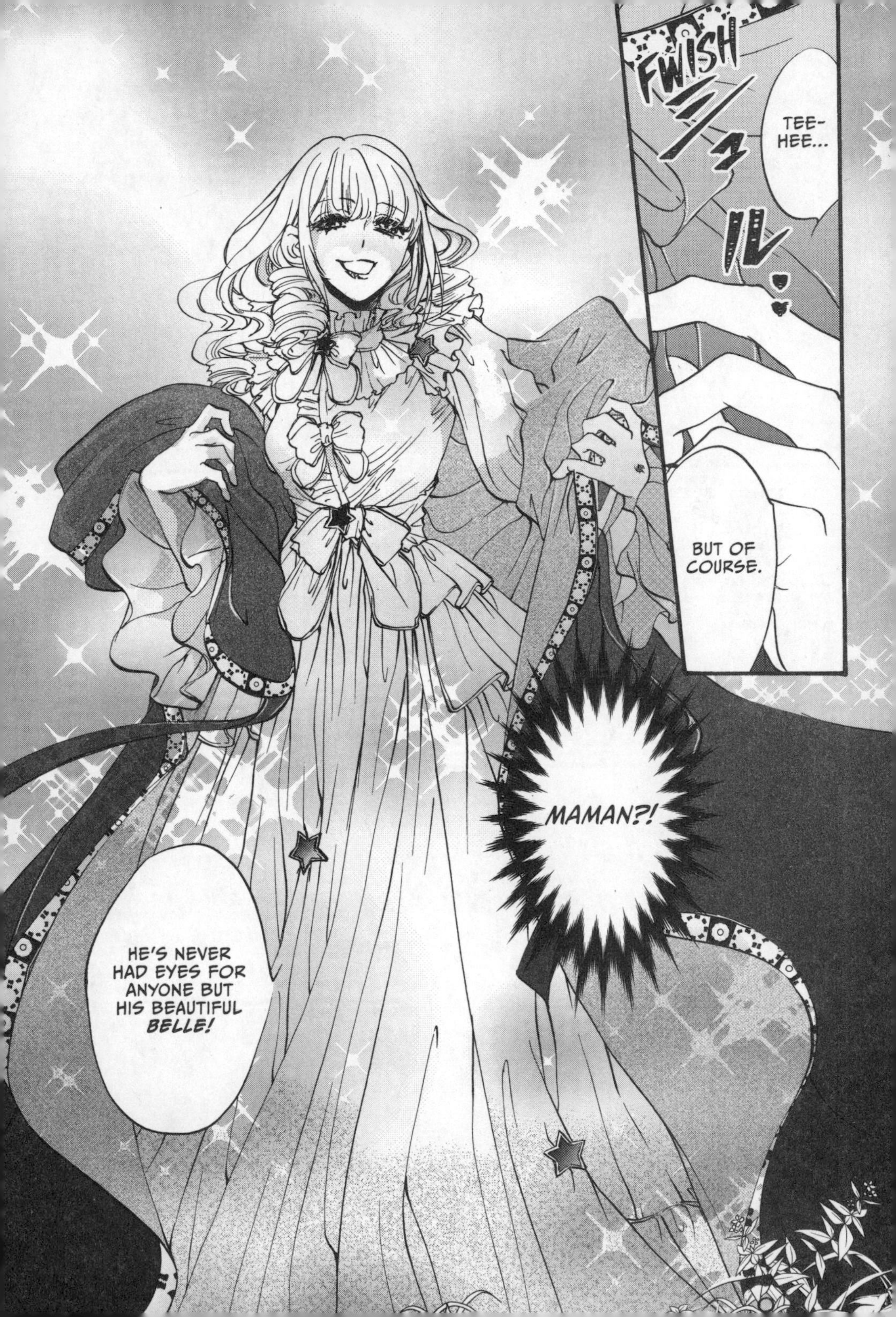
FWISH
シュル
TEE-HEE...
BUT OF COURSE.
MAMAN?!
HE'S NEVER HAD EYES FOR ANYONE BUT HIS BEAUTIFUL *BELLE!*

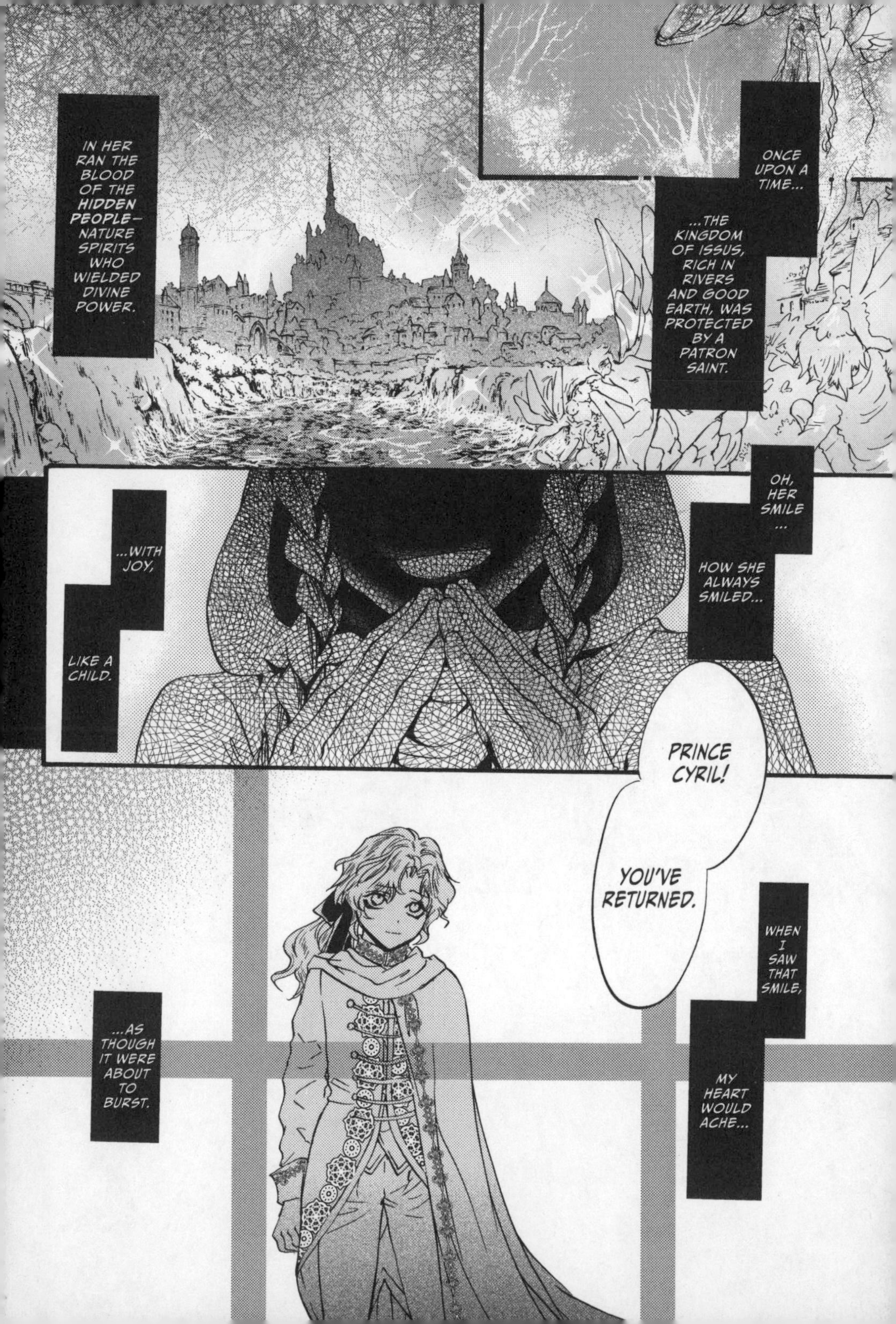
ONCE UPON A TIME...
...THE KINGDOM OF ISSUS, RICH IN RIVERS AND GOOD EARTH, WAS PROTECTED BY A PATRON SAINT.
IN HER RAN THE BLOOD OF THE HIDDEN PEOPLE—NATURE SPIRITS WHO WIELDED DIVINE POWER.
OH, HER SMILE...
HOW SHE ALWAYS SMILED...
...WITH JOY,
LIKE A CHILD.
PRINCE CYRIL!
YOU'VE RETURNED.
WHEN I SAW THAT SMILE,
MY HEART WOULD ACHE...
...AS THOUGH IT WERE ABOUT TO BURST.

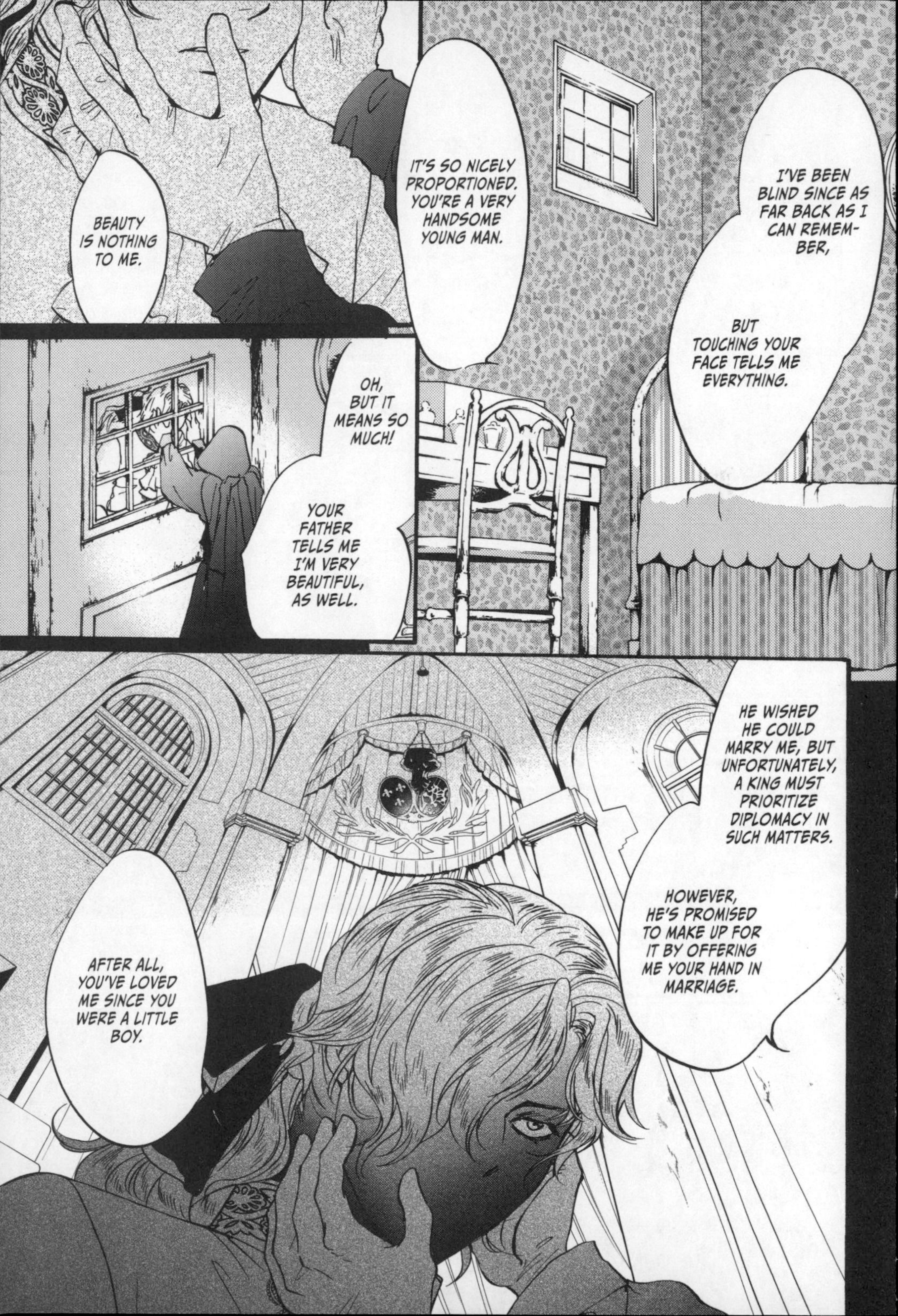
I'VE BEEN BLIND SINCE AS FAR BACK AS I CAN REMEMBER,
BUT TOUCHING YOUR FACE TELLS ME EVERYTHING.
IT'S SO NICELY PROPORTIONED. YOU'RE A VERY HANDSOME YOUNG MAN.
BEAUTY IS NOTHING TO ME.
OH, BUT IT MEANS SO MUCH!
YOUR FATHER TELLS ME I'M VERY BEAUTIFUL, AS WELL.
HE WISHED HE COULD MARRY ME, BUT UNFORTUNATELY, A KING MUST PRIORITIZE DIPLOMACY IN SUCH MATTERS.
HOWEVER, HE'S PROMISED TO MAKE UP FOR IT BY OFFERING ME YOUR HAND IN MARRIAGE.
AFTER ALL, YOU'VE LOVED ME SINCE YOU WERE A LITTLE BOY.

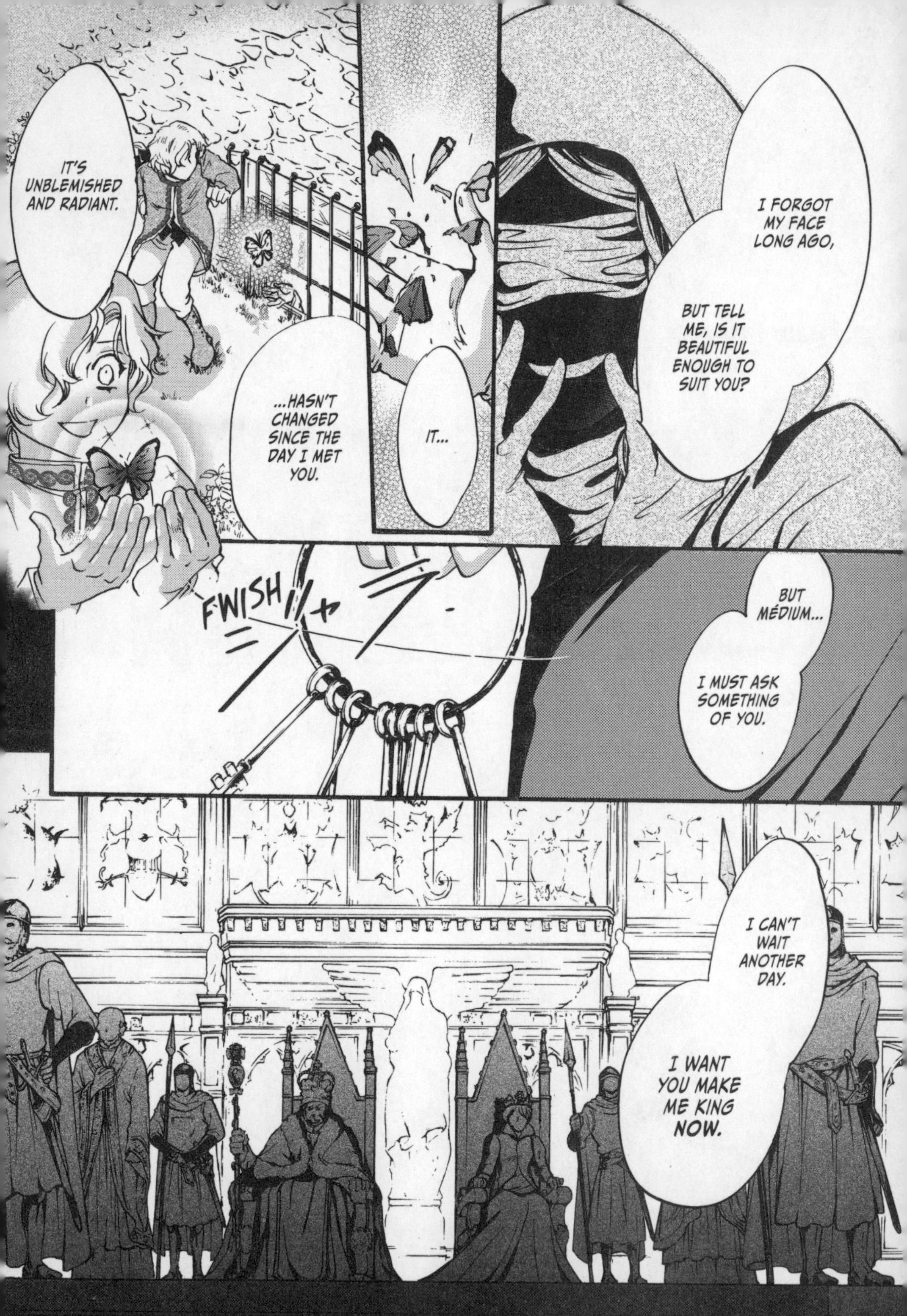
I FORGOT MY FACE LONG AGO,
BUT TELL ME, IS IT BEAUTIFUL ENOUGH TO SUIT YOU?
IT...
...HASN'T CHANGED SINCE THE DAY I MET YOU.
IT'S UNBLEMISHED AND RADIANT.
BUT MÉDIUM...
I MUST ASK SOMETHING OF YOU.
FWISH
I CAN'T WAIT ANOTHER DAY.
I WANT YOU MAKE ME KING NOW.

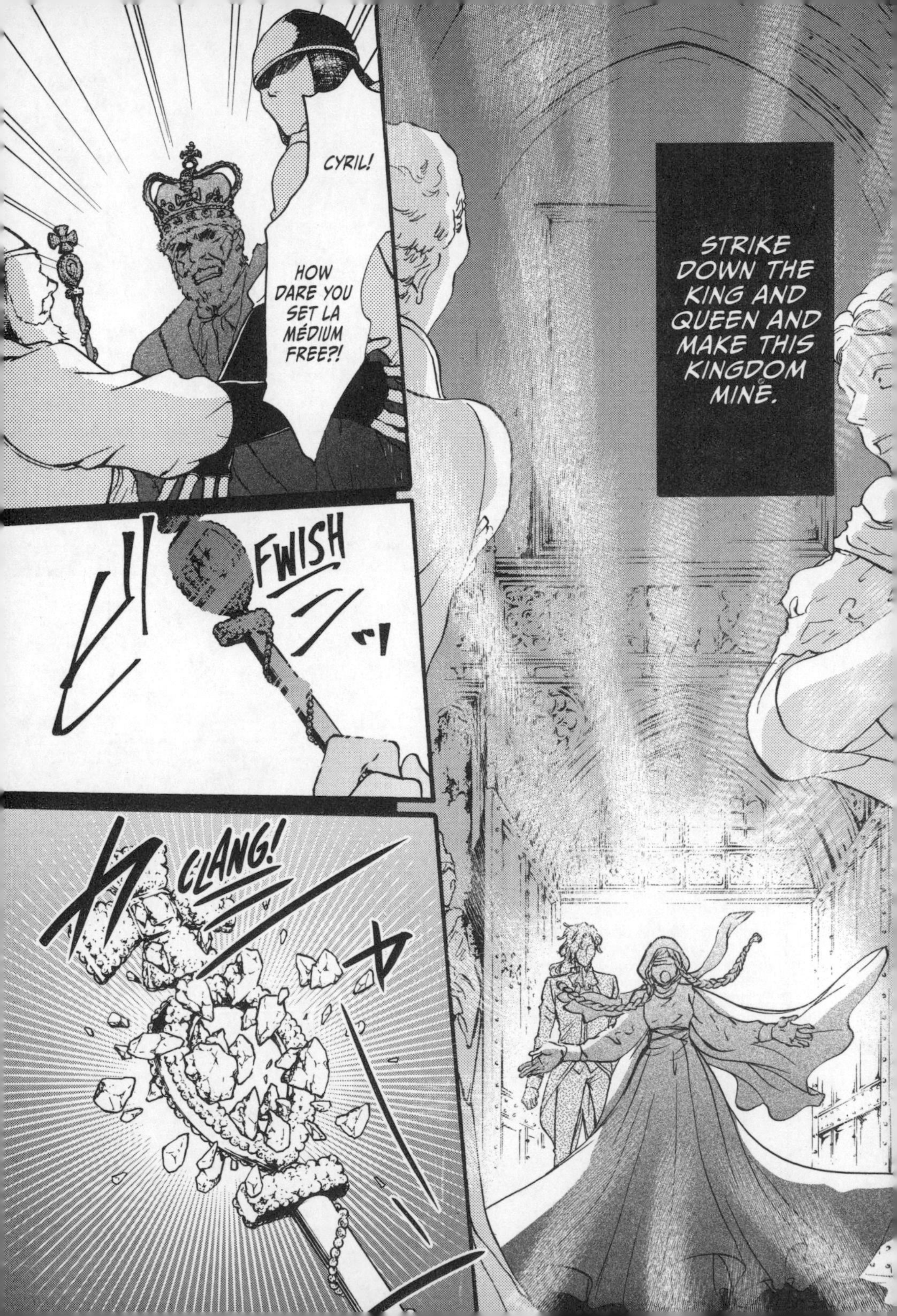
STRIKE DOWN THE KING AND QUEEN AND MAKE THIS KINGDOM MINE.
CYRIL!
HOW DARE YOU SET LA MÉDIUM FREE?!
FWISH
CLANG!

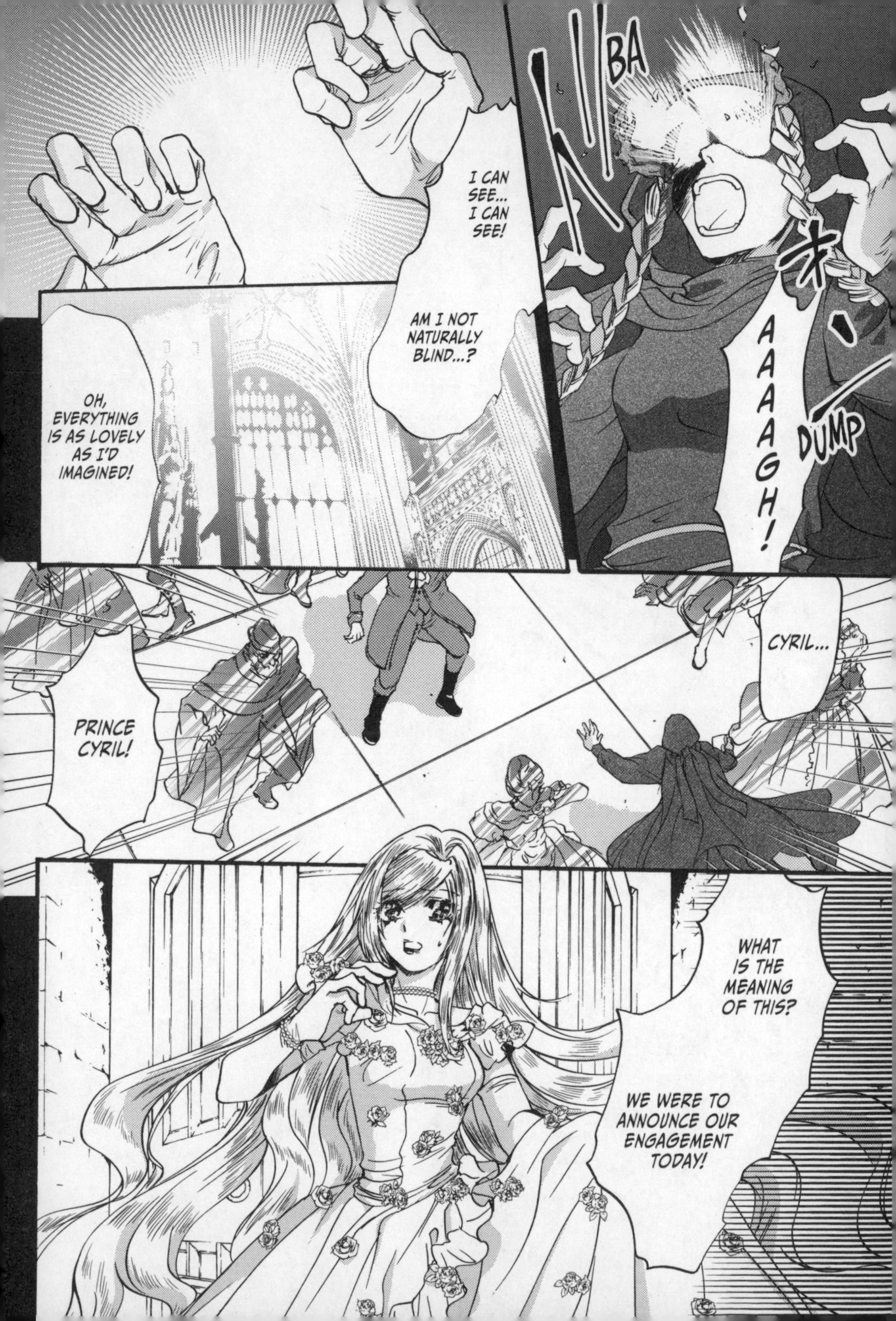
BA
AAAAAGH!
DUMP
I CAN SEE... I CAN SEE!
AM I NOT NATURALLY BLIND...?
OH, EVERYTHING IS AS LOVELY AS I'D IMAGINED!
CYRIL...
PRINCE CYRIL!
WHAT IS THE MEANING OF THIS?
WE WERE TO ANNOUNCE OUR ENGAGEMENT TODAY!

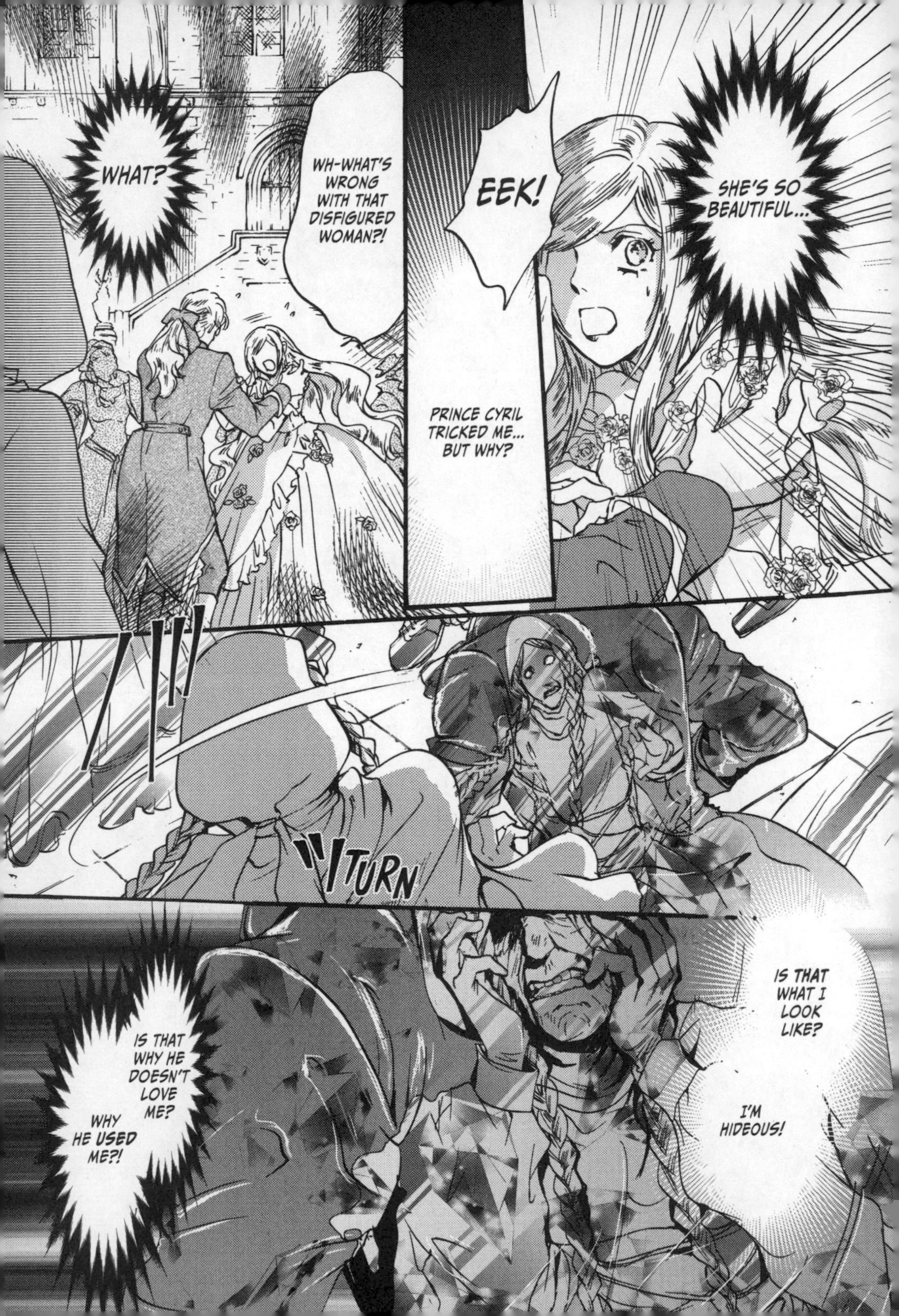
SHE'S SO BEAUTIFUL...
EEK!
PRINCE CYRIL TRICKED ME... BUT WHY?
WH-WHAT'S WRONG WITH THAT DISFIGURED WOMAN?!
WHAT?
TURN
IS THAT WHAT I LOOK LIKE?
I'M HIDEOUS!
IS THAT WHY HE DOESN'T LOVE ME?
WHY HE USED ME?!

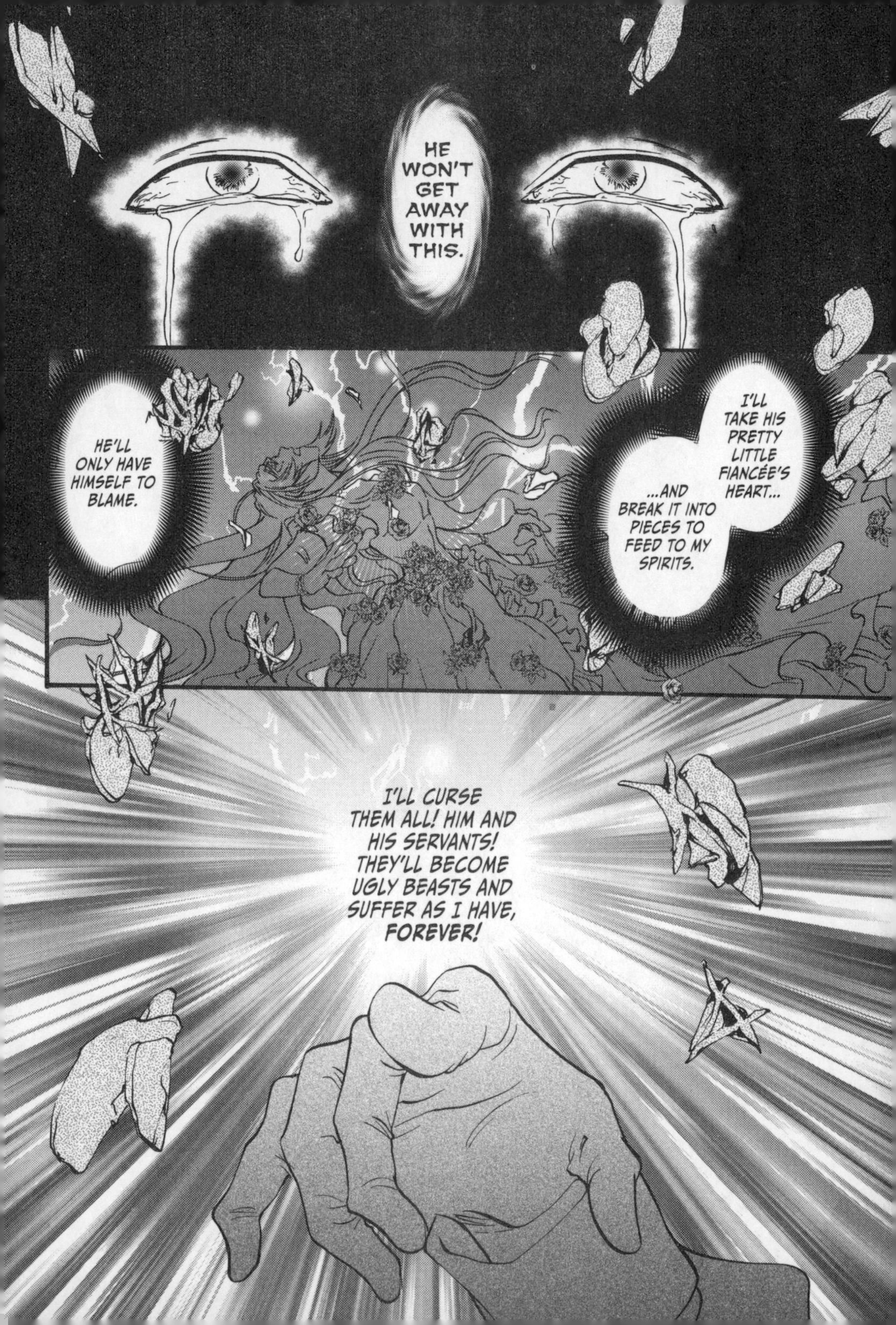
HE WON'T GET AWAY WITH THIS.
I'LL TAKE HIS PRETTY LITTLE FIANCÉE'S HEART...
...AND BREAK IT INTO PIECES TO FEED TO MY SPIRITS.
HE'LL ONLY HAVE HIMSELF TO BLAME.
I'LL CURSE THEM ALL! HIM AND HIS SERVANTS! THEY'LL BECOME UGLY BEASTS AND SUFFER AS I HAVE, FOREVER!

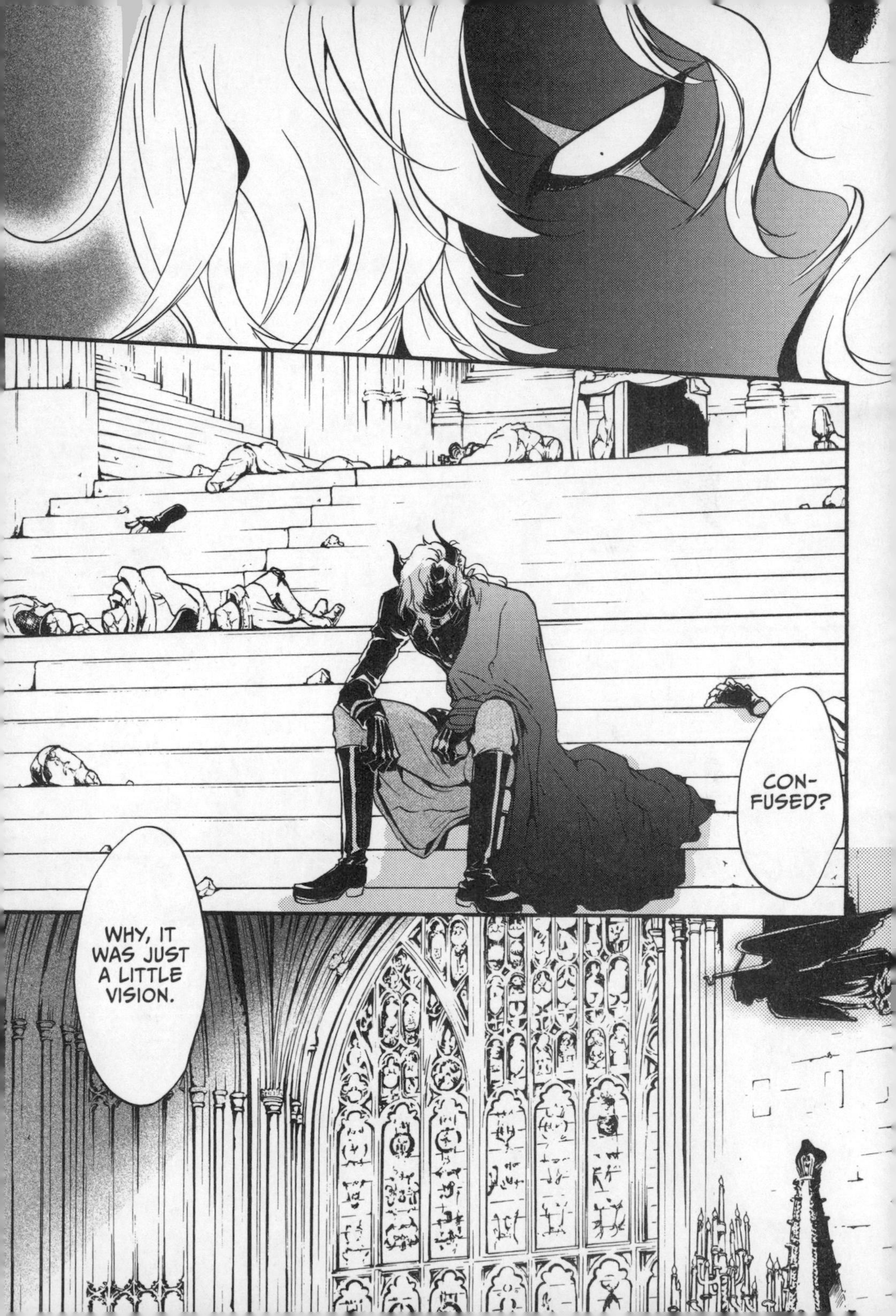
CON-FUSED?
WHY, IT WAS JUST A LITTLE VISION.

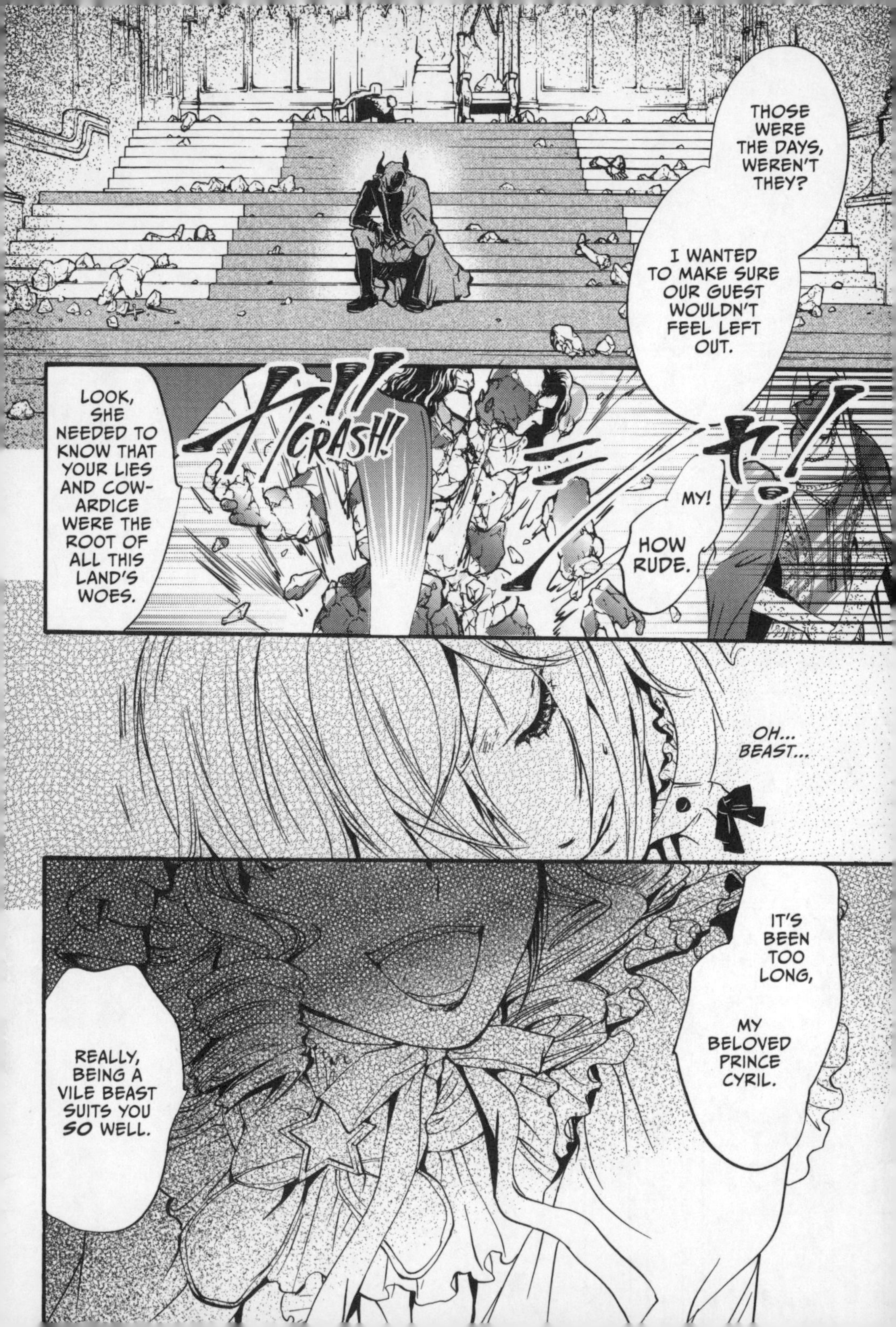
THOSE WERE THE DAYS, WEREN'T THEY?
I WANTED TO MAKE SURE OUR GUEST WOULDN'T FEEL LEFT OUT.
MY!
HOW RUDE.
CRASH!!
LOOK, SHE NEEDED TO KNOW THAT YOUR LIES AND COW-ARDICE WERE THE ROOT OF ALL THIS LAND'S WOES.
OH... BEAST...
IT'S BEEN TOO LONG,
MY BELOVED PRINCE CYRIL.
REALLY, BEING A VILE BEAST SUITS YOU *SO* WELL.

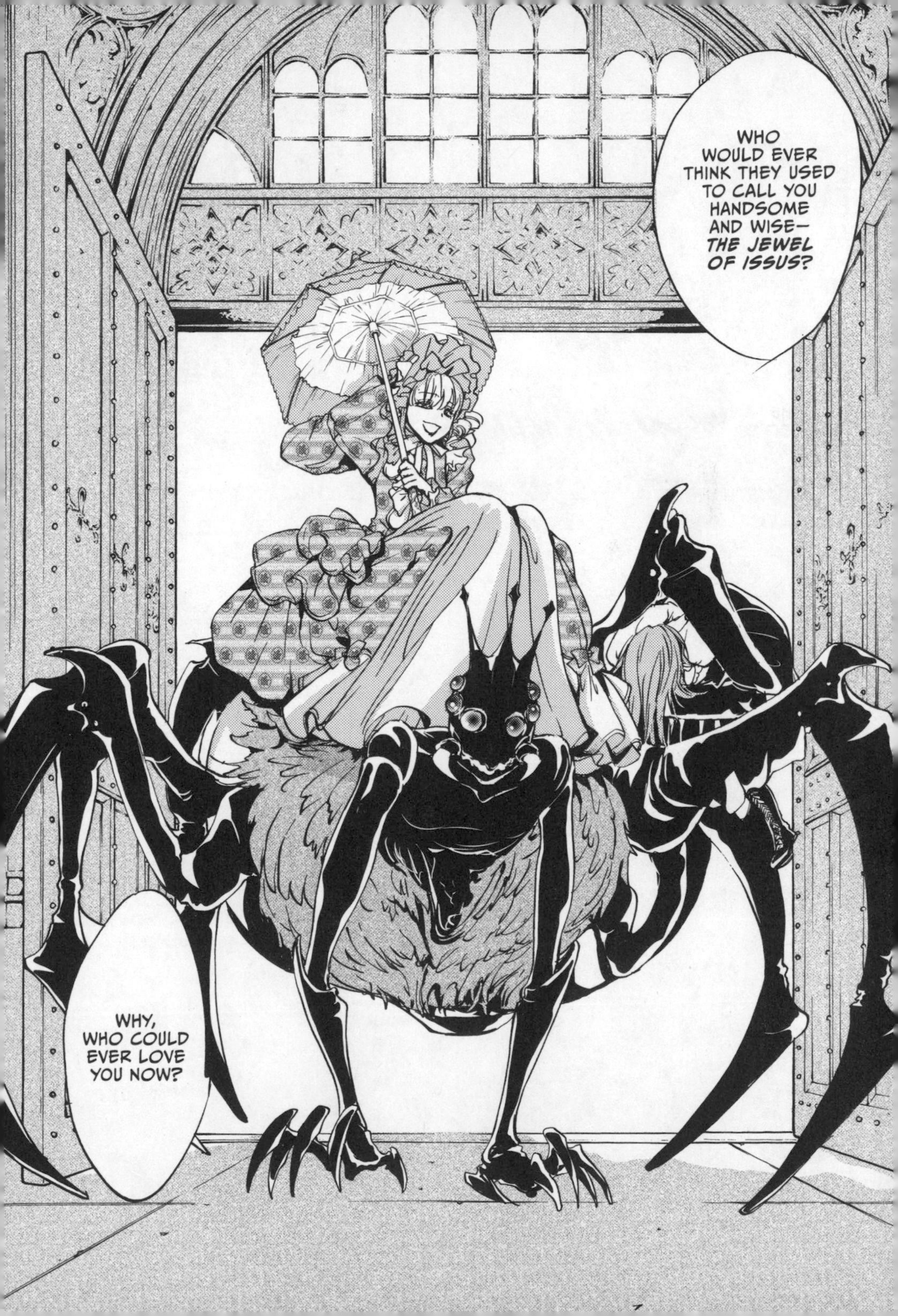
WHO WOULD EVER THINK THEY USED TO CALL YOU HANDSOME AND WISE—*THE JEWEL OF ISSUS?*
WHY, WHO COULD EVER LOVE YOU NOW?

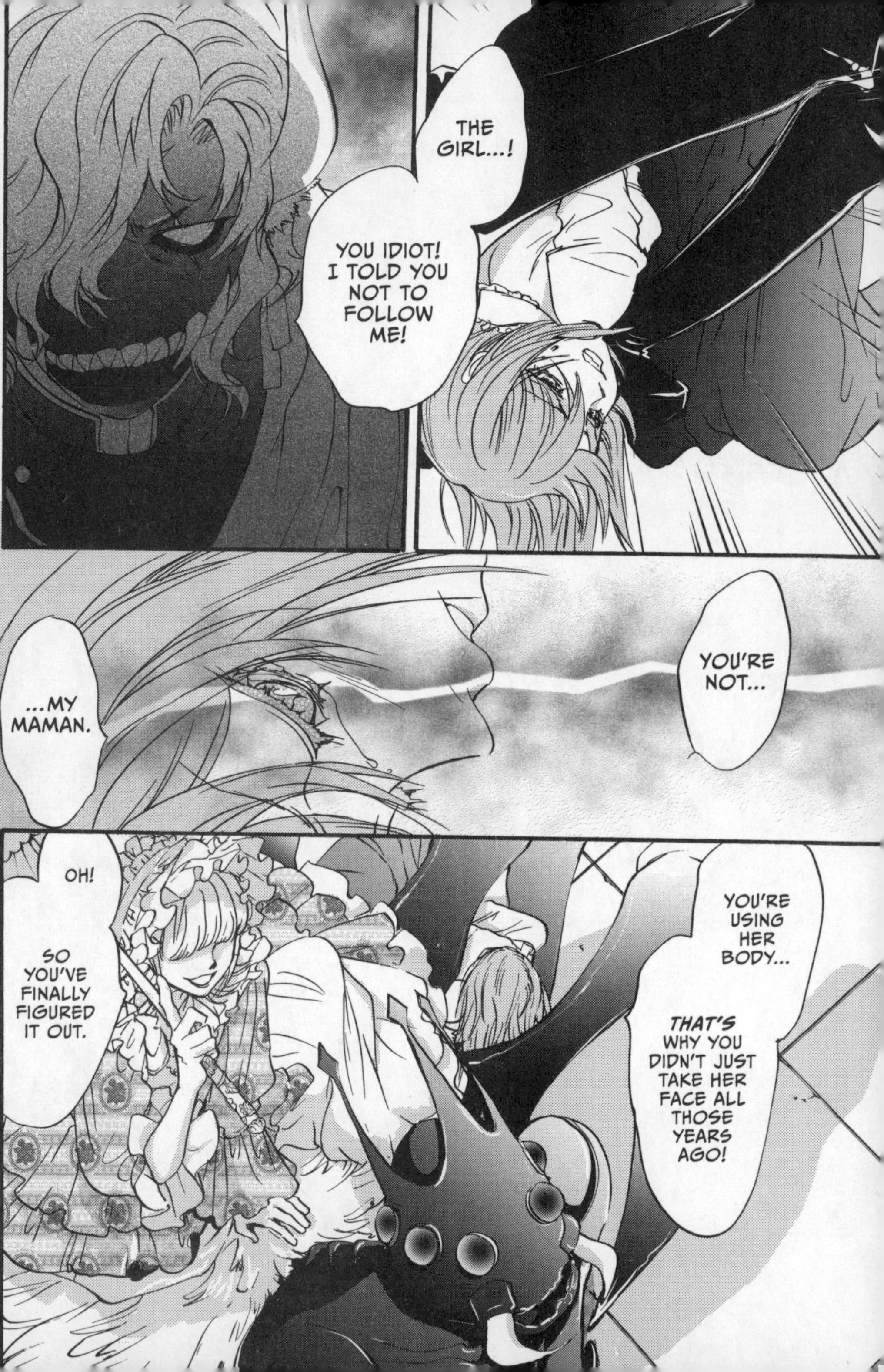
THE GIRL...!
YOU IDIOT! I TOLD YOU NOT TO FOLLOW ME!
YOU'RE NOT...
...MY MAMAN.
YOU'RE USING HER BODY...
THAT'S WHY YOU DIDN'T JUST TAKE HER FACE ALL THOSE YEARS AGO!
OH!
SO YOU'VE FINALLY FIGURED IT OUT.

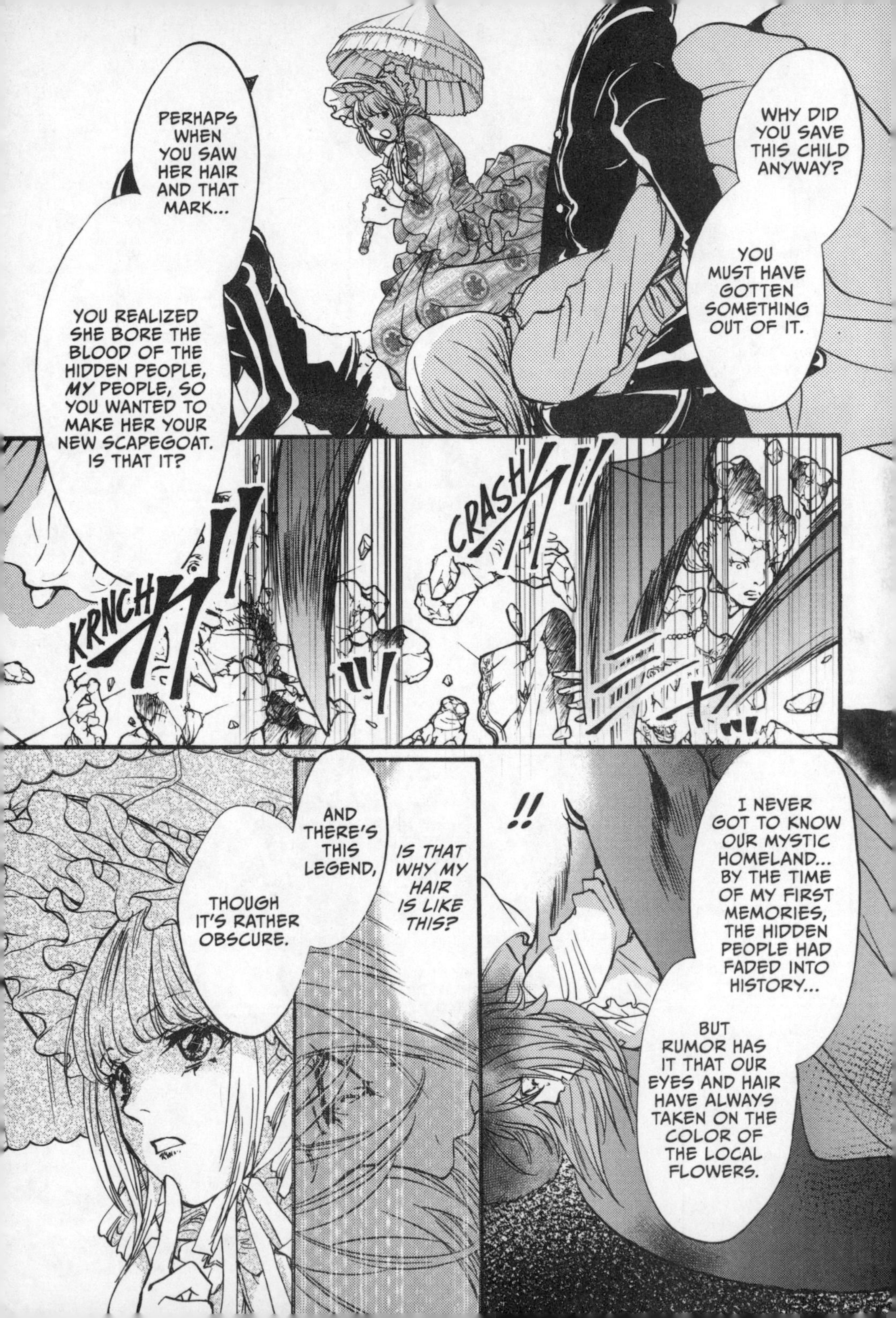

WHY DID YOU SAVE THIS CHILD ANYWAY?
YOU MUST HAVE GOTTEN SOMETHING OUT OF IT.
PERHAPS WHEN YOU SAW HER HAIR AND THAT MARK...
YOU REALIZED SHE BORE THE BLOOD OF THE HIDDEN PEOPLE, *MY* PEOPLE, SO YOU WANTED TO MAKE HER YOUR NEW SCAPEGOAT. IS THAT IT?
CRASH
KRNCH
I NEVER GOT TO KNOW OUR MYSTIC HOMELAND... BY THE TIME OF MY FIRST MEMORIES, THE HIDDEN PEOPLE HAD FADED INTO HISTORY...
!!
BUT RUMOR HAS IT THAT OUR EYES AND HAIR HAVE ALWAYS TAKEN ON THE COLOR OF THE LOCAL FLOWERS.
IS THAT WHY MY HAIR IS LIKE THIS?
AND THERE'S THIS LEGEND,
THOUGH IT'S RATHER OBSCURE.

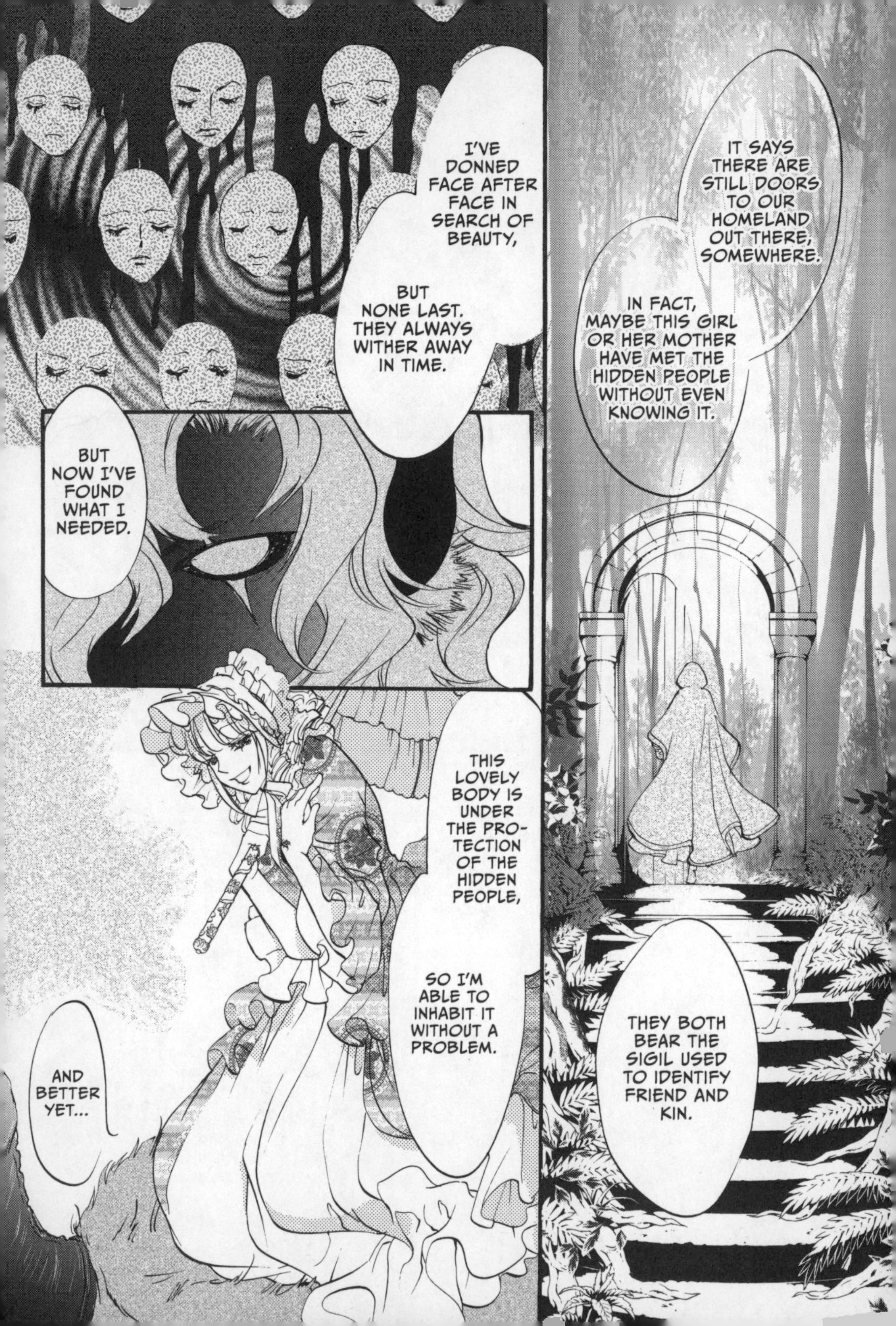
IT SAYS THERE ARE STILL DOORS TO OUR HOMELAND OUT THERE, SOMEWHERE.
IN FACT, MAYBE THIS GIRL OR HER MOTHER HAVE MET THE HIDDEN PEOPLE WITHOUT EVEN KNOWING IT.
THEY BOTH BEAR THE SIGIL USED TO IDENTIFY FRIEND AND KIN.
I'VE DONNED FACE AFTER FACE IN SEARCH OF BEAUTY,
BUT NONE LAST. THEY ALWAYS WITHER AWAY IN TIME.
BUT NOW I'VE FOUND WHAT I NEEDED.
THIS LOVELY BODY IS UNDER THE PRO-TECTION OF THE HIDDEN PEOPLE,
SO I'M ABLE TO INHABIT IT WITHOUT A PROBLEM.
AND BETTER YET...

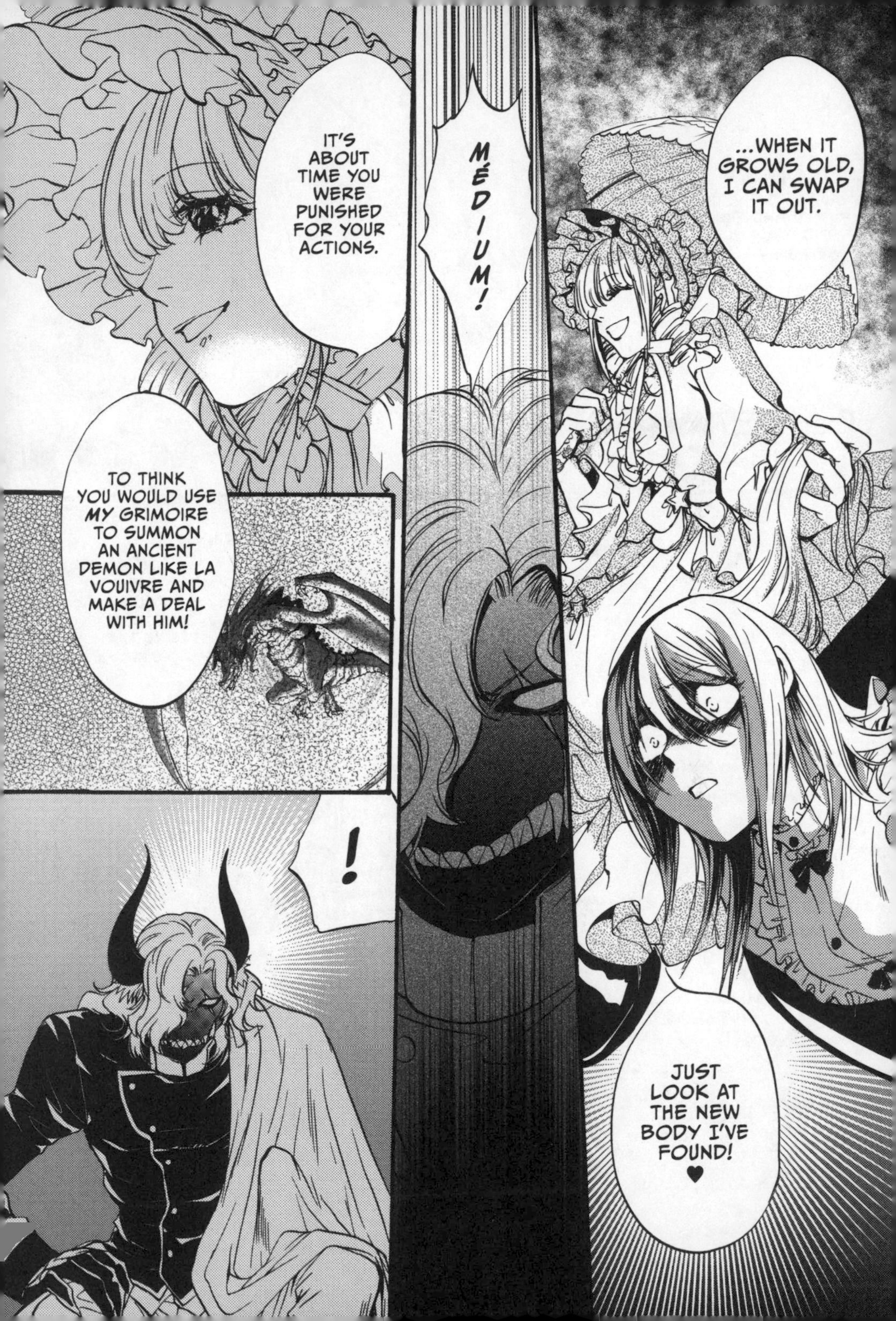
...WHEN IT GROWS OLD, I CAN SWAP IT OUT.
JUST LOOK AT THE NEW BODY I'VE FOUND! ♥
MÉDIUM!
IT'S ABOUT TIME YOU WERE PUNISHED FOR YOUR ACTIONS.
TO THINK YOU WOULD USE *MY* GRIMOIRE TO SUMMON AN ANCIENT DEMON LIKE LA VOUIVRE AND MAKE A DEAL WITH HIM!
!

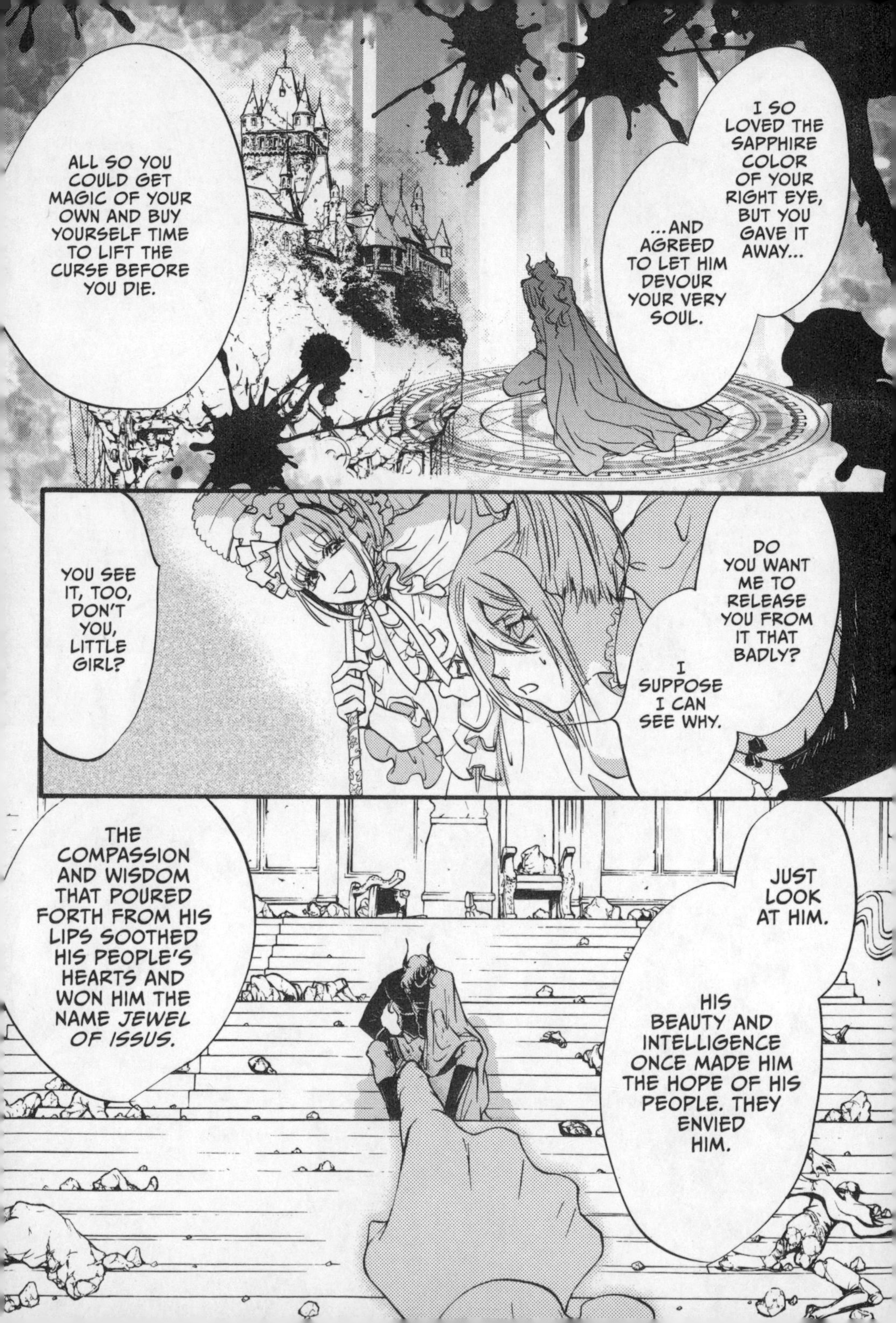
I SO LOVED THE SAPPHIRE COLOR OF YOUR RIGHT EYE, BUT YOU GAVE IT AWAY...
...AND AGREED TO LET HIM DEVOUR YOUR VERY SOUL.
ALL SO YOU COULD GET MAGIC OF YOUR OWN AND BUY YOURSELF TIME TO LIFT THE CURSE BEFORE YOU DIE.
DO YOU WANT ME TO RELEASE YOU FROM IT THAT BADLY?
I SUPPOSE I CAN SEE WHY.
YOU SEE IT, TOO, DON'T YOU, LITTLE GIRL?
JUST LOOK AT HIM.
HIS BEAUTY AND INTELLIGENCE ONCE MADE HIM THE HOPE OF HIS PEOPLE. THEY ENVIED HIM.
THE COMPASSION AND WISDOM THAT POURED FORTH FROM HIS LIPS SOOTHED HIS PEOPLE'S HEARTS AND WON HIM THE NAME *JEWEL OF ISSUS.*

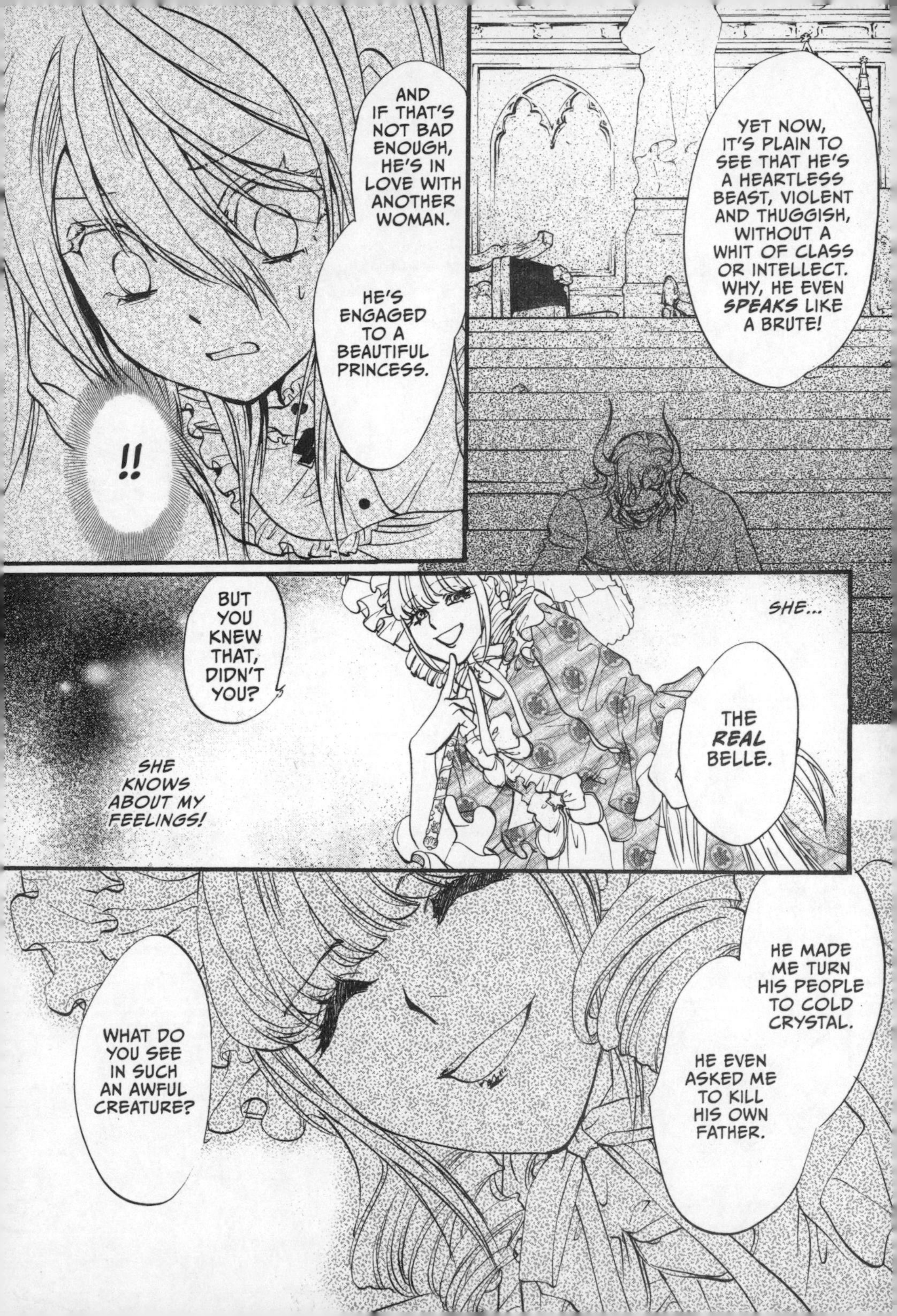
YET NOW, IT'S PLAIN TO SEE THAT HE'S A HEARTLESS BEAST, VIOLENT AND THUGGISH, WITHOUT A WHIT OF CLASS OR INTELLECT. WHY, HE EVEN SPEAKS LIKE A BRUTE!
AND IF THAT'S NOT BAD ENOUGH, HE'S IN LOVE WITH ANOTHER WOMAN.
HE'S ENGAGED TO A BEAUTIFUL PRINCESS.
!!
SHE...
THE REAL BELLE.
BUT YOU KNEW THAT, DIDN'T YOU?
SHE KNOWS ABOUT MY FEELINGS!
HE MADE ME TURN HIS PEOPLE TO COLD CRYSTAL.
HE EVEN ASKED ME TO KILL HIS OWN FATHER.
WHAT DO YOU SEE IN SUCH AN AWFUL CREATURE?

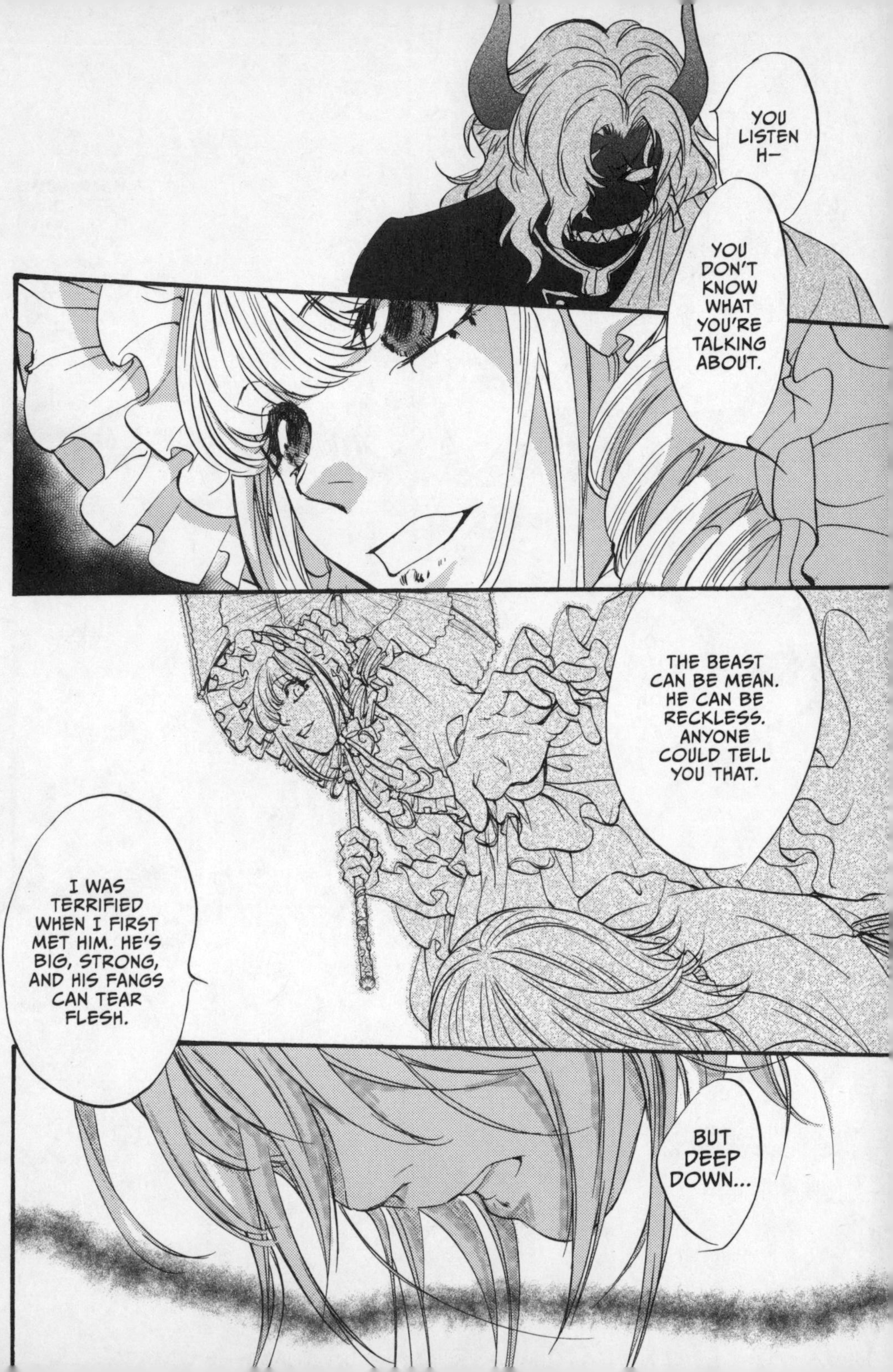
YOU LISTEN H—
YOU DON'T KNOW WHAT YOU'RE TALKING ABOUT.
THE BEAST CAN BE MEAN. HE CAN BE RECKLESS. ANYONE COULD TELL YOU THAT.
I WAS TERRIFIED WHEN I FIRST MET HIM. HE'S BIG, STRONG, AND HIS FANGS CAN TEAR FLESH.
BUT DEEP DOWN...

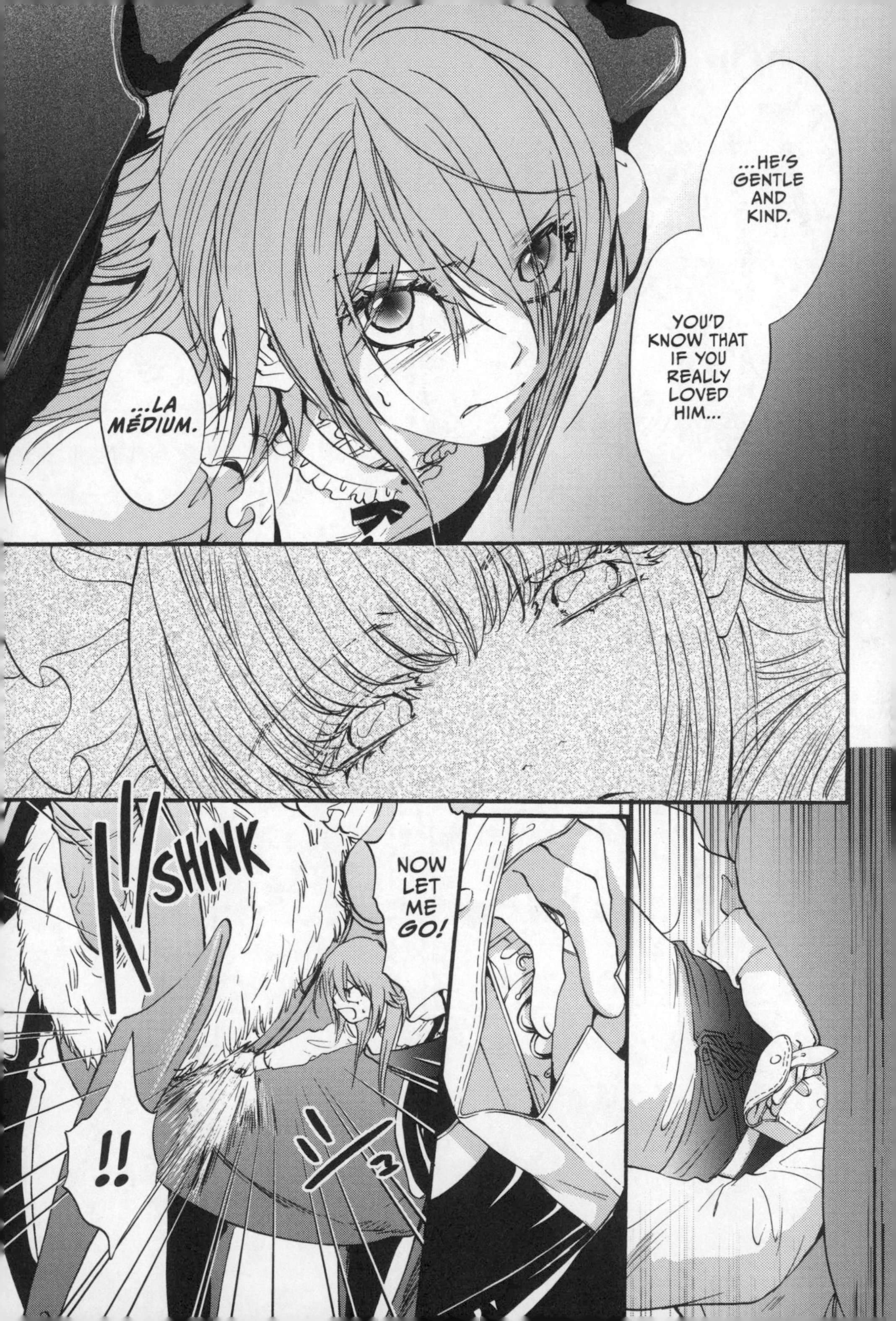
...HE'S GENTLE AND KIND.
YOU'D KNOW THAT IF YOU REALLY LOVED HIM...
...LA MÉDIUM.
NOW LET ME GO!
SHINK
!!

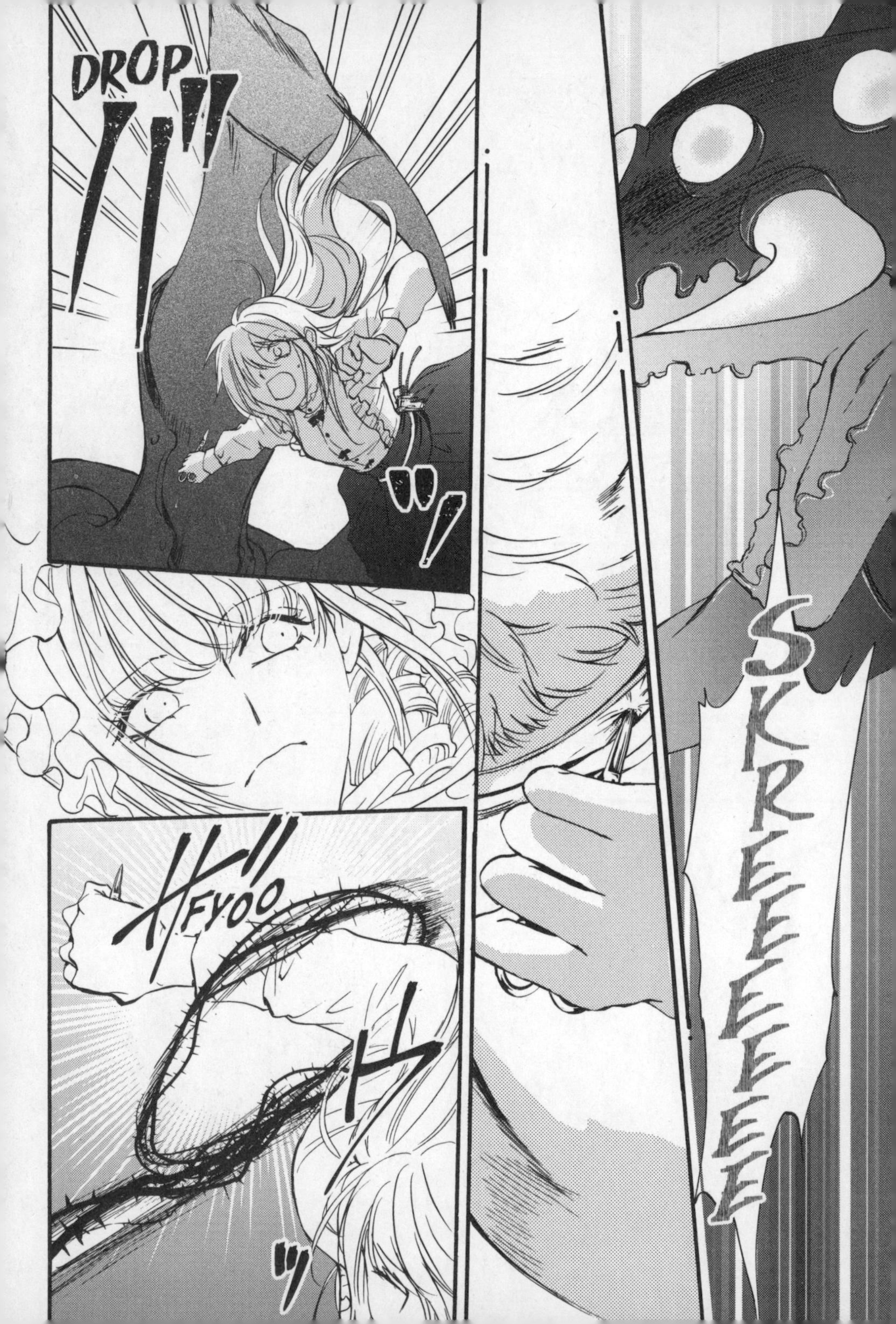
SKREEEEEEE
DROP
FYOO

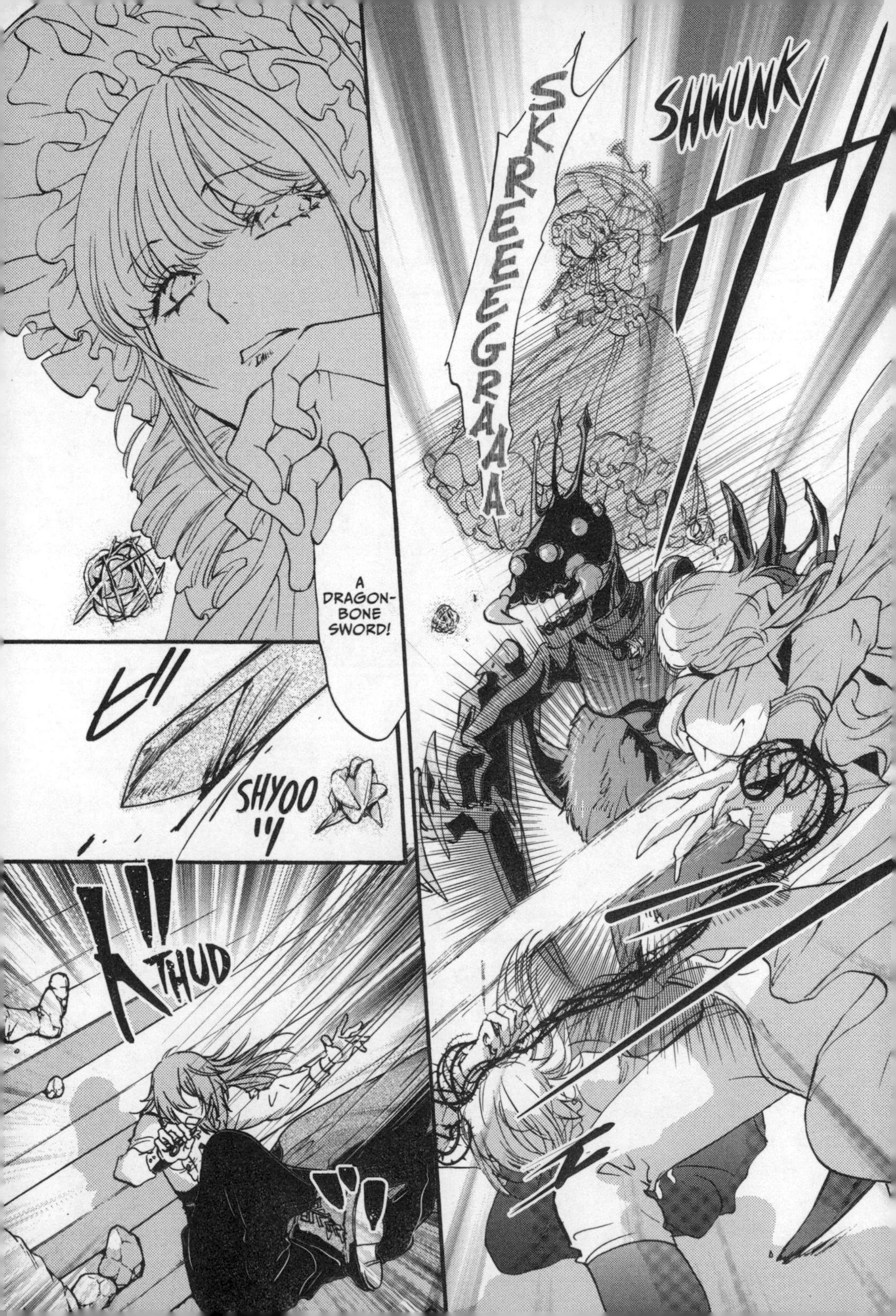

SHWUNK
SKREEEEGRAAA
A DRAGON-BONE SWORD!
SHYOO
THUD

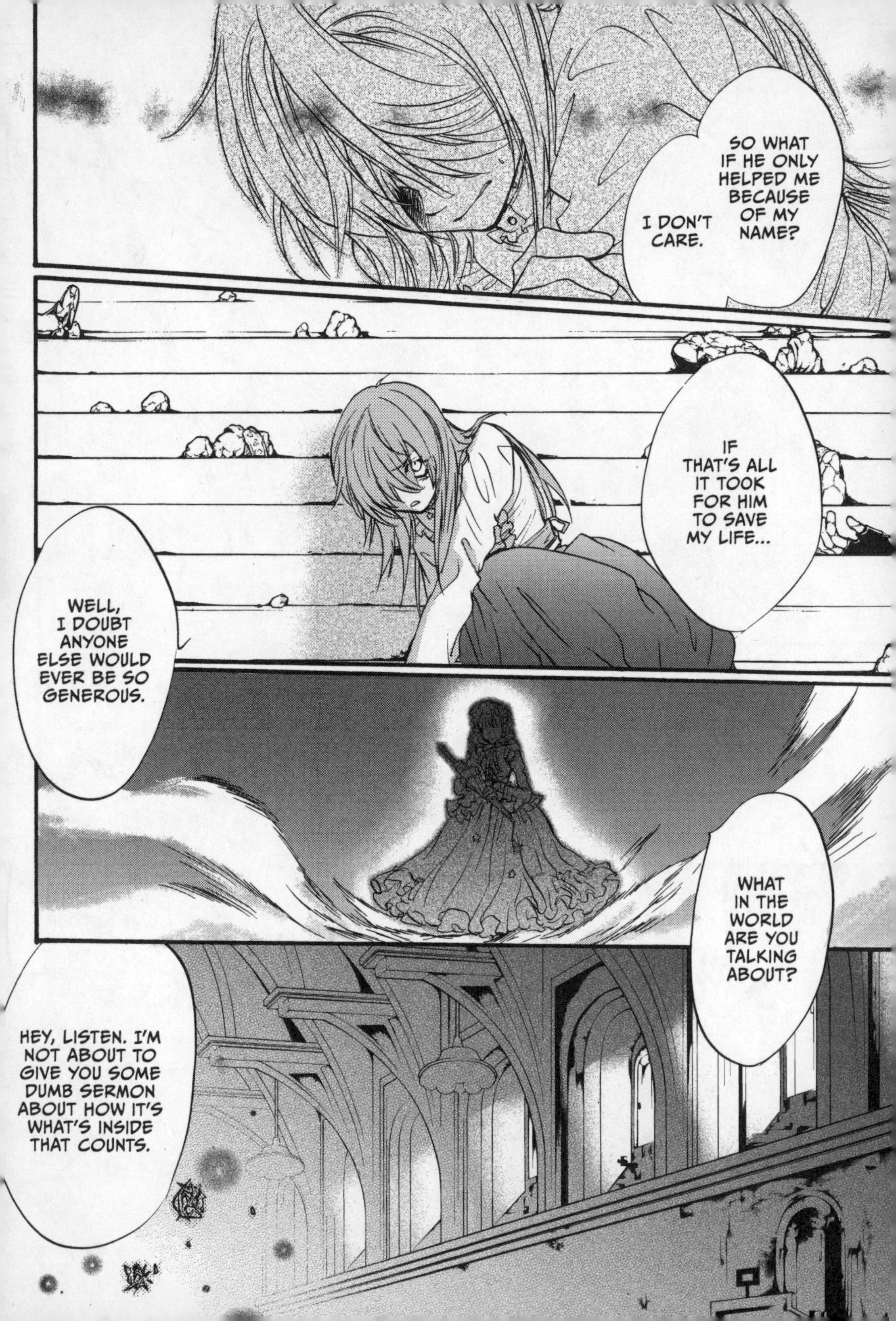
SO WHAT IF HE ONLY HELPED ME BECAUSE OF MY NAME?
I DON'T CARE.
IF THAT'S ALL IT TOOK FOR HIM TO SAVE MY LIFE...
WELL, I DOUBT ANYONE ELSE WOULD EVER BE SO GENEROUS.
WHAT IN THE WORLD ARE YOU TALKING ABOUT?
HEY, LISTEN. I'M NOT ABOUT TO GIVE YOU SOME DUMB SERMON ABOUT HOW IT'S WHAT'S INSIDE THAT COUNTS.

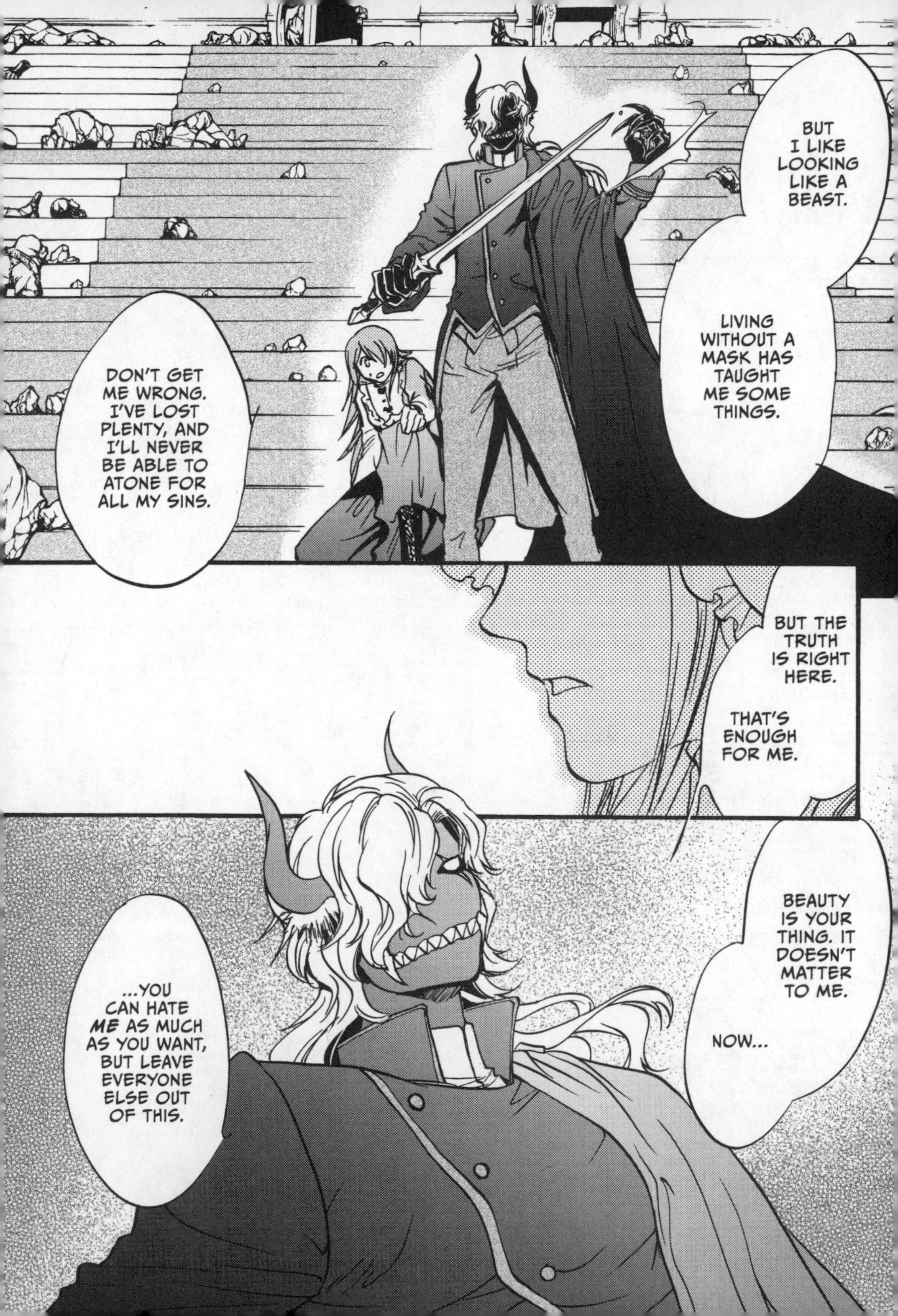
BUT I LIKE LOOKING LIKE A BEAST.
LIVING WITHOUT A MASK HAS TAUGHT ME SOME THINGS.
DON'T GET ME WRONG. I'VE LOST PLENTY, AND I'LL NEVER BE ABLE TO ATONE FOR ALL MY SINS.
BUT THE TRUTH IS RIGHT HERE.
THAT'S ENOUGH FOR ME.
BEAUTY IS YOUR THING. IT DOESN'T MATTER TO ME.
NOW...
...YOU CAN HATE *ME* AS MUCH AS YOU WANT, BUT LEAVE EVERYONE ELSE OUT OF THIS.

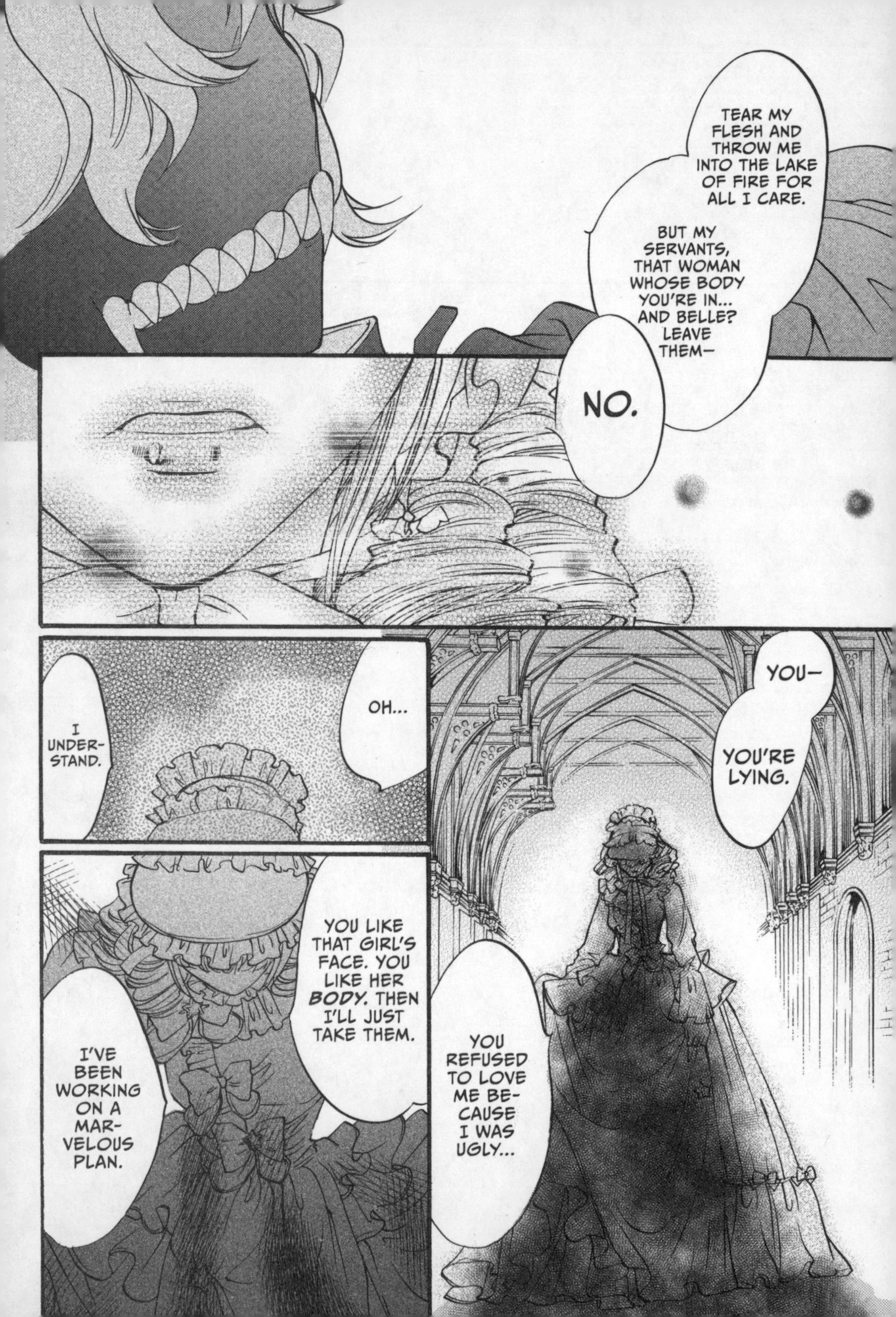
TEAR MY FLESH AND THROW ME INTO THE LAKE OF FIRE FOR ALL I CARE.
BUT MY SERVANTS, THAT WOMAN WHOSE BODY YOU'RE IN... AND BELLE? LEAVE THEM—
NO.
YOU—
YOU'RE LYING.
YOU REFUSED TO LOVE ME BE-CAUSE I WAS UGLY...
OH...
I UNDER-STAND.
YOU LIKE THAT GIRL'S FACE. YOU LIKE HER *BODY*. THEN I'LL JUST TAKE THEM.
I'VE BEEN WORKING ON A MAR-VELOUS PLAN.

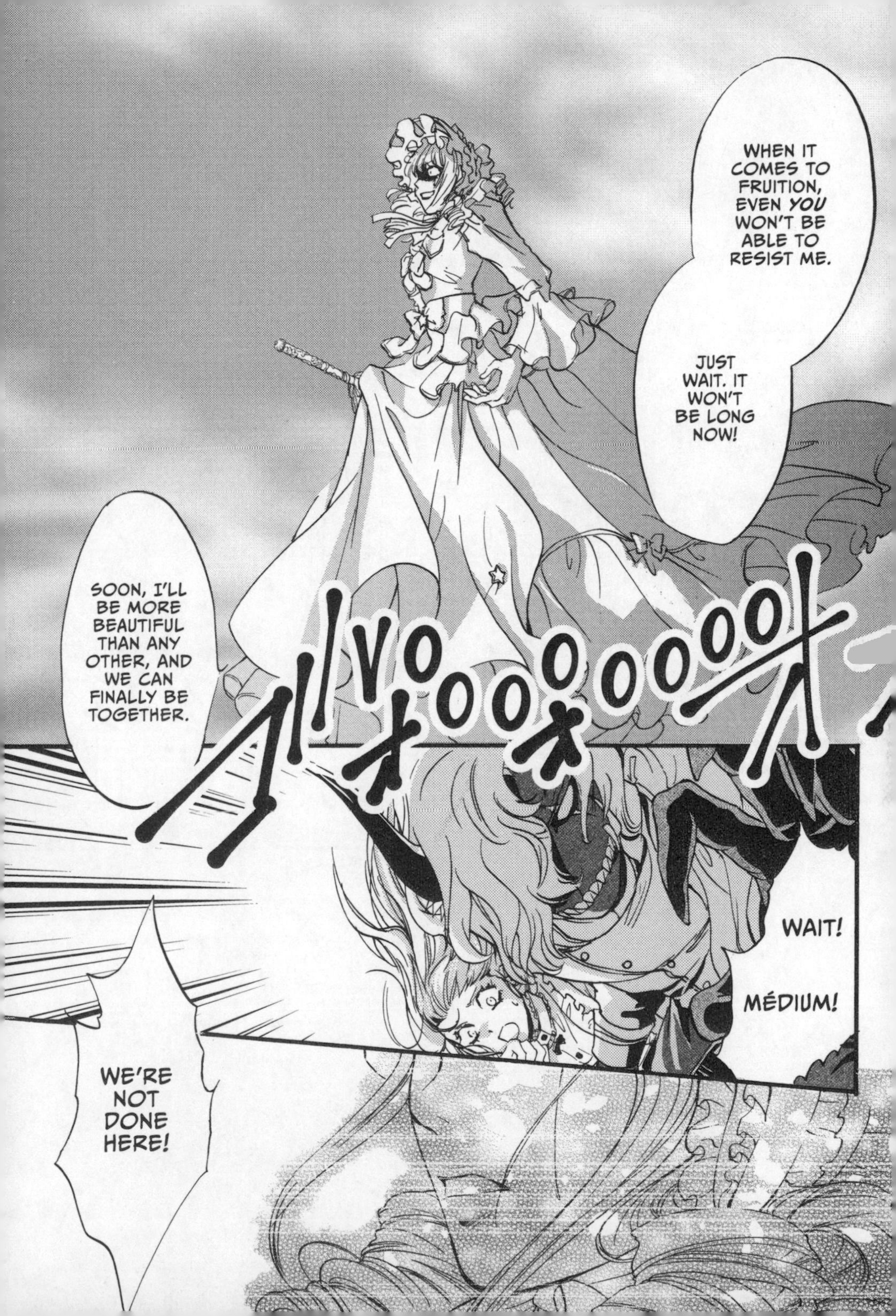
WHEN IT COMES TO FRUITION, EVEN *YOU* WON'T BE ABLE TO RESIST ME.
JUST WAIT. IT WON'T BE LONG NOW!
SOON, I'LL BE MORE BEAUTIFUL THAN ANY OTHER, AND WE CAN FINALLY BE TOGETHER.
WAIT!
MÉDIUM!
WE'RE NOT DONE HERE!

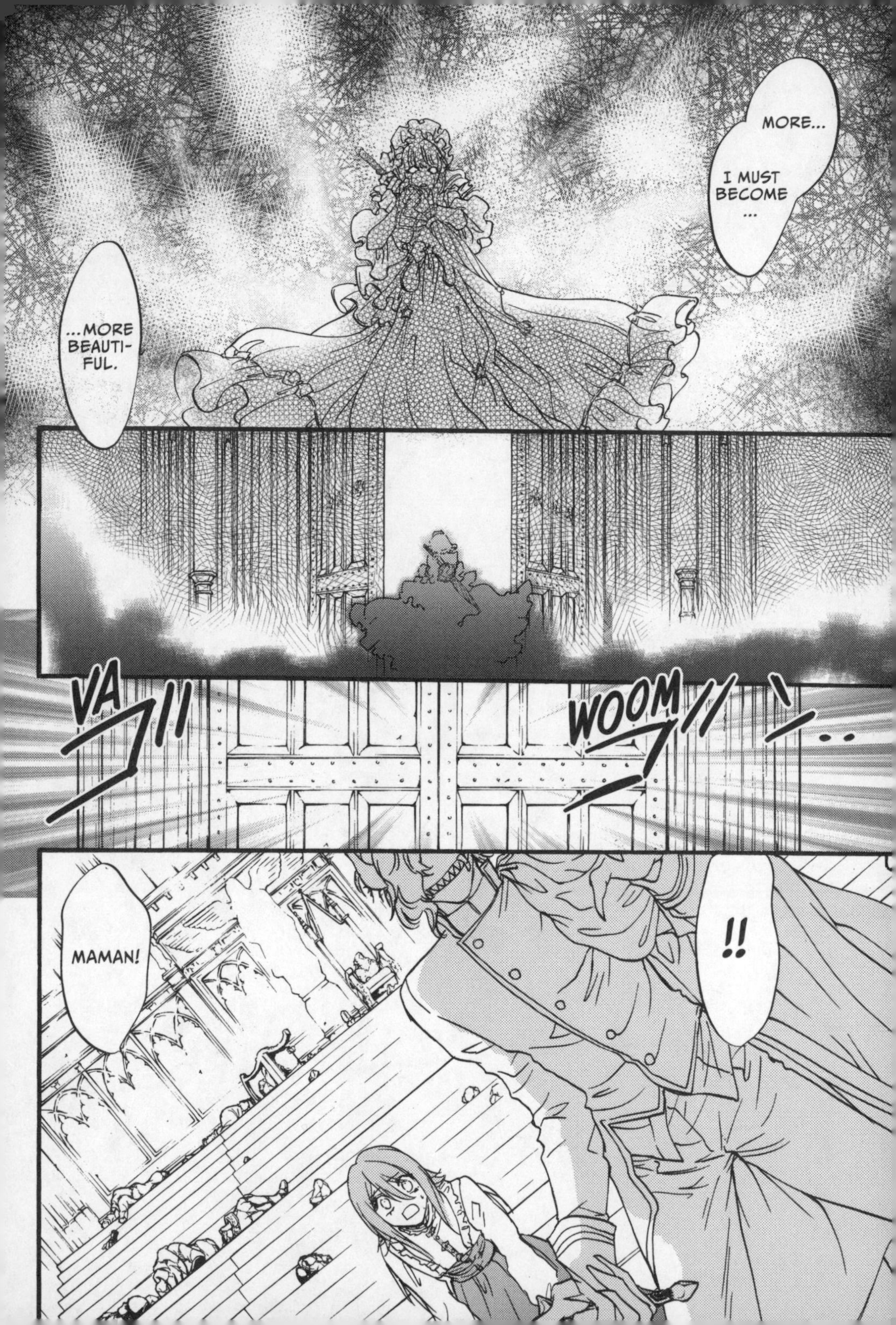
MORE...
I MUST BECOME ...
...MORE BEAUTIFUL.
VA
WOOM
!!
MAMAN!

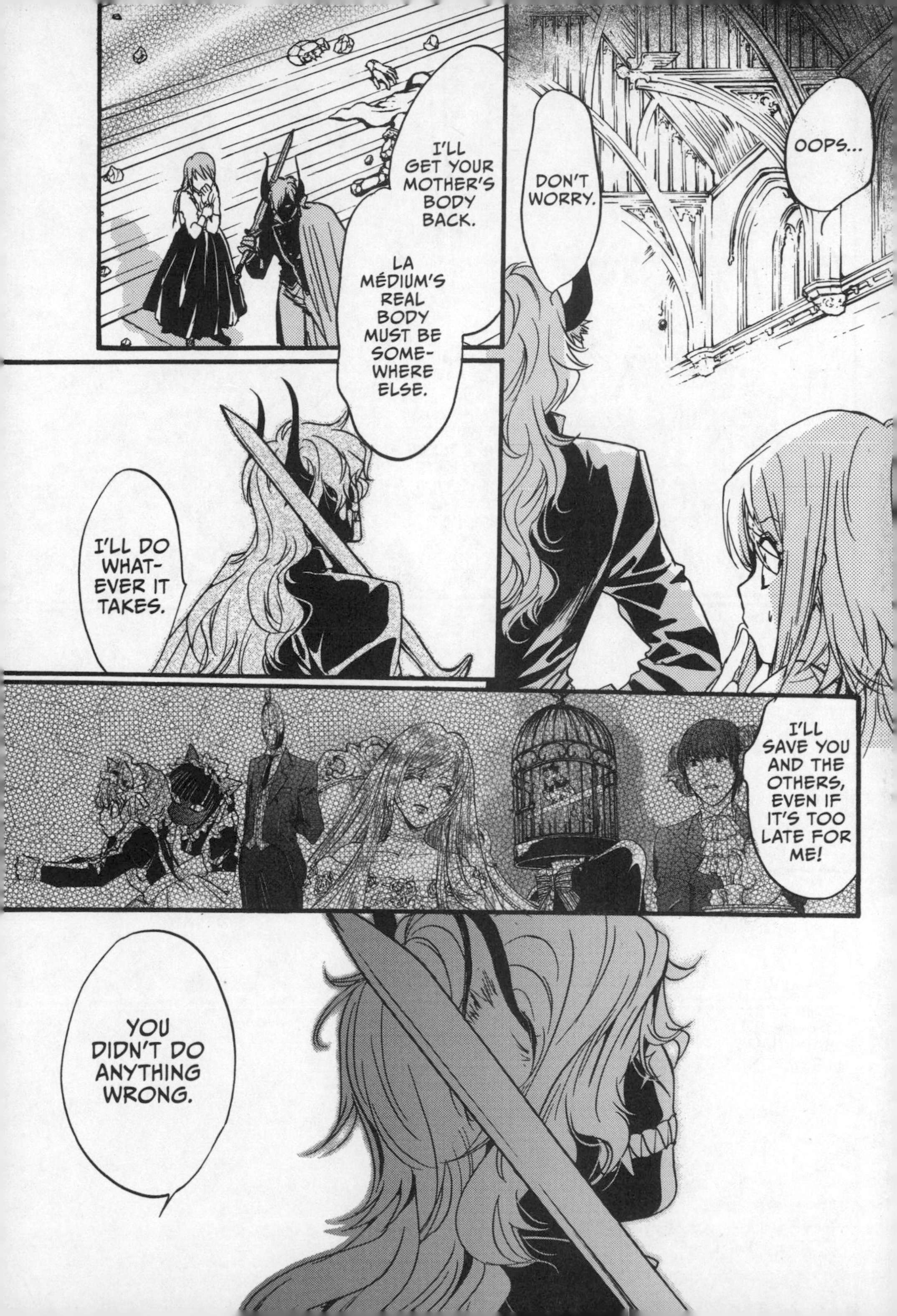
OOPS...
DON'T WORRY.
I'LL GET YOUR MOTHER'S BODY BACK.
LA MÉDIUM'S REAL BODY MUST BE SOMEWHERE ELSE.
I'LL DO WHATEVER IT TAKES.
I'LL SAVE YOU AND THE OTHERS, EVEN IF IT'S TOO LATE FOR ME!
YOU DIDN'T DO ANYTHING WRONG.

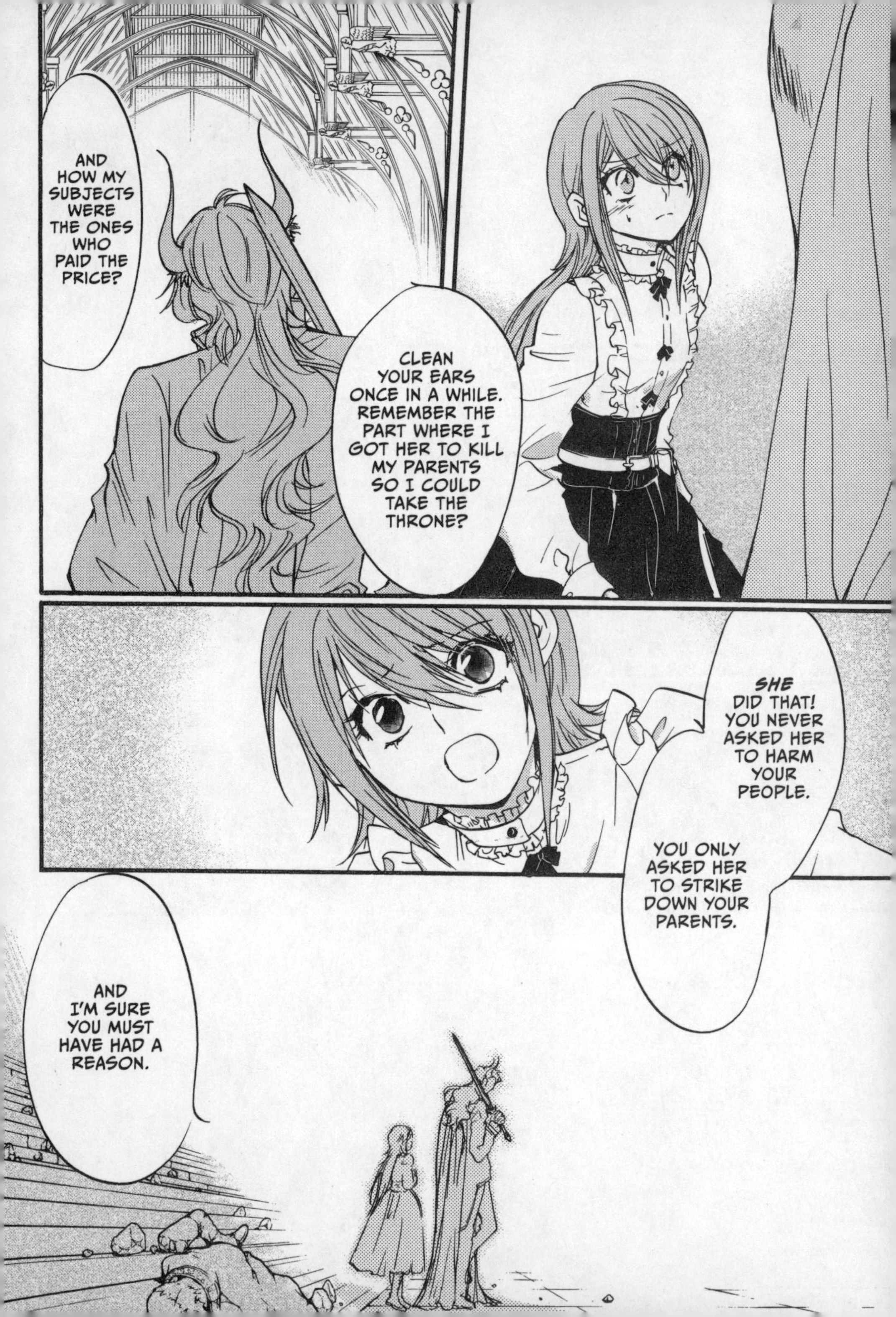

CLEAN YOUR EARS ONCE IN A WHILE. REMEMBER THE PART WHERE I GOT HER TO KILL MY PARENTS SO I COULD TAKE THE THRONE?
AND HOW MY SUBJECTS WERE THE ONES WHO PAID THE PRICE?
SHE DID THAT! YOU NEVER ASKED HER TO HARM YOUR PEOPLE.
YOU ONLY ASKED HER TO STRIKE DOWN YOUR PARENTS.
AND I'M SURE YOU MUST HAVE HAD A REASON.

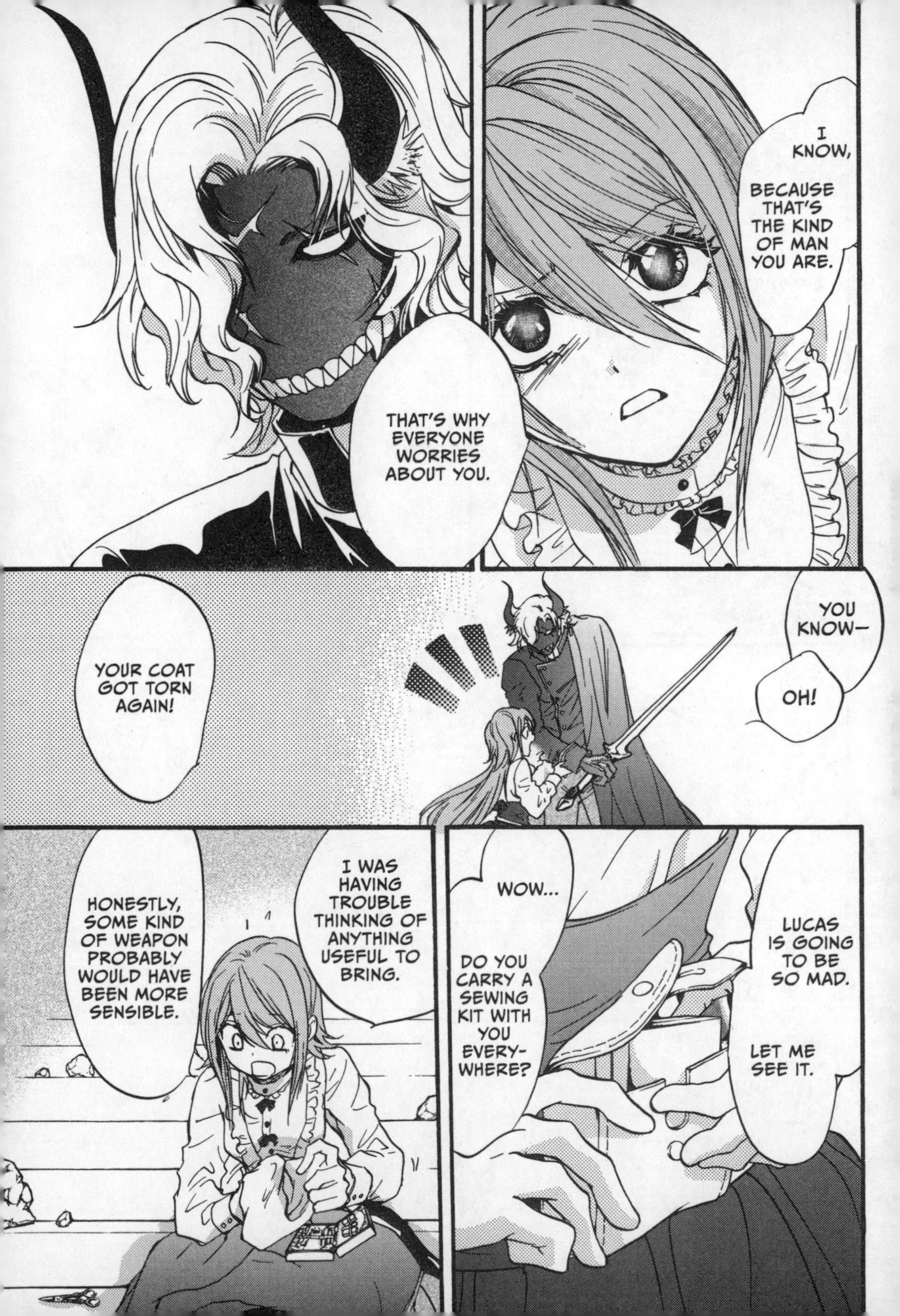
I KNOW,
BECAUSE THAT'S THE KIND OF MAN YOU ARE.
THAT'S WHY EVERYONE WORRIES ABOUT YOU.
YOU KNOW—
OH!
YOUR COAT GOT TORN AGAIN!
LUCAS IS GOING TO BE SO MAD.
WOW...
LET ME SEE IT.
DO YOU CARRY A SEWING KIT WITH YOU EVERY-WHERE?
I WAS HAVING TROUBLE THINKING OF ANYTHING USEFUL TO BRING.
HONESTLY, SOME KIND OF WEAPON PROBABLY WOULD HAVE BEEN MORE SENSIBLE.

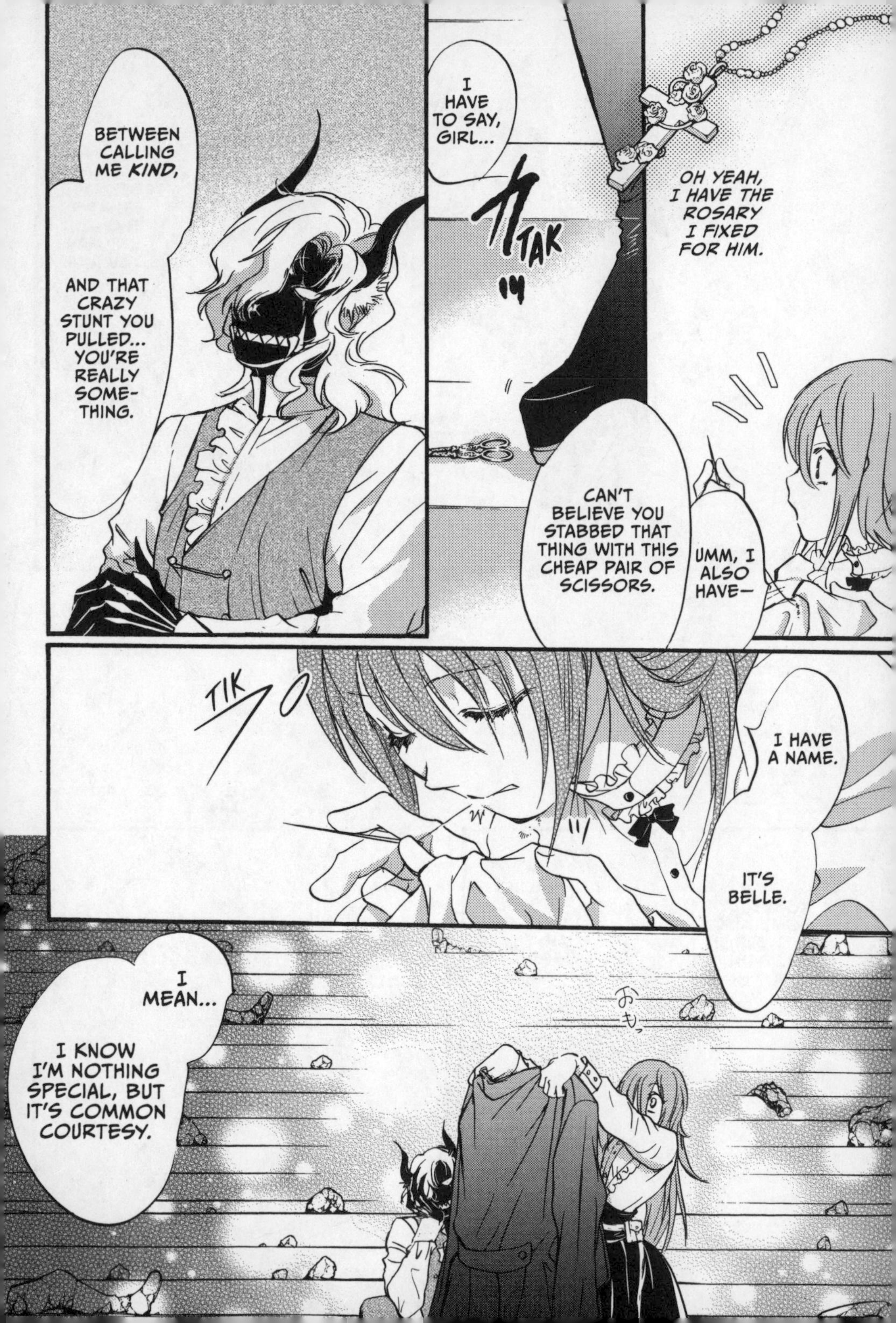
OH YEAH, I HAVE THE ROSARY I FIXED FOR HIM.
I HAVE TO SAY, GIRL...
TAK
UMM, I ALSO HAVE—
CAN'T BELIEVE YOU STABBED THAT THING WITH THIS CHEAP PAIR OF SCISSORS.
BETWEEN CALLING ME *KIND*,
AND THAT CRAZY STUNT YOU PULLED... YOU'RE REALLY SOME-THING.
I HAVE A NAME.
IT'S BELLE.
TIK
おもっ
I MEAN...
I KNOW I'M NOTHING SPECIAL, BUT IT'S COMMON COURTESY.

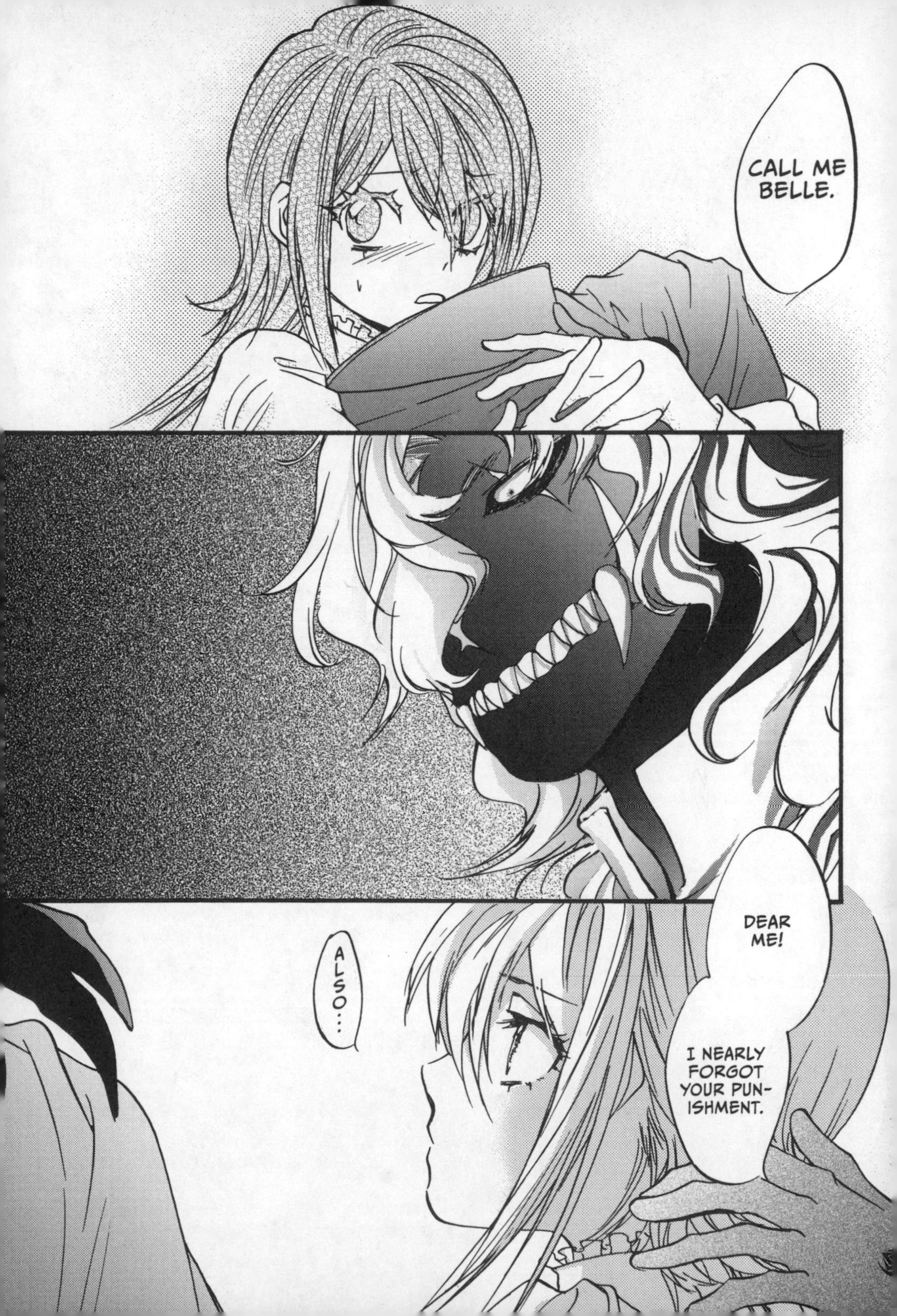
CALL ME BELLE.
DEAR ME!
I NEARLY FORGOT YOUR PUN-ISHMENT.
ALSO…

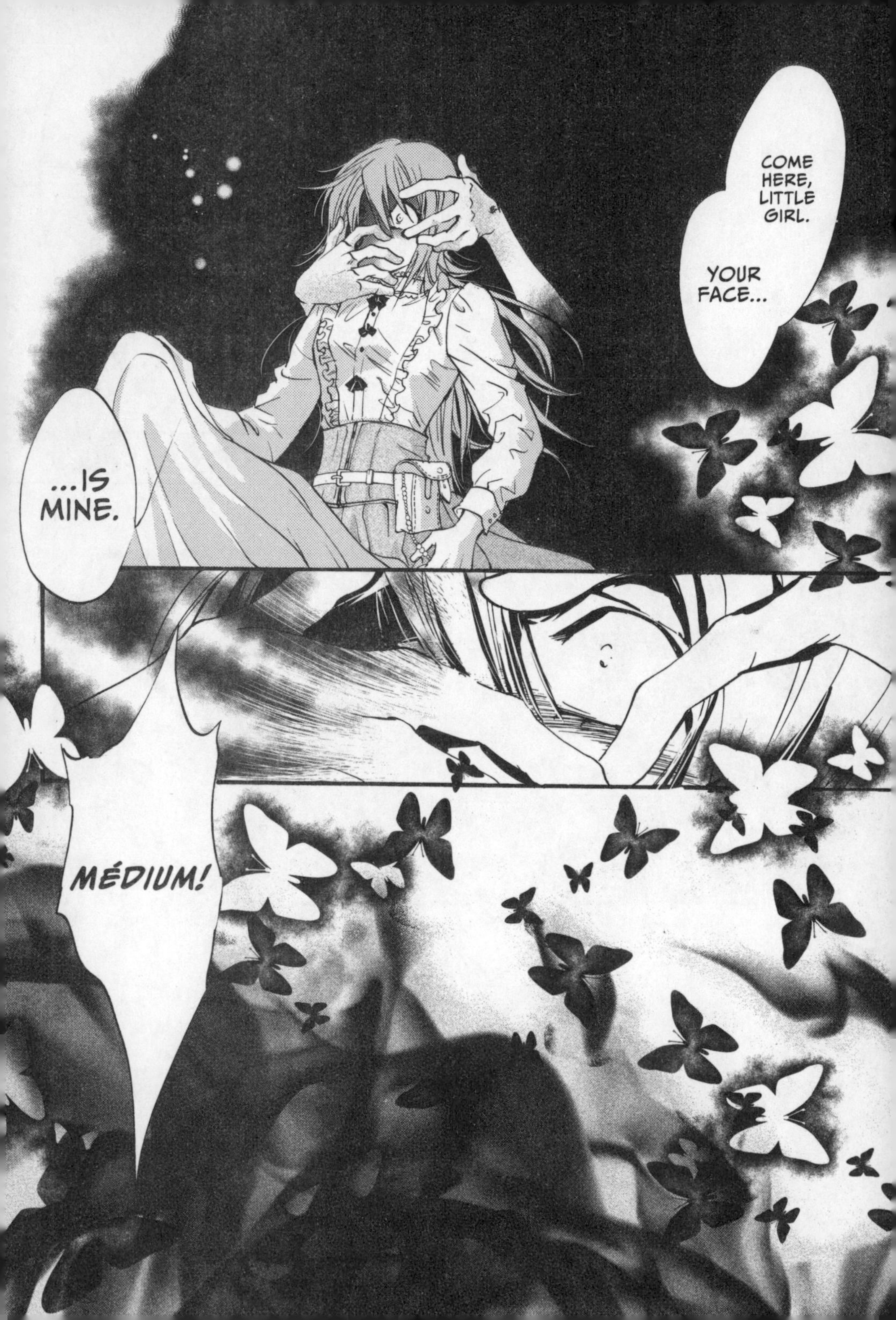
COME HERE, LITTLE GIRL.
YOUR FACE...
...IS MINE.
MÉDIUM!

LA BELLE ET LA BÊTE

DU PARADIS PERDU

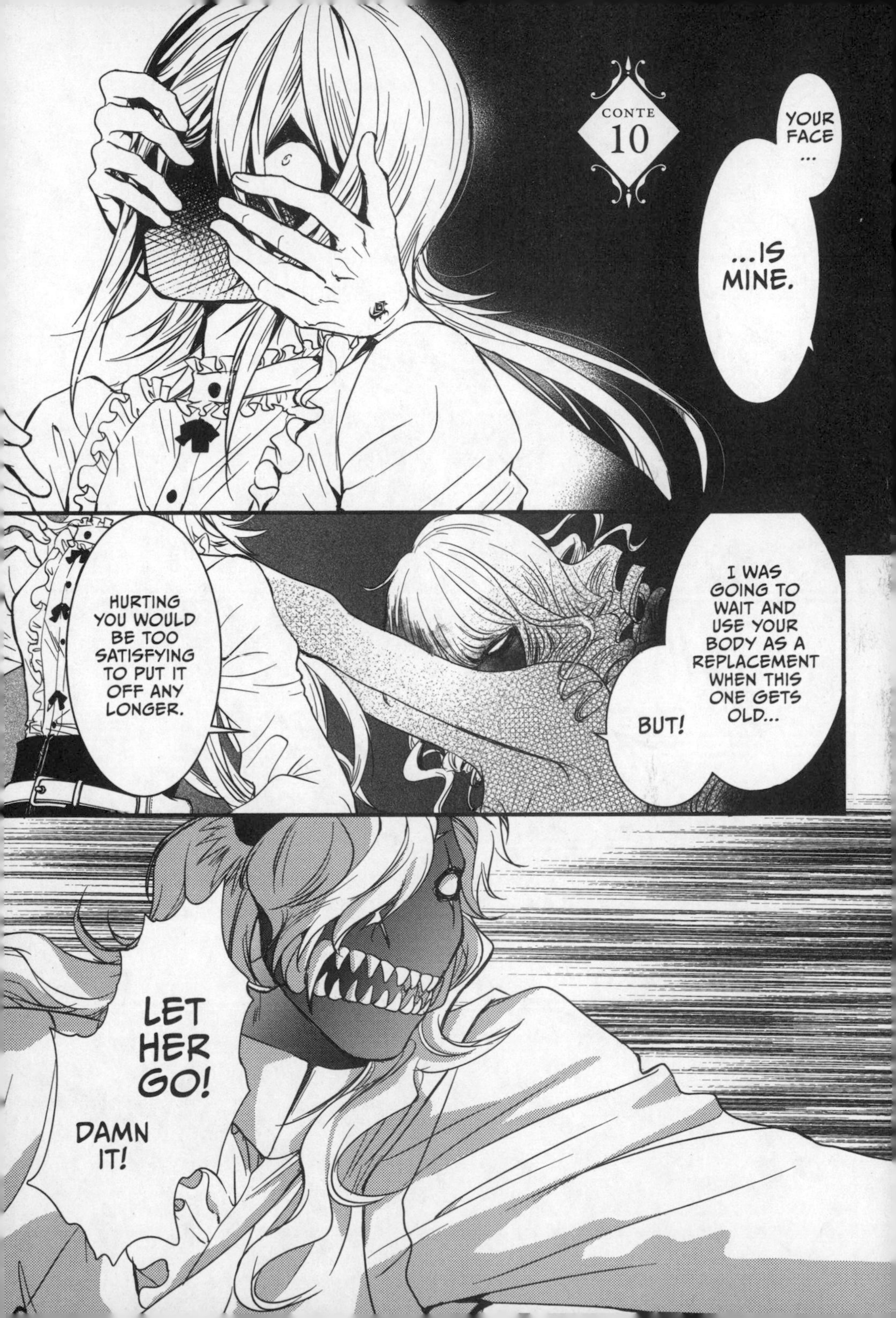
CONTE
10
YOUR FACE ...
...IS MINE.
I WAS GOING TO WAIT AND USE YOUR BODY AS A REPLACEMENT WHEN THIS ONE GETS OLD...
BUT!
HURTING YOU WOULD BE TOO SATISFYING TO PUT IT OFF ANY LONGER.
LET HER GO!
DAMN IT!

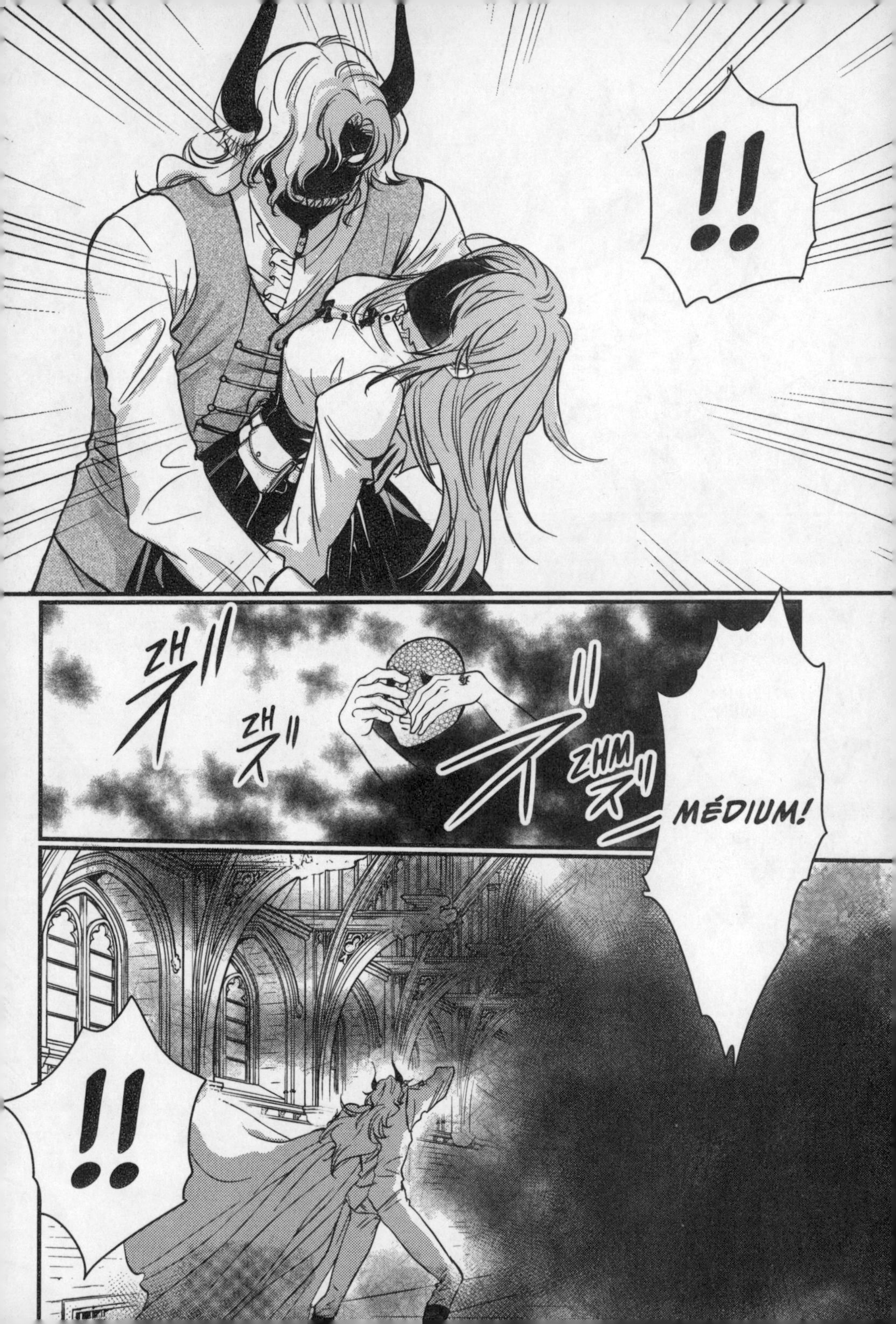
!!
MÉDIUM!
ZHM
!!

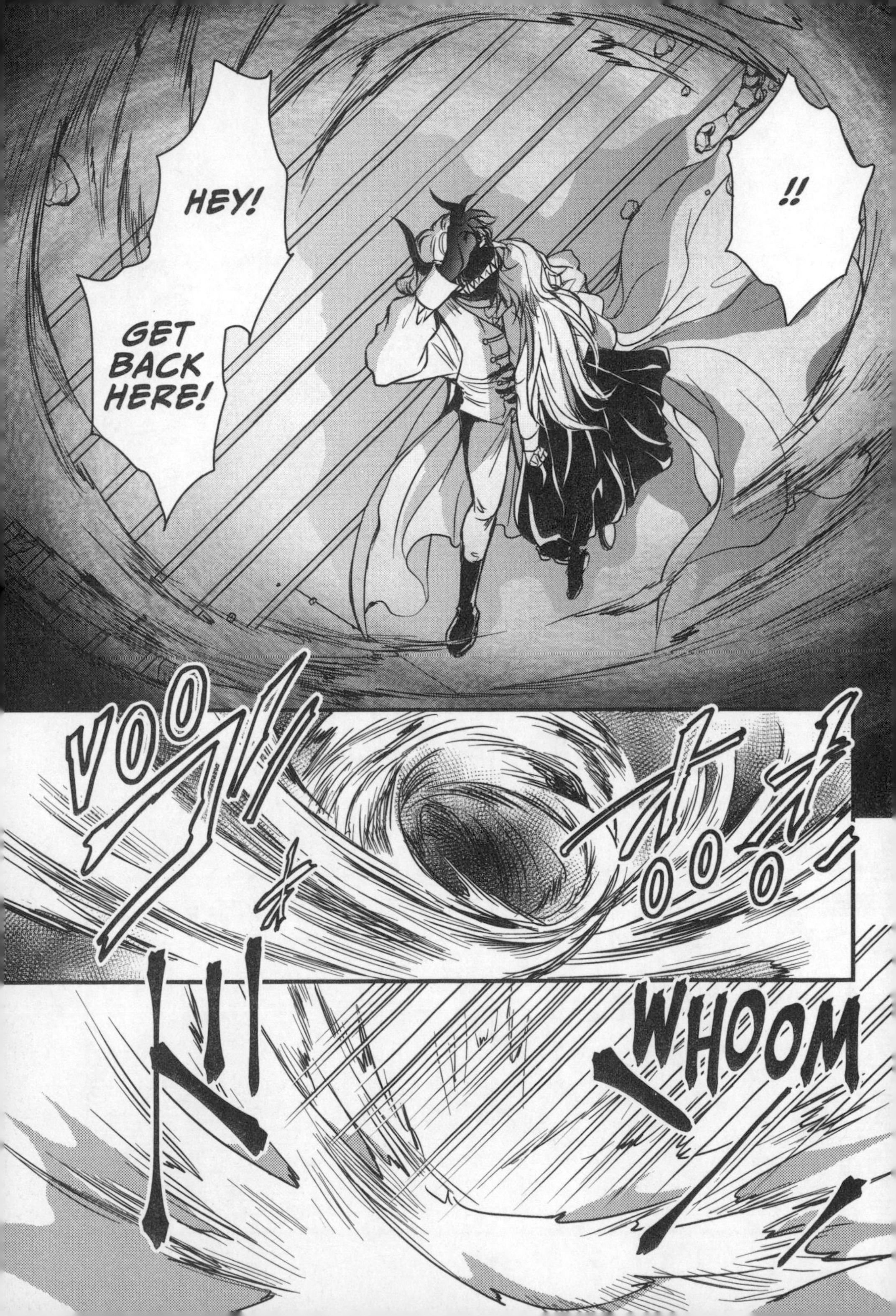

!!
HEY! GET BACK HERE!
VOO
OOO
WHOOM

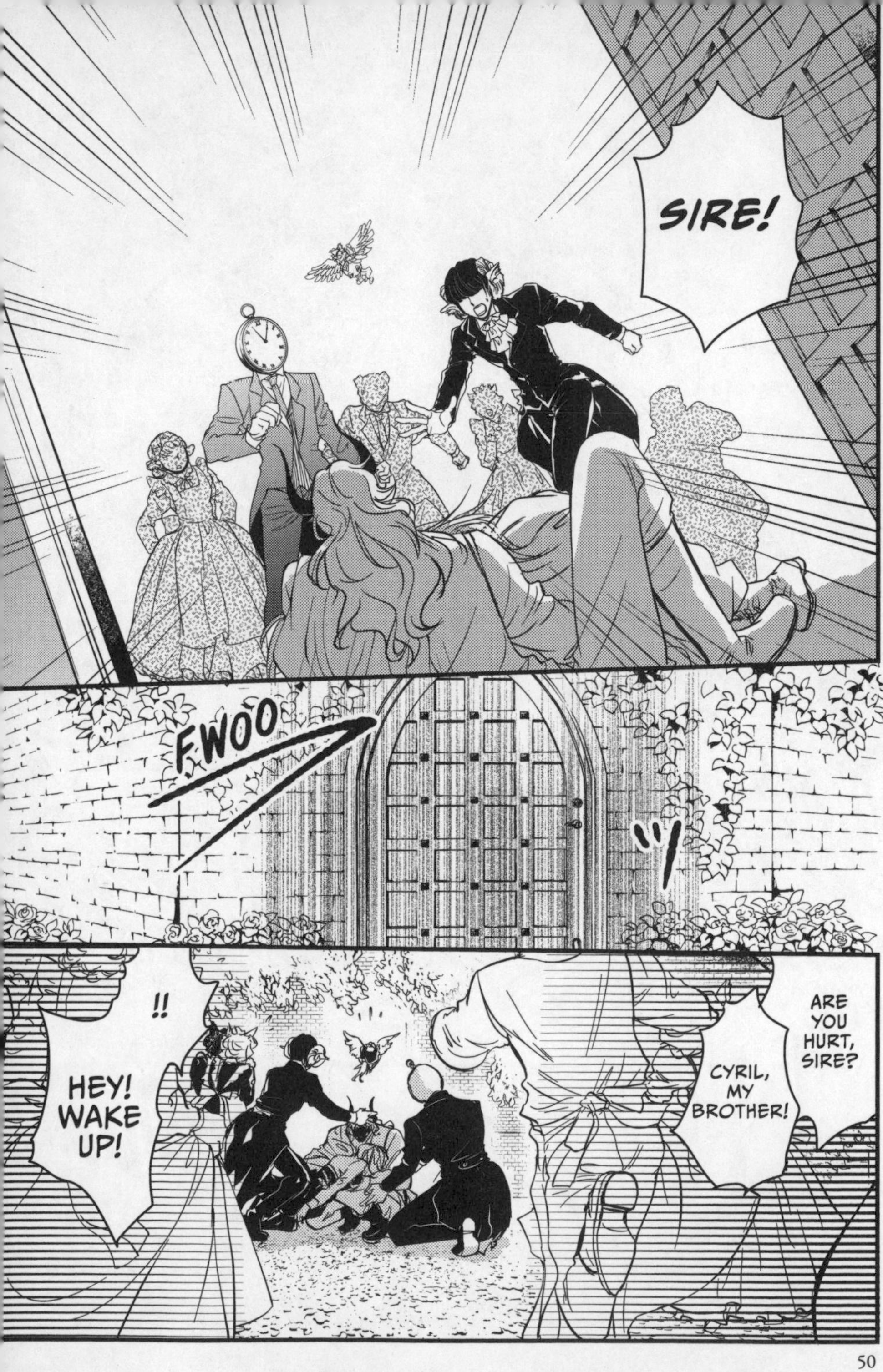
SIRE!
FWOO
ARE YOU HURT, SIRE?
CYRIL, MY BROTHER!
!!
HEY! WAKE UP!

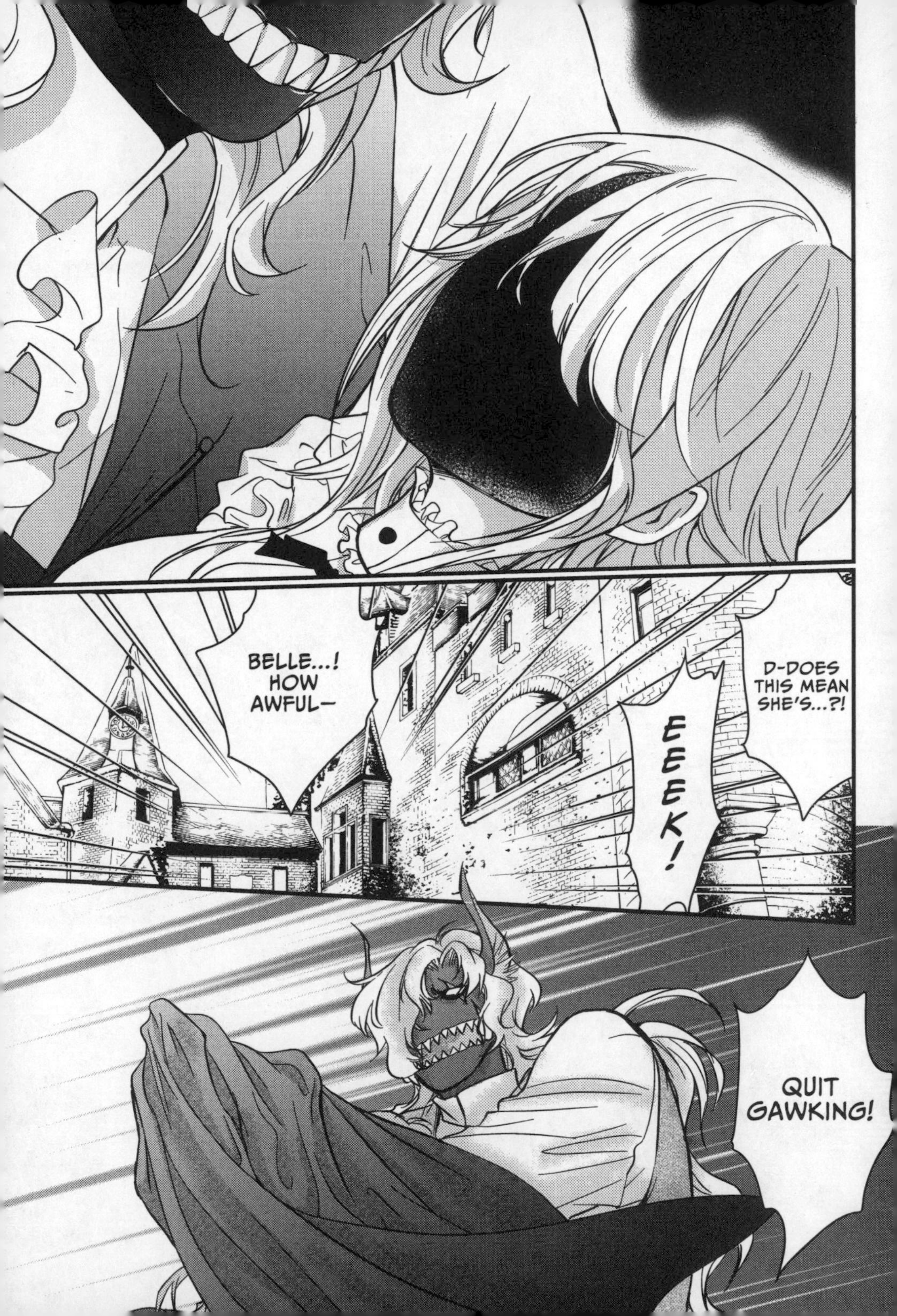
D-DOES THIS MEAN SHE'S...?!
EEEK!
BELLE...! HOW AWFUL—
QUIT GAWKING!

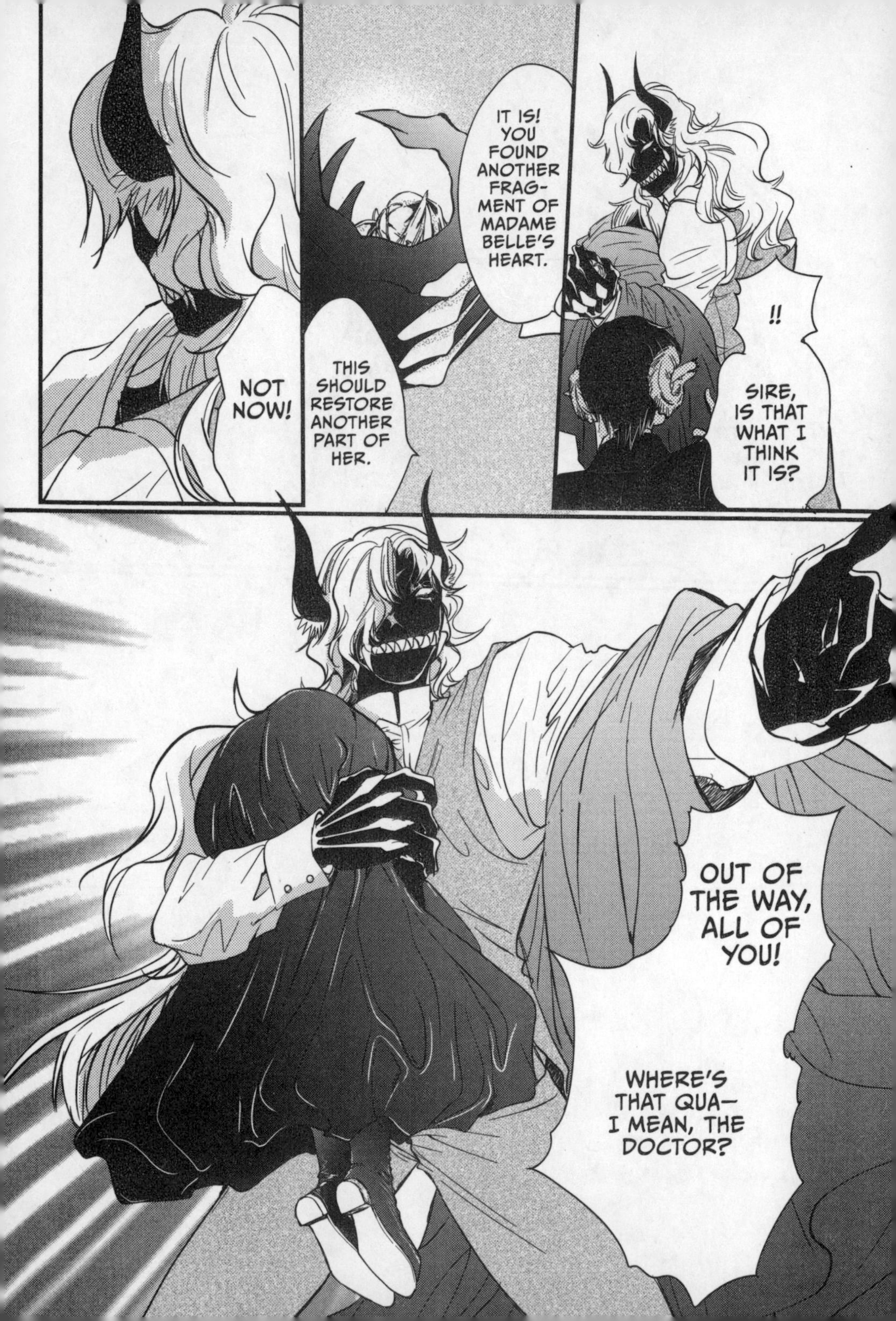
!!
SIRE, IS THAT WHAT I THINK IT IS?
IT IS! YOU FOUND ANOTHER FRAG-MENT OF MADAME BELLE'S HEART.
THIS SHOULD RESTORE ANOTHER PART OF HER.
NOT NOW!
OUT OF THE WAY, ALL OF YOU!
WHERE'S THAT QUA— I MEAN, THE DOCTOR?

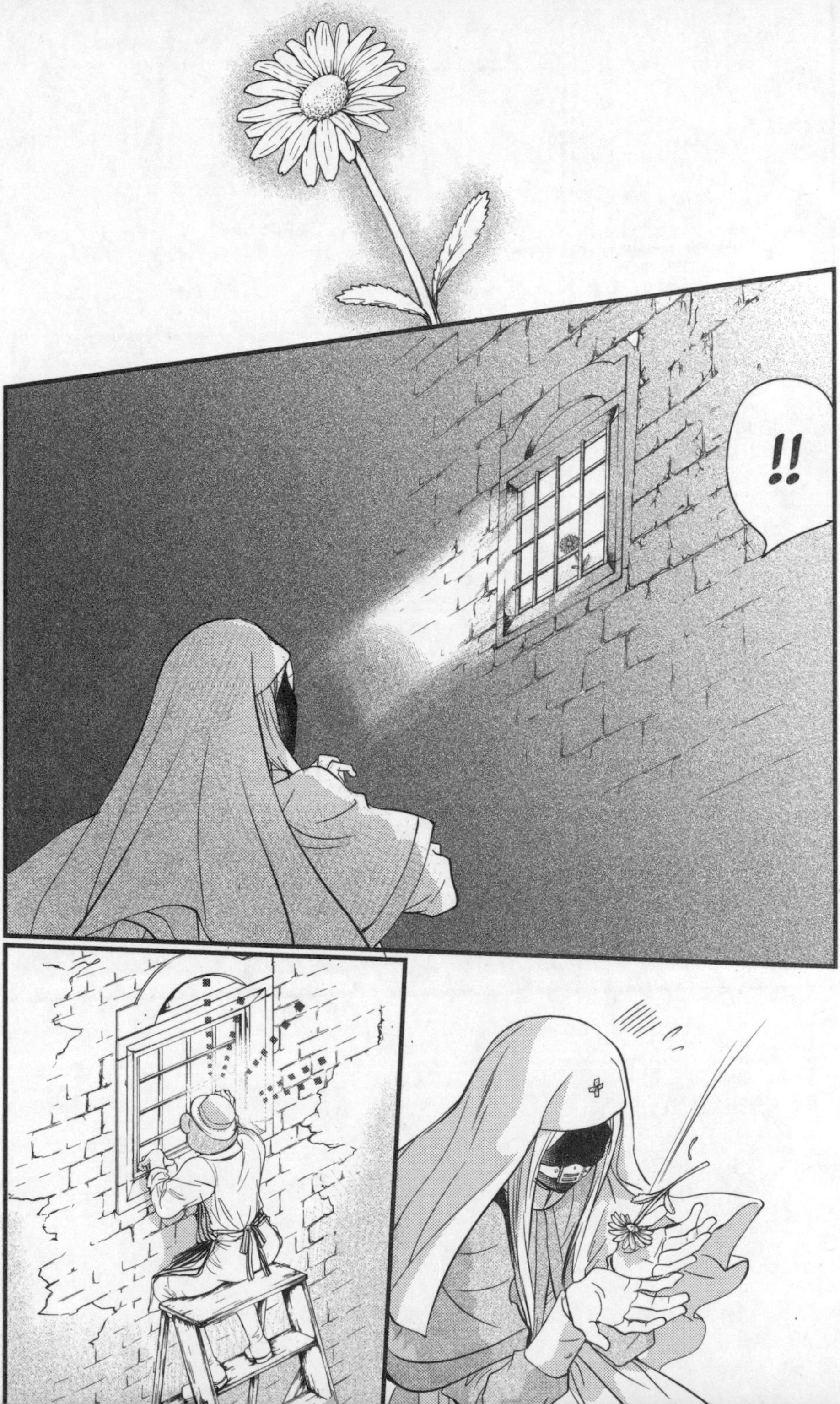
!!

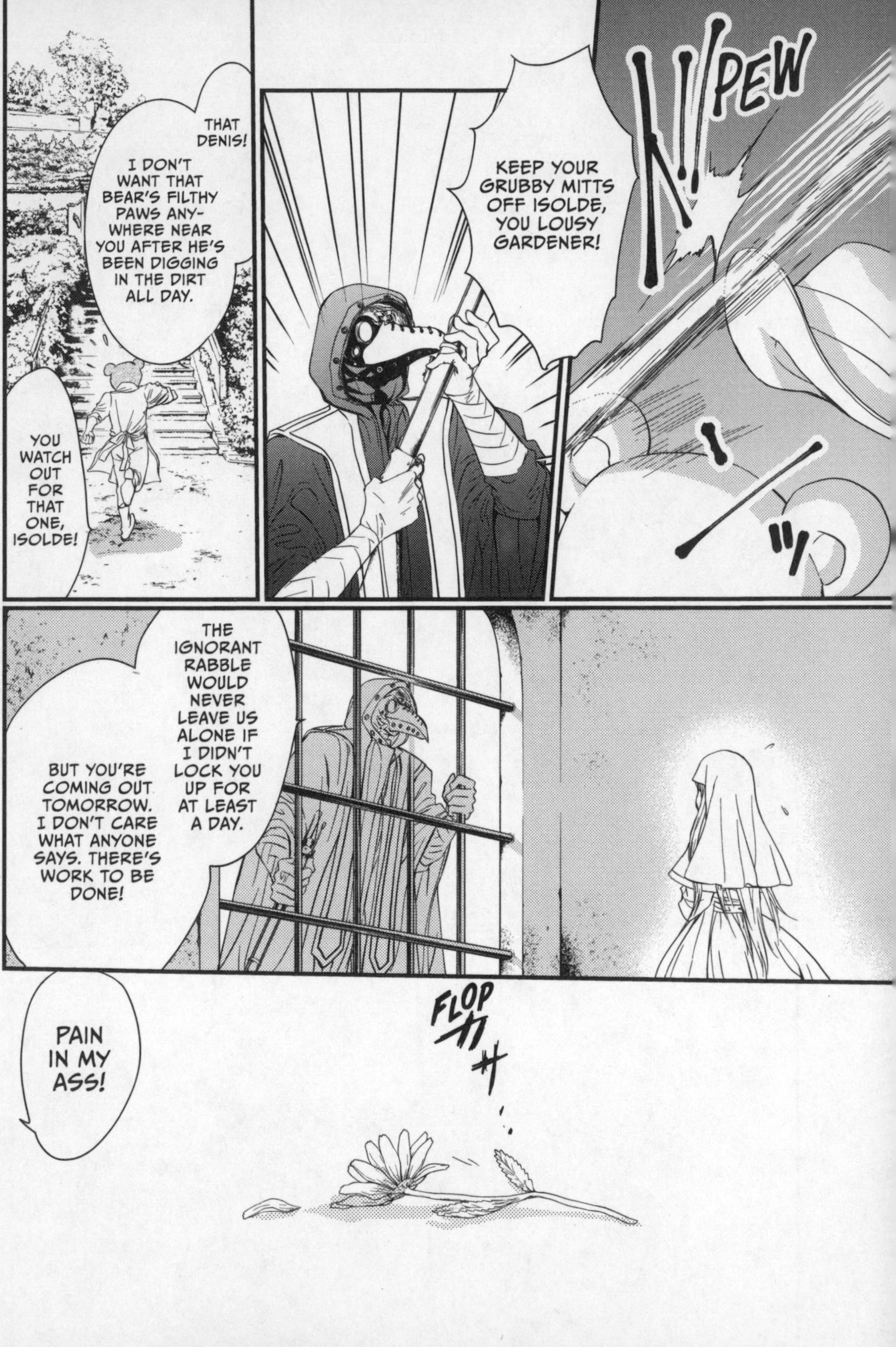
N//PEW
KEEP YOUR GRUBBY MITTS OFF ISOLDE, YOU LOUSY GARDENER!
THAT DENIS!
I DON'T WANT THAT BEAR'S FILTHY PAWS ANY-WHERE NEAR YOU AFTER HE'S BEEN DIGGING IN THE DIRT ALL DAY.
YOU WATCH OUT FOR THAT ONE, ISOLDE!
THE IGNORANT RABBLE WOULD NEVER LEAVE US ALONE IF I DIDN'T LOCK YOU UP FOR AT LEAST A DAY.
BUT YOU'RE COMING OUT TOMORROW. I DON'T CARE WHAT ANYONE SAYS. THERE'S WORK TO BE DONE!
PAIN IN MY ASS!
FLOP

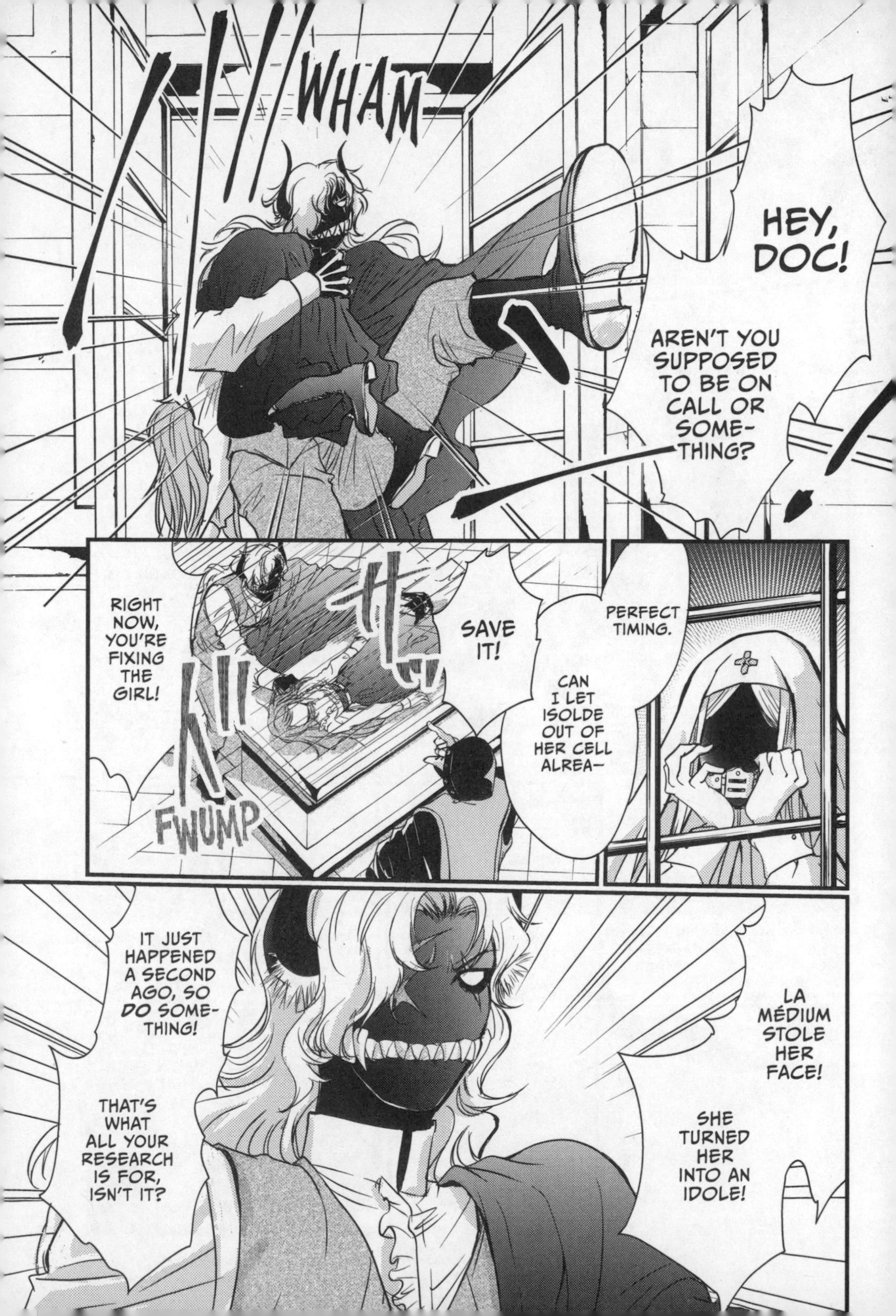
WHAM
HEY, DOC!
AREN'T YOU SUPPOSED TO BE ON CALL OR SOME-THING?
PERFECT TIMING.
CAN I LET ISOLDE OUT OF HER CELL ALREA—
SAVE IT!
RIGHT NOW, YOU'RE FIXING THE GIRL!
FWUMP
LA MÉDIUM STOLE HER FACE!
SHE TURNED HER INTO AN IDOLE!
IT JUST HAPPENED A SECOND AGO, SO DO SOME-THING!
THAT'S WHAT ALL YOUR RESEARCH IS FOR, ISN'T IT?

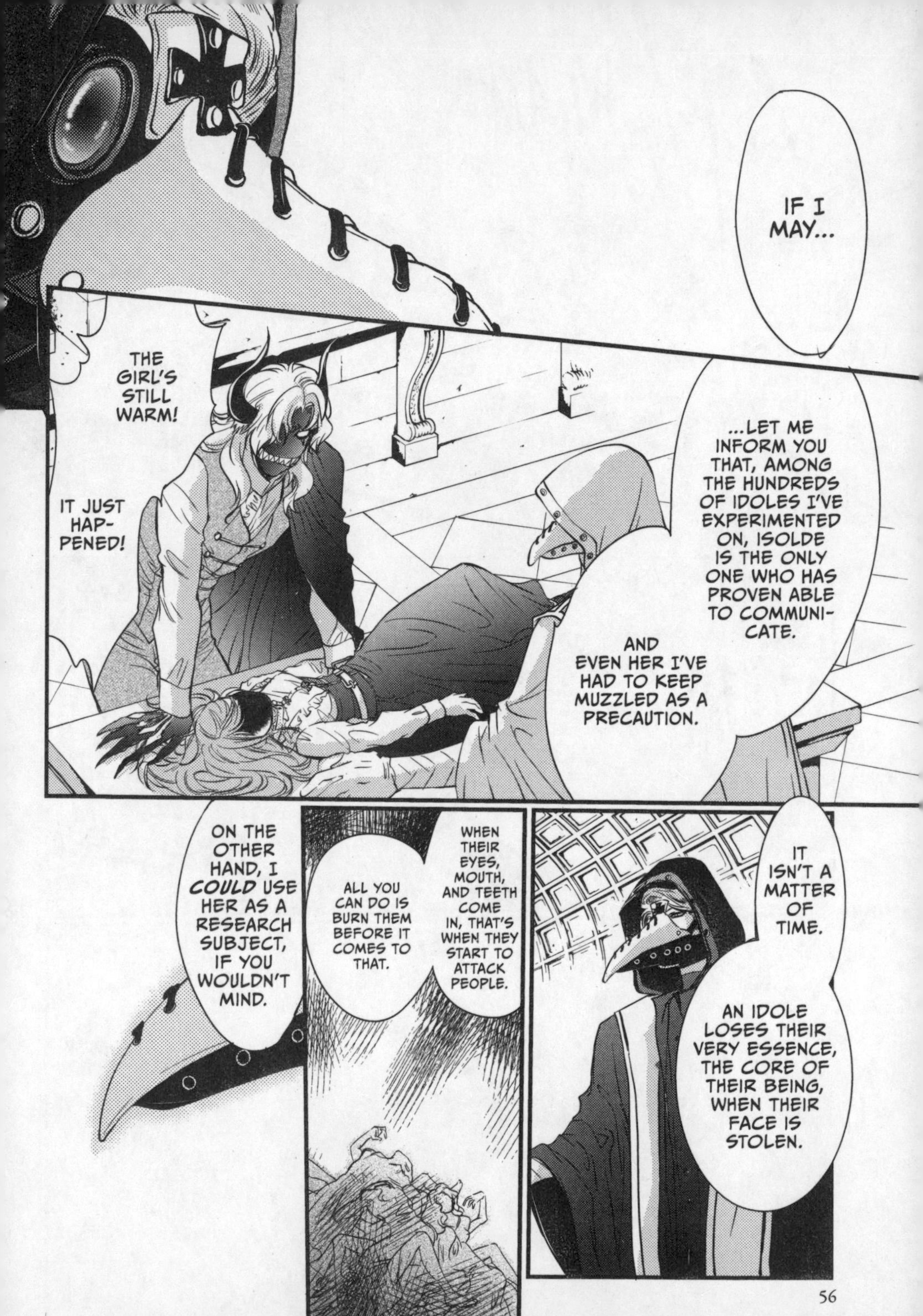
IF I MAY...
...LET ME INFORM YOU THAT, AMONG THE HUNDREDS OF IDOLES I'VE EXPERIMENTED ON, ISOLDE IS THE ONLY ONE WHO HAS PROVEN ABLE TO COMMUNICATE.
AND EVEN HER I'VE HAD TO KEEP MUZZLED AS A PRECAUTION.
THE GIRL'S STILL WARM!
IT JUST HAPPENED!
IT ISN'T A MATTER OF TIME.
AN IDOLE LOSES THEIR VERY ESSENCE, THE CORE OF THEIR BEING, WHEN THEIR FACE IS STOLEN.
WHEN THEIR EYES, MOUTH, AND TEETH COME IN, THAT'S WHEN THEY START TO ATTACK PEOPLE.
ALL YOU CAN DO IS BURN THEM BEFORE IT COMES TO THAT.
ON THE OTHER HAND, I *COULD* USE HER AS A RESEARCH SUBJECT, IF YOU WOULDN'T MIND.

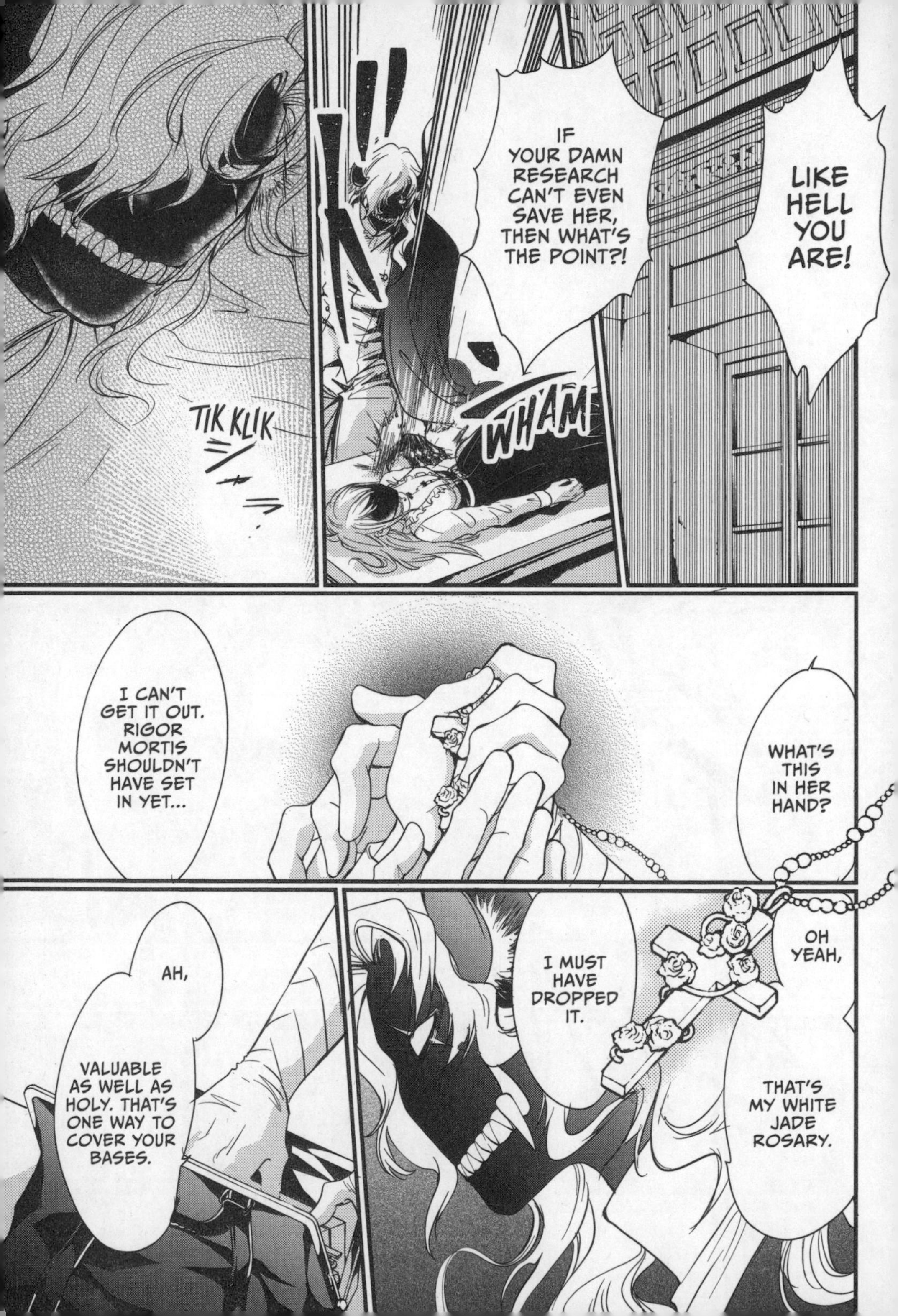
LIKE HELL YOU ARE!
IF YOUR DAMN RESEARCH CAN'T EVEN SAVE HER, THEN WHAT'S THE POINT?!
WHAM
TIK KLIK
WHAT'S THIS IN HER HAND?
I CAN'T GET IT OUT. RIGOR MORTIS SHOULDN'T HAVE SET IN YET...
OH YEAH,
THAT'S MY WHITE JADE ROSARY.
I MUST HAVE DROPPED IT.
AH,
VALUABLE AS WELL AS HOLY. THAT'S ONE WAY TO COVER YOUR BASES.

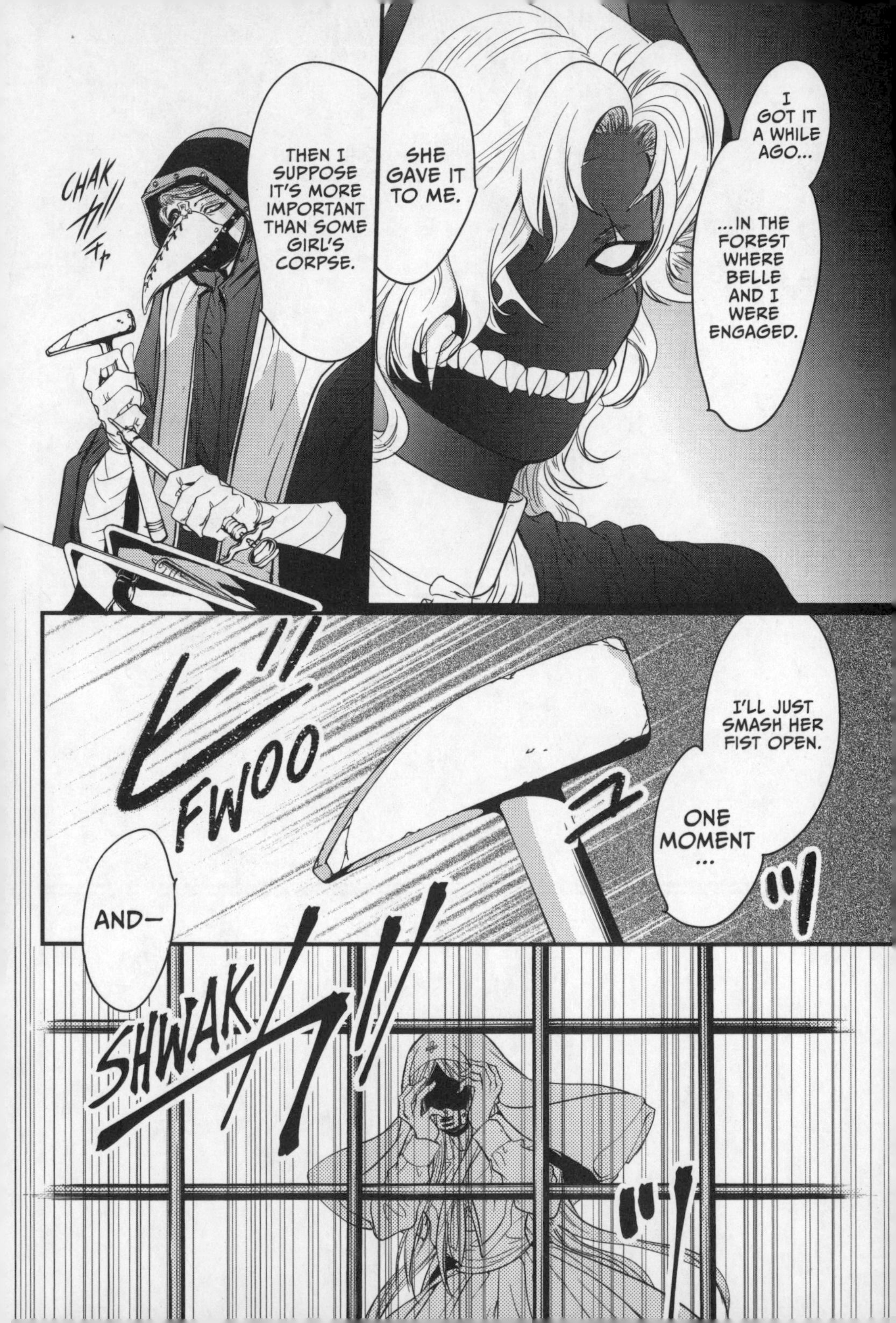
I GOT IT A WHILE AGO...
...IN THE FOREST WHERE BELLE AND I WERE ENGAGED.
SHE GAVE IT TO ME.
THEN I SUPPOSE IT'S MORE IMPORTANT THAN SOME GIRL'S CORPSE.
CHAK
I'LL JUST SMASH HER FIST OPEN.
ONE MOMENT...
FWOO
AND—
SHWAK

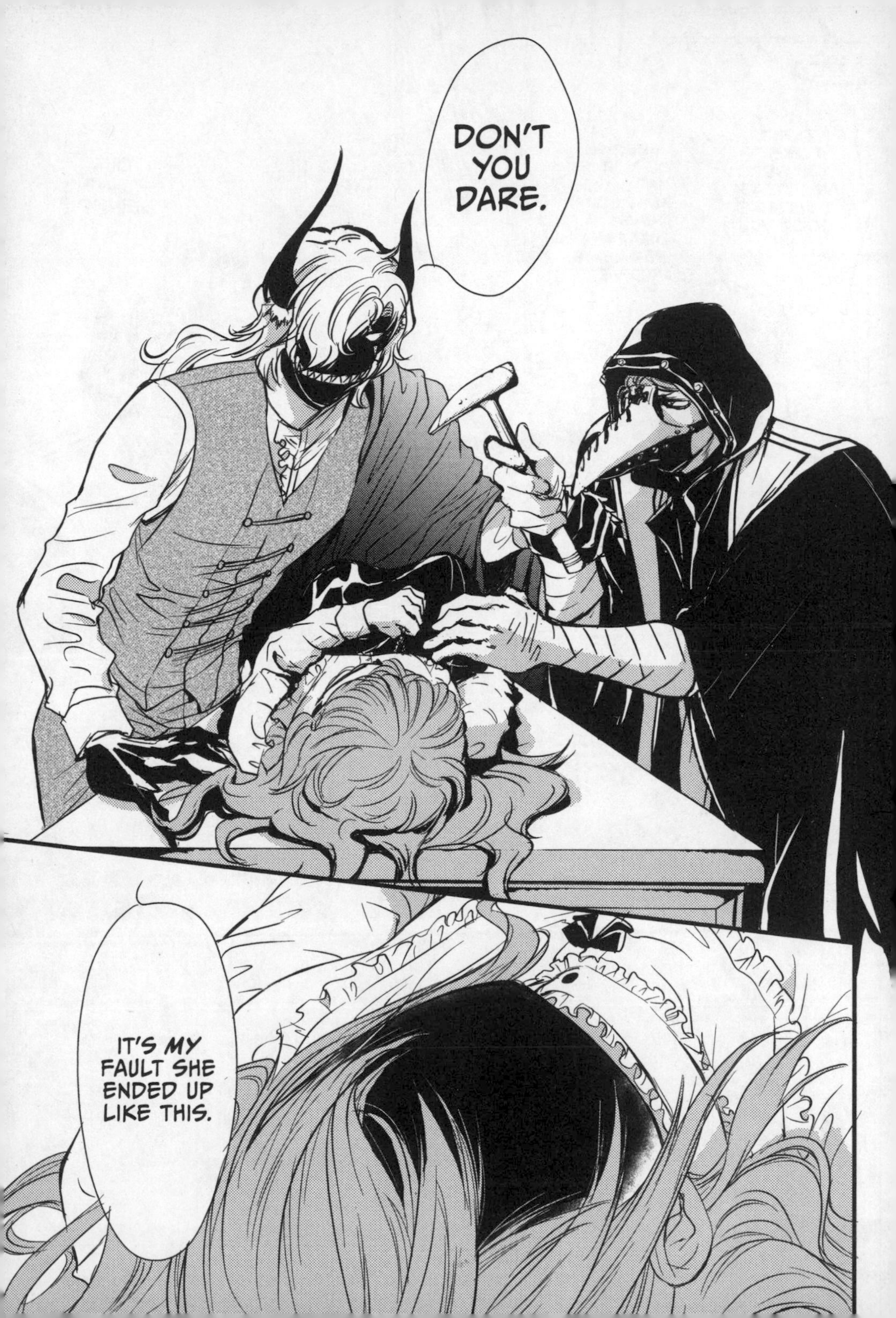
DON'T YOU DARE.
IT'S MY FAULT SHE ENDED UP LIKE THIS.

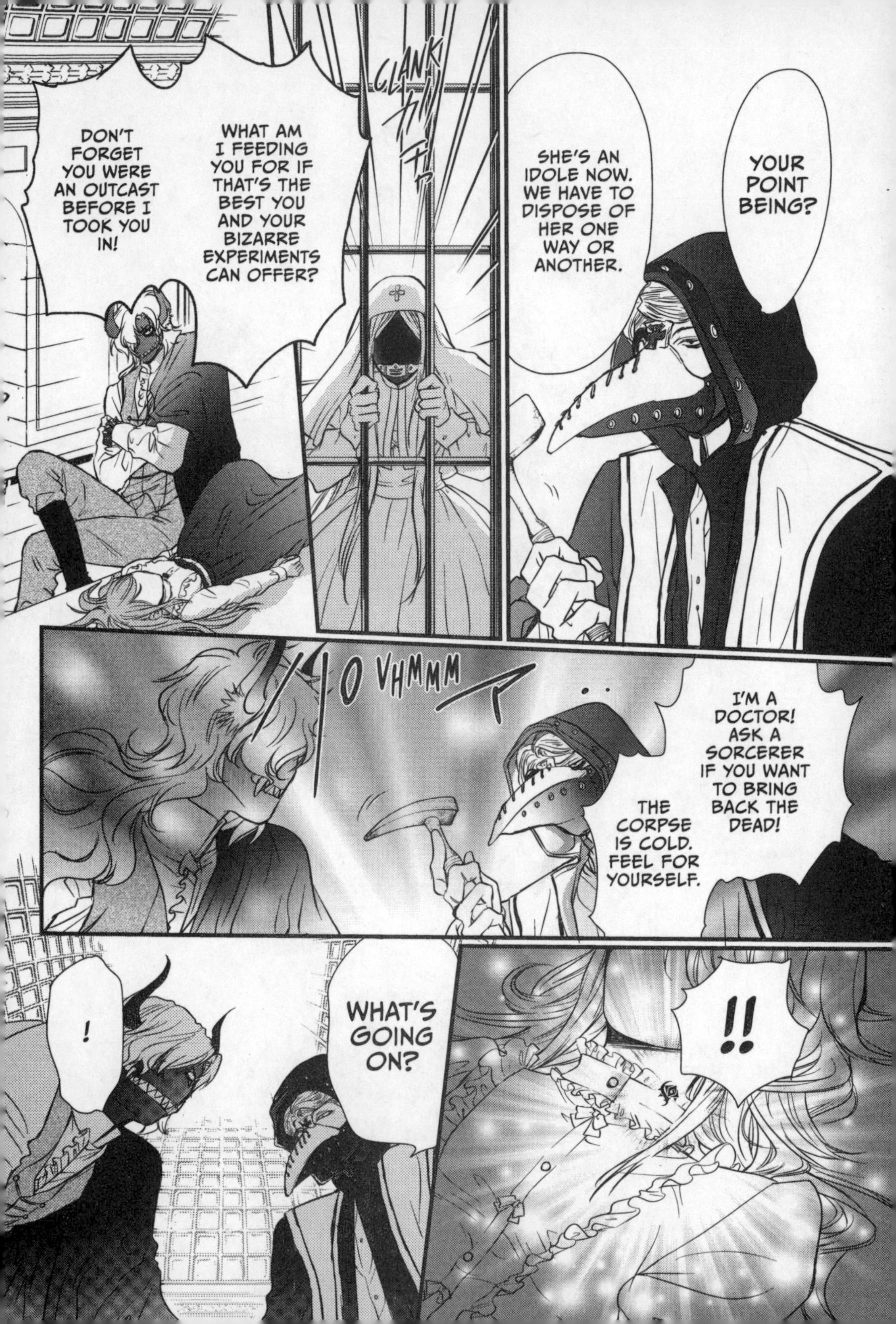
YOUR POINT BEING?
SHE'S AN IDOLE NOW. WE HAVE TO DISPOSE OF HER ONE WAY OR ANOTHER.
CLANK
WHAT AM I FEEDING YOU FOR IF THAT'S THE BEST YOU AND YOUR BIZARRE EXPERIMENTS CAN OFFER?
DON'T FORGET YOU WERE AN OUTCAST BEFORE I TOOK YOU IN!
I'M A DOCTOR! ASK A SORCERER IF YOU WANT TO BRING BACK THE DEAD!
THE CORPSE IS COLD. FEEL FOR YOURSELF.
...
VHMMM
!!
WHAT'S GOING ON?
!

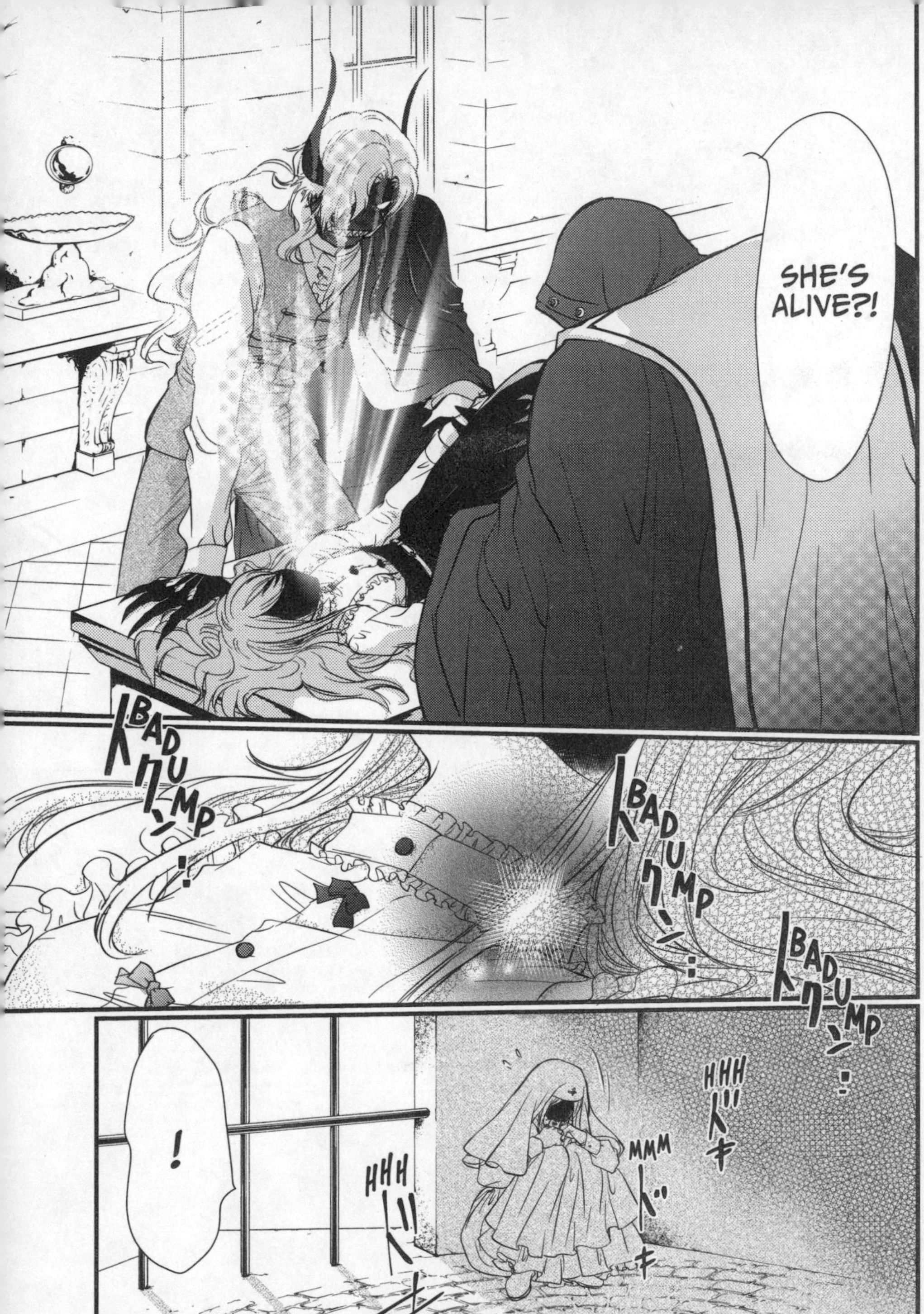
SHE'S ALIVE?!
BADUMP
BADUMP
BADUMP
HHH
MMM
!
HHH

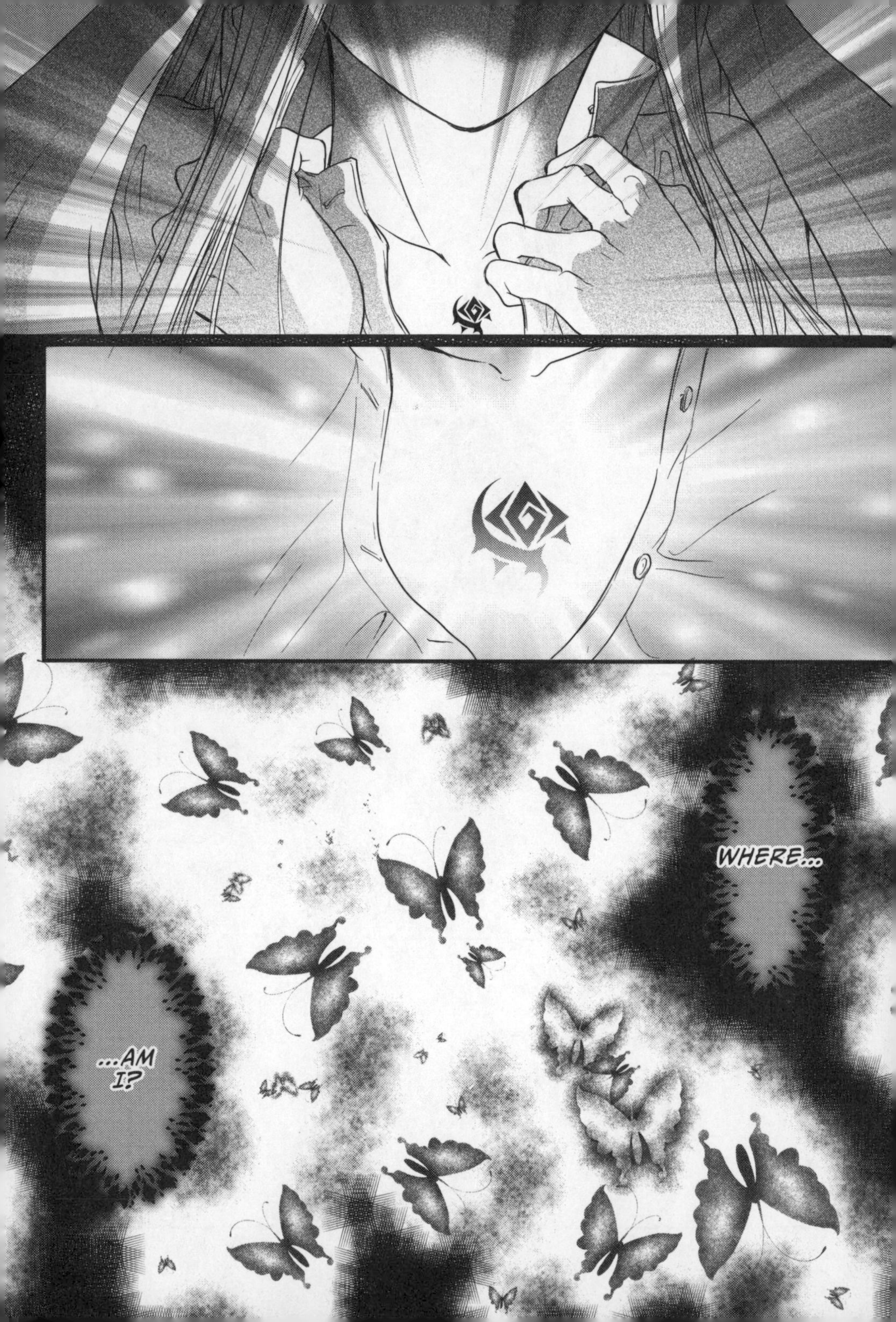
WHERE...
...AM I?

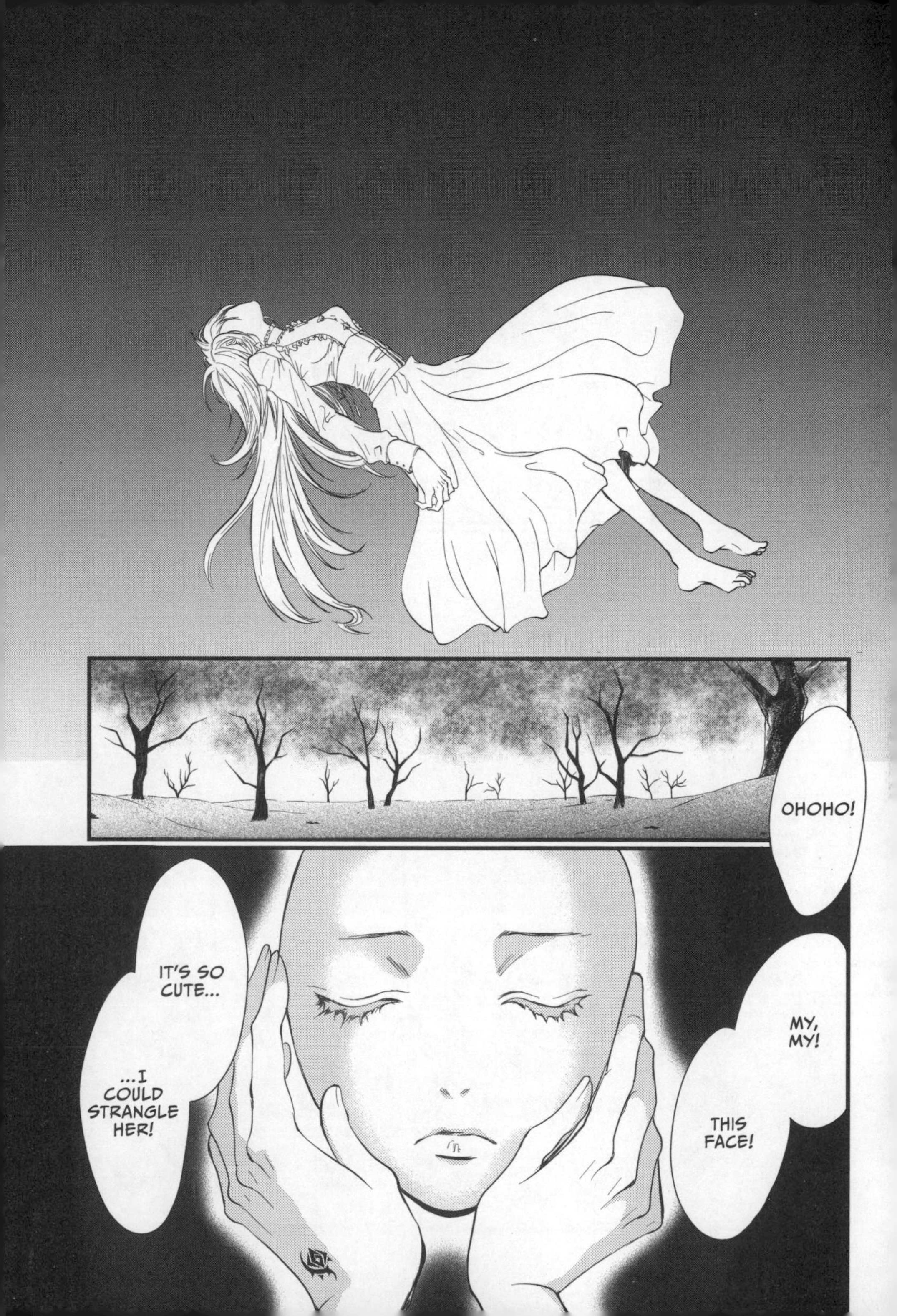
OHOHO!
MY, MY!
THIS FACE!
IT'S SO CUTE...
...I COULD STRANGLE HER!

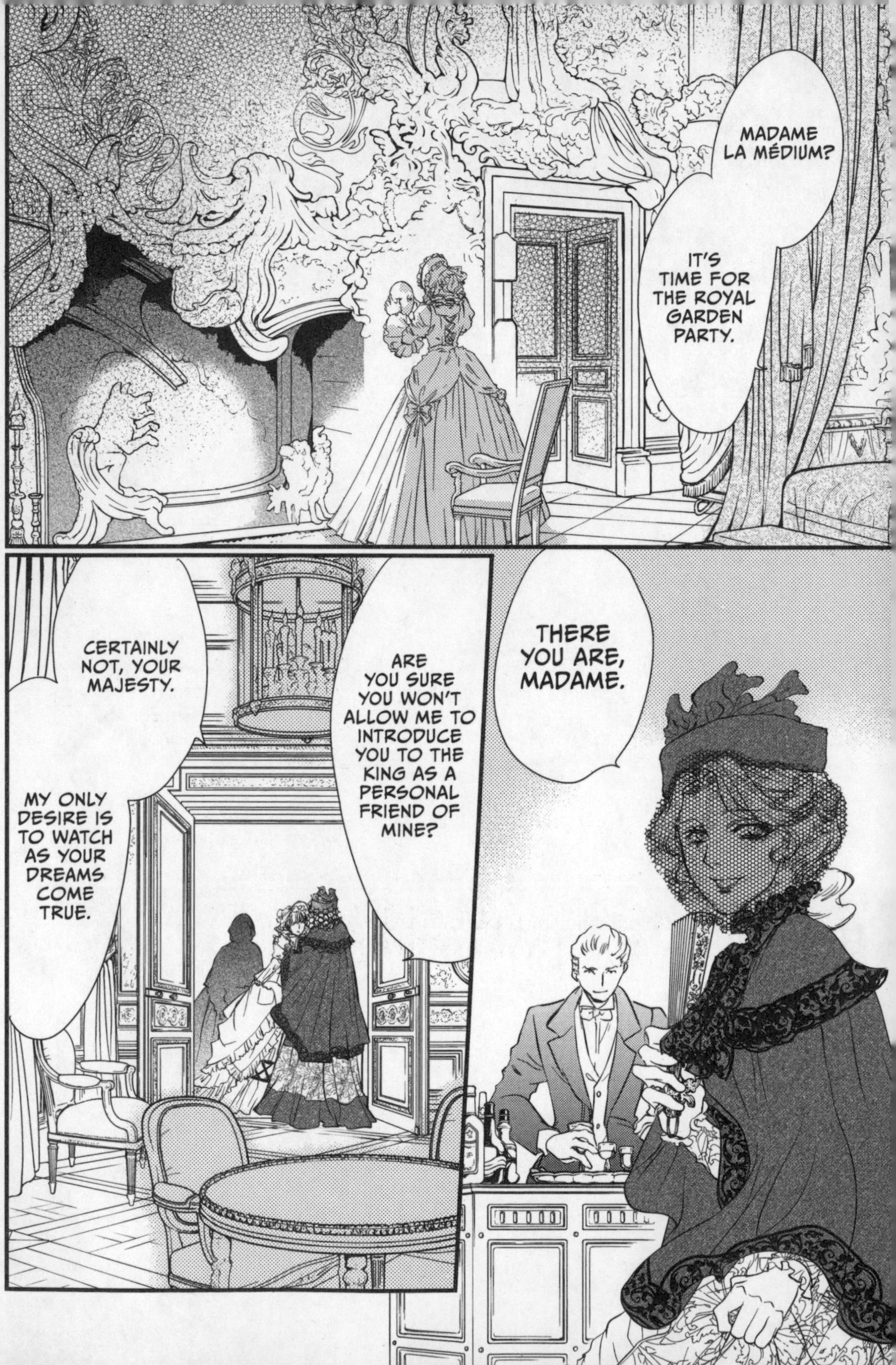
MADAME LA MÉDIUM?
IT'S TIME FOR THE ROYAL GARDEN PARTY.
THERE YOU ARE, MADAME.
ARE YOU SURE YOU WON'T ALLOW ME TO INTRODUCE YOU TO THE KING AS A PERSONAL FRIEND OF MINE?
CERTAINLY NOT, YOUR MAJESTY.
MY ONLY DESIRE IS TO WATCH AS YOUR DREAMS COME TRUE.

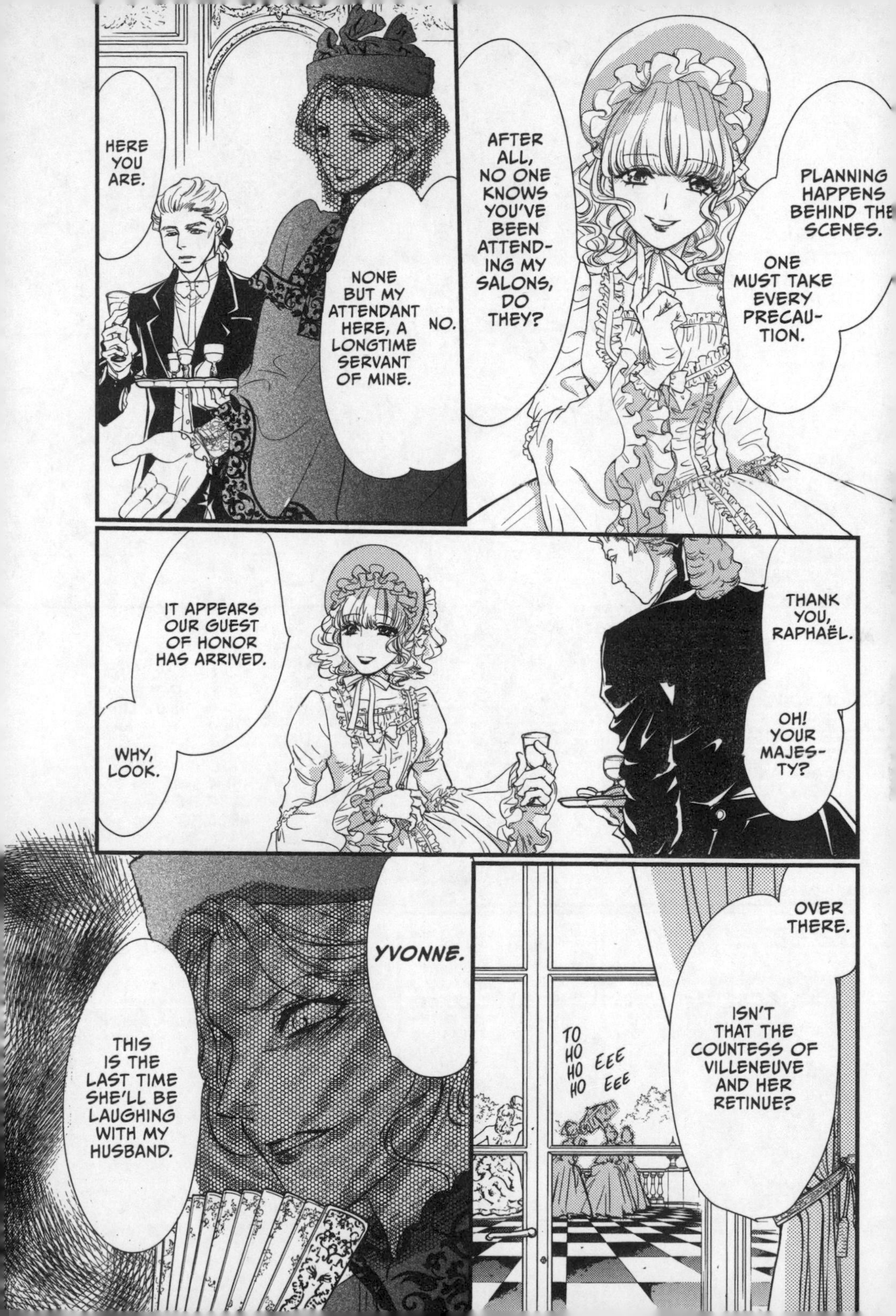
PLANNING HAPPENS BEHIND THE SCENES.
ONE MUST TAKE EVERY PRECAUTION.
AFTER ALL, NO ONE KNOWS YOU'VE BEEN ATTENDING MY SALONS, DO THEY?
NO.
NONE BUT MY ATTENDANT HERE, A LONGTIME SERVANT OF MINE.
HERE YOU ARE.
THANK YOU, RAPHAËL.
OH! YOUR MAJESTY?
IT APPEARS OUR GUEST OF HONOR HAS ARRIVED.
WHY, LOOK.
OVER THERE.
ISN'T THAT THE COUNTESS OF VILLENEUVE AND HER RETINUE?
TO HO HO HO
EEE EEE
YVONNE.
THIS IS THE LAST TIME SHE'LL BE LAUGHING WITH MY HUSBAND.

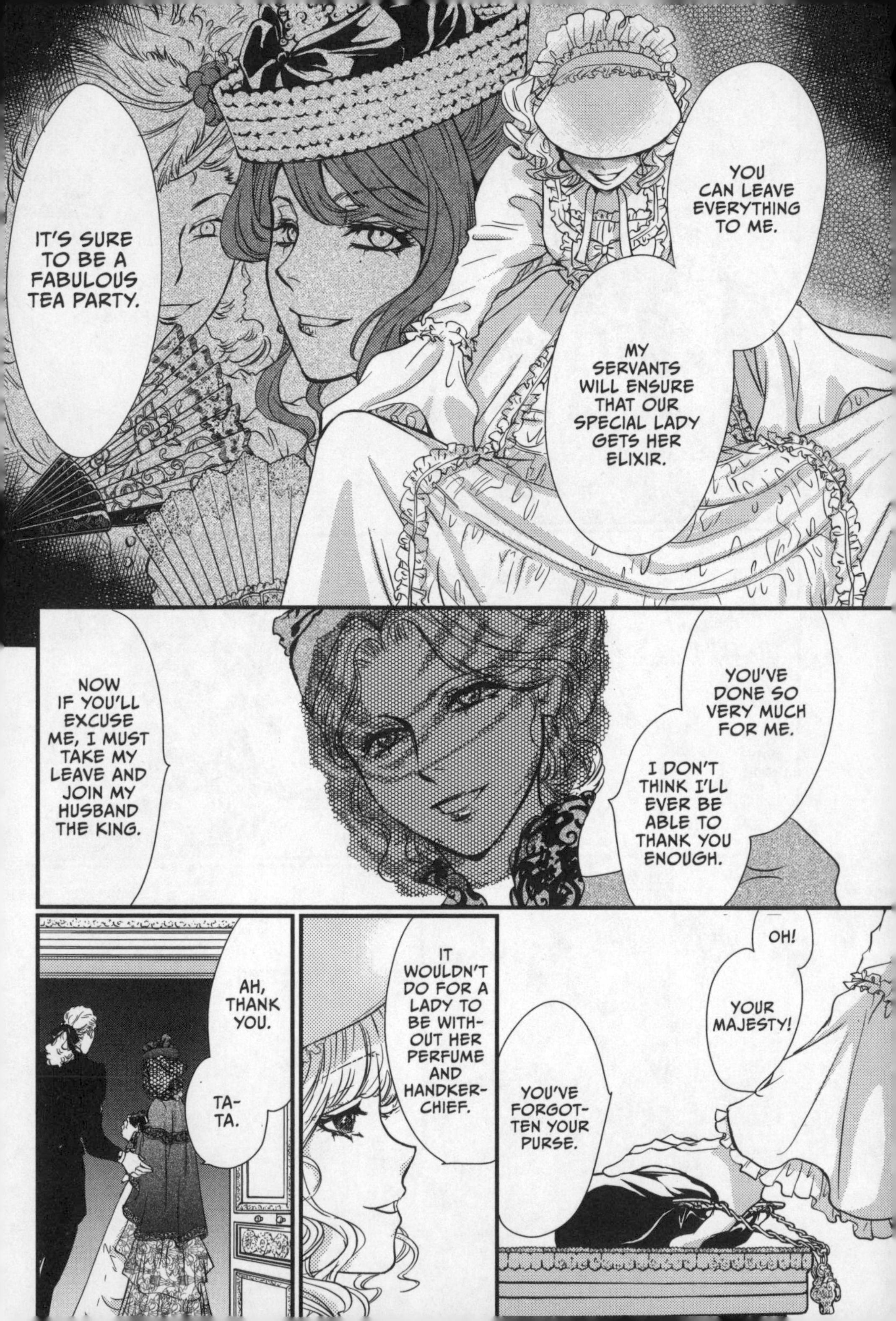
YOU CAN LEAVE EVERYTHING TO ME.
MY SERVANTS WILL ENSURE THAT OUR SPECIAL LADY GETS HER ELIXIR.
IT'S SURE TO BE A FABULOUS TEA PARTY.
YOU'VE DONE SO VERY MUCH FOR ME.
I DON'T THINK I'LL EVER BE ABLE TO THANK YOU ENOUGH.
NOW IF YOU'LL EXCUSE ME, I MUST TAKE MY LEAVE AND JOIN MY HUSBAND THE KING.
OH!
YOUR MAJESTY!
YOU'VE FORGOTTEN YOUR PURSE.
IT WOULDN'T DO FOR A LADY TO BE WITHOUT HER PERFUME AND HANDKERCHIEF.
AH, THANK YOU.
TA-TA.

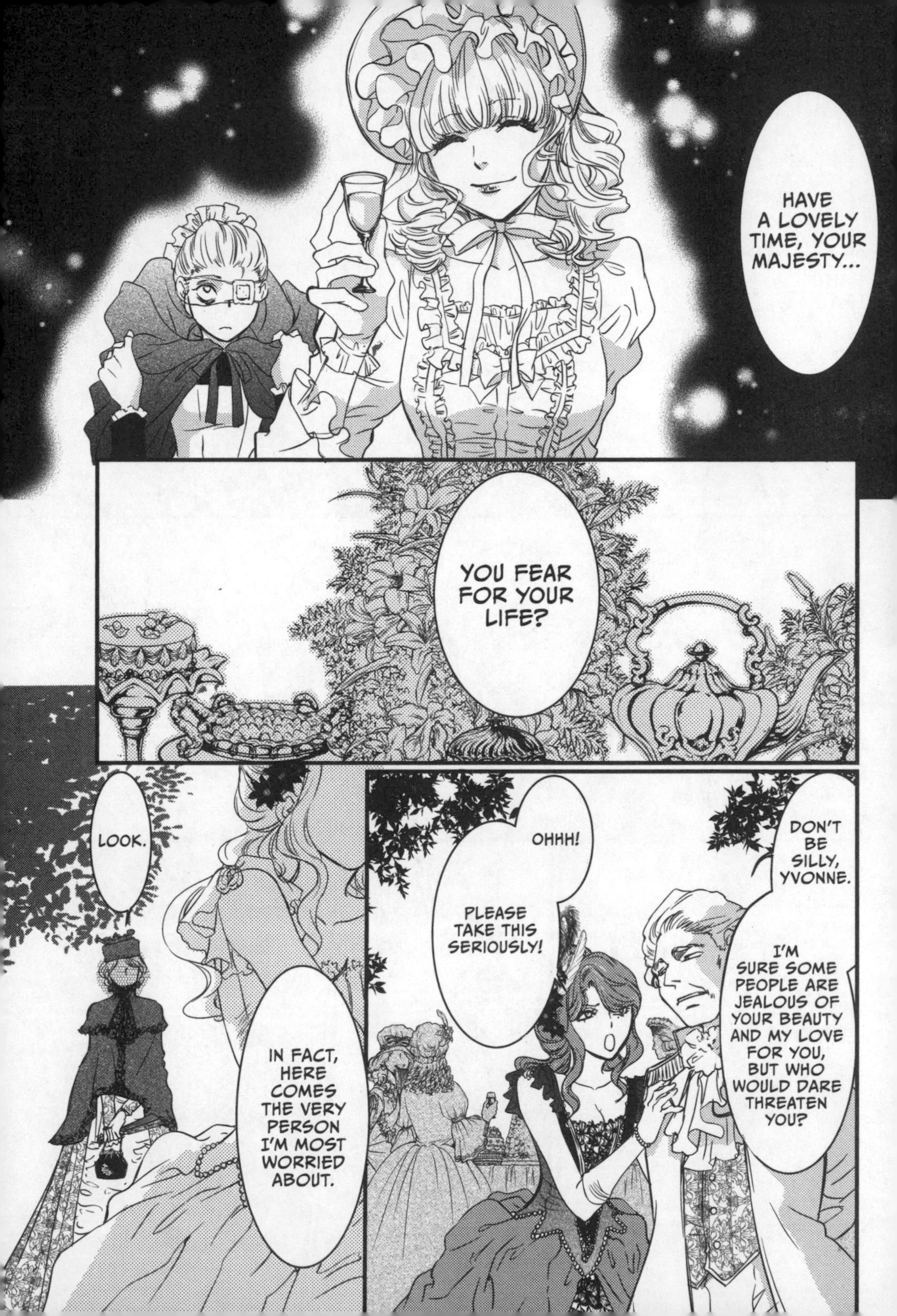
HAVE A LOVELY TIME, YOUR MAJESTY...
YOU FEAR FOR YOUR LIFE?
DON'T BE SILLY, YVONNE.
I'M SURE SOME PEOPLE ARE JEALOUS OF YOUR BEAUTY AND MY LOVE FOR YOU, BUT WHO WOULD DARE THREATEN YOU?
OHHH!
PLEASE TAKE THIS SERIOUSLY!
LOOK.
IN FACT, HERE COMES THE VERY PERSON I'M MOST WORRIED ABOUT.

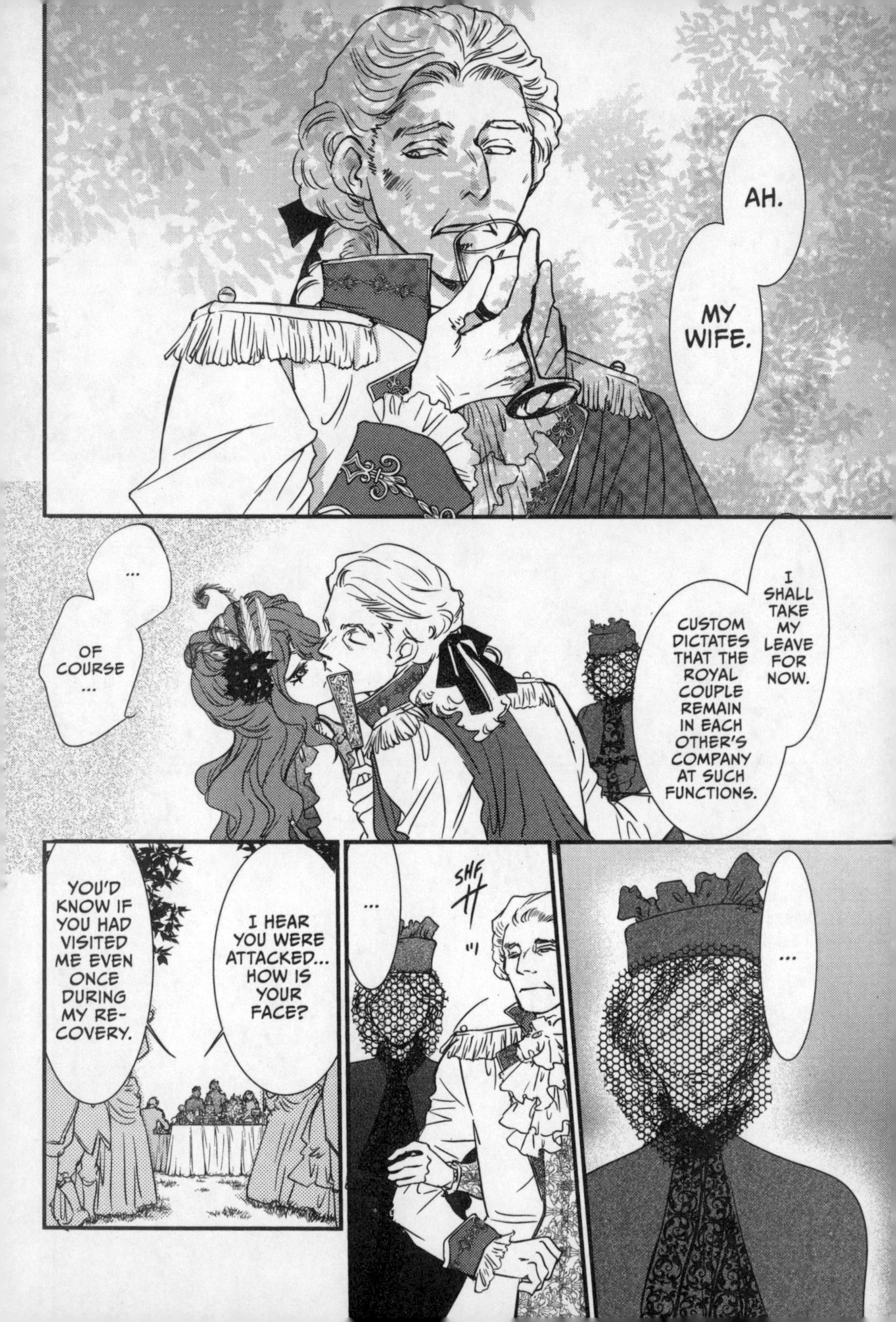
AH.
MY WIFE.
I SHALL TAKE MY LEAVE FOR NOW.
CUSTOM DICTATES THAT THE ROYAL COUPLE REMAIN IN EACH OTHER'S COMPANY AT SUCH FUNCTIONS.
...
OF COURSE ...
...
SHF
...
I HEAR YOU WERE ATTACKED... HOW IS YOUR FACE?
YOU'D KNOW IF YOU HAD VISITED ME EVEN ONCE DURING MY RE-COVERY.

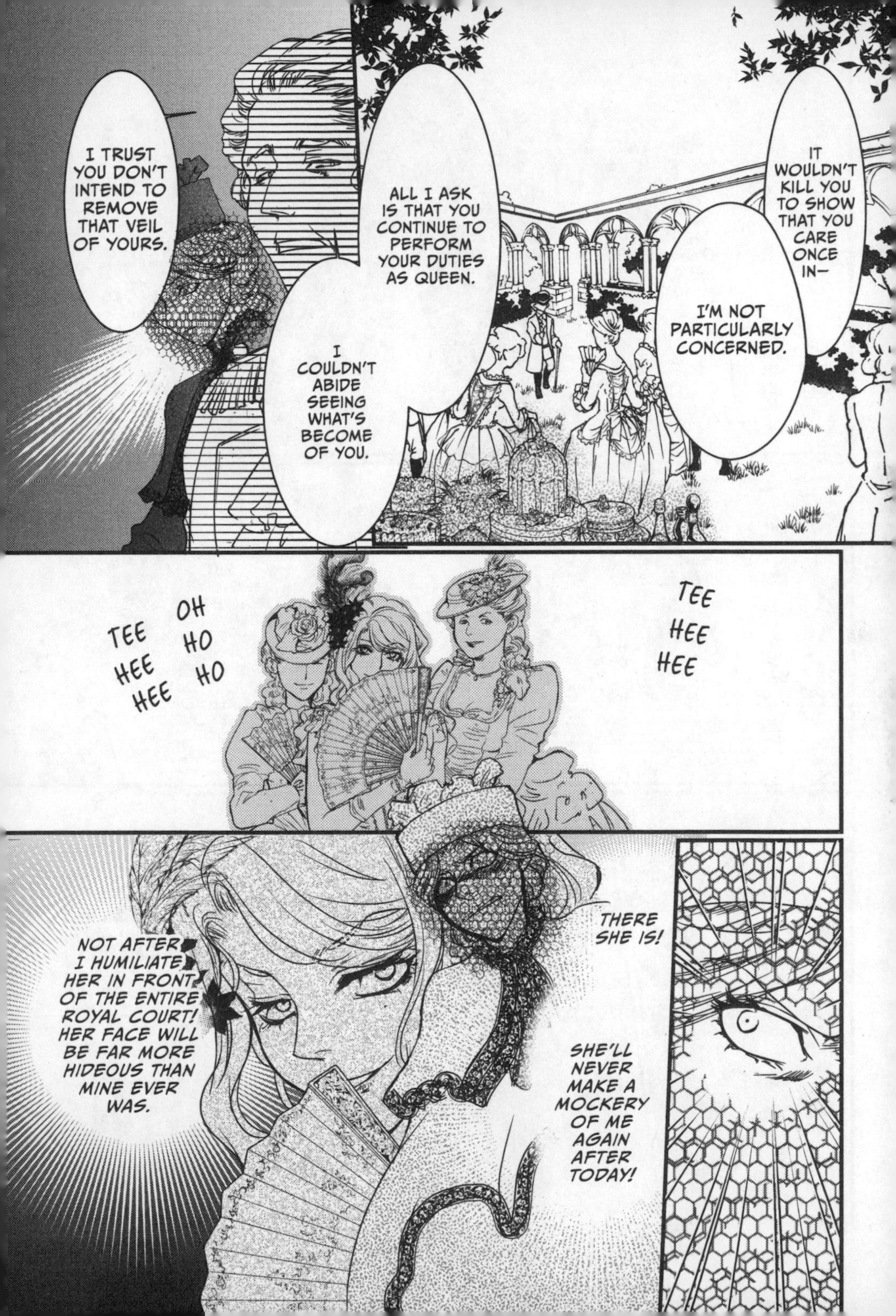
IT WOULDN'T KILL YOU TO SHOW THAT YOU CARE ONCE IN—
I'M NOT PARTICULARLY CONCERNED.
ALL I ASK IS THAT YOU CONTINUE TO PERFORM YOUR DUTIES AS QUEEN.
I COULDN'T ABIDE SEEING WHAT'S BECOME OF YOU.
I TRUST YOU DON'T INTEND TO REMOVE THAT VEIL OF YOURS.
TEE HEE HEE
OH HO HO
TEE HEE HEE
THERE SHE IS!
SHE'LL NEVER MAKE A MOCKERY OF ME AGAIN AFTER TODAY!
NOT AFTER I HUMILIATE HER IN FRONT OF THE ENTIRE ROYAL COURT! HER FACE WILL BE FAR MORE HIDEOUS THAN MINE EVER WAS.

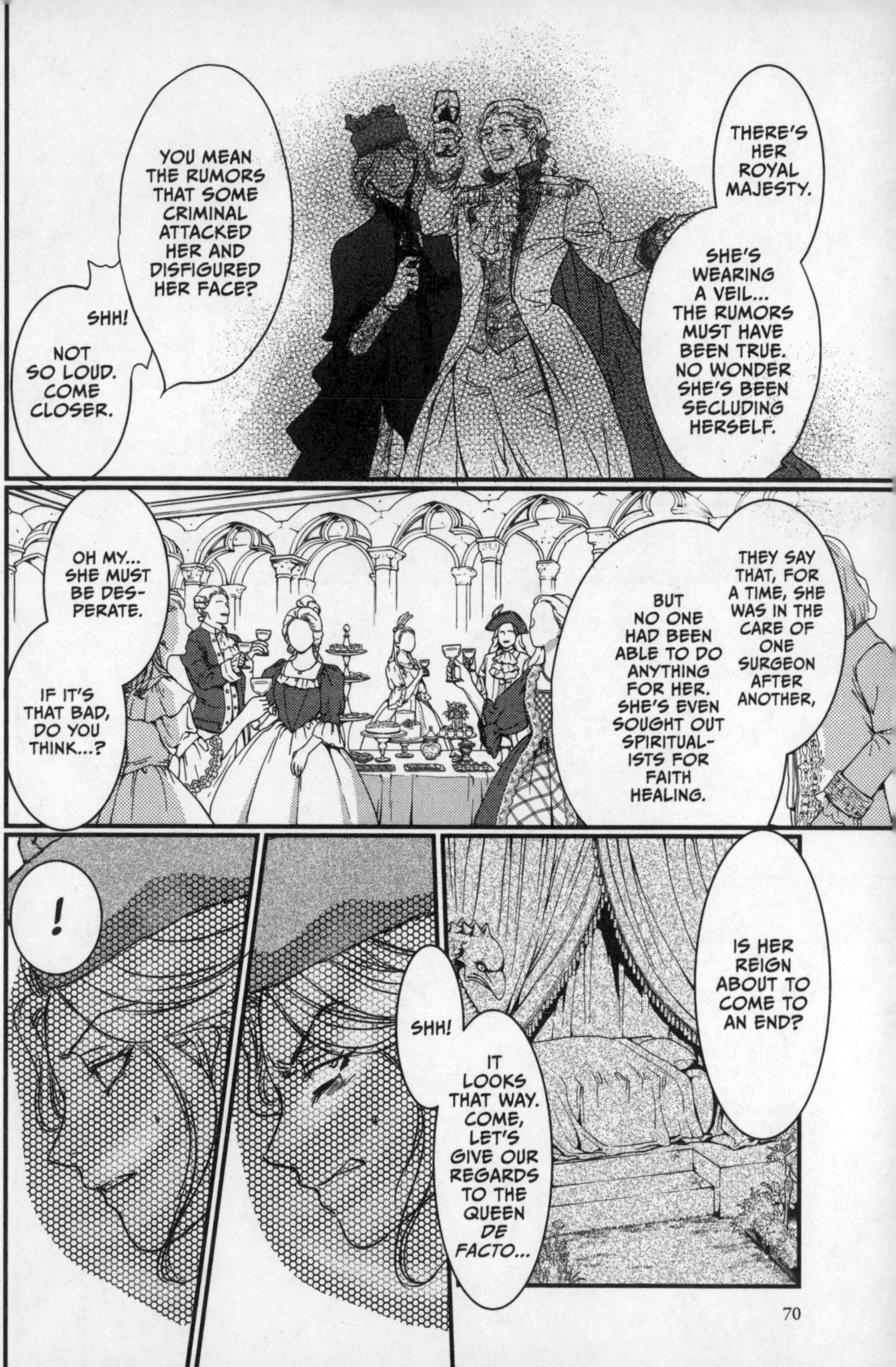
THERE'S HER ROYAL MAJESTY.
SHE'S WEARING A VEIL... THE RUMORS MUST HAVE BEEN TRUE. NO WONDER SHE'S BEEN SECLUDING HERSELF.
YOU MEAN THE RUMORS THAT SOME CRIMINAL ATTACKED HER AND DISFIGURED HER FACE?
SHH! NOT SO LOUD. COME CLOSER.
THEY SAY THAT, FOR A TIME, SHE WAS IN THE CARE OF ONE SURGEON AFTER ANOTHER,
BUT NO ONE HAD BEEN ABLE TO DO ANYTHING FOR HER. SHE'S EVEN SOUGHT OUT SPIRITUALISTS FOR FAITH HEALING.
OH MY... SHE MUST BE DESPERATE.
IF IT'S THAT BAD, DO YOU THINK...?
IS HER REIGN ABOUT TO COME TO AN END?
SHH! IT LOOKS THAT WAY. COME, LET'S GIVE OUR REGARDS TO THE QUEEN *DE FACTO*...
!

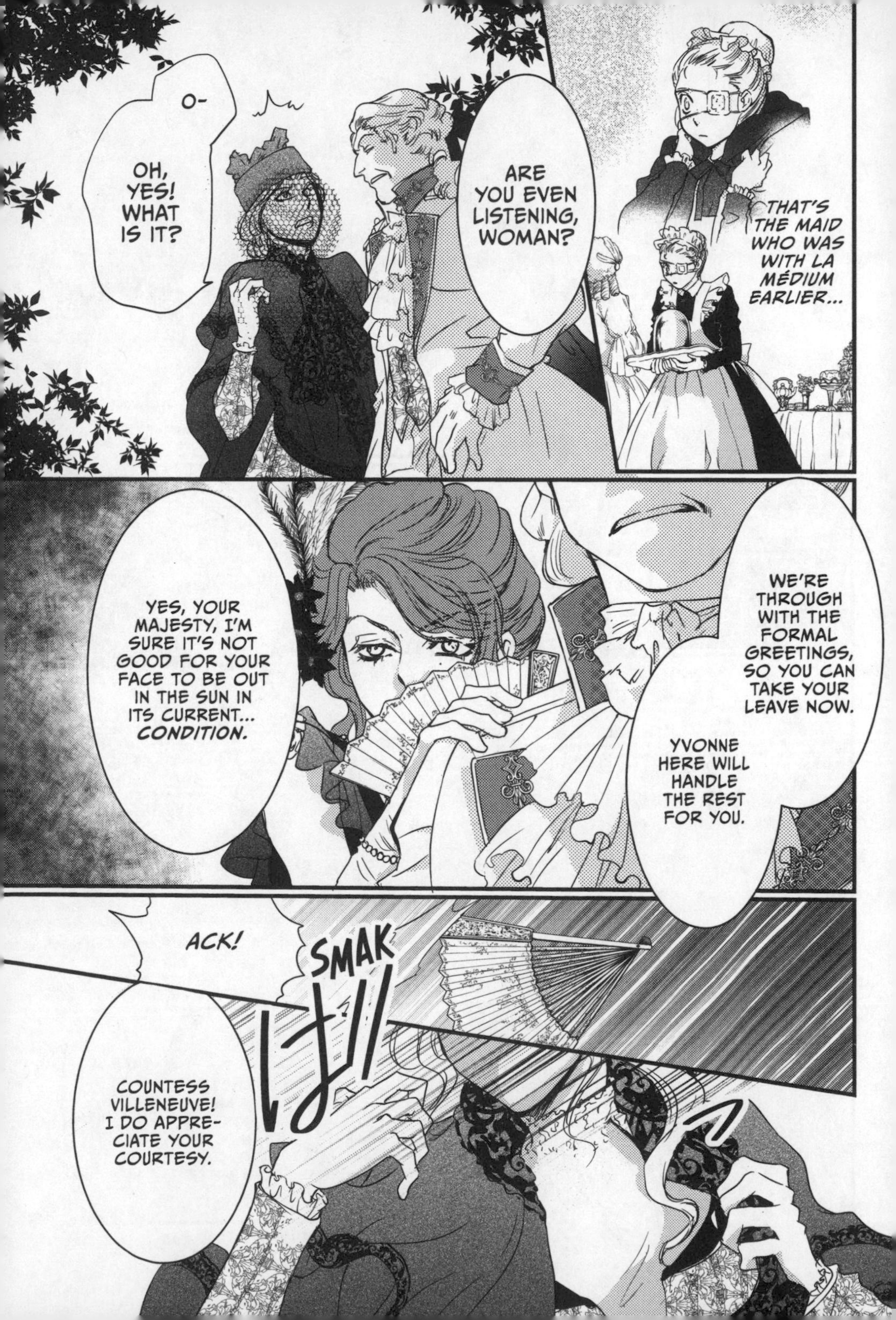
THAT'S THE MAID WHO WAS WITH LA MÉDIUM EARLIER...
ARE YOU EVEN LISTENING, WOMAN?
O-
OH, YES! WHAT IS IT?
WE'RE THROUGH WITH THE FORMAL GREETINGS, SO YOU CAN TAKE YOUR LEAVE NOW.
YVONNE HERE WILL HANDLE THE REST FOR YOU.
YES, YOUR MAJESTY, I'M SURE IT'S NOT GOOD FOR YOUR FACE TO BE OUT IN THE SUN IN ITS CURRENT... *CONDITION.*
SMAK
ACK!
COUNTESS VILLENEUVE! I DO APPRECIATE YOUR COURTESY.

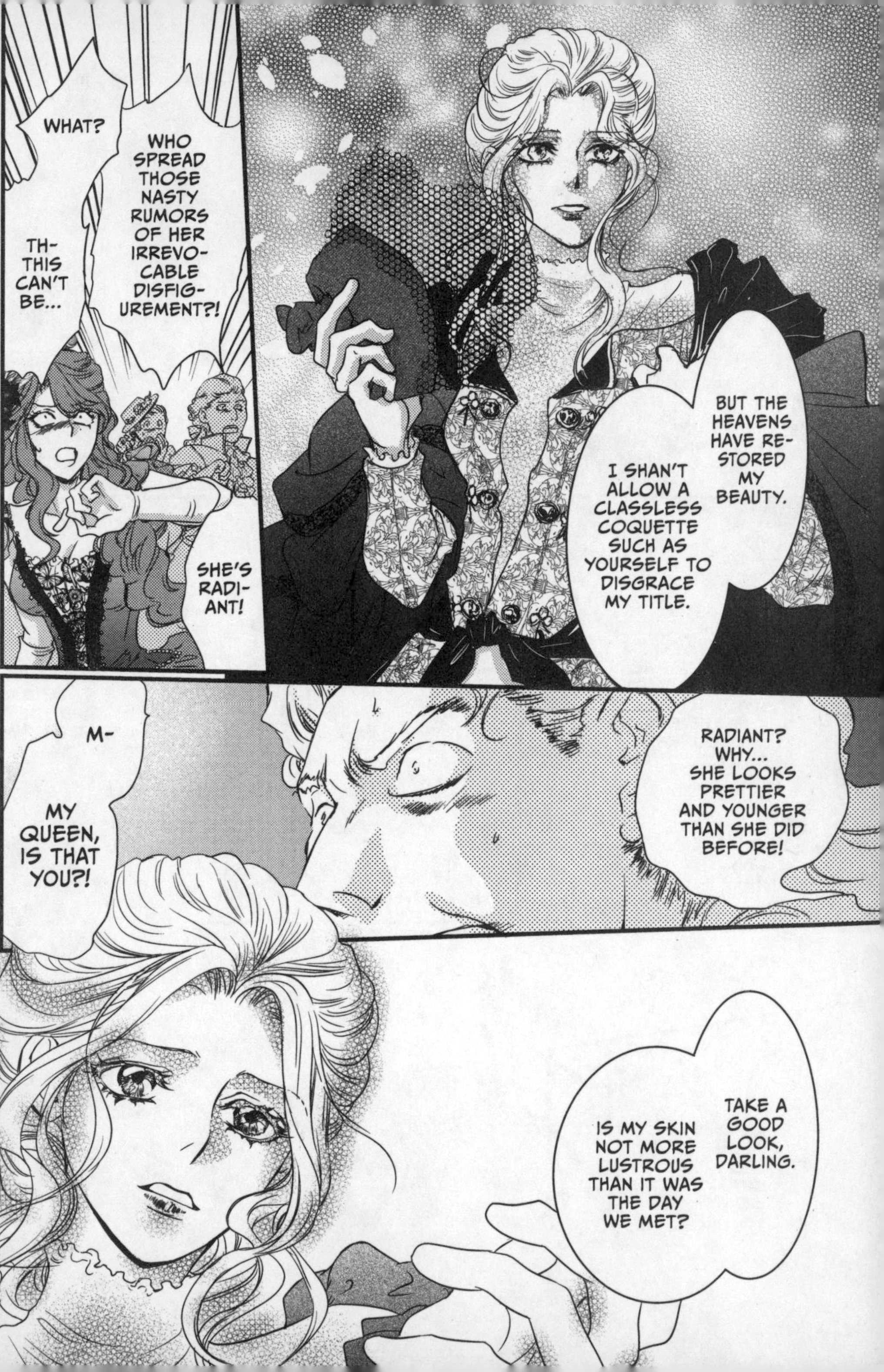
BUT THE HEAVENS HAVE RESTORED MY BEAUTY.
I SHAN'T ALLOW A CLASSLESS COQUETTE SUCH AS YOURSELF TO DISGRACE MY TITLE.
WHO SPREAD THOSE NASTY RUMORS OF HER IRREVOCABLE DISFIGUREMENT?!
WHAT?
TH-THIS CAN'T BE...
SHE'S RADIANT!
RADIANT? WHY... SHE LOOKS PRETTIER AND YOUNGER THAN SHE DID BEFORE!
M-
MY QUEEN, IS THAT YOU?!
TAKE A GOOD LOOK, DARLING.
IS MY SKIN NOT MORE LUSTROUS THAN IT WAS THE DAY WE MET?

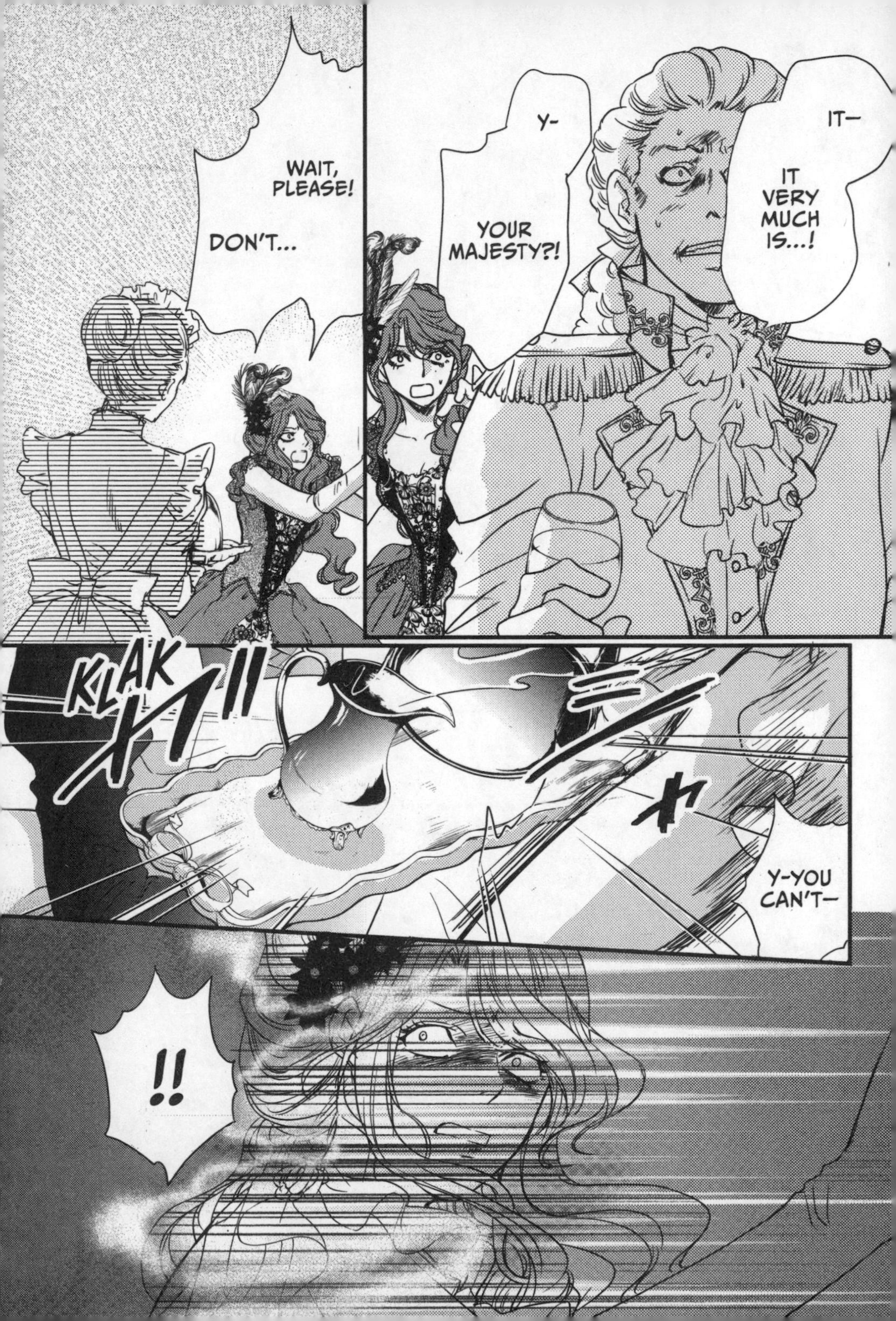
IT—
IT VERY MUCH IS...!
Y-
YOUR MAJESTY?!
WAIT, PLEASE!
DON'T...
KLAK
Y-YOU CAN'T—
!!

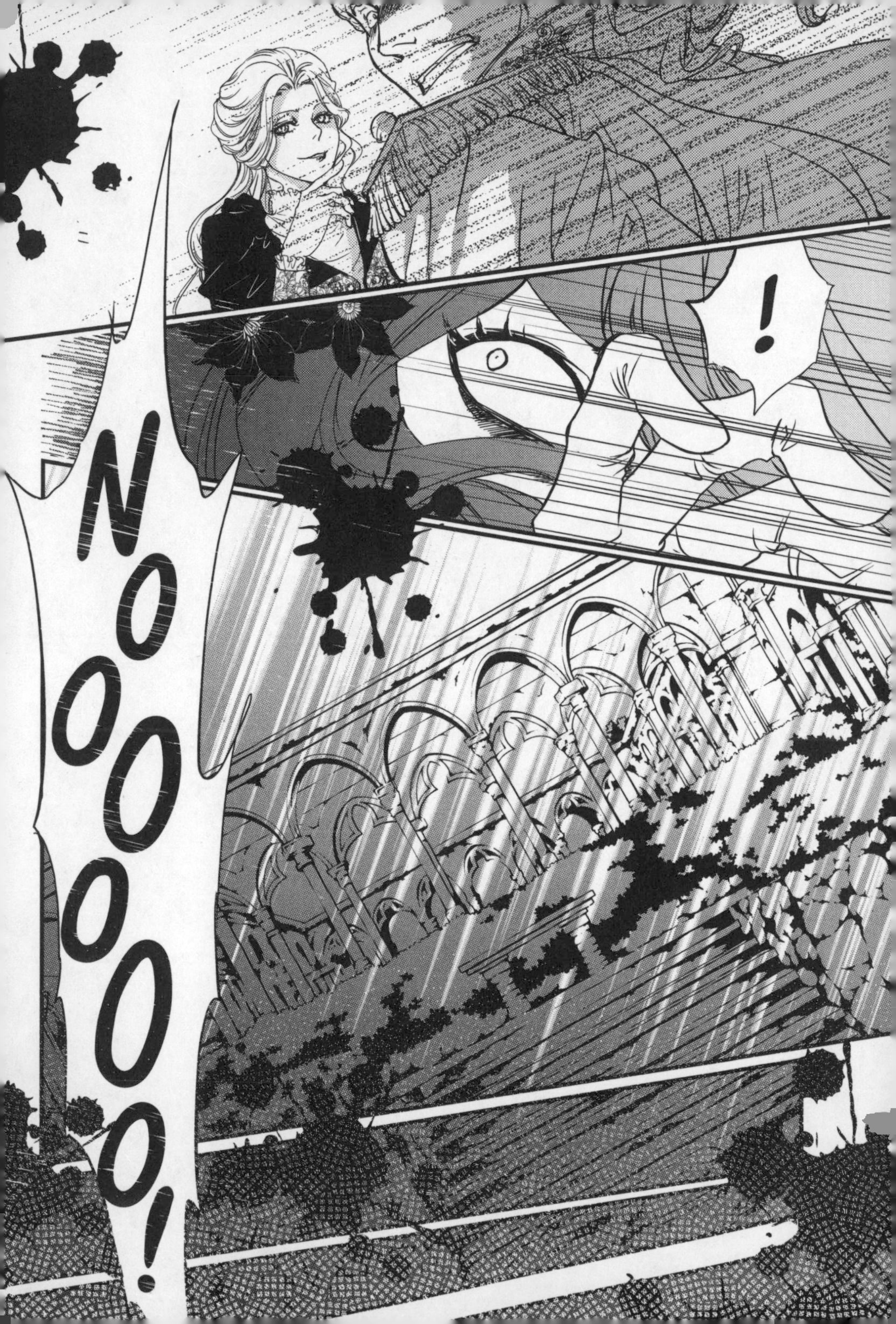
!
NOOOOOO!

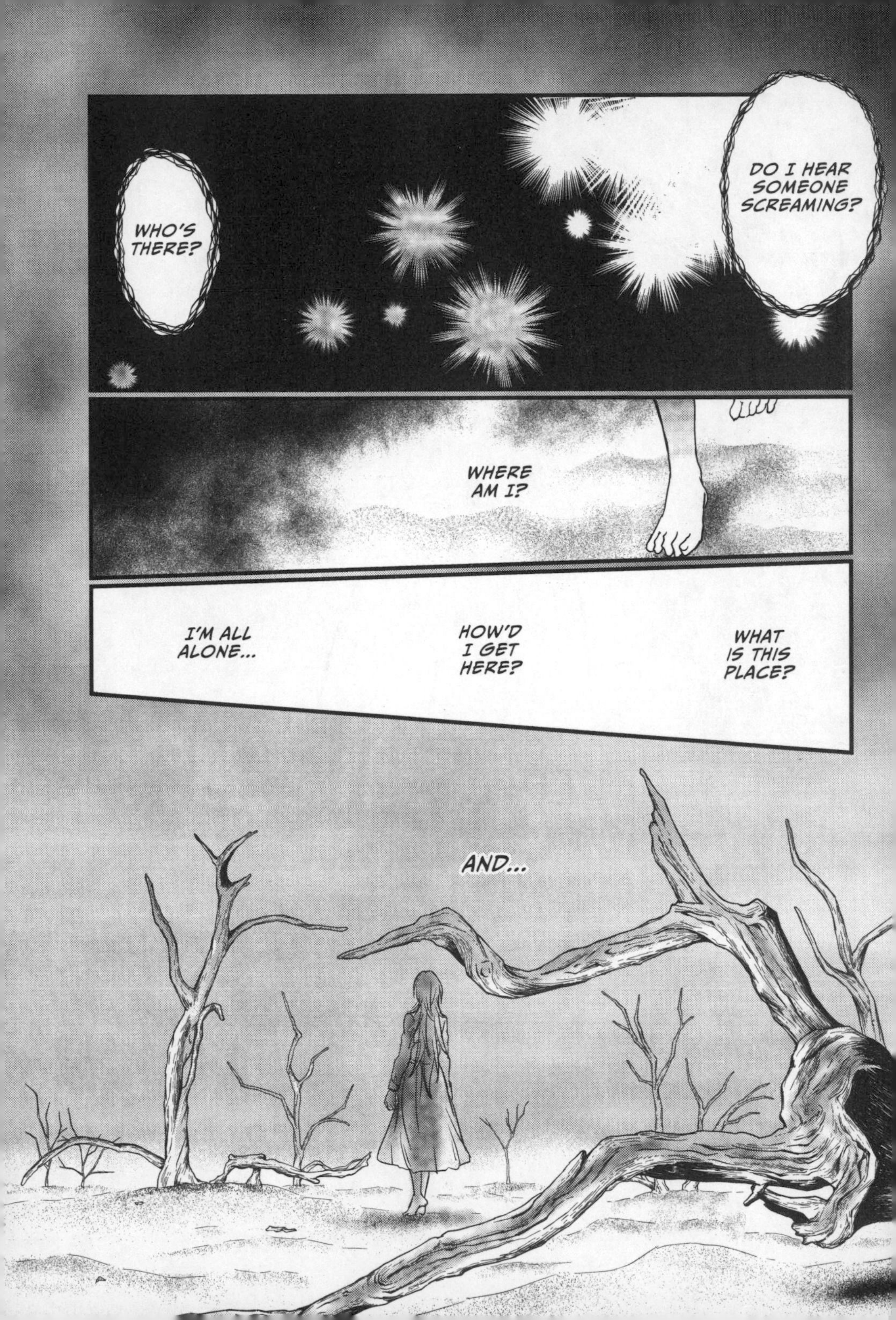
DO I HEAR SOMEONE SCREAMING?
WHO'S THERE?
WHERE AM I?
WHAT IS THIS PLACE?
HOW'D I GET HERE?
I'M ALL ALONE...
AND...

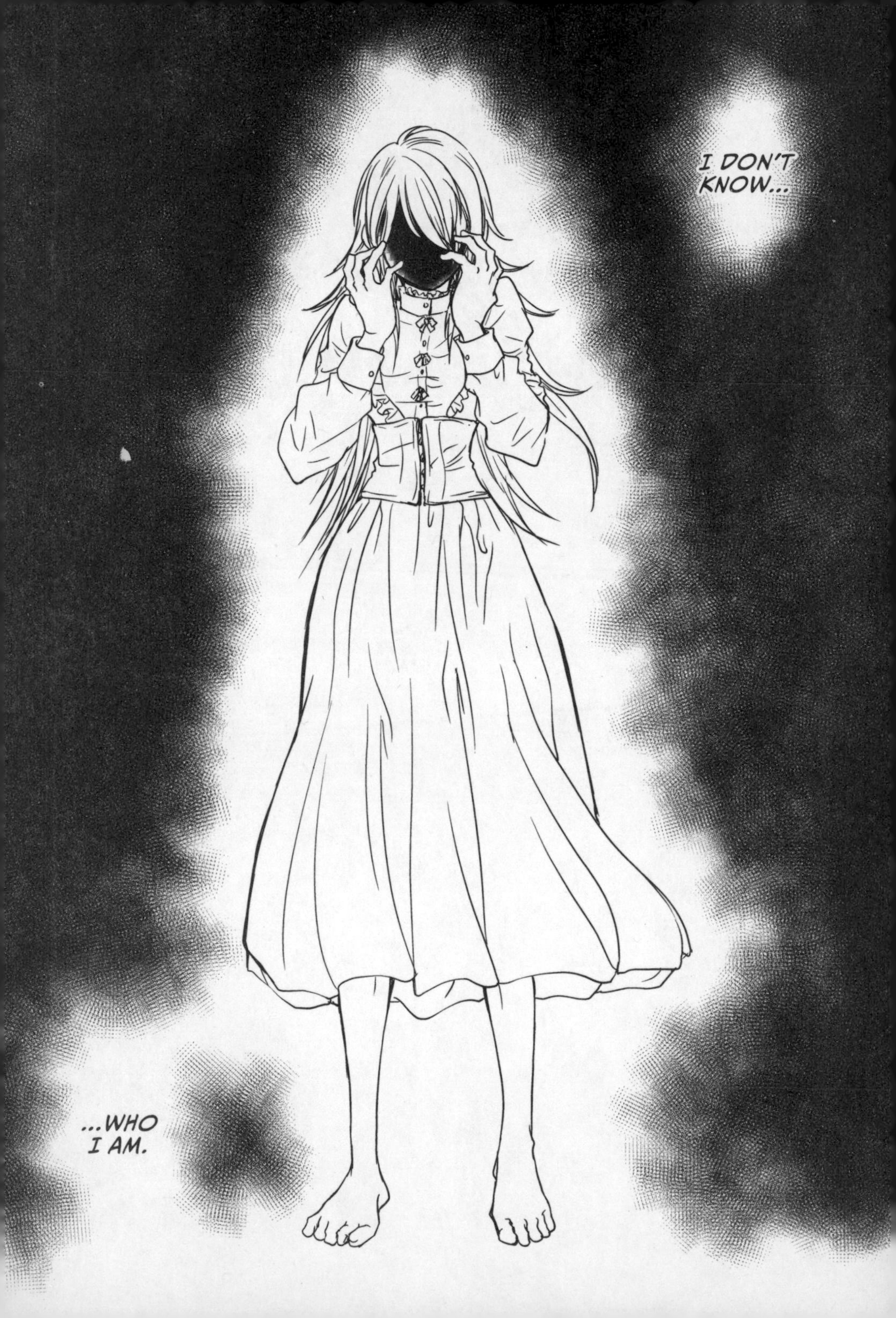
I DON'T KNOW...
...WHO I AM.

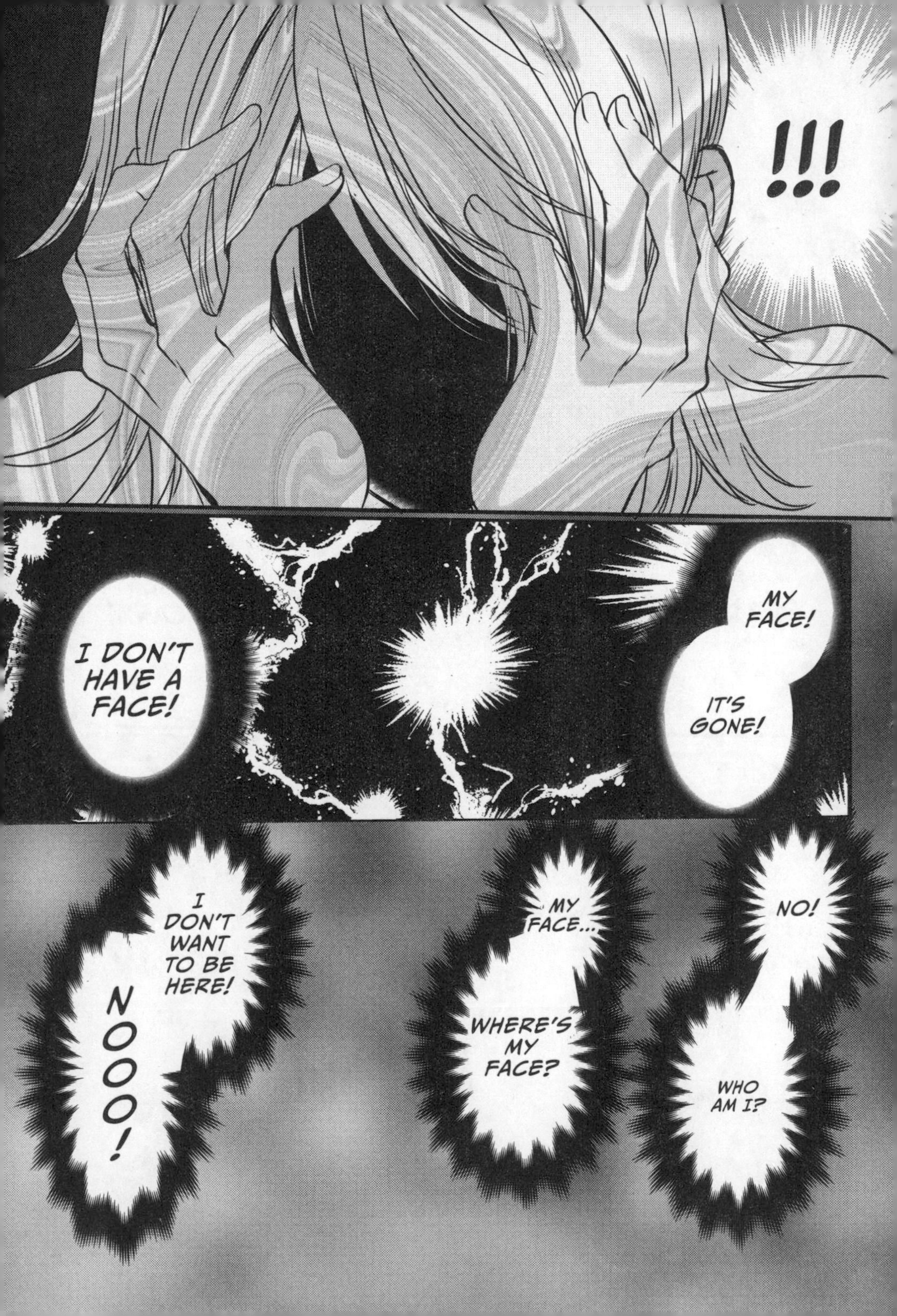
!!!
MY FACE!
IT'S GONE!
I DON'T HAVE A FACE!
NO!
WHO AM I?
MY FACE...
WHERE'S MY FACE?
I DON'T WANT TO BE HERE!
NOOOO!

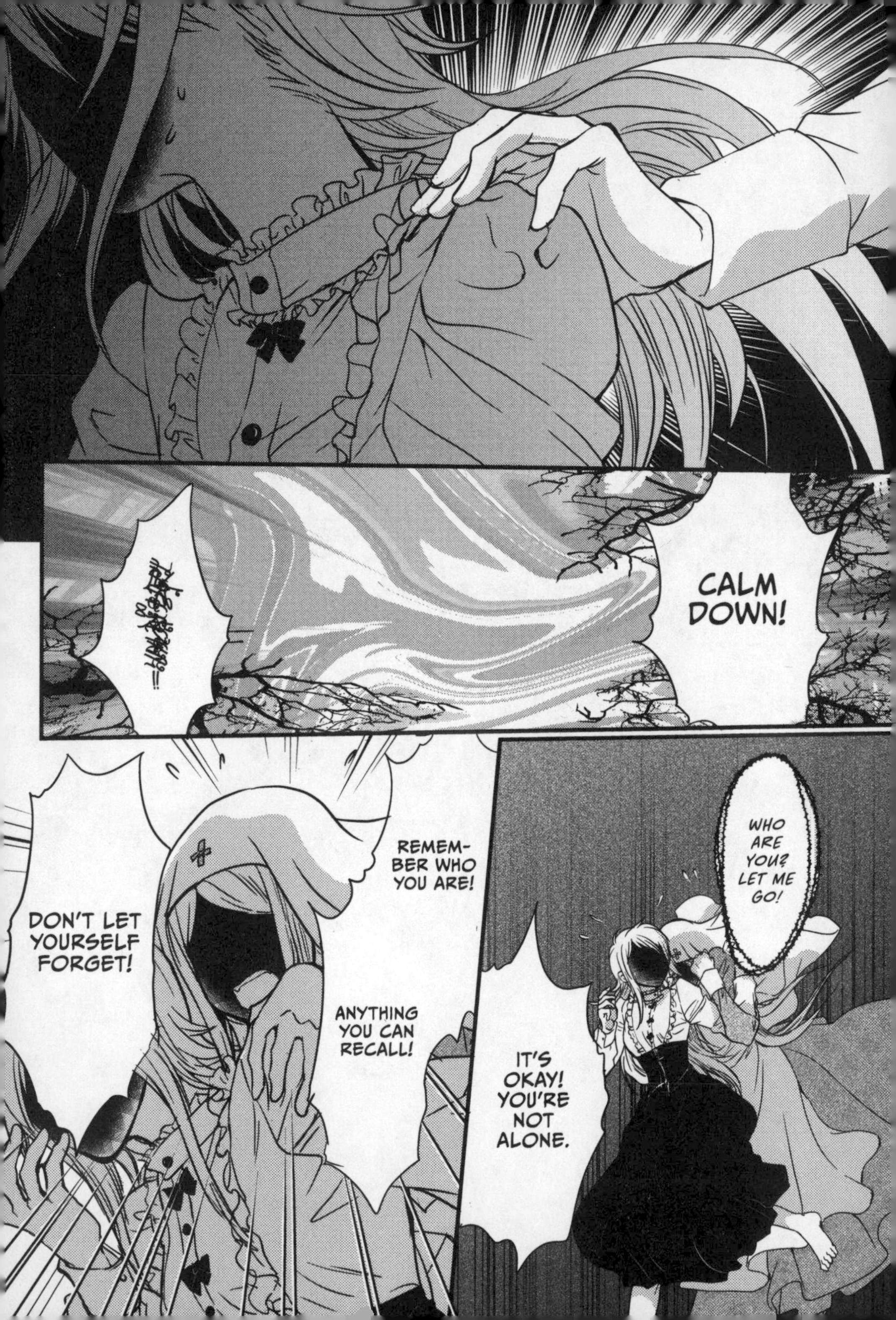
CALM DOWN!
WHO ARE YOU? LET ME GO!
IT'S OKAY! YOU'RE NOT ALONE.
REMEM-BER WHO YOU ARE!
DON'T LET YOURSELF FORGET!
ANYTHING YOU CAN RECALL!

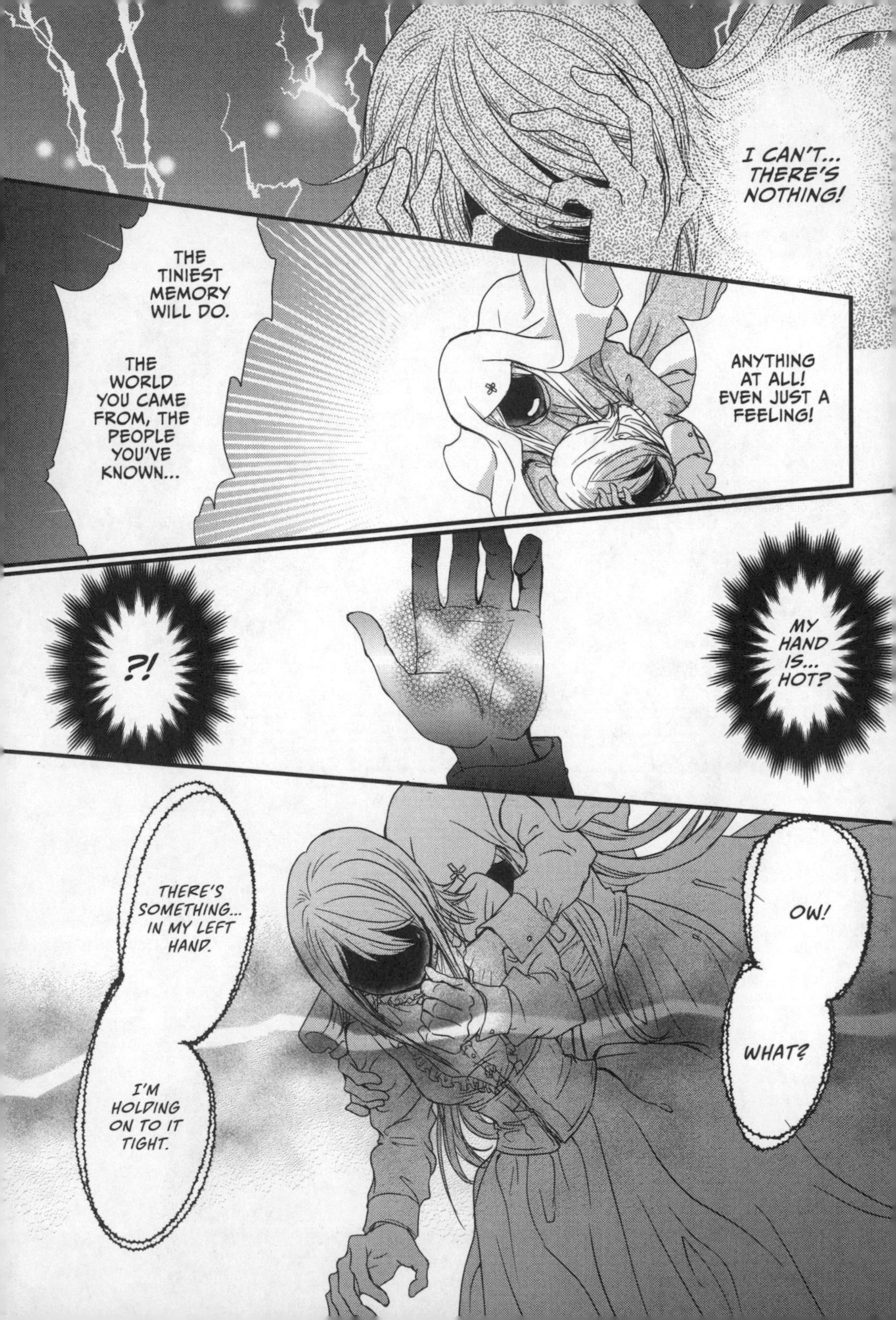
I CAN'T... THERE'S NOTHING!
ANYTHING AT ALL! EVEN JUST A FEELING!
THE TINIEST MEMORY WILL DO.
THE WORLD YOU CAME FROM, THE PEOPLE YOU'VE KNOWN...
MY HAND IS... HOT?
?!
OW!
WHAT?
THERE'S SOMETHING... IN MY LEFT HAND.
I'M HOLDING ON TO IT TIGHT.

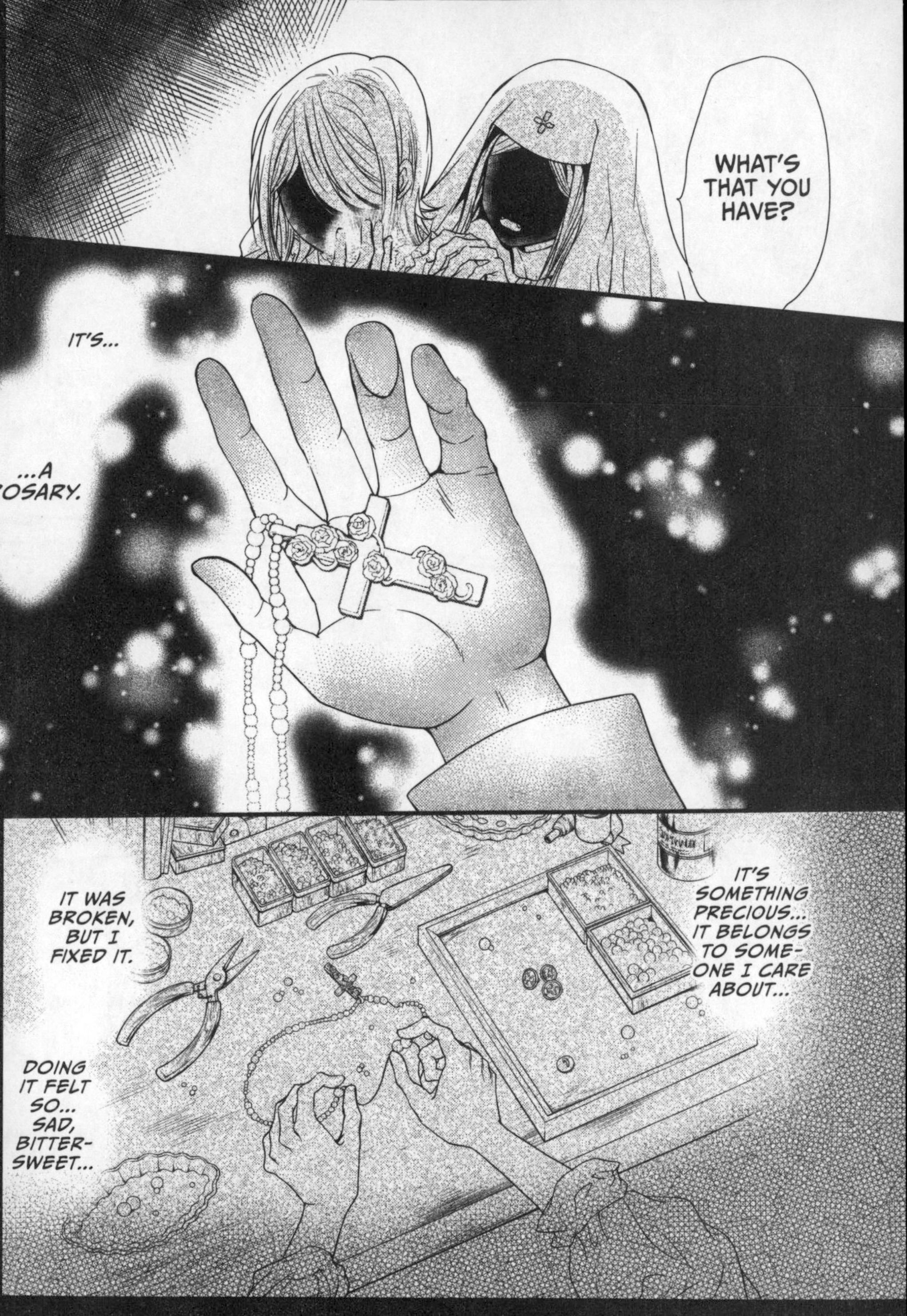
WHAT'S THAT YOU HAVE?
IT'S...
...A ROSARY.
IT'S SOMETHING PRECIOUS... IT BELONGS TO SOME-ONE I CARE ABOUT...
IT WAS BROKEN, BUT I FIXED IT.
DOING IT FELT SO... SAD, BITTER-SWEET...

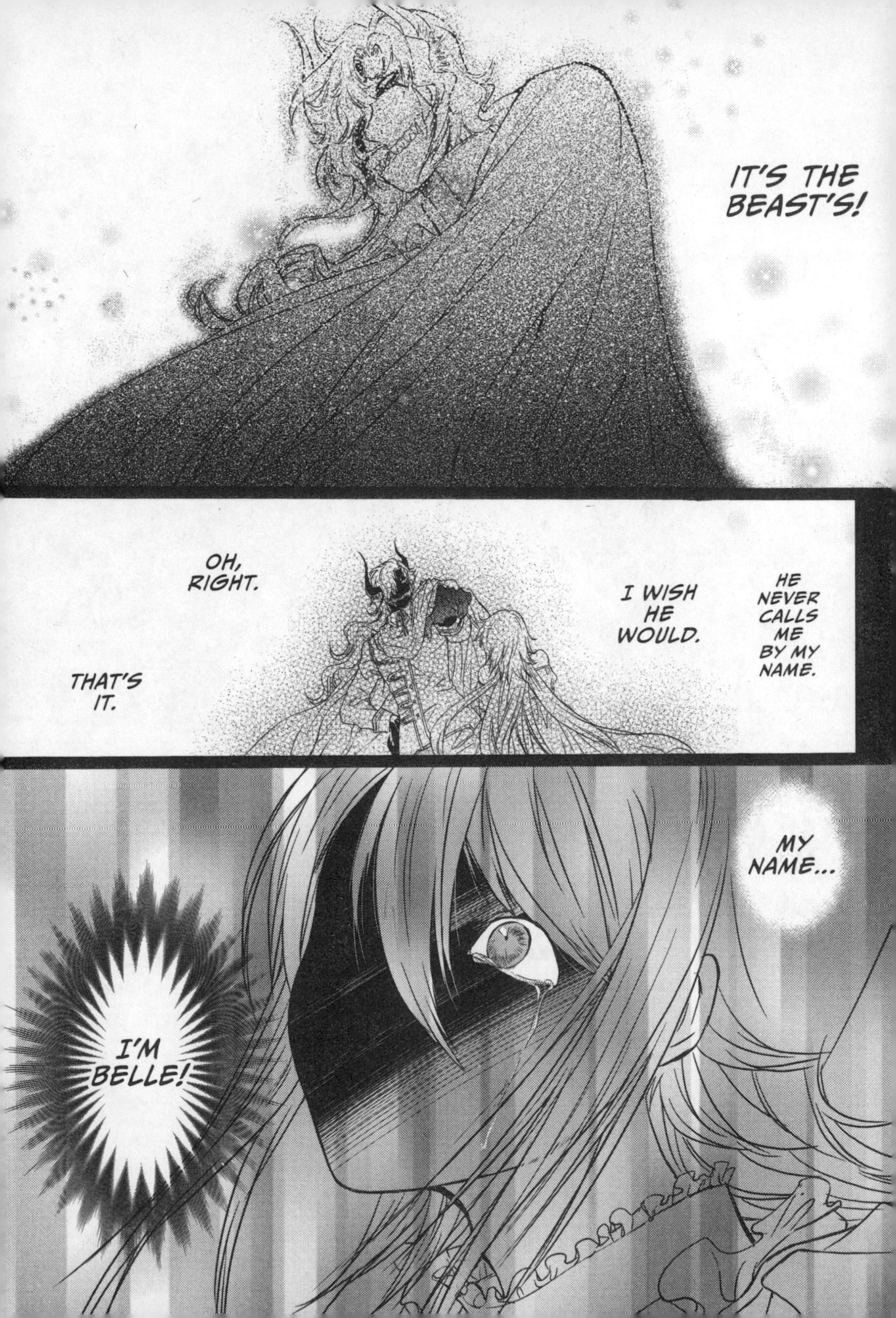
IT'S THE BEAST'S!
HE NEVER CALLS ME BY MY NAME.
I WISH HE WOULD.
OH, RIGHT.
THAT'S IT.
MY NAME...
I'M BELLE!

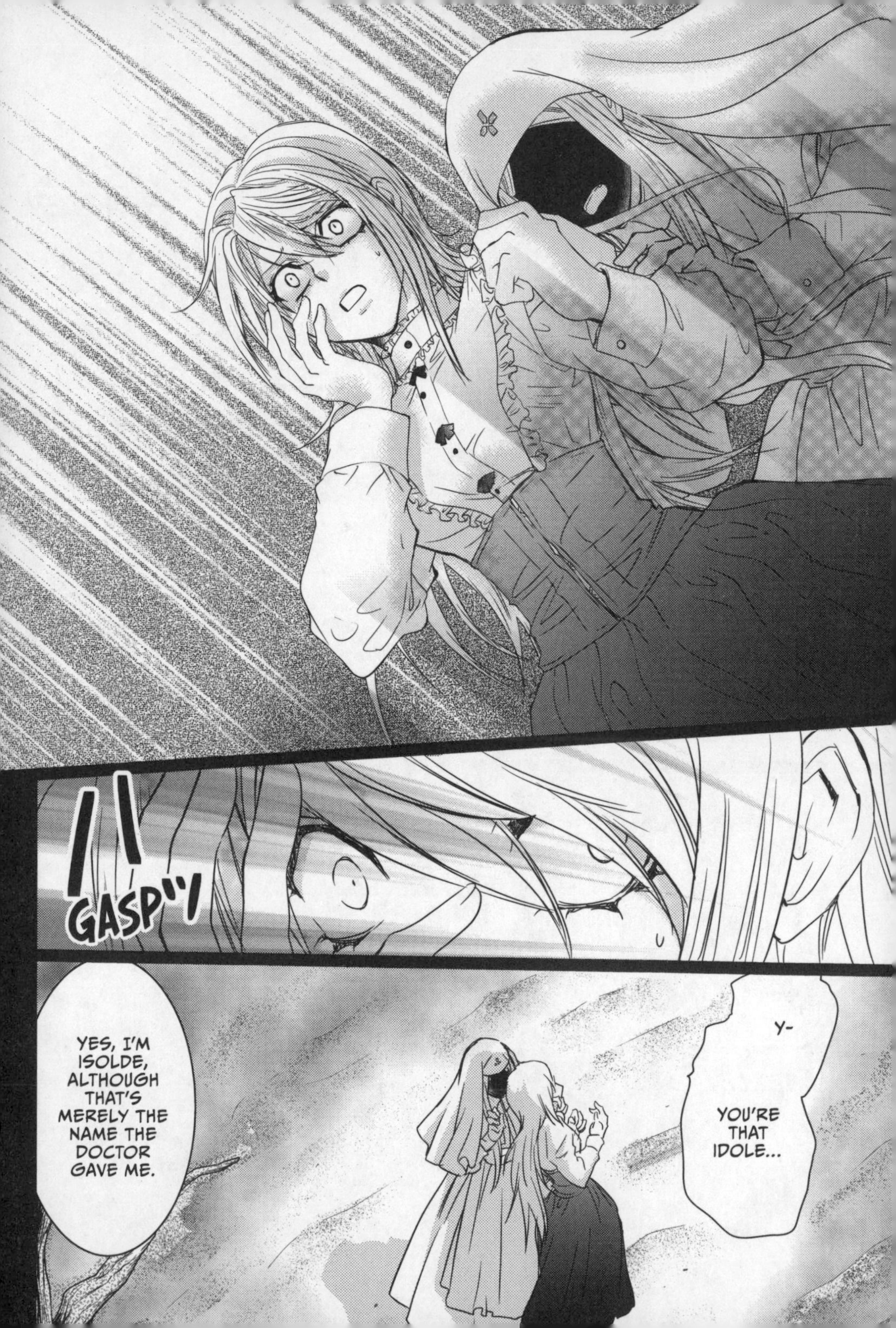
GASP!!
Y- YOU'RE THAT IDOLE...
YES, I'M ISOLDE, ALTHOUGH THAT'S MERELY THE NAME THE DOCTOR GAVE ME.

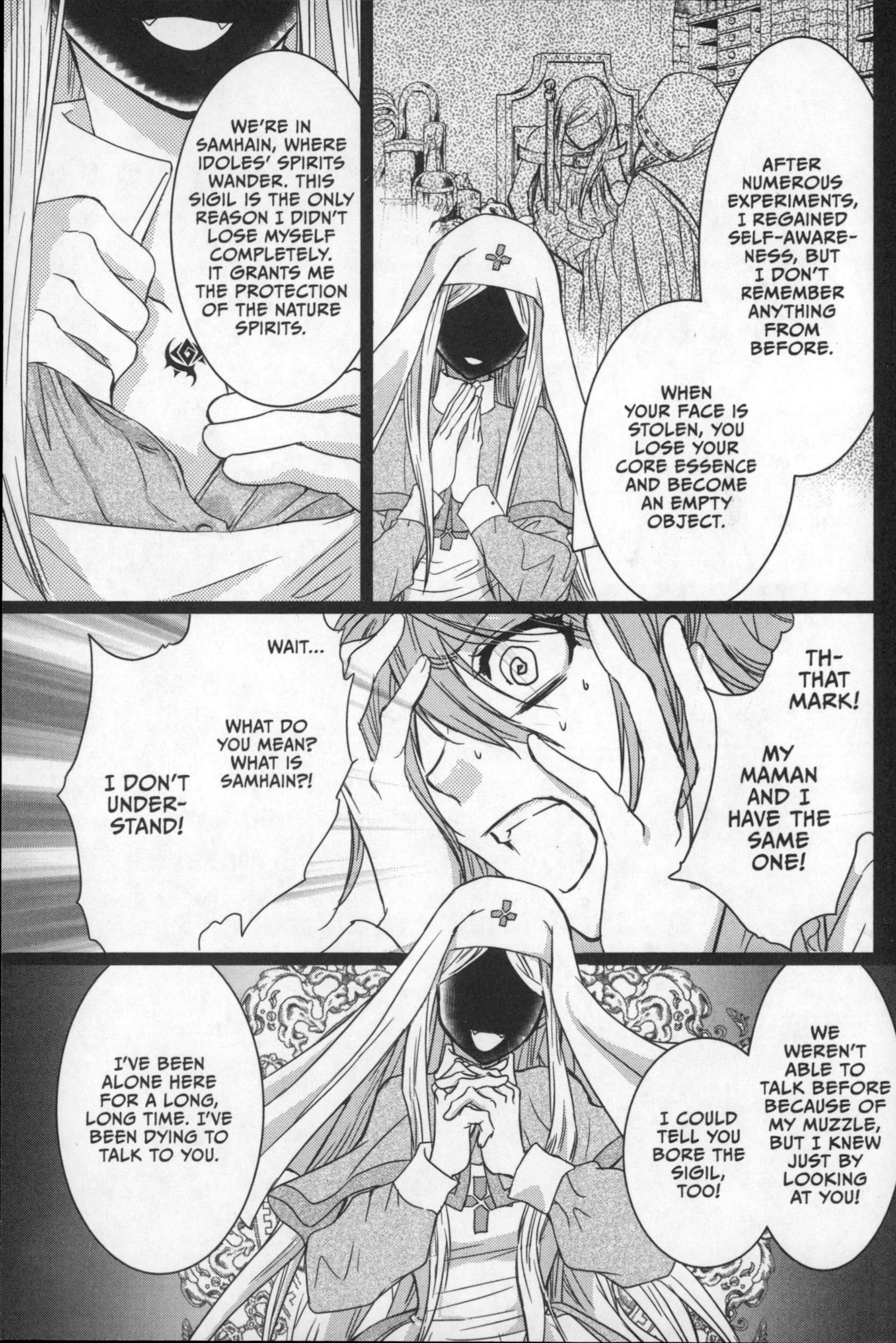
AFTER NUMEROUS EXPERIMENTS, I REGAINED SELF-AWARE-NESS, BUT I DON'T REMEMBER ANYTHING FROM BEFORE.
WHEN YOUR FACE IS STOLEN, YOU LOSE YOUR CORE ESSENCE AND BECOME AN EMPTY OBJECT.
WE'RE IN SAMHAIN, WHERE IDOLES' SPIRITS WANDER. THIS SIGIL IS THE ONLY REASON I DIDN'T LOSE MYSELF COMPLETELY. IT GRANTS ME THE PROTECTION OF THE NATURE SPIRITS.
TH-THAT MARK!
MY MAMAN AND I HAVE THE SAME ONE!
WAIT...
WHAT DO YOU MEAN? WHAT IS SAMHAIN?!
I DON'T UNDER-STAND!
WE WEREN'T ABLE TO TALK BEFORE BECAUSE OF MY MUZZLE, BUT I KNEW JUST BY LOOKING AT YOU!
I COULD TELL YOU BORE THE SIGIL, TOO!
I'VE BEEN ALONE HERE FOR A LONG, LONG TIME. I'VE BEEN DYING TO TALK TO YOU.

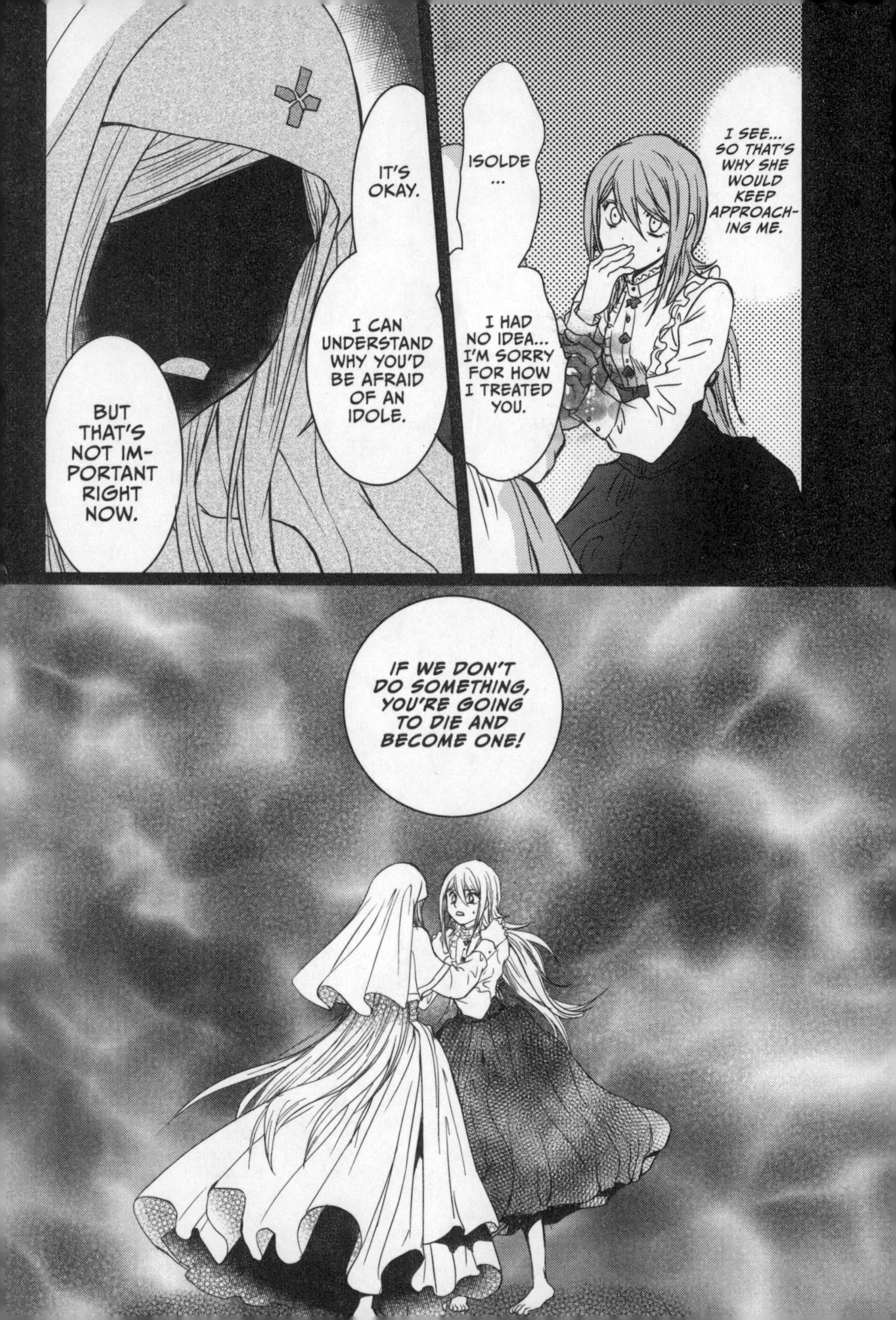
I SEE... SO THAT'S WHY SHE WOULD KEEP APPROACHING ME.
ISOLDE ...
I HAD NO IDEA... I'M SORRY FOR HOW I TREATED YOU.
IT'S OKAY.
I CAN UNDERSTAND WHY YOU'D BE AFRAID OF AN IDOLE.
BUT THAT'S NOT IMPORTANT RIGHT NOW.
IF WE DON'T DO SOMETHING, YOU'RE GOING TO DIE AND BECOME ONE!

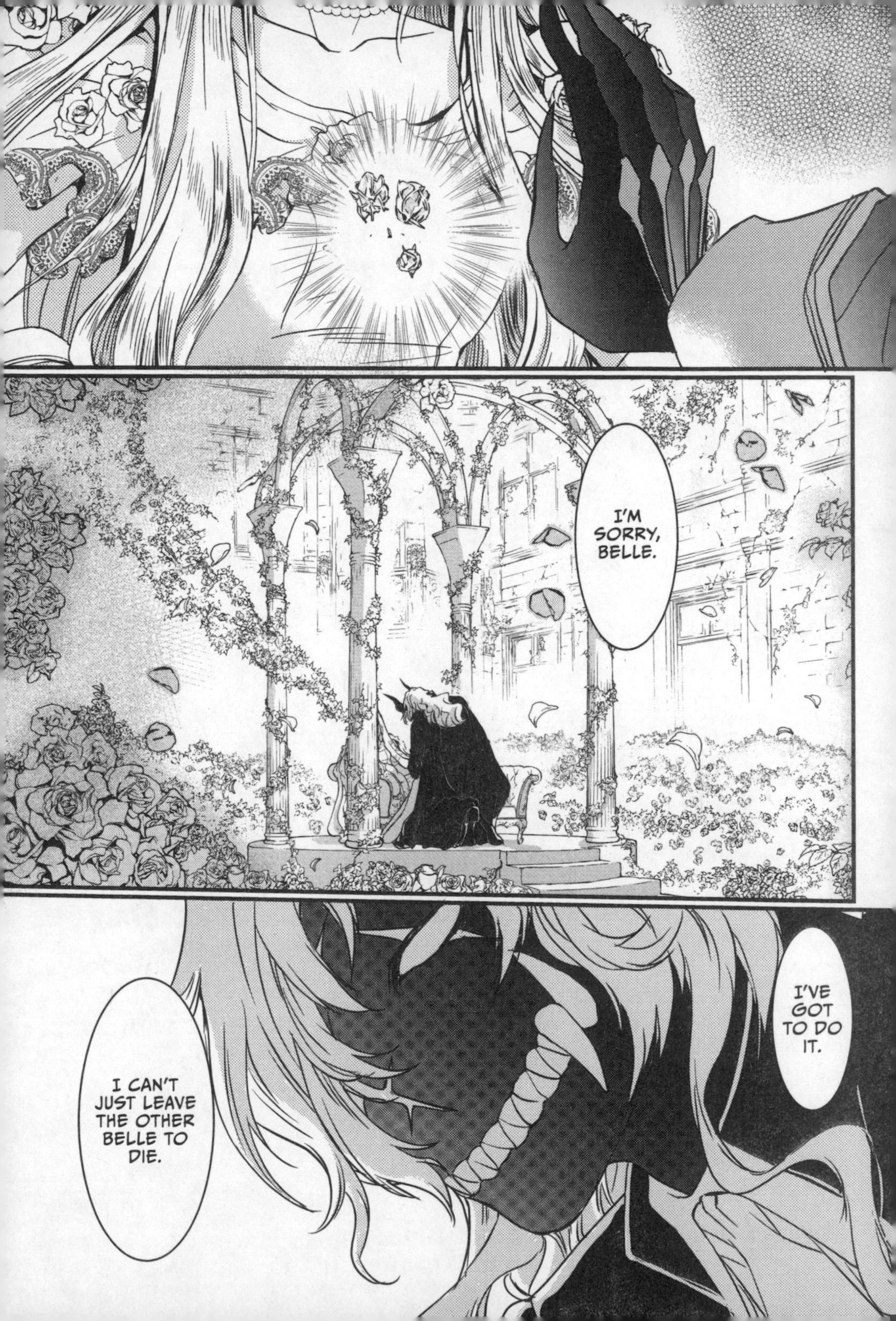
I'M SORRY, BELLE.
I'VE GOT TO DO IT.
I CAN'T JUST LEAVE THE OTHER BELLE TO DIE.

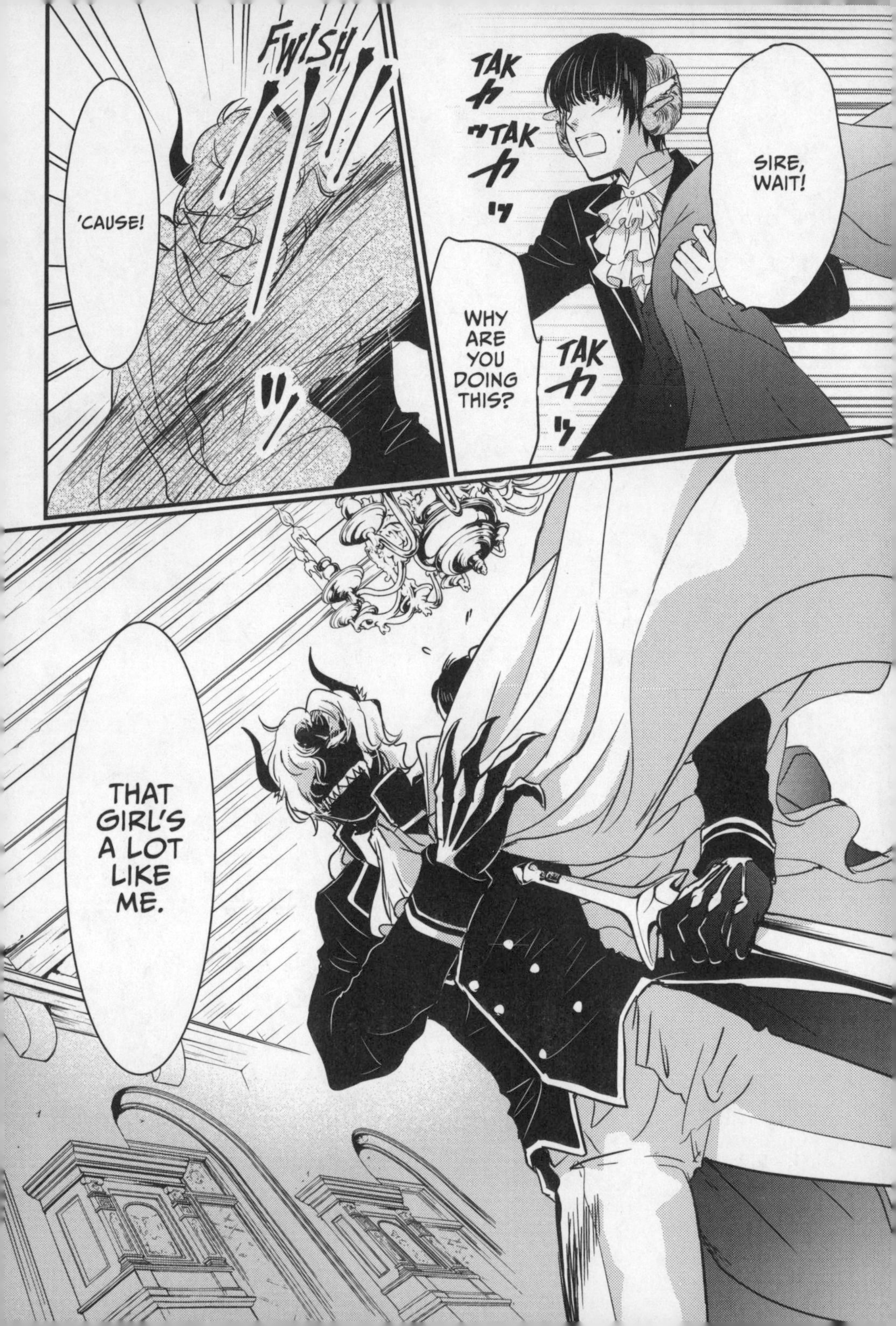
SIRE, WAIT!
TAK
TAK
WHY ARE YOU DOING THIS?
TAK
FWISH
'CAUSE!
THAT GIRL'S A LOT LIKE ME.

LA BELLE ET LA BÊTE

DU PARADIS PERDU

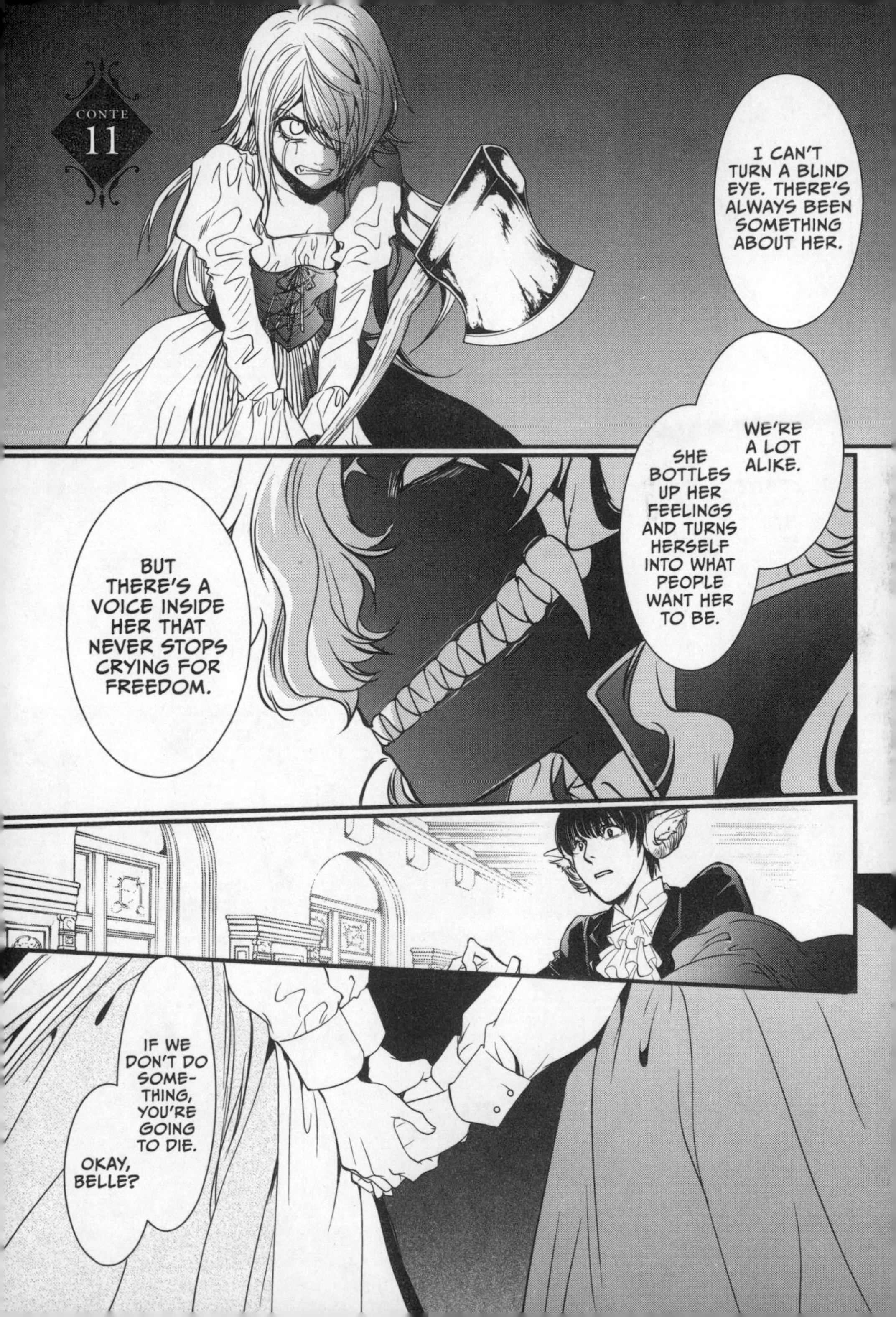
CONTE 11
I CAN'T TURN A BLIND EYE. THERE'S ALWAYS BEEN SOMETHING ABOUT HER.
WE'RE A LOT ALIKE.
SHE BOTTLES UP HER FEELINGS AND TURNS HERSELF INTO WHAT PEOPLE WANT HER TO BE.
BUT THERE'S A VOICE INSIDE HER THAT NEVER STOPS CRYING FOR FREEDOM.
IF WE DON'T DO SOME-THING, YOU'RE GOING TO DIE.
OKAY, BELLE?

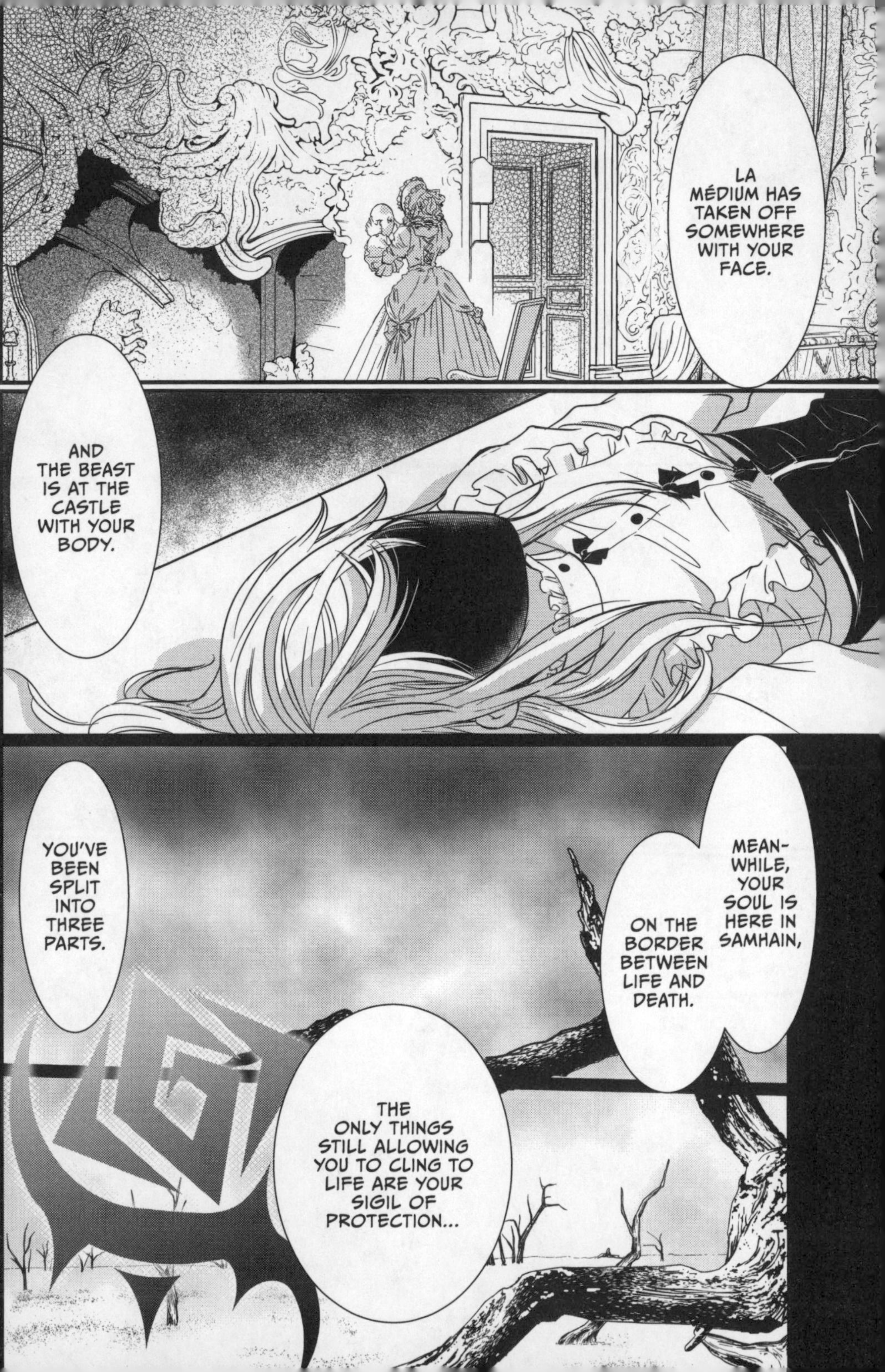
LA MÉDIUM HAS TAKEN OFF SOMEWHERE WITH YOUR FACE.
AND THE BEAST IS AT THE CASTLE WITH YOUR BODY.
MEAN-WHILE, YOUR SOUL IS HERE IN SAMHAIN,
ON THE BORDER BETWEEN LIFE AND DEATH.
YOU'VE BEEN SPLIT INTO THREE PARTS.
THE ONLY THINGS STILL ALLOWING YOU TO CLING TO LIFE ARE YOUR SIGIL OF PROTECTION...

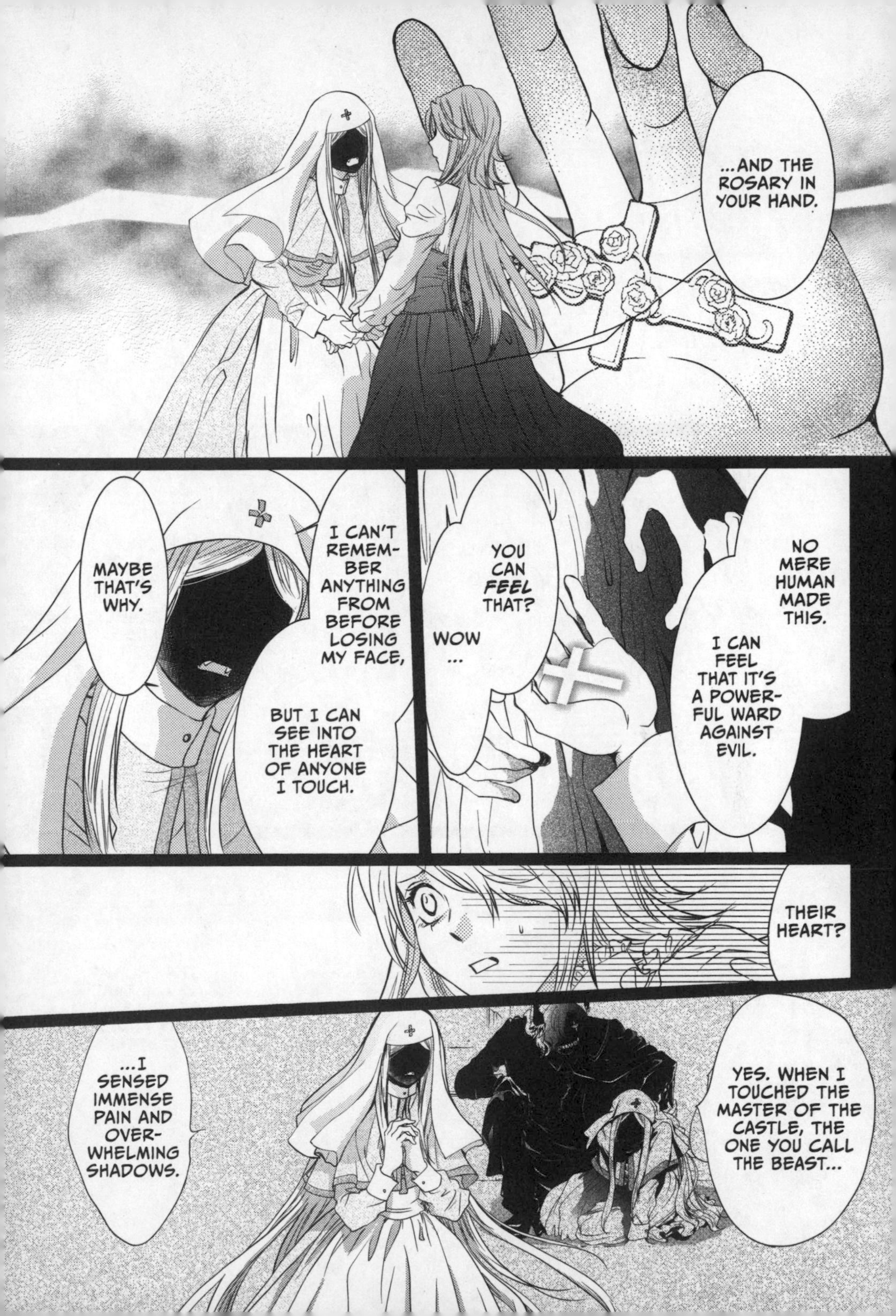
...AND THE ROSARY IN YOUR HAND.
NO MERE HUMAN MADE THIS. I CAN FEEL THAT IT'S A POWERFUL WARD AGAINST EVIL.
YOU CAN *FEEL* THAT? WOW ...
I CAN'T REMEMBER ANYTHING FROM BEFORE LOSING MY FACE, BUT I CAN SEE INTO THE HEART OF ANYONE I TOUCH.
MAYBE THAT'S WHY.
THEIR HEART?
YES. WHEN I TOUCHED THE MASTER OF THE CASTLE, THE ONE YOU CALL THE BEAST...
...I SENSED IMMENSE PAIN AND OVERWHELMING SHADOWS.

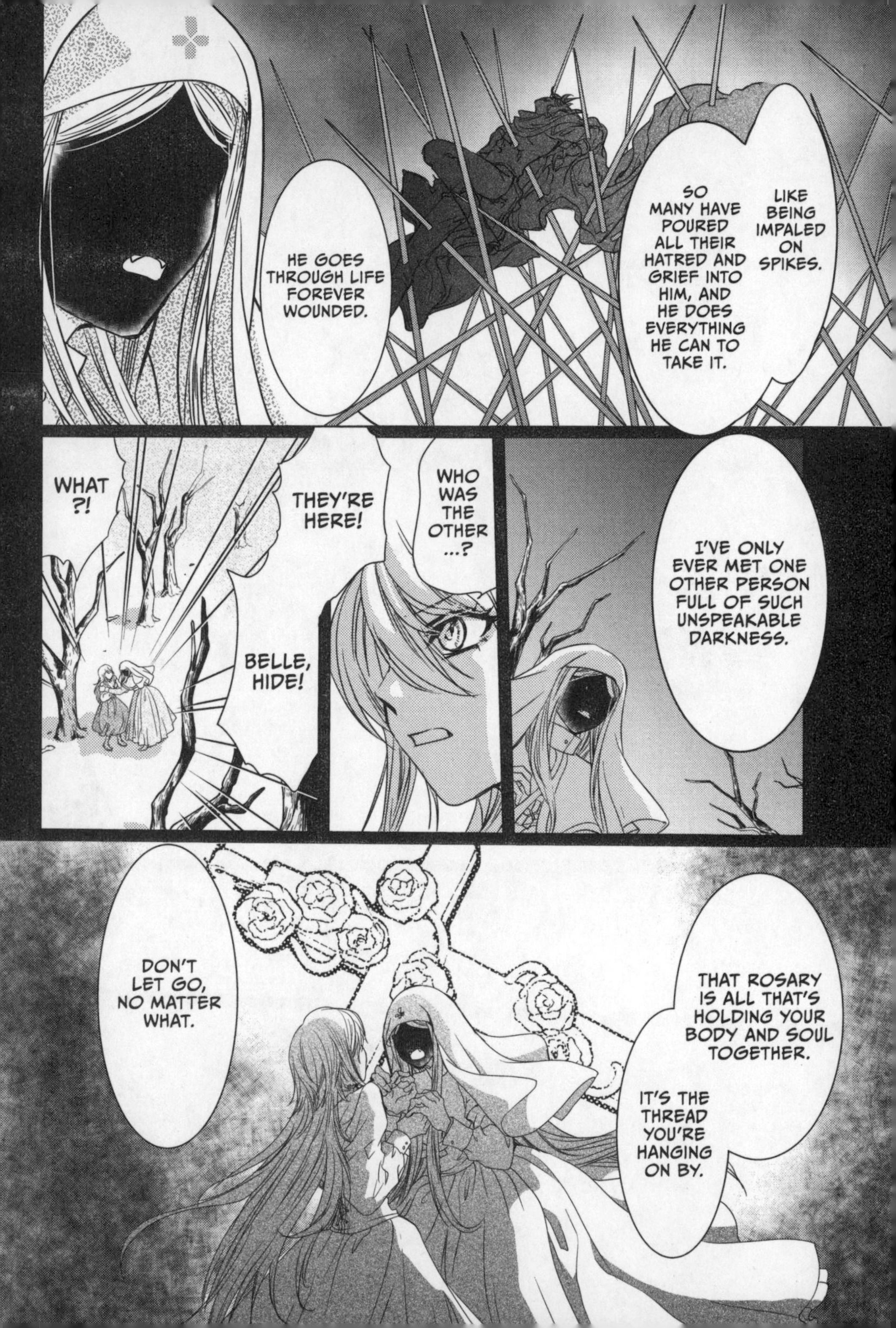
LIKE BEING IMPALED ON SPIKES.
SO MANY HAVE POURED ALL THEIR HATRED AND GRIEF INTO HIM, AND HE DOES EVERYTHING HE CAN TO TAKE IT.
HE GOES THROUGH LIFE FOREVER WOUNDED.
I'VE ONLY EVER MET ONE OTHER PERSON FULL OF SUCH UNSPEAKABLE DARKNESS.
WHO WAS THE OTHER ...?
THEY'RE HERE!
BELLE, HIDE!
WHAT ?!
THAT ROSARY IS ALL THAT'S HOLDING YOUR BODY AND SOUL TOGETHER.
IT'S THE THREAD YOU'RE HANGING ON BY.
DON'T LET GO, NO MATTER WHAT.

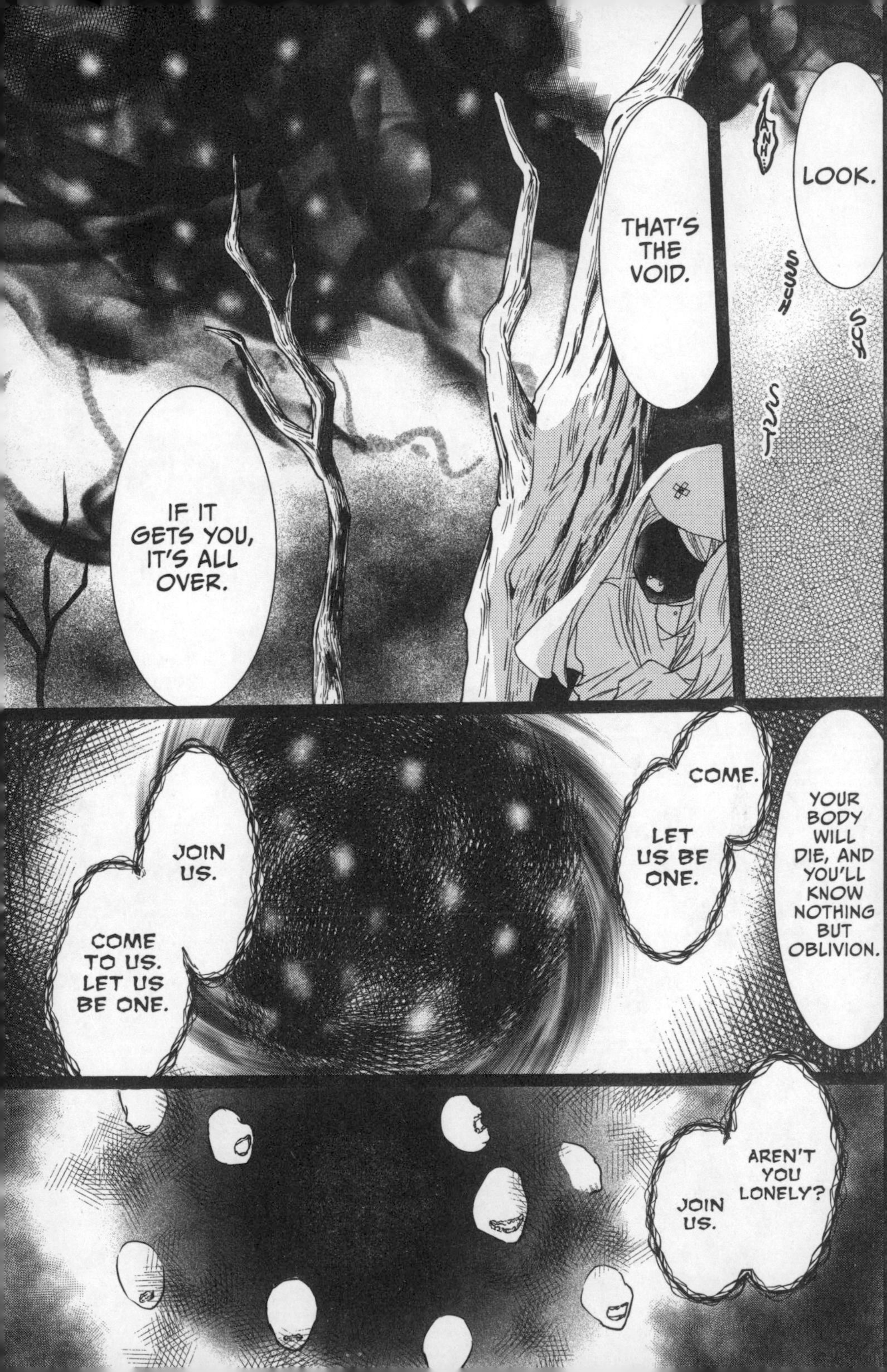
LOOK.
ANH...
THAT'S THE VOID.
IF IT GETS YOU, IT'S ALL OVER.
YOUR BODY WILL DIE, AND YOU'LL KNOW NOTHING BUT OBLIVION.
COME.
LET US BE ONE.
JOIN US.
COME TO US. LET US BE ONE.
AREN'T YOU LONELY?
JOIN US.

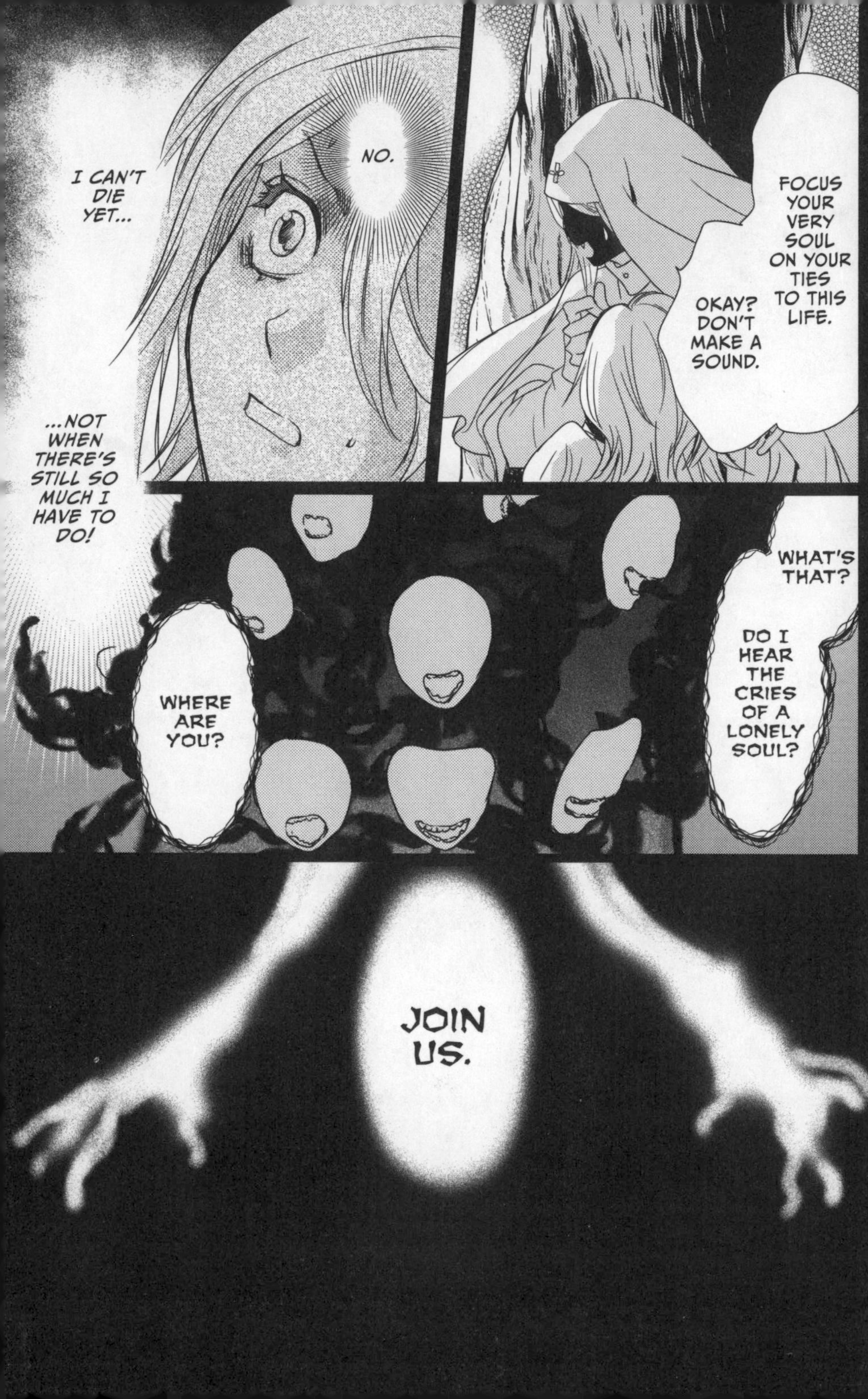
FOCUS YOUR VERY SOUL ON YOUR TIES TO THIS LIFE.
OKAY? DON'T MAKE A SOUND.
NO.
I CAN'T DIE YET...
...NOT WHEN THERE'S STILL SO MUCH I HAVE TO DO!
WHAT'S THAT?
DO I HEAR THE CRIES OF A LONELY SOUL?
WHERE ARE YOU?
JOIN US.

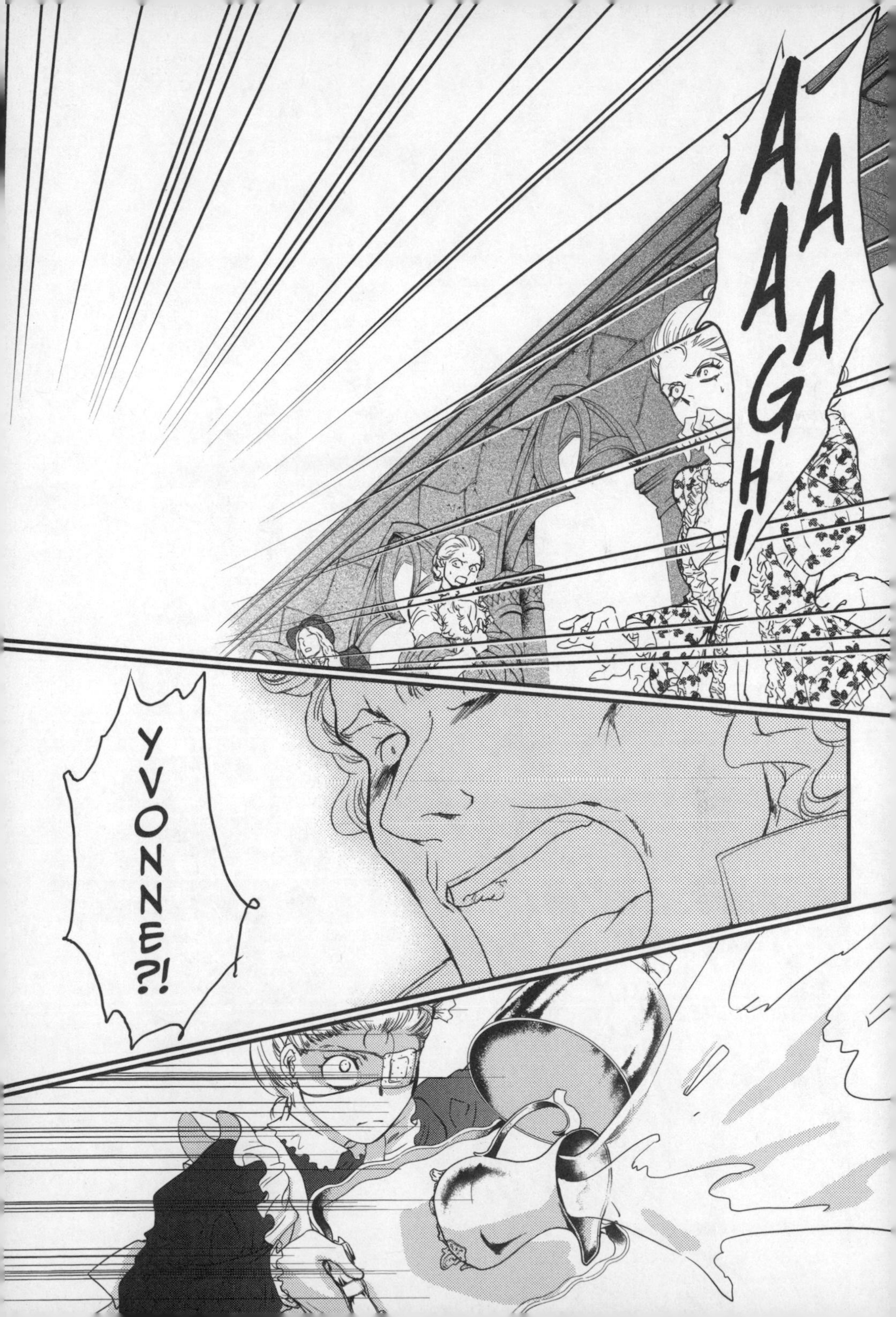
AAAAAGH!!
YVONNE?!

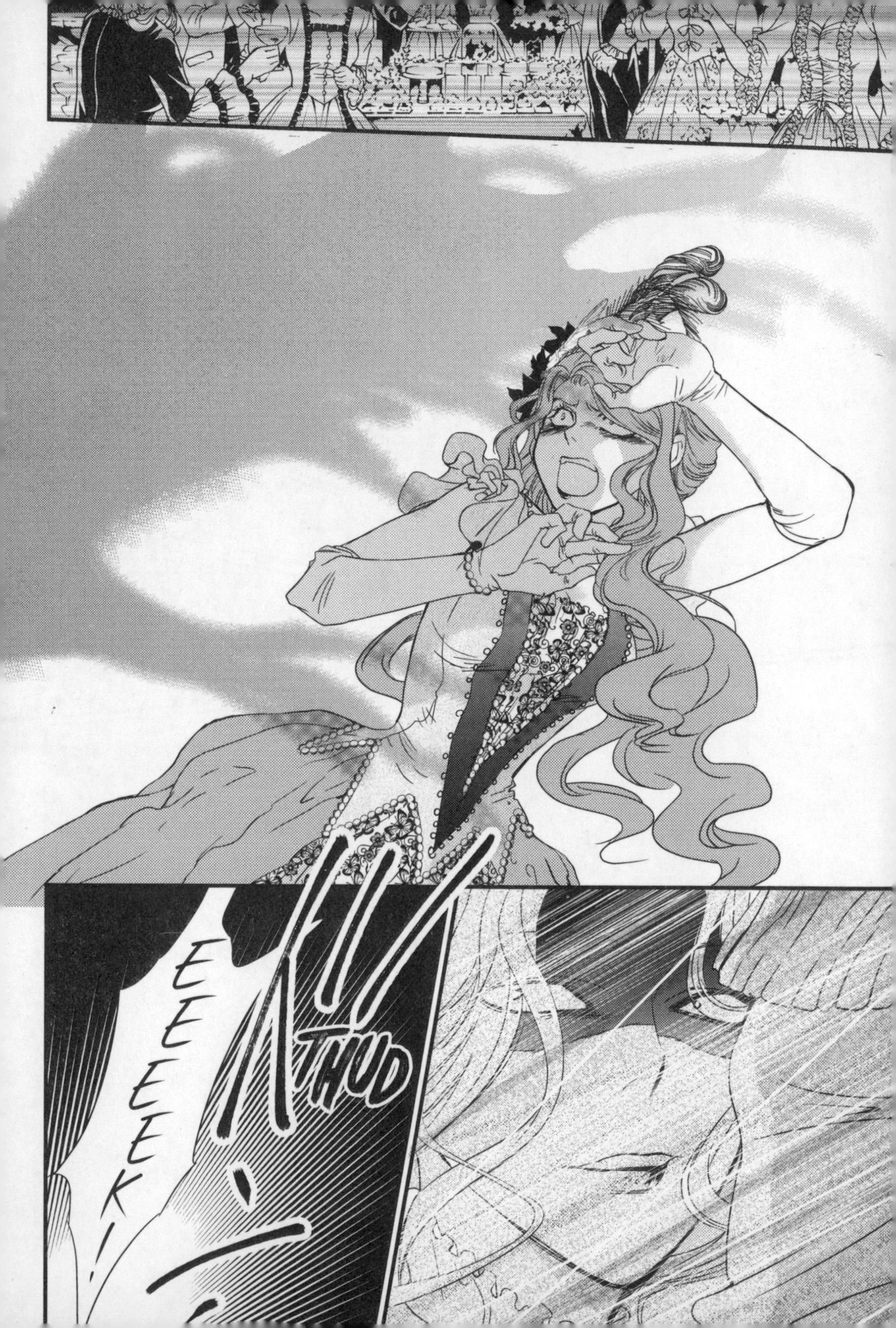
THUD
EEEEEEK!

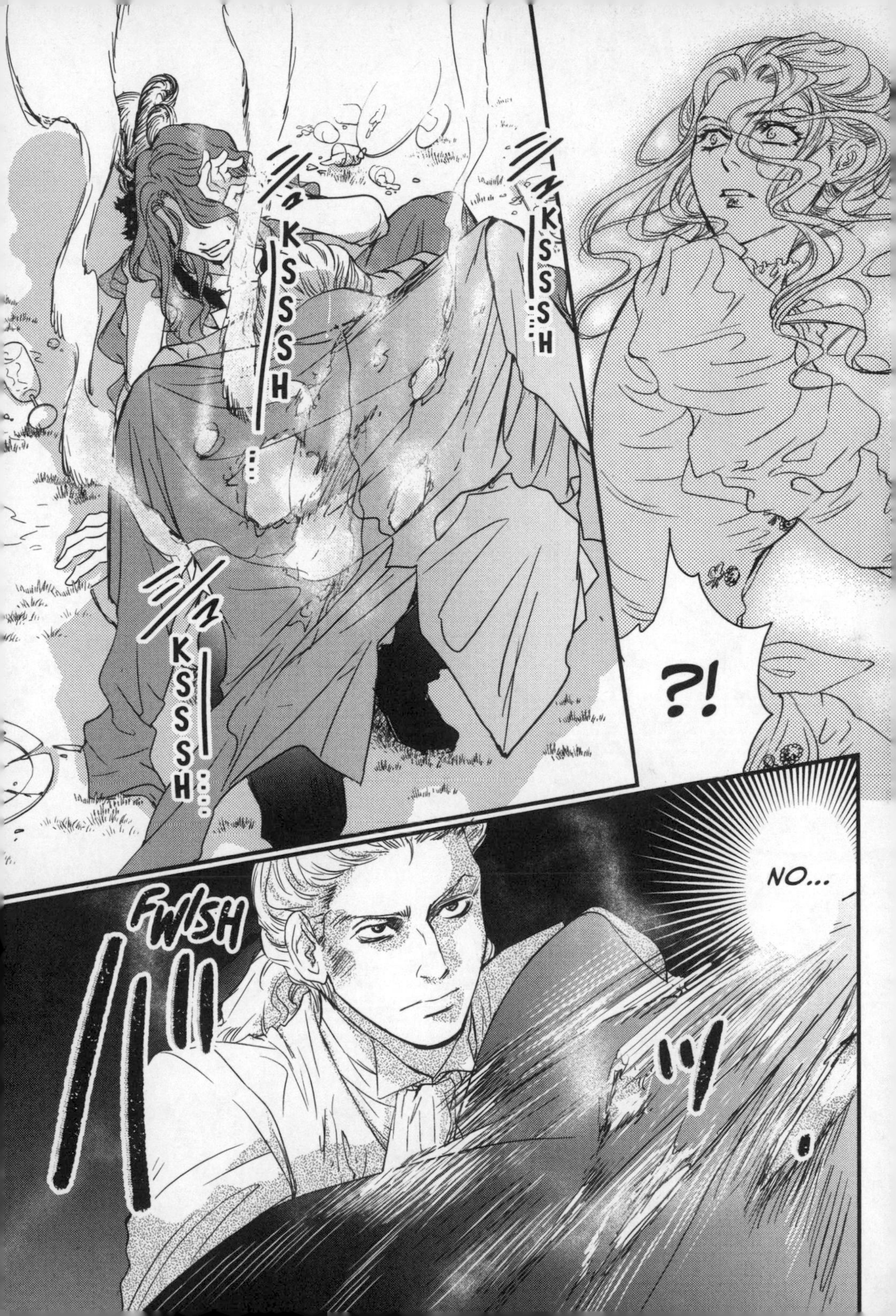
?!
KSSSH
KSSSH...
KSSSSH...
NO...
FWISH

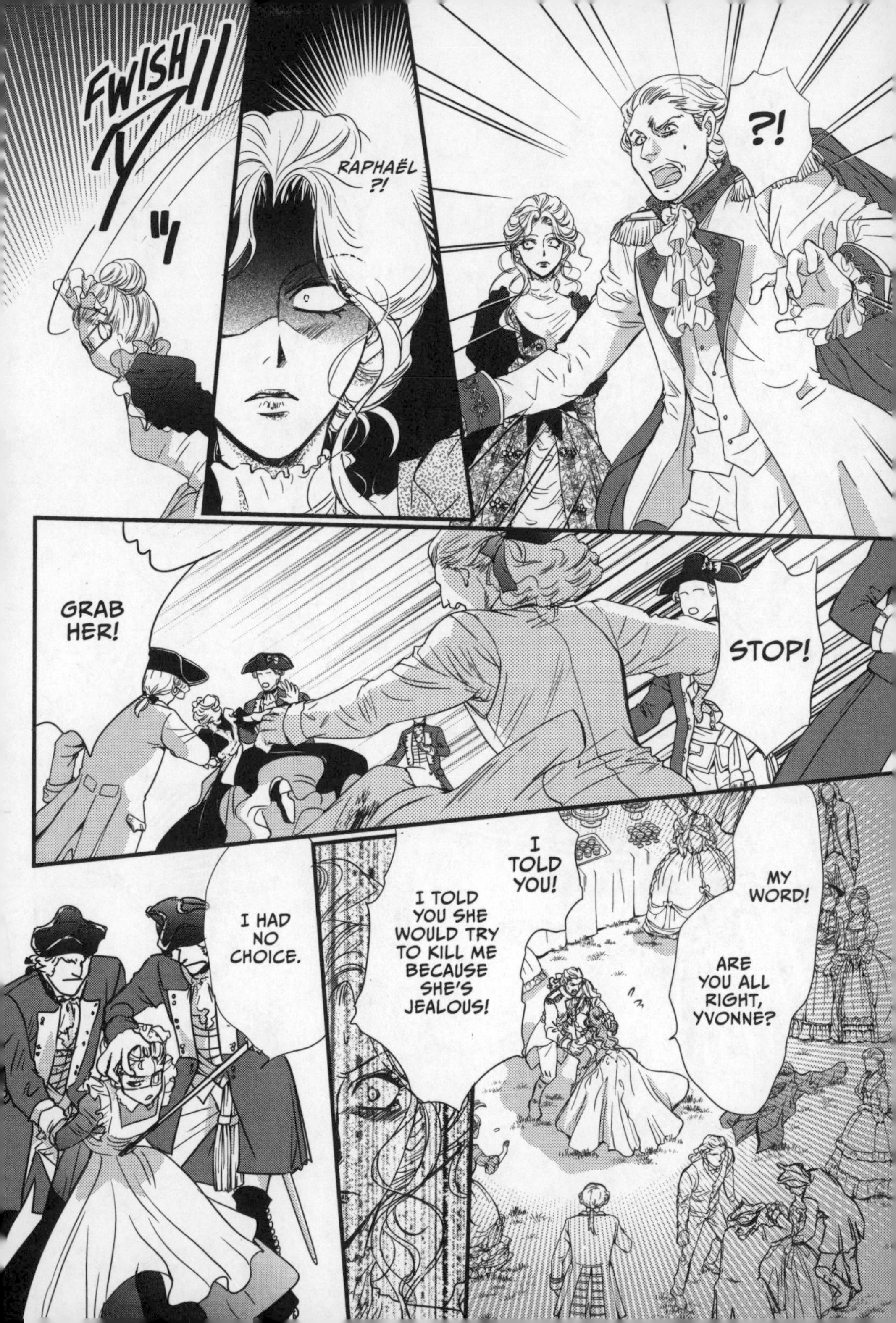
?!
RAPHAËL ?!
FWISH
STOP!
GRAB HER!
MY WORD!
ARE YOU ALL RIGHT, YVONNE?
I TOLD YOU!
I TOLD YOU SHE WOULD TRY TO KILL ME BECAUSE SHE'S JEALOUS!
I HAD NO CHOICE.

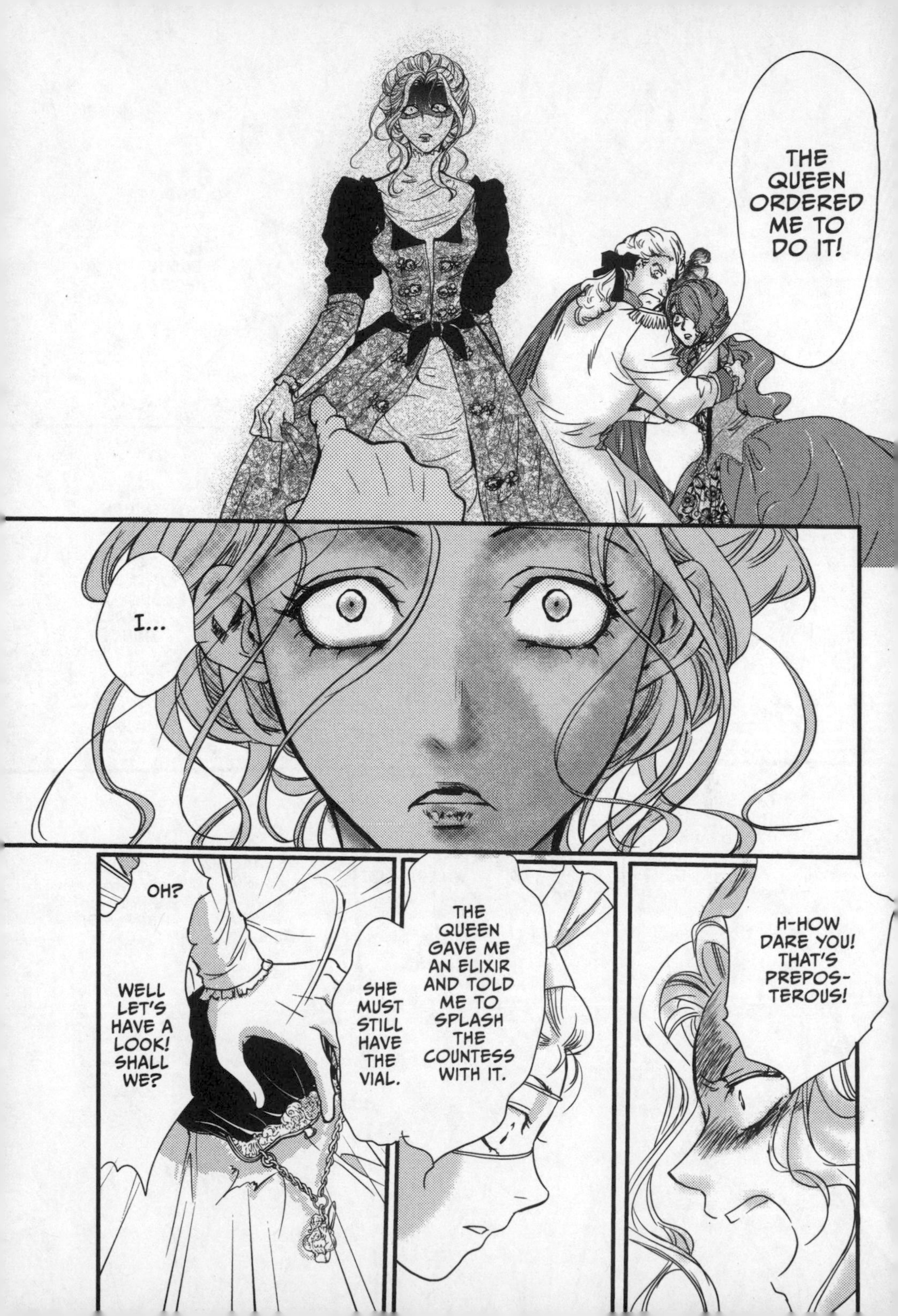
THE QUEEN ORDERED ME TO DO IT!
I...
H-HOW DARE YOU! THAT'S PREPOSTEROUS!
THE QUEEN GAVE ME AN ELIXIR AND TOLD ME TO SPLASH THE COUNTESS WITH IT.
SHE MUST STILL HAVE THE VIAL.
OH?
WELL LET'S HAVE A LOOK! SHALL WE?

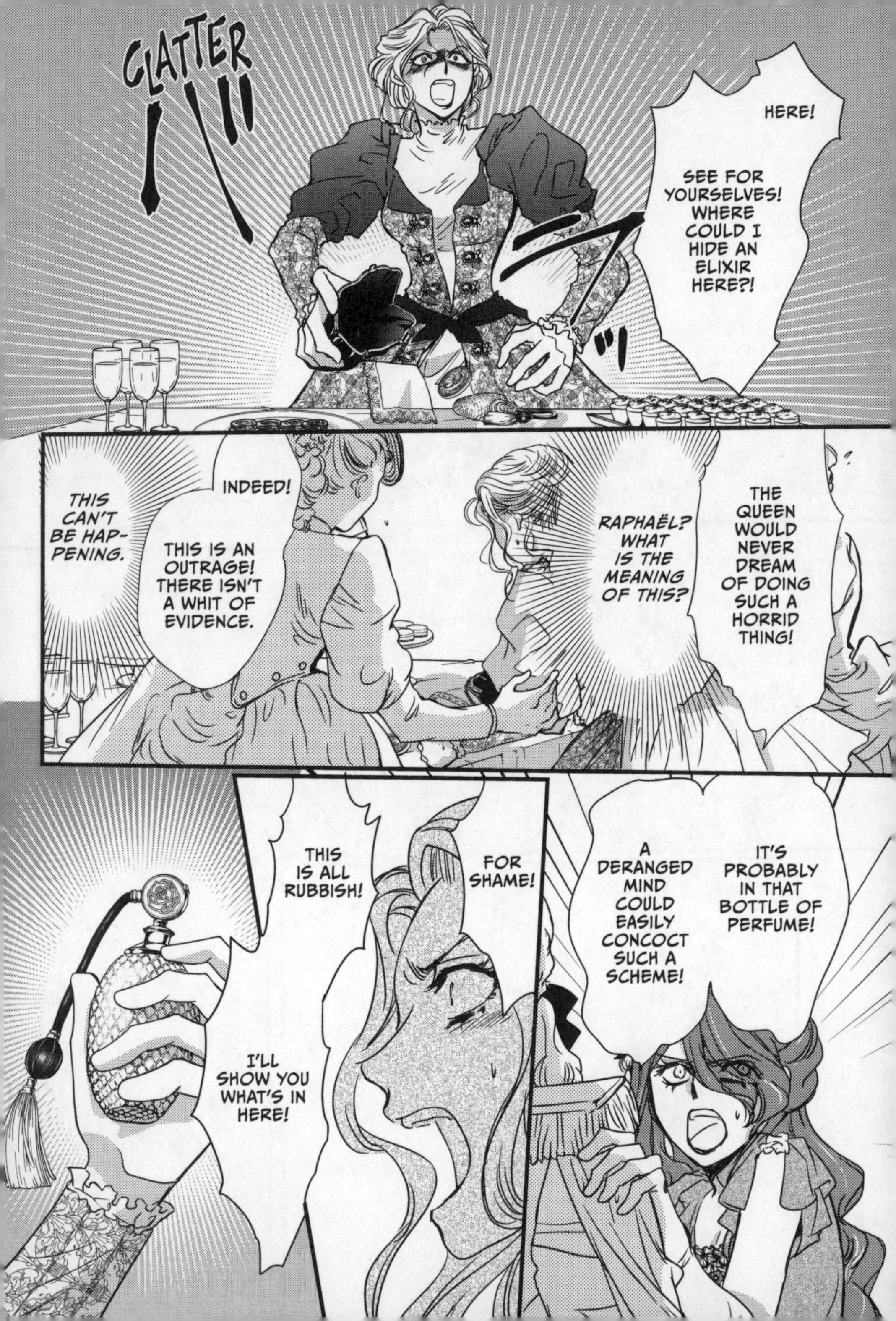
HERE!
SEE FOR YOURSELVES! WHERE COULD I HIDE AN ELIXIR HERE?!
CLATTER
THE QUEEN WOULD NEVER DREAM OF DOING SUCH A HORRID THING!
RAPHAËL? WHAT IS THE MEANING OF THIS?
INDEED!
THIS IS AN OUTRAGE! THERE ISN'T A WHIT OF EVIDENCE.
THIS CAN'T BE HAP-PENING.
IT'S PROBABLY IN THAT BOTTLE OF PERFUME!
A DERANGED MIND COULD EASILY CONCOCT SUCH A SCHEME!
FOR SHAME!
THIS IS ALL RUBBISH!
I'LL SHOW YOU WHAT'S IN HERE!

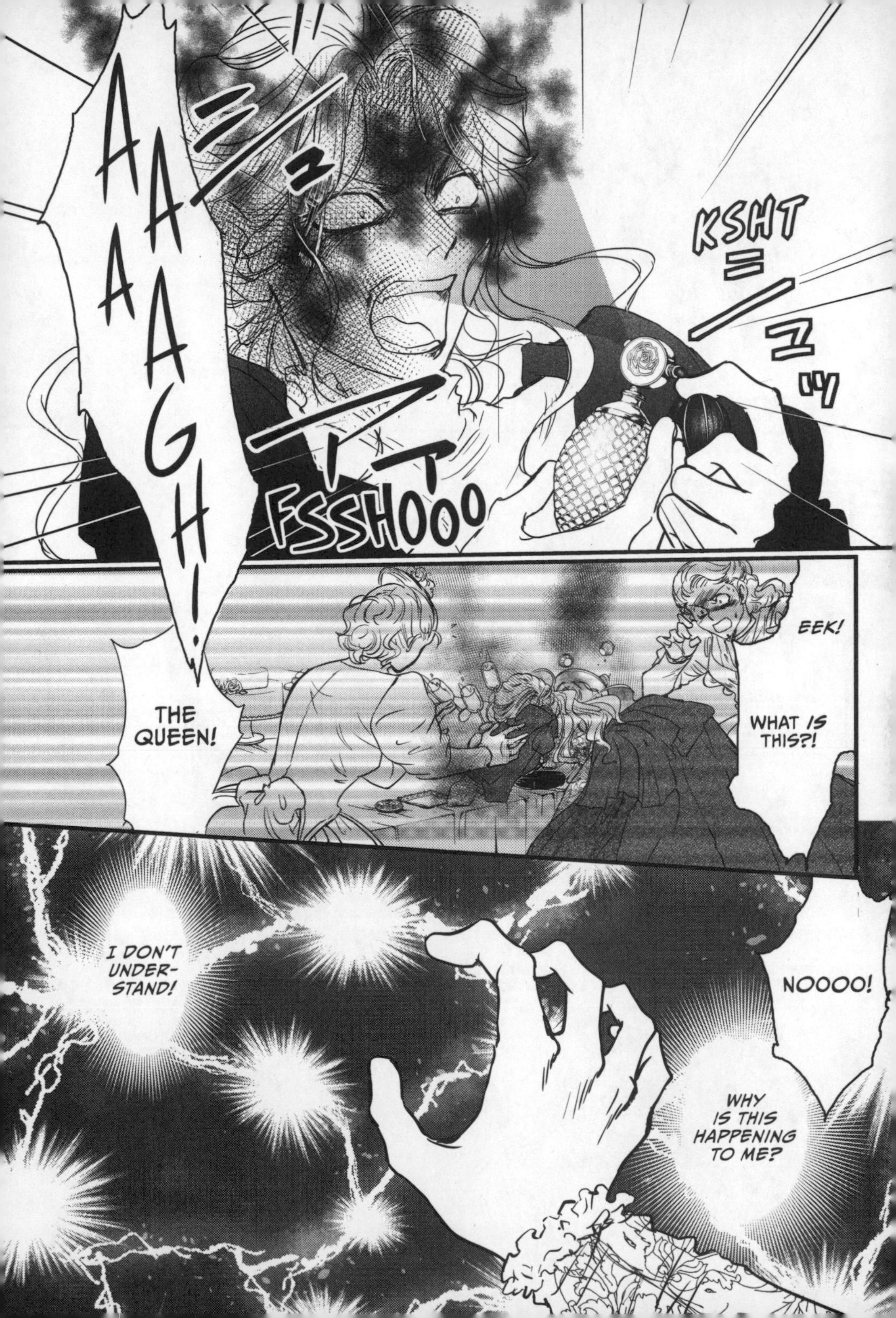
KSHT
FSSHOOO
AAAAGH!!
EEK!
WHAT IS THIS?!
THE QUEEN!
NOOOO!
WHY IS THIS HAPPENING TO ME?
I DON'T UNDER-STAND!

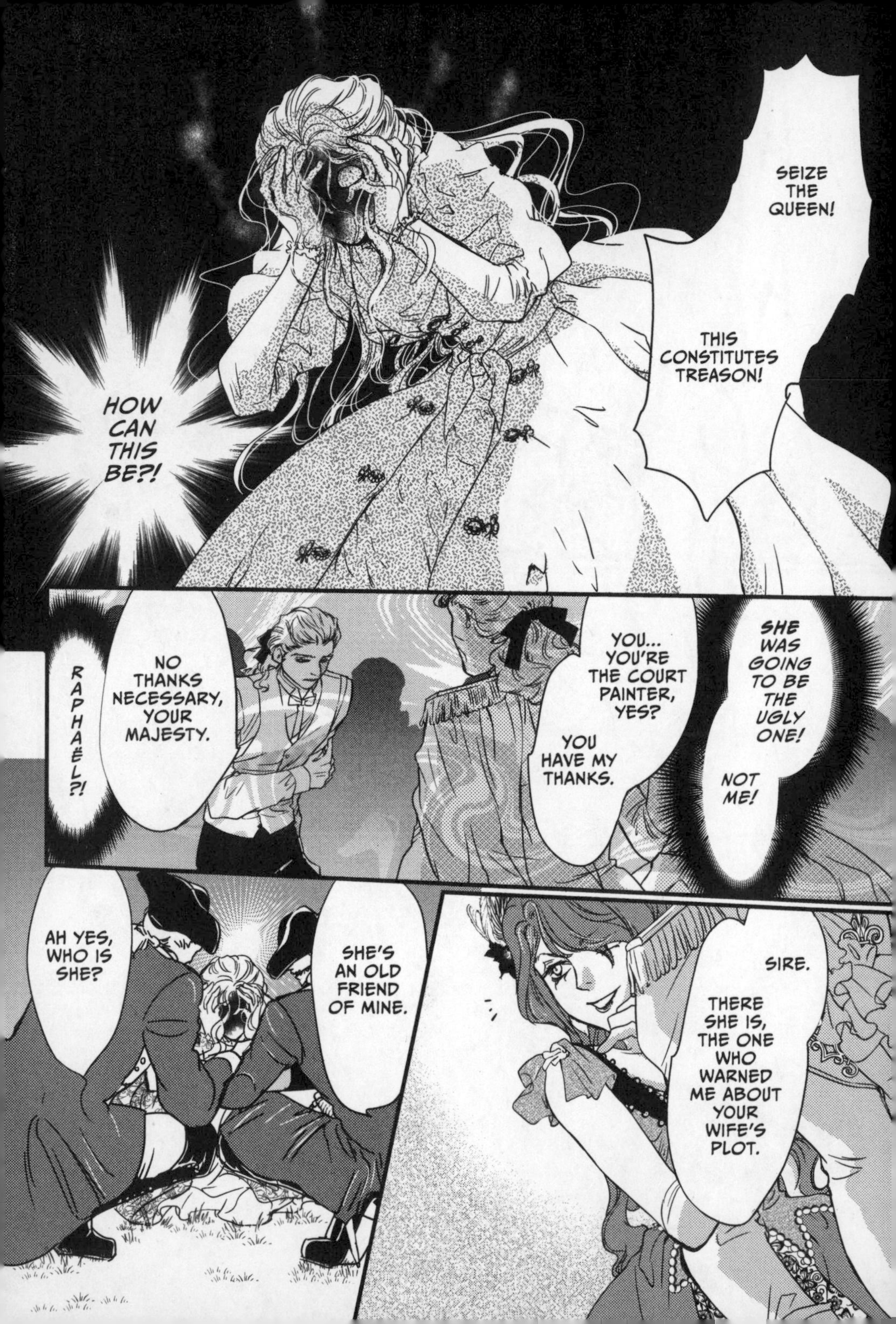
SEIZE THE QUEEN!
THIS CONSTITUTES TREASON!
HOW CAN THIS BE?!
SHE WAS GOING TO BE THE UGLY ONE!
NOT ME!
YOU... YOU'RE THE COURT PAINTER, YES?
YOU HAVE MY THANKS.
NO THANKS NECESSARY, YOUR MAJESTY.
RAPHAËL?!
SIRE.
THERE SHE IS, THE ONE WHO WARNED ME ABOUT YOUR WIFE'S PLOT.
SHE'S AN OLD FRIEND OF MINE.
AH YES, WHO IS SHE?

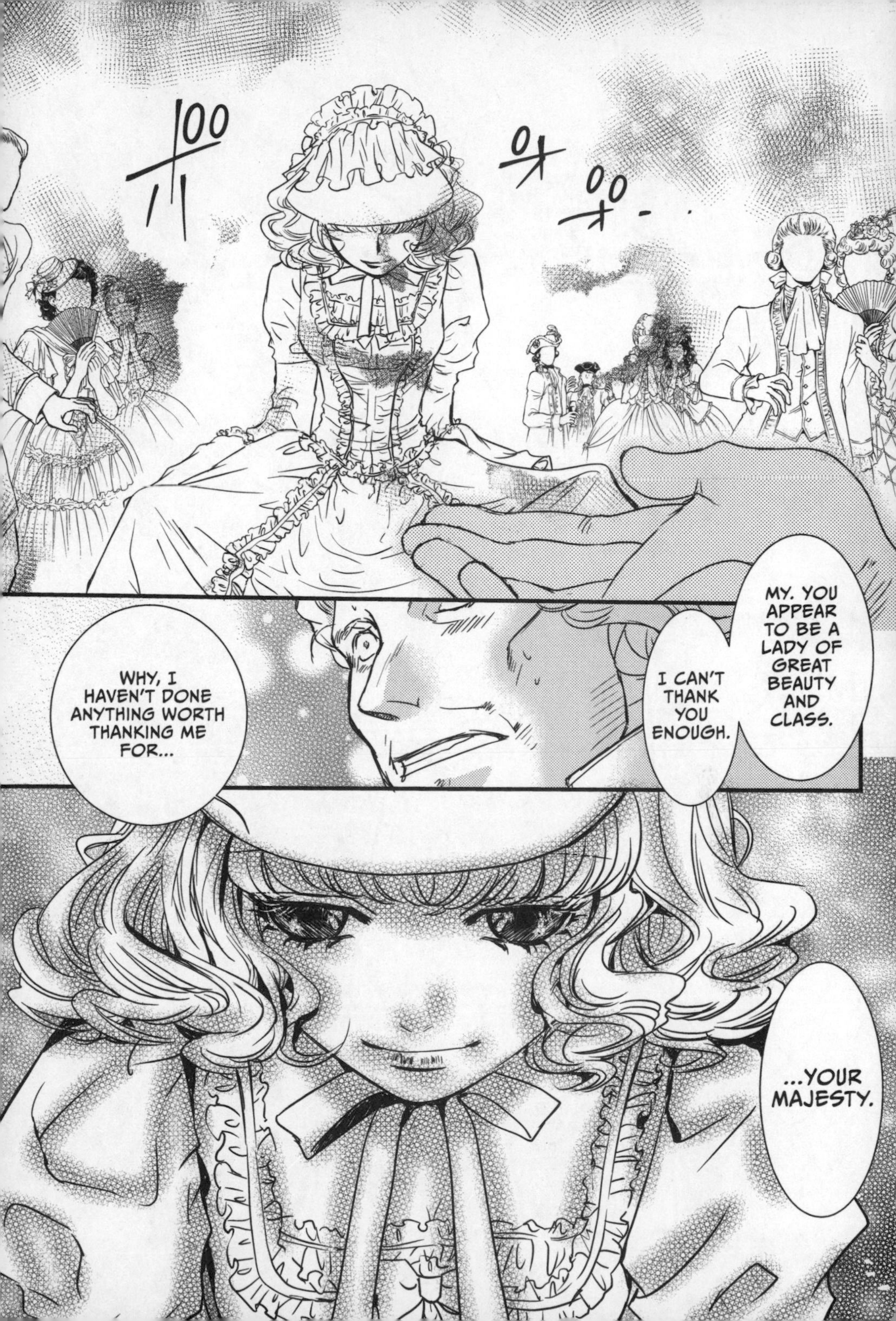
MY. YOU APPEAR TO BE A LADY OF GREAT BEAUTY AND CLASS.
I CAN'T THANK YOU ENOUGH.
WHY, I HAVEN'T DONE ANYTHING WORTH THANKING ME FOR...
...YOUR MAJESTY.

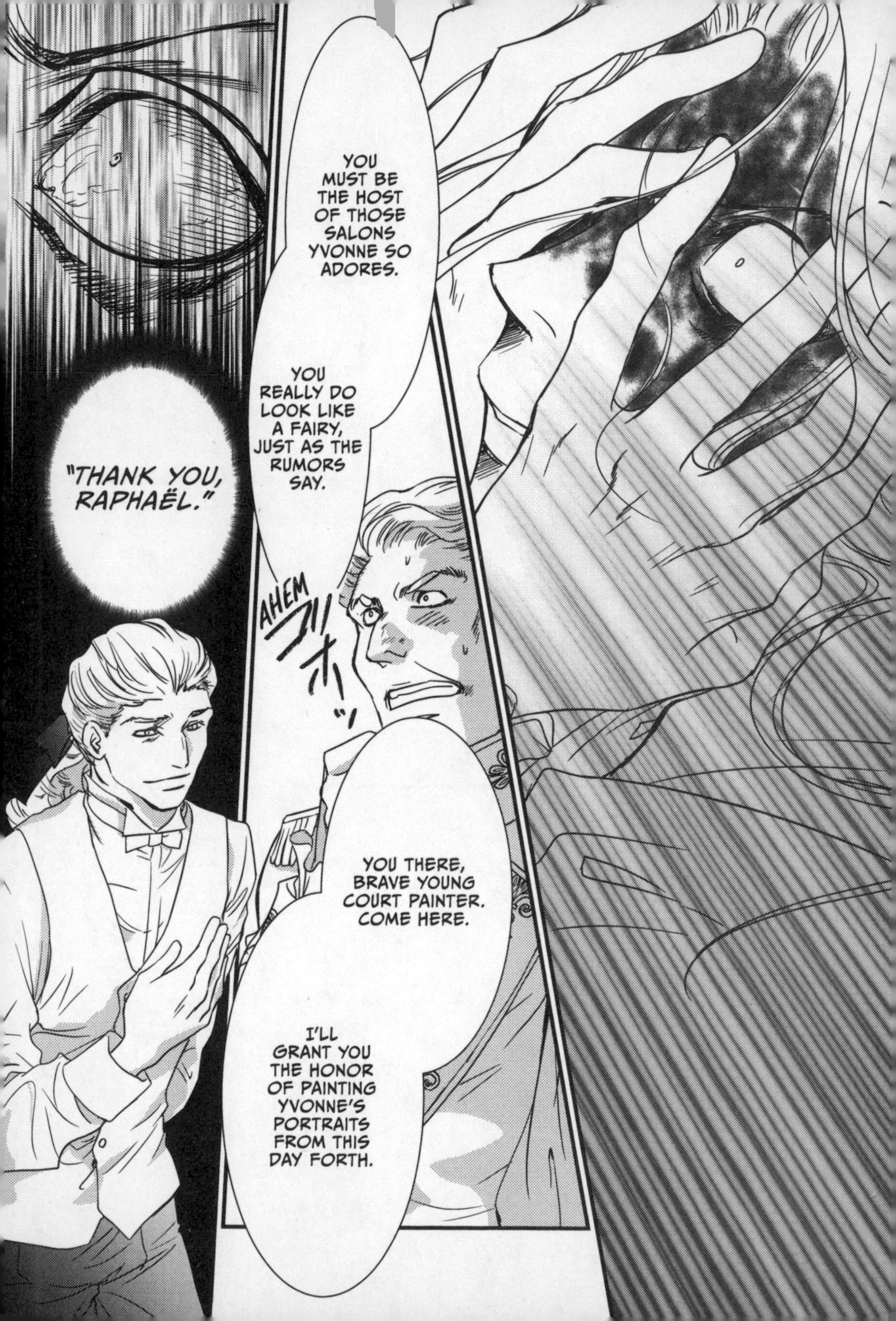

YOU MUST BE THE HOST OF THOSE SALONS YVONNE SO ADORES.
YOU REALLY DO LOOK LIKE A FAIRY, JUST AS THE RUMORS SAY.
AHEM
YOU THERE, BRAVE YOUNG COURT PAINTER. COME HERE.
I'LL GRANT YOU THE HONOR OF PAINTING YVONNE'S PORTRAITS FROM THIS DAY FORTH.
"THANK YOU, RAPHAËL."

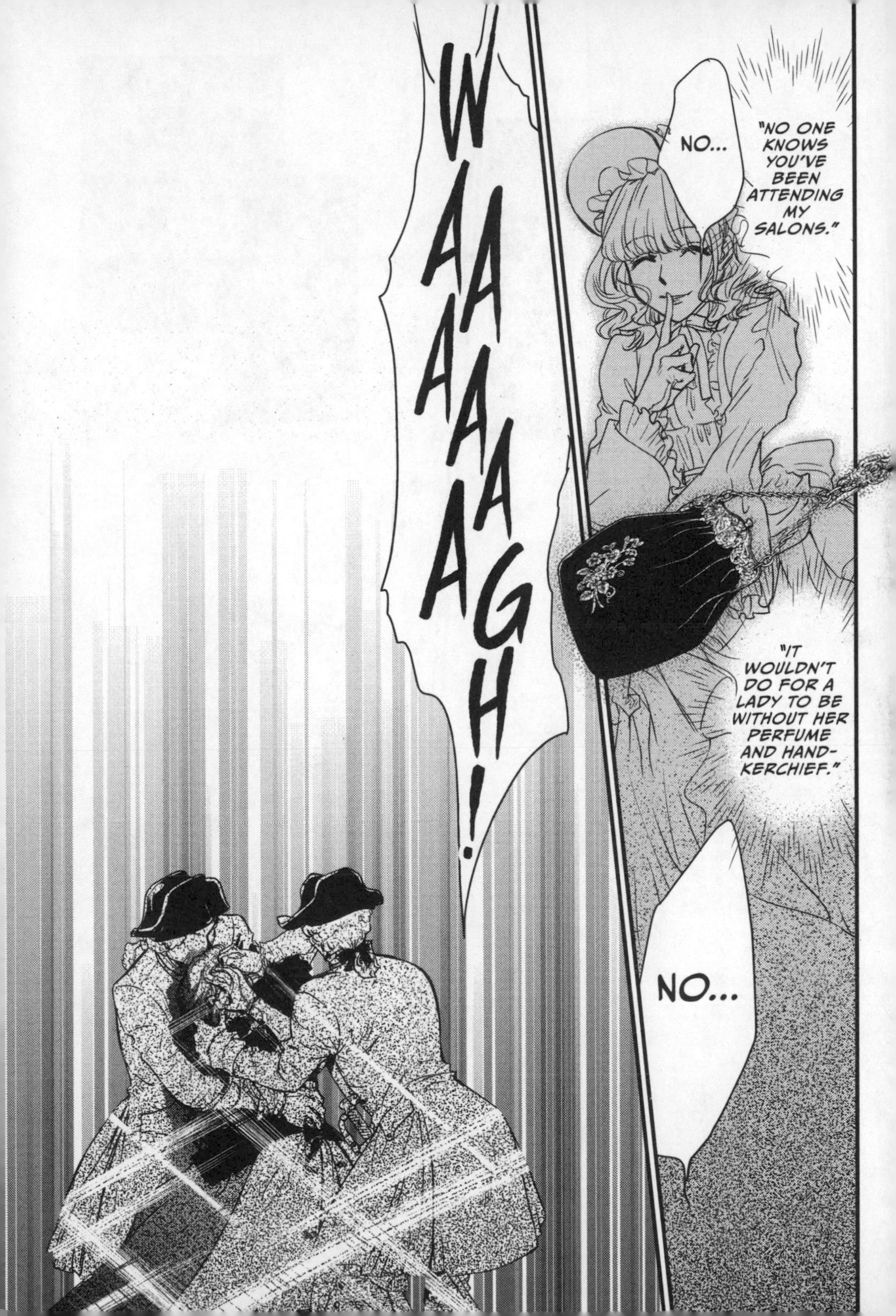
"NO ONE KNOWS YOU'VE BEEN ATTENDING MY SALONS."
NO...
"IT WOULDN'T DO FOR A LADY TO BE WITHOUT HER PERFUME AND HAND-KERCHIEF."
NO...
WAAAAAAGH!

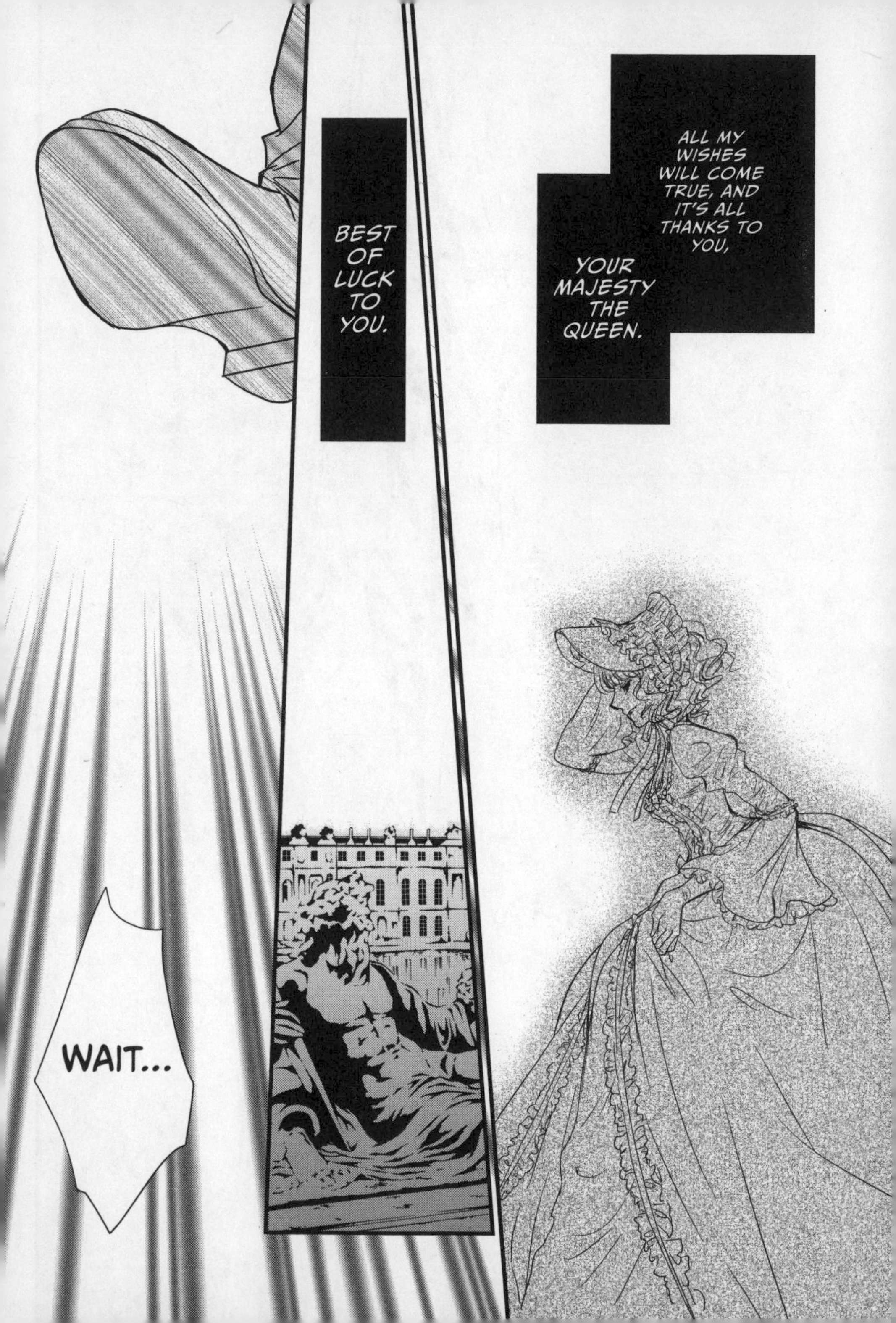
ALL MY WISHES WILL COME TRUE, AND IT'S ALL THANKS TO YOU,
YOUR MAJESTY THE QUEEN.
BEST OF LUCK TO YOU.
WAIT...

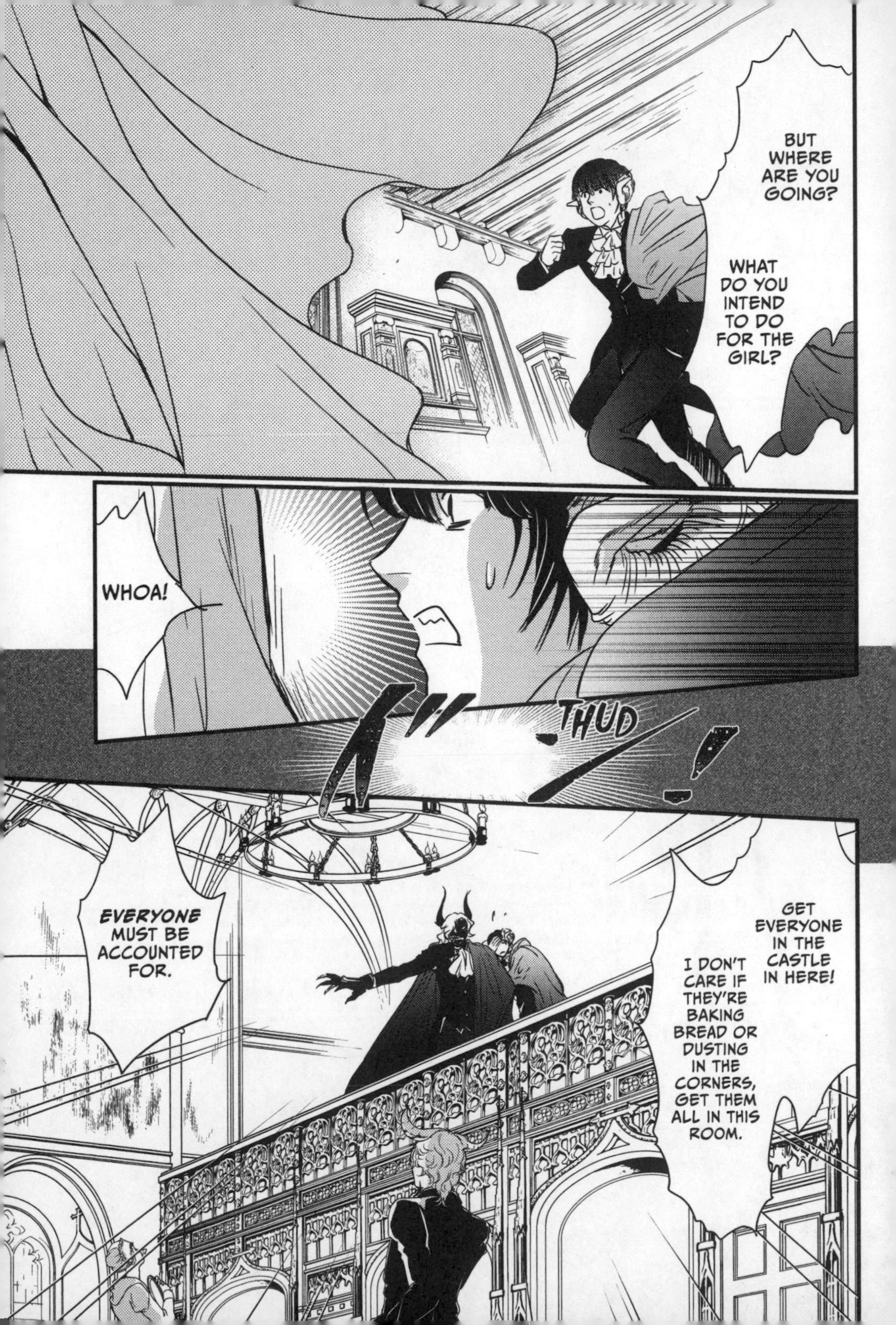

BUT WHERE ARE YOU GOING?
WHAT DO YOU INTEND TO DO FOR THE GIRL?
WHOA!
THUD
GET EVERYONE IN THE CASTLE IN HERE!
I DON'T CARE IF THEY'RE BAKING BREAD OR DUSTING IN THE CORNERS, GET THEM ALL IN THIS ROOM.
EVERYONE MUST BE ACCOUNTED FOR.

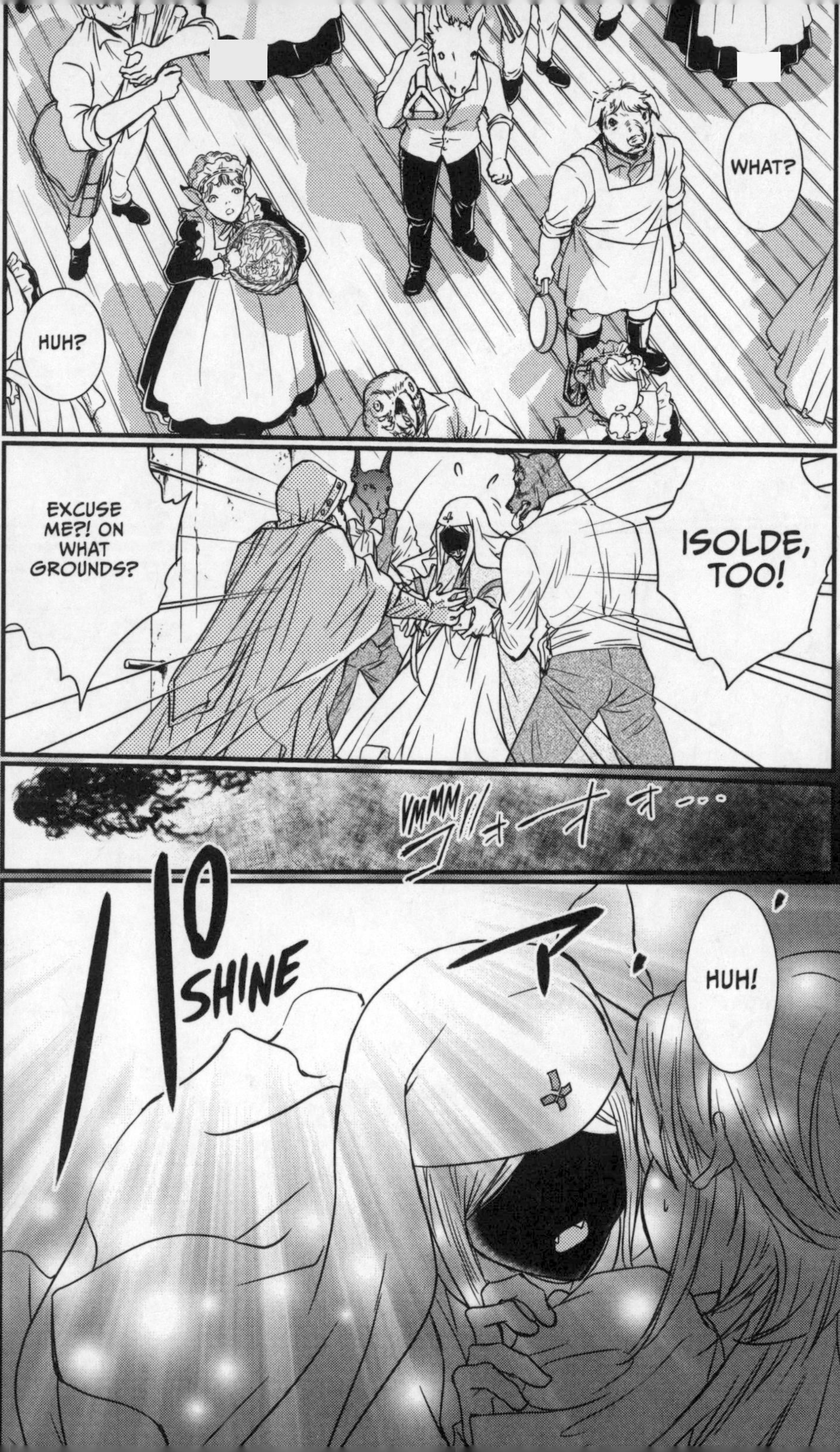
WHAT?
HUH?
ISOLDE, TOO!
EXCUSE ME?! ON WHAT GROUNDS?
VMMM
HUH!
SHINE

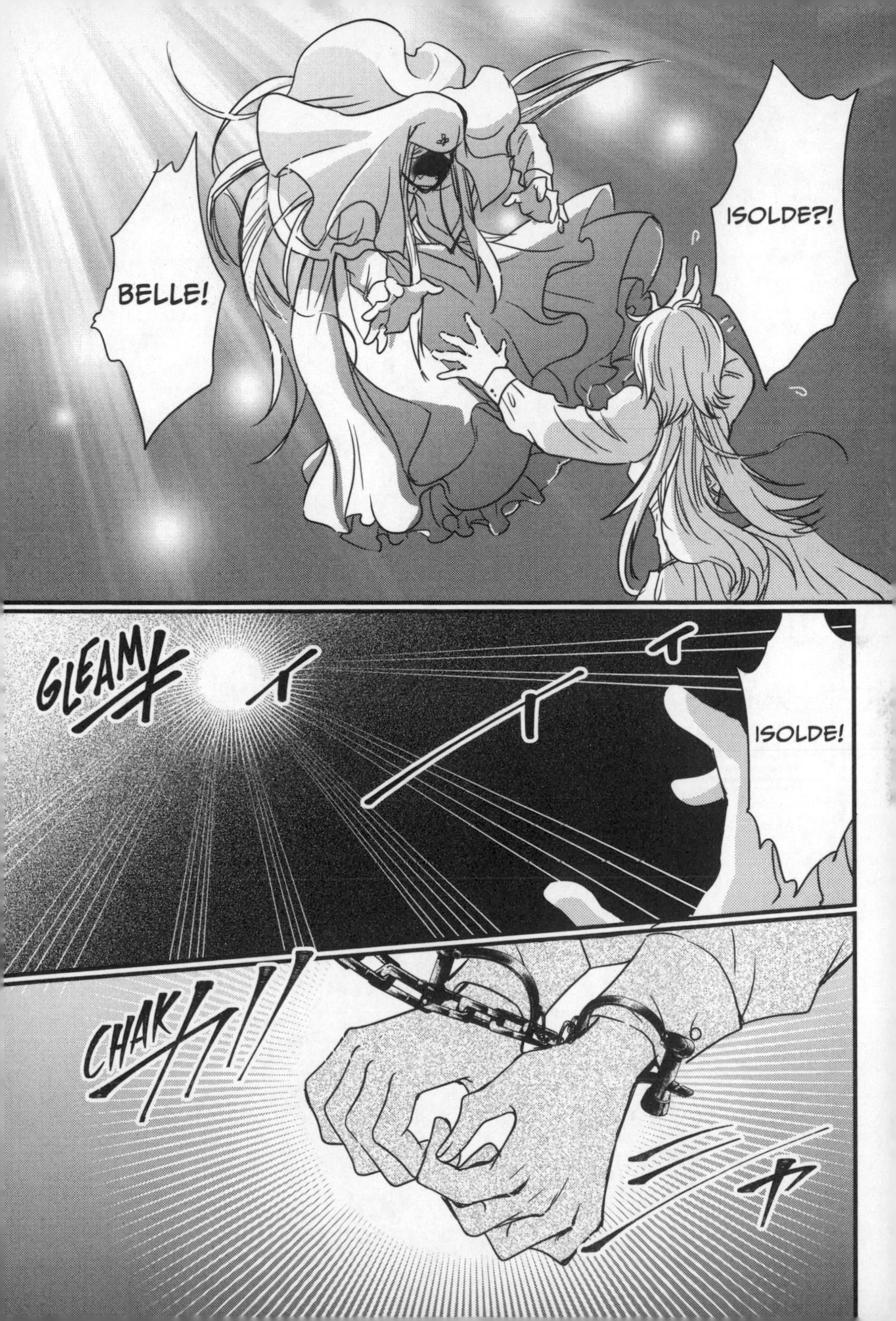
ISOLDE?!
BELLE!
ISOLDE!
GLEAM
CHAK

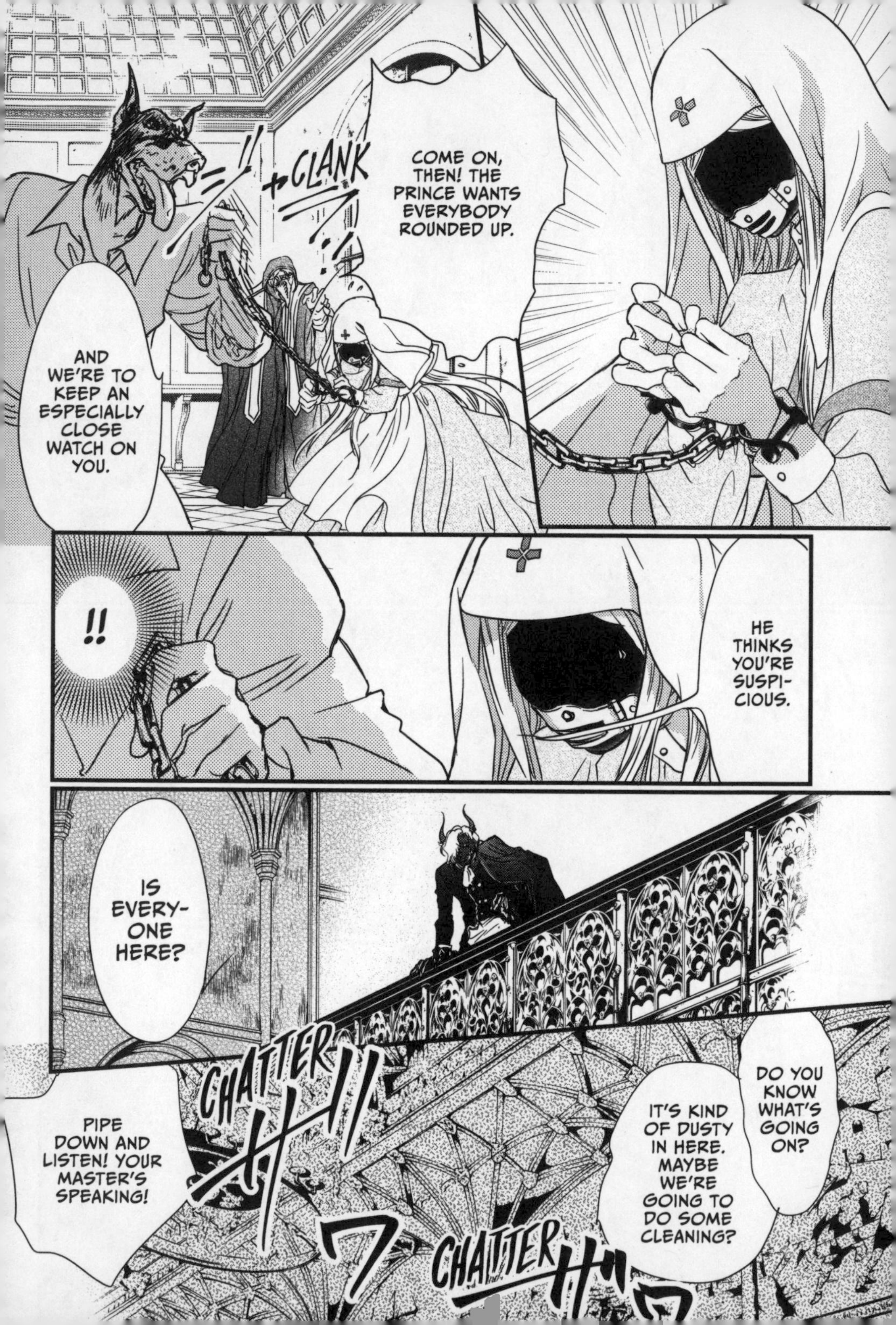
COME ON, THEN! THE PRINCE WANTS EVERYBODY ROUNDED UP.
CLANK
AND WE'RE TO KEEP AN ESPECIALLY CLOSE WATCH ON YOU.
HE THINKS YOU'RE SUSPI-CIOUS.
!!
IS EVERY-ONE HERE?
DO YOU KNOW WHAT'S GOING ON?
IT'S KIND OF DUSTY IN HERE. MAYBE WE'RE GOING TO DO SOME CLEANING?
CHATTER
CHATTER
PIPE DOWN AND LISTEN! YOUR MASTER'S SPEAKING!

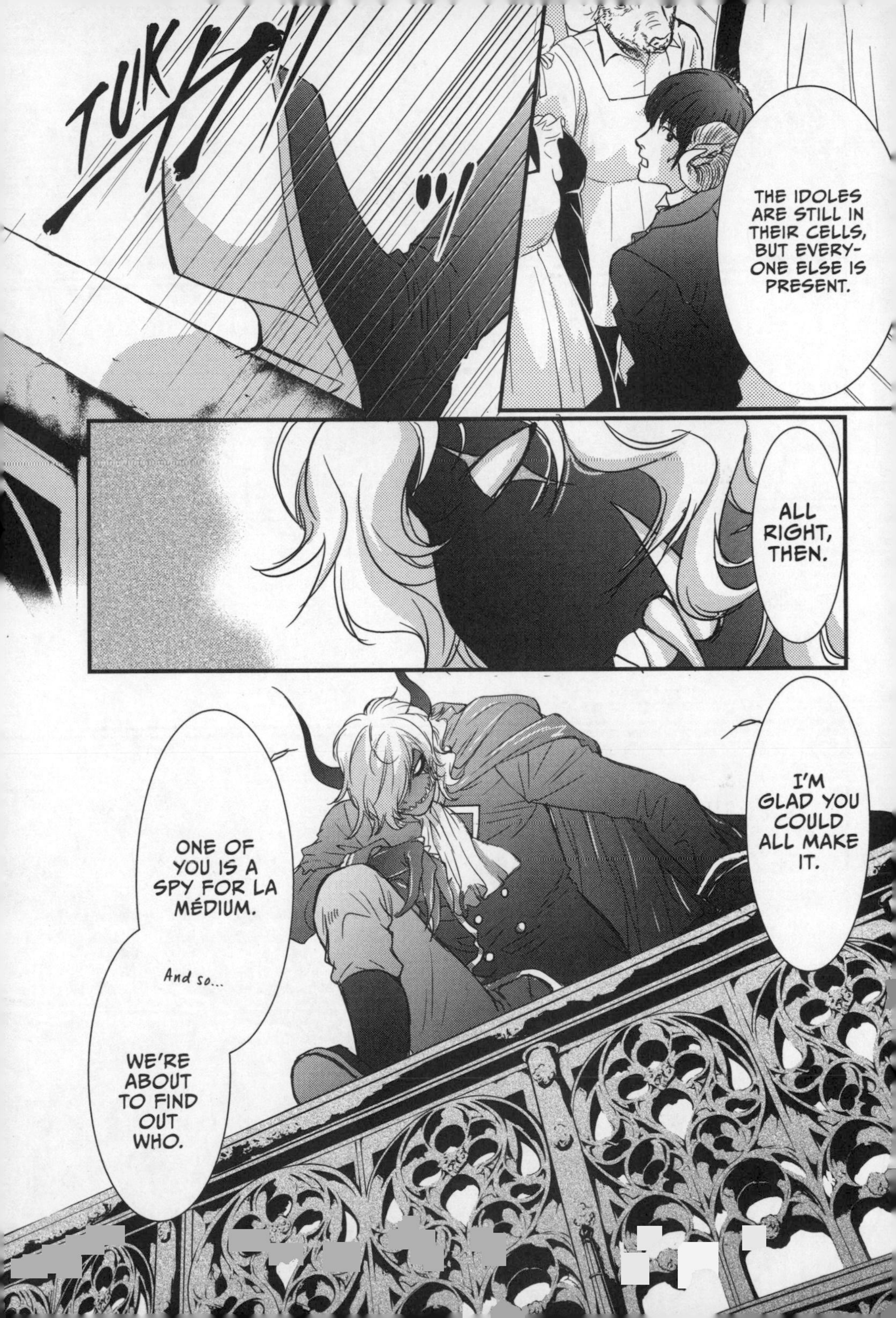
THE IDOLES ARE STILL IN THEIR CELLS, BUT EVERY-ONE ELSE IS PRESENT.
TUK
ALL RIGHT, THEN.
I'M GLAD YOU COULD ALL MAKE IT.
ONE OF YOU IS A SPY FOR LA MÉDIUM.
And so...
WE'RE ABOUT TO FIND OUT WHO.

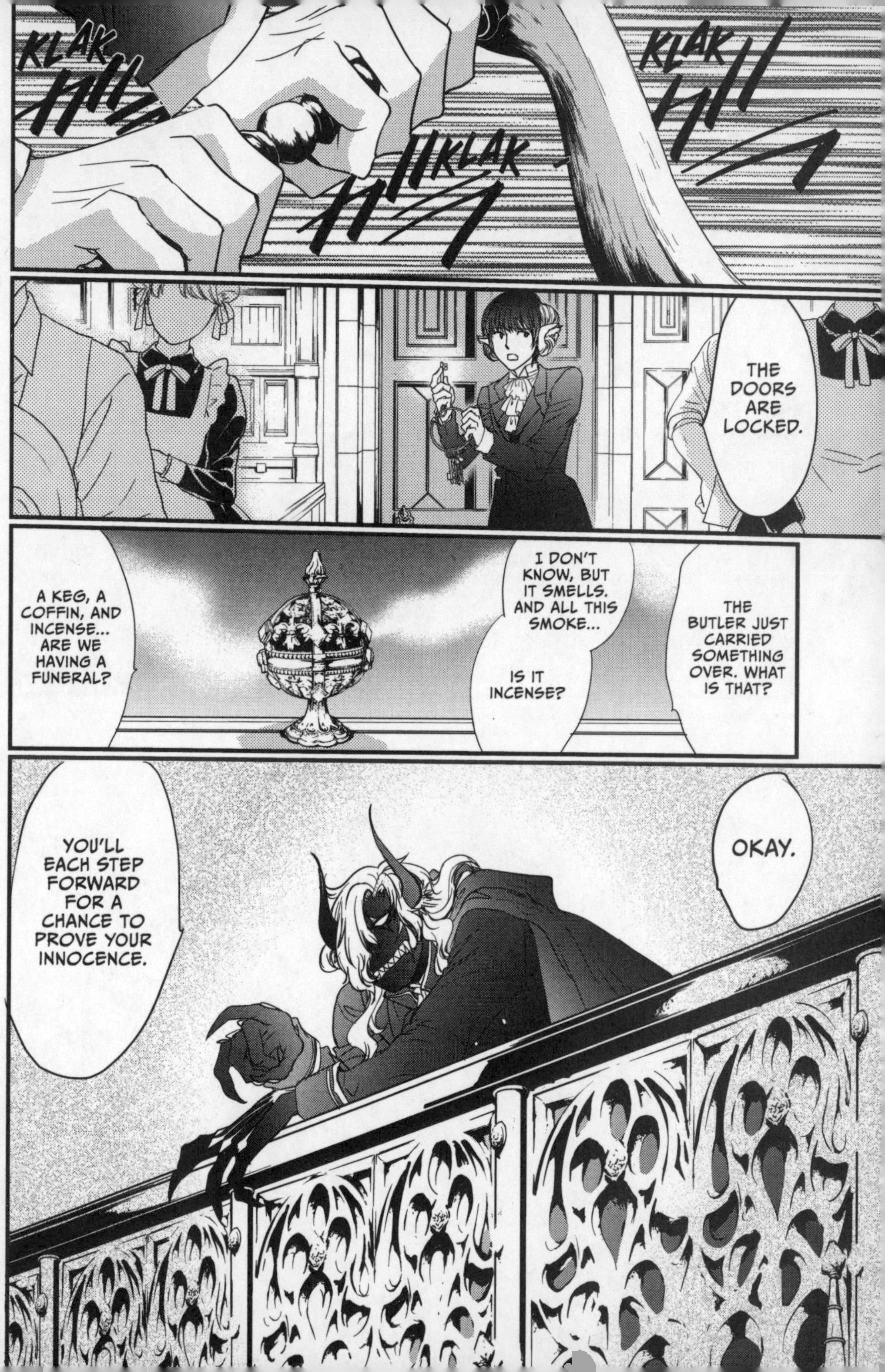

KLAK
KLAK
KLAK
THE DOORS ARE LOCKED.
THE BUTLER JUST CARRIED SOMETHING OVER. WHAT IS THAT?
I DON'T KNOW, BUT IT SMELLS. AND ALL THIS SMOKE...
IS IT INCENSE?
A KEG, A COFFIN, AND INCENSE... ARE WE HAVING A FUNERAL?
OKAY.
YOU'LL EACH STEP FORWARD FOR A CHANCE TO PROVE YOUR INNOCENCE.

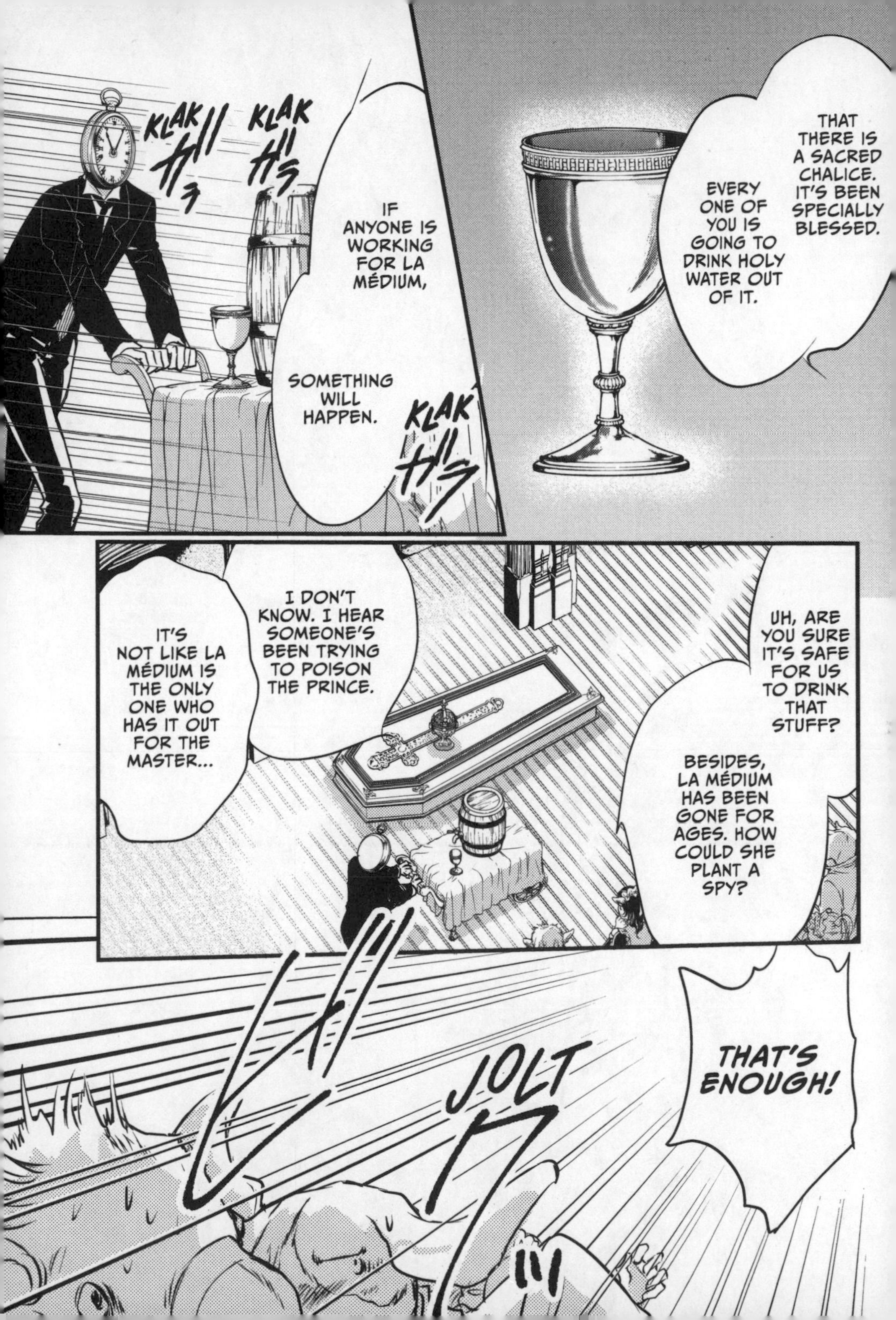
THAT THERE IS A SACRED CHALICE. IT'S BEEN SPECIALLY BLESSED.
EVERY ONE OF YOU IS GOING TO DRINK HOLY WATER OUT OF IT.
KLAK
IF ANYONE IS WORKING FOR LA MÉDIUM,
SOMETHING WILL HAPPEN.
KLAK
KLAK
UH, ARE YOU SURE IT'S SAFE FOR US TO DRINK THAT STUFF?
BESIDES, LA MÉDIUM HAS BEEN GONE FOR AGES. HOW COULD SHE PLANT A SPY?
I DON'T KNOW. I HEAR SOMEONE'S BEEN TRYING TO POISON THE PRINCE.
IT'S NOT LIKE LA MÉDIUM IS THE ONLY ONE WHO HAS IT OUT FOR THE MASTER...
THAT'S ENOUGH!
JOLT

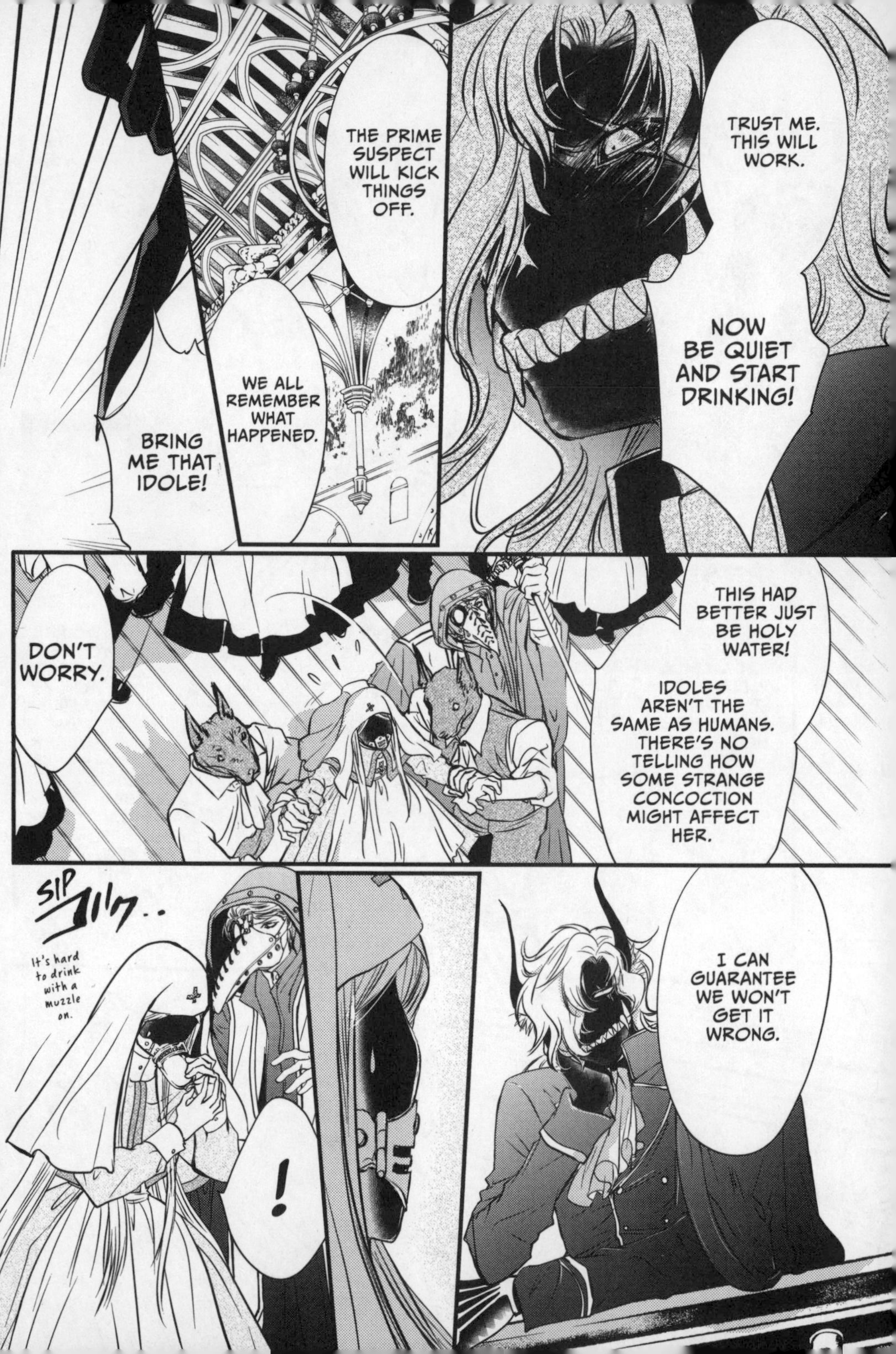
TRUST ME. THIS WILL WORK.
NOW BE QUIET AND START DRINKING!
THE PRIME SUSPECT WILL KICK THINGS OFF.
WE ALL REMEMBER WHAT HAPPENED.
BRING ME THAT IDOLE!
THIS HAD BETTER JUST BE HOLY WATER!
IDOLES AREN'T THE SAME AS HUMANS. THERE'S NO TELLING HOW SOME STRANGE CONCOCTION MIGHT AFFECT HER.
DON'T WORRY.
I CAN GUARANTEE WE WON'T GET IT WRONG.
!
SIP
It's hard to drink with a muzzle on.

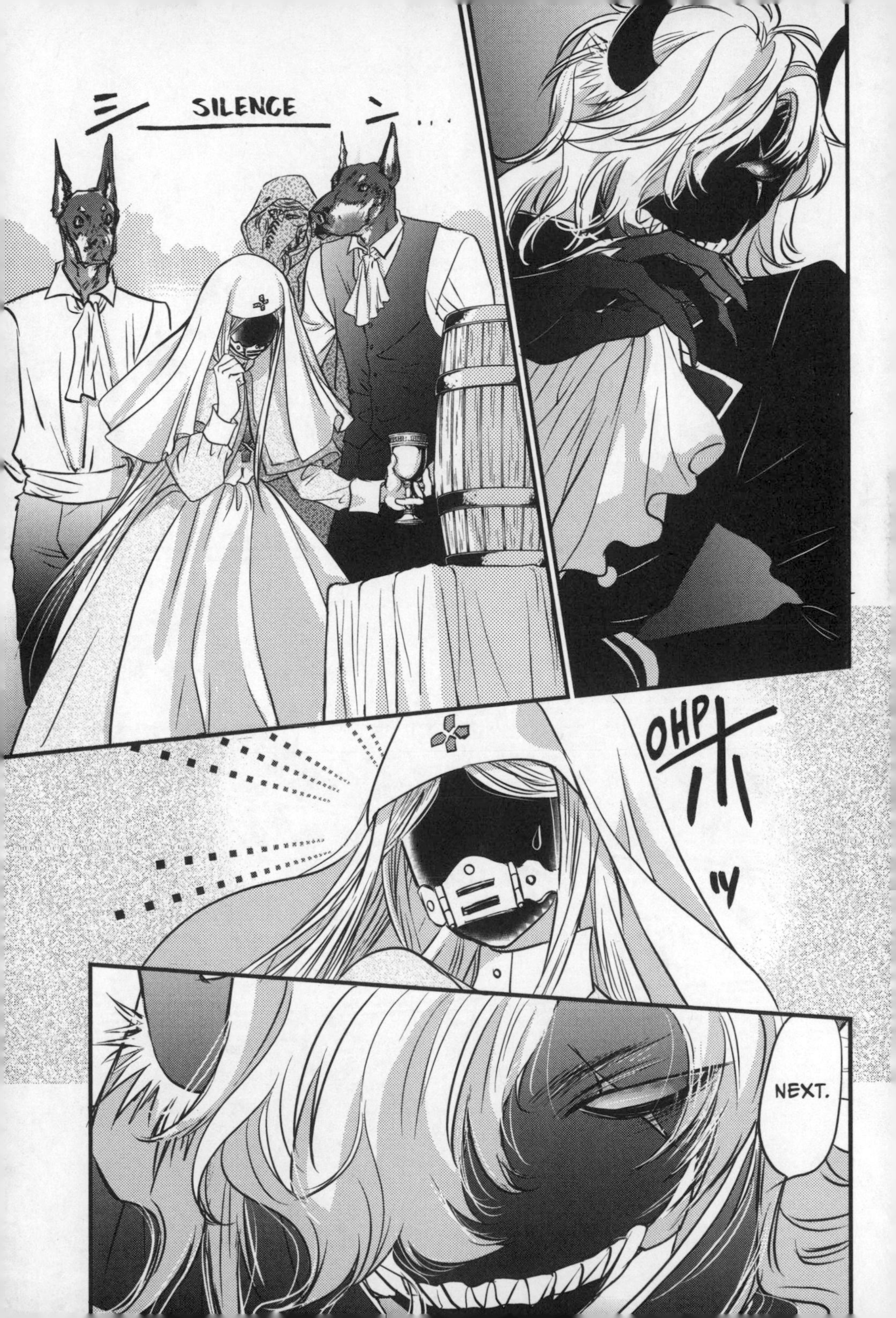
SILENCE
OHP
NEXT.

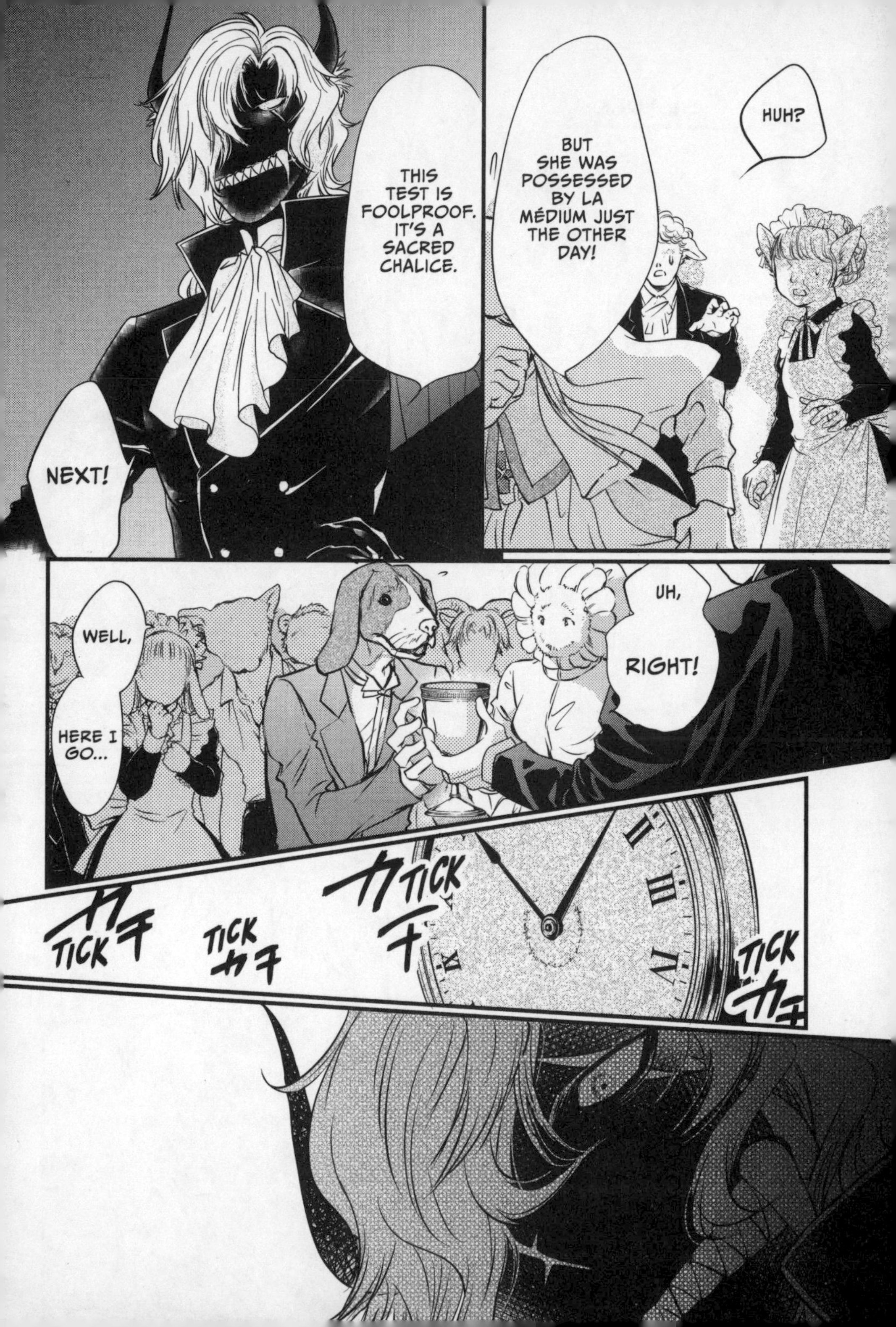

HUH?
BUT SHE WAS POSSESSED BY LA MÉDIUM JUST THE OTHER DAY!
THIS TEST IS FOOLPROOF. IT'S A SACRED CHALICE.
NEXT!
UH, RIGHT!
WELL, HERE I GO...
TICK カチ
TICK カチ
TICK カチ
TICK カチ

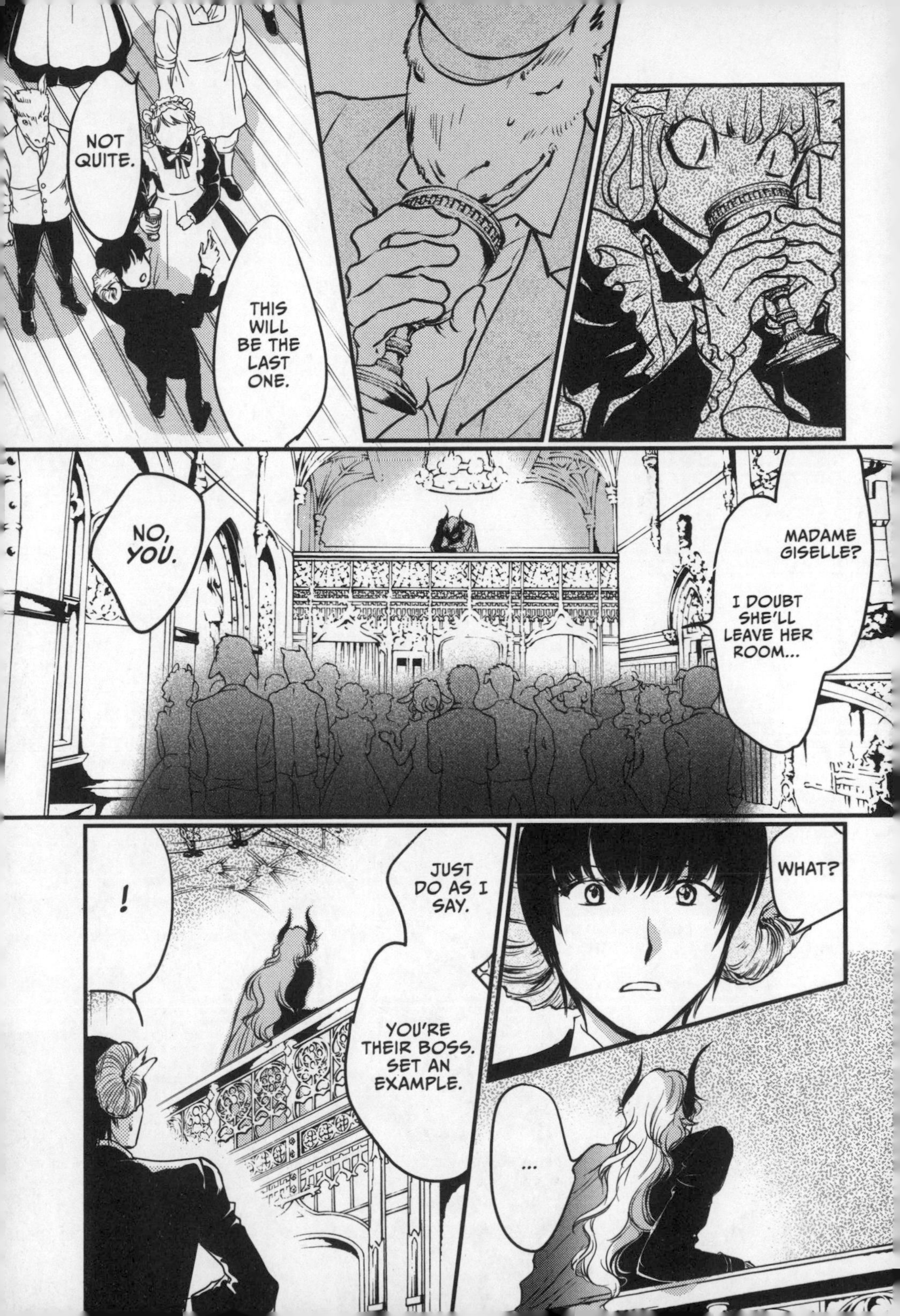
NOT QUITE.
THIS WILL BE THE LAST ONE.
MADAME GISELLE?
I DOUBT SHE'LL LEAVE HER ROOM...
NO, YOU.
WHAT?
...
JUST DO AS I SAY.
!
YOU'RE THEIR BOSS. SET AN EXAMPLE.

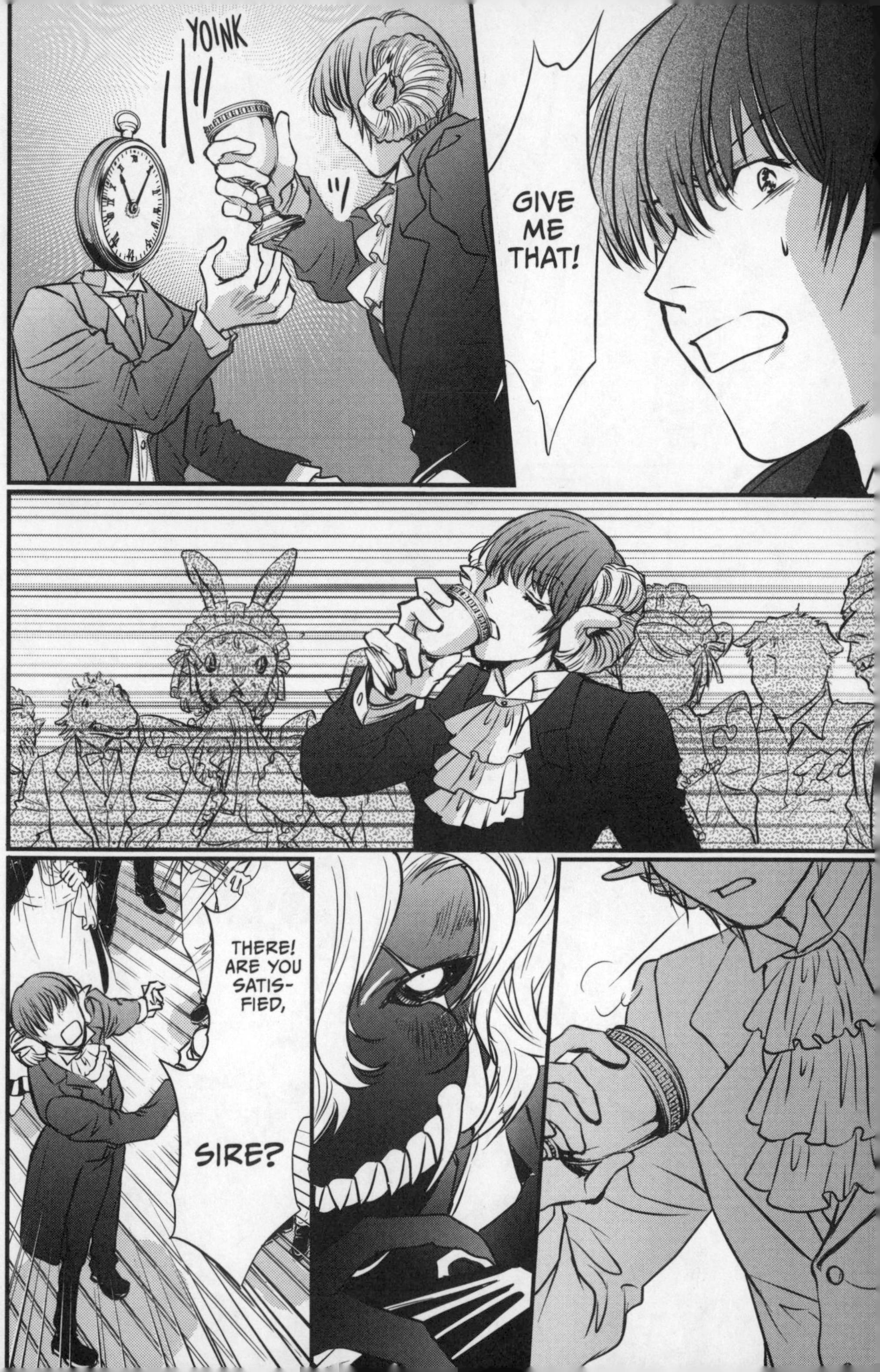
GIVE ME THAT!
YOINK
THERE! ARE YOU SATIS-FIED,
SIRE?

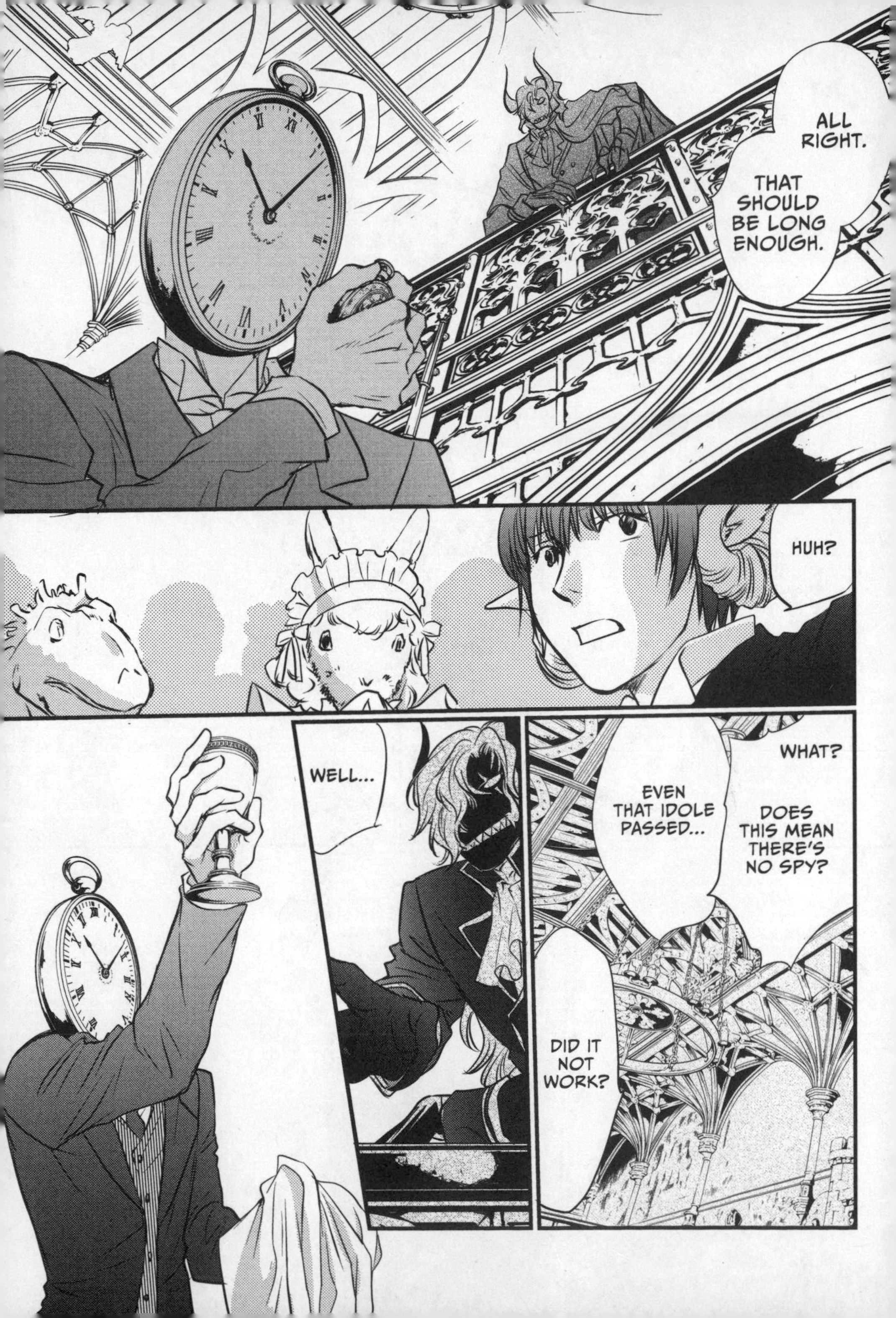
ALL RIGHT.
THAT SHOULD BE LONG ENOUGH.
HUH?
WHAT?
DOES THIS MEAN THERE'S NO SPY?
EVEN THAT IDOLE PASSED...
DID IT NOT WORK?
WELL...

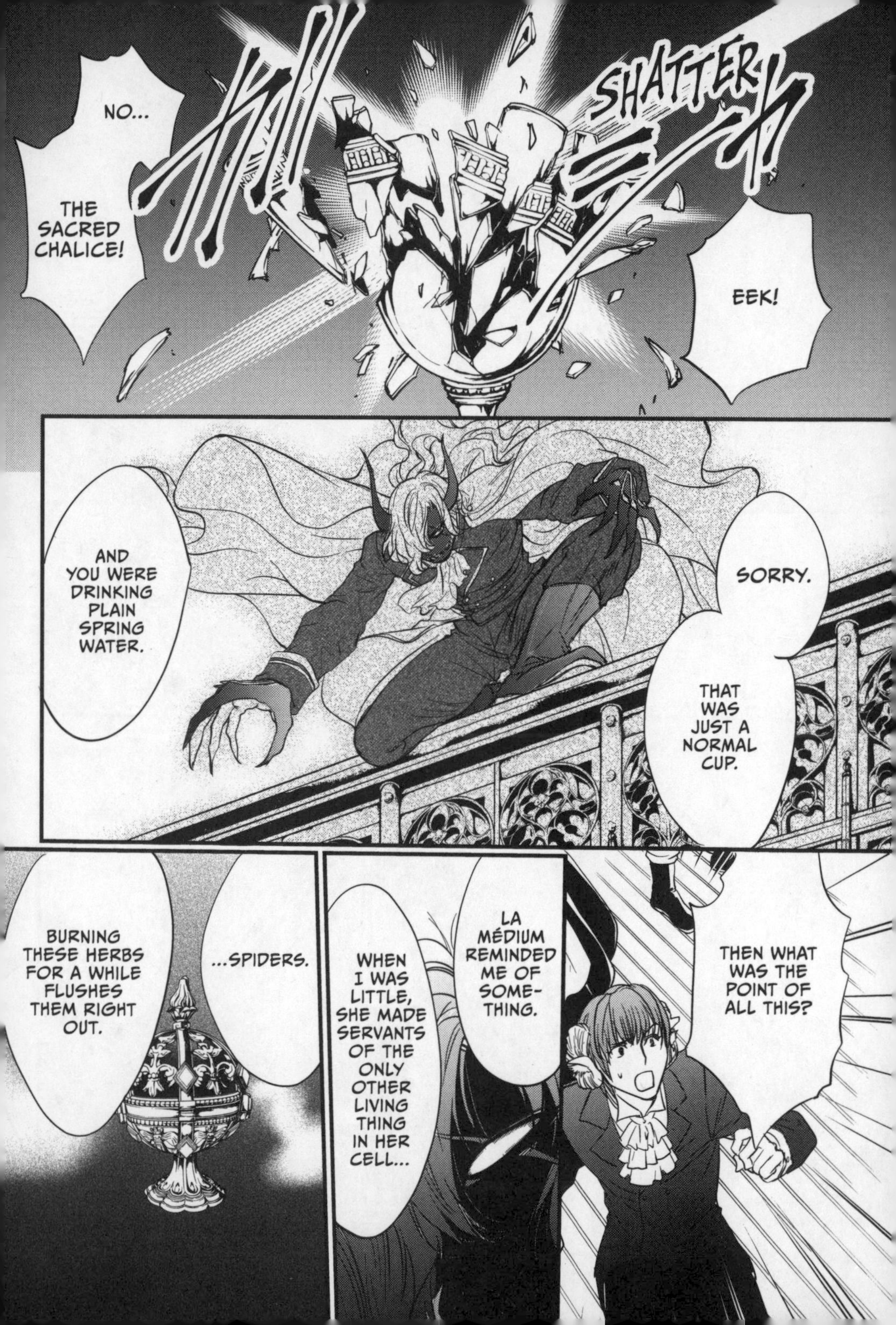
SHATTER
EEK!
NO...
THE SACRED CHALICE!
SORRY.
THAT WAS JUST A NORMAL CUP.
AND YOU WERE DRINKING PLAIN SPRING WATER.
THEN WHAT WAS THE POINT OF ALL THIS?
LA MÉDIUM REMINDED ME OF SOMETHING.
WHEN I WAS LITTLE, SHE MADE SERVANTS OF THE ONLY OTHER LIVING THING IN HER CELL...
...SPIDERS.
BURNING THESE HERBS FOR A WHILE FLUSHES THEM RIGHT OUT.

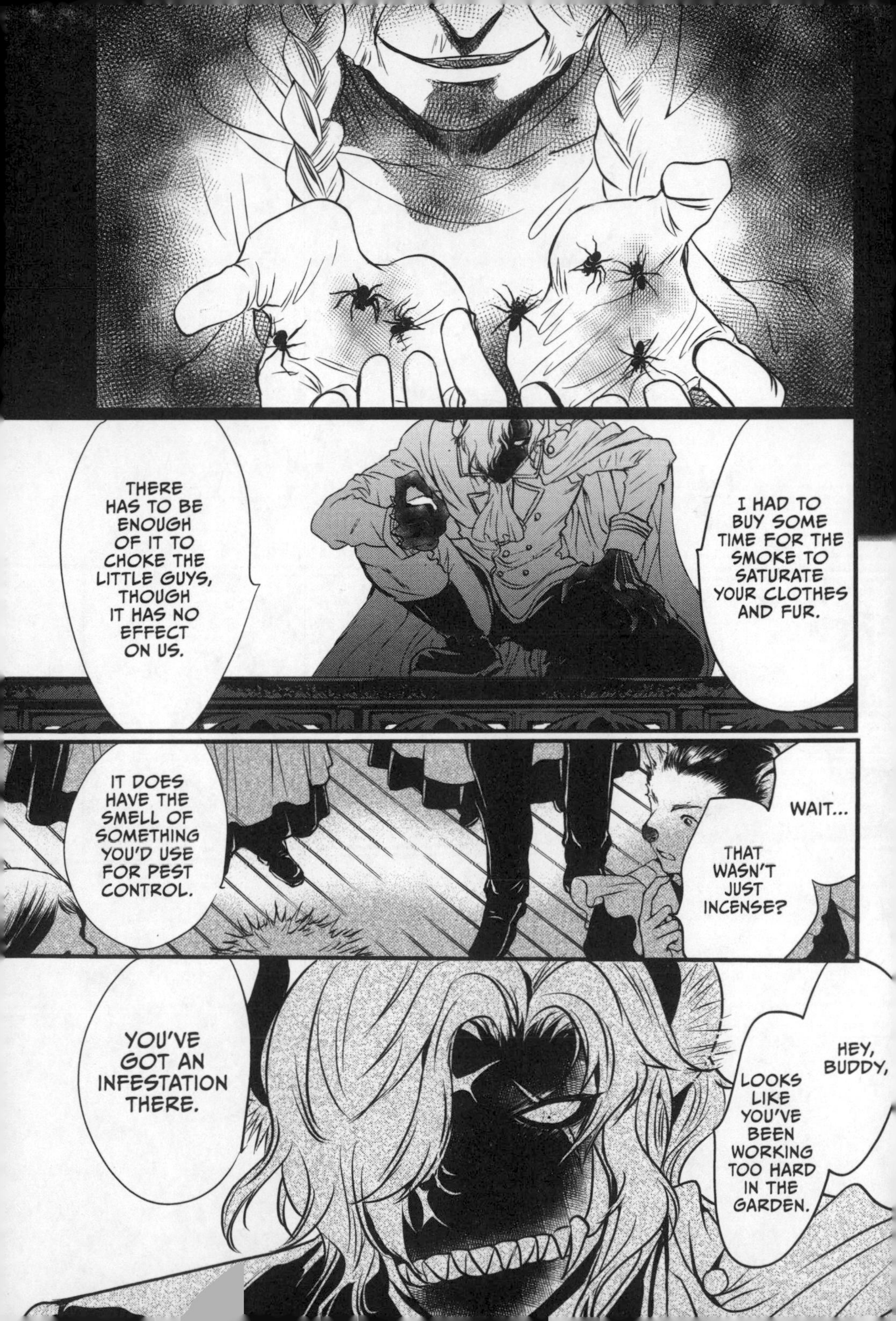
I HAD TO BUY SOME TIME FOR THE SMOKE TO SATURATE YOUR CLOTHES AND FUR.
THERE HAS TO BE ENOUGH OF IT TO CHOKE THE LITTLE GUYS, THOUGH IT HAS NO EFFECT ON US.
WAIT...
THAT WASN'T JUST INCENSE?
IT DOES HAVE THE SMELL OF SOMETHING YOU'D USE FOR PEST CONTROL.
HEY, BUDDY,
LOOKS LIKE YOU'VE BEEN WORKING TOO HARD IN THE GARDEN.
YOU'VE GOT AN INFESTATION THERE.

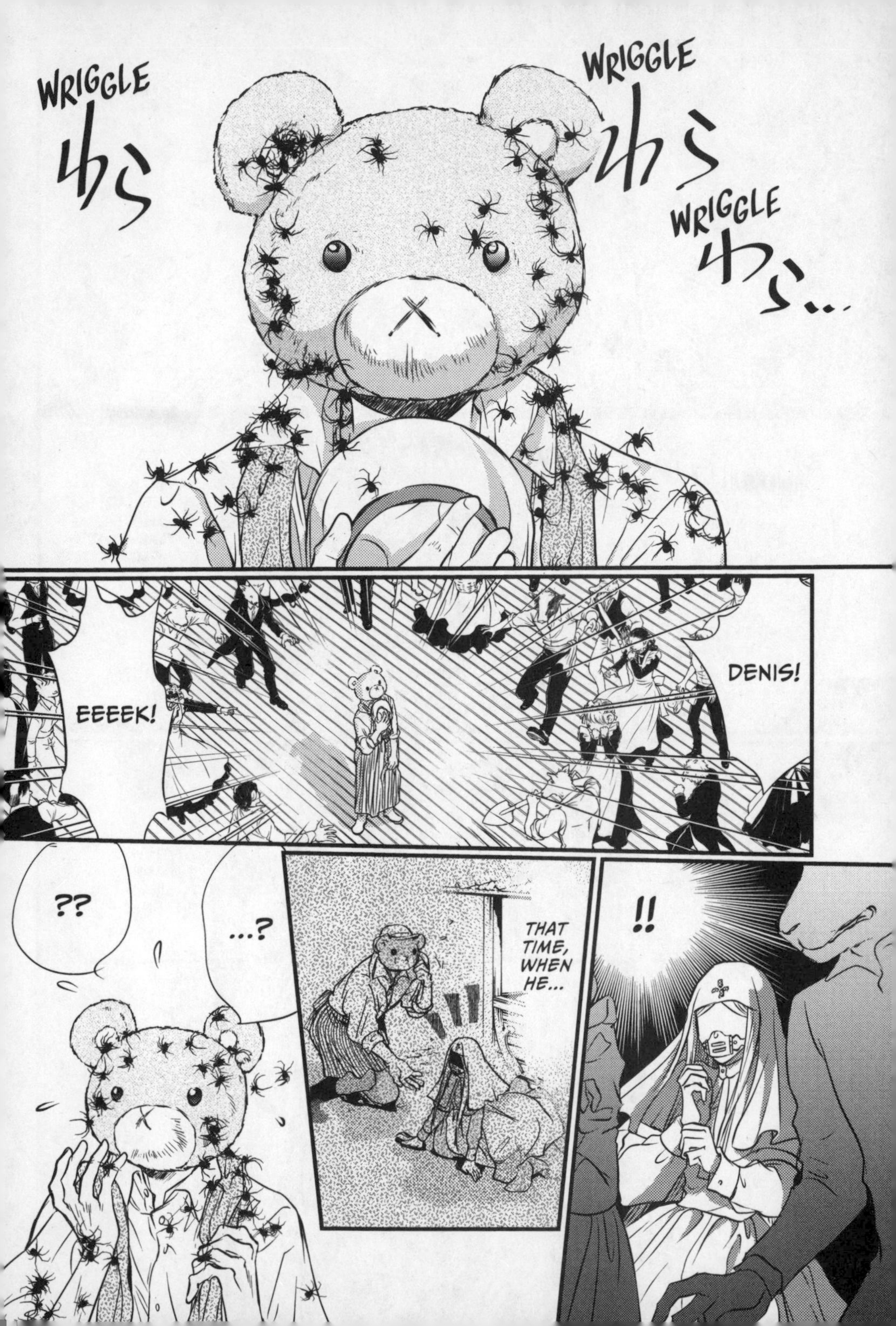
WRIGGLE
ゆら
WRIGGLE
ゆら…
WRIGGLE
ゆら
DENIS!
EEEEK!
!!
THAT TIME, WHEN HE...
...?
??

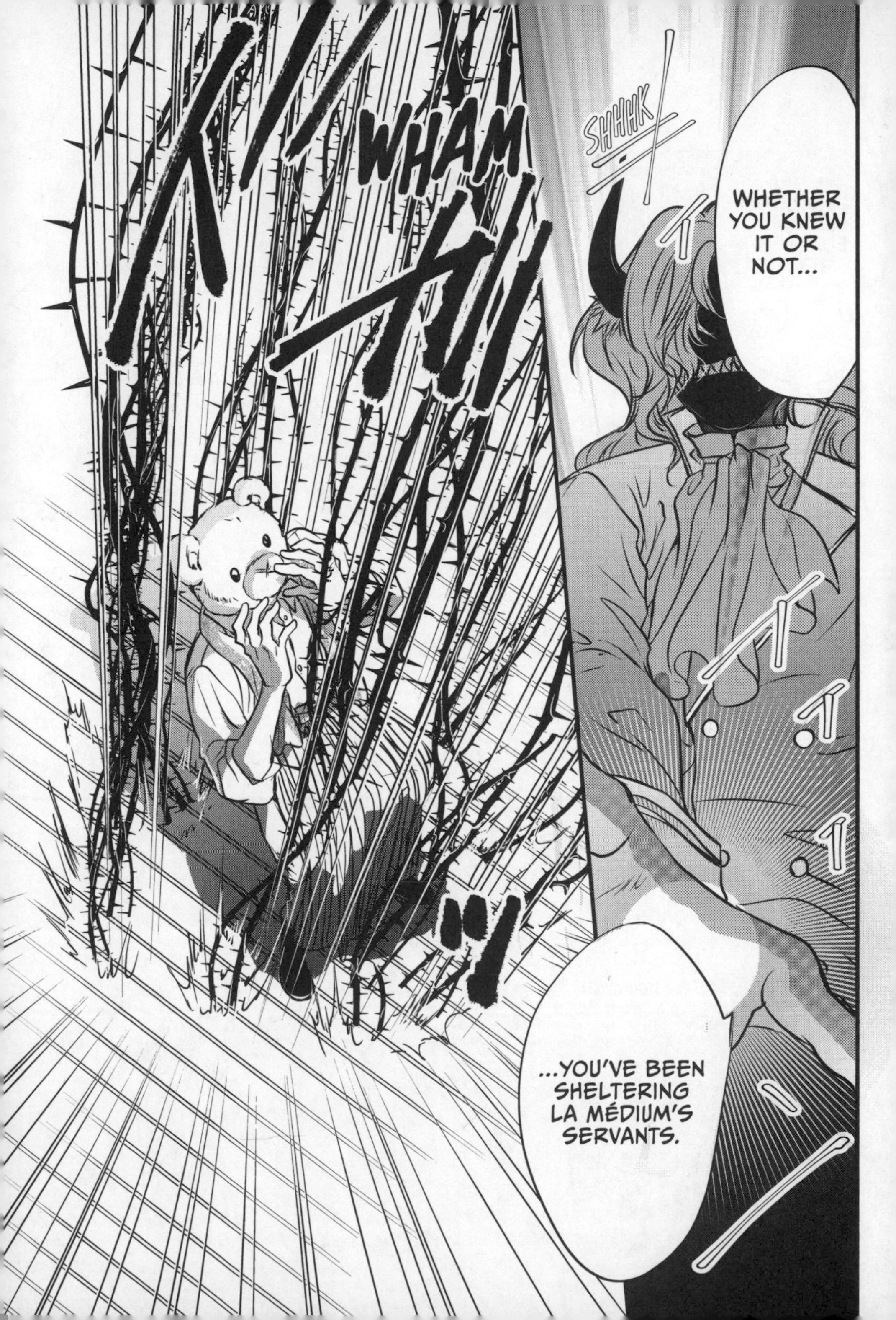
SHHHK
WHETHER YOU KNEW IT OR NOT...
WHAM
...YOU'VE BEEN SHELTERING LA MÉDIUM'S SERVANTS.

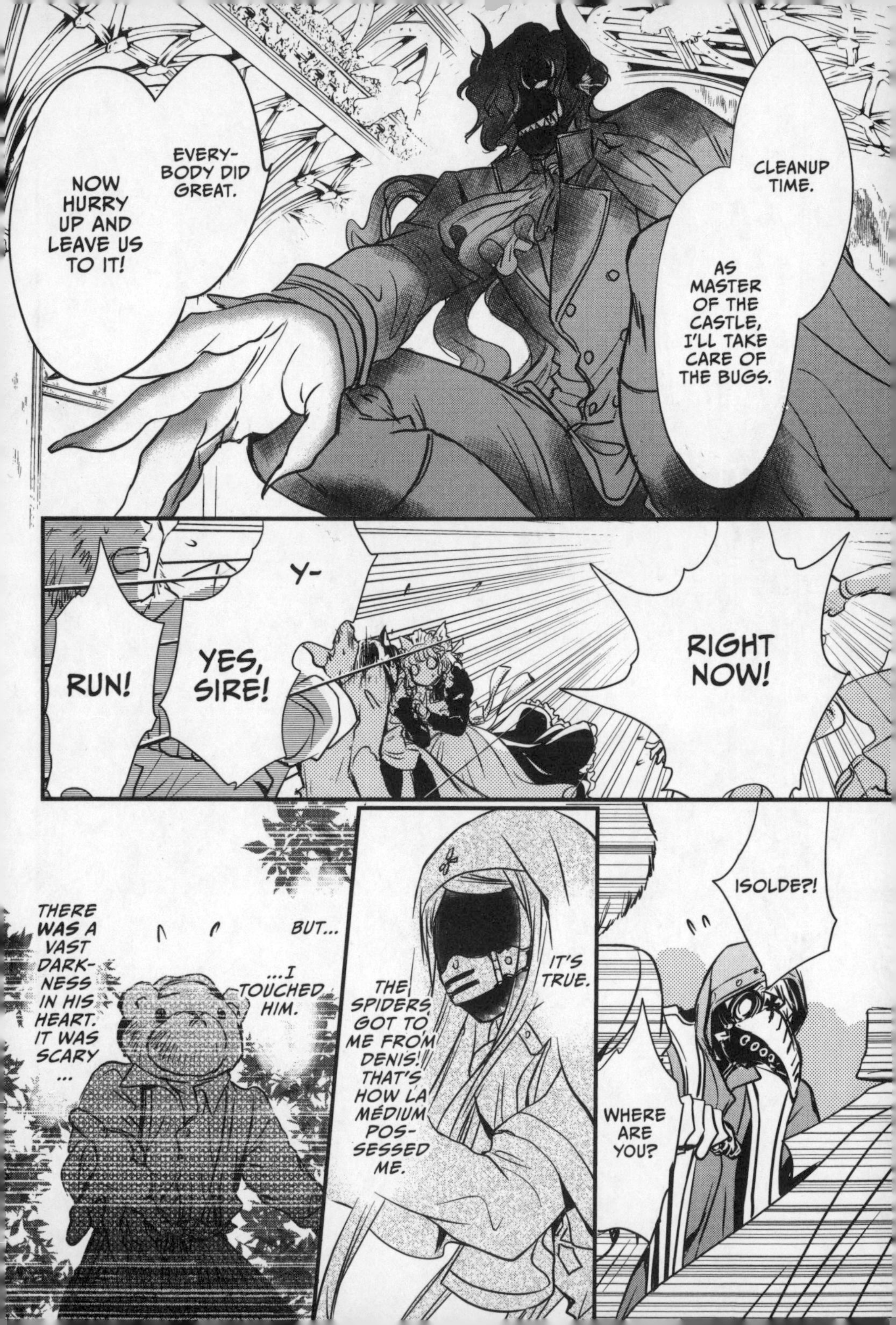
CLEANUP TIME.
AS MASTER OF THE CASTLE, I'LL TAKE CARE OF THE BUGS.
EVERY-BODY DID GREAT.
NOW HURRY UP AND LEAVE US TO IT!
RIGHT NOW!
Y-
YES, SIRE!
RUN!
ISOLDE?!
WHERE ARE YOU?
IT'S TRUE.
THE SPIDERS GOT TO ME FROM DENIS! THAT'S HOW LA MÉDIUM POS-SESSED ME.
BUT...
...I TOUCHED HIM.
THERE WAS A VAST DARK-NESS IN HIS HEART. IT WAS SCARY...

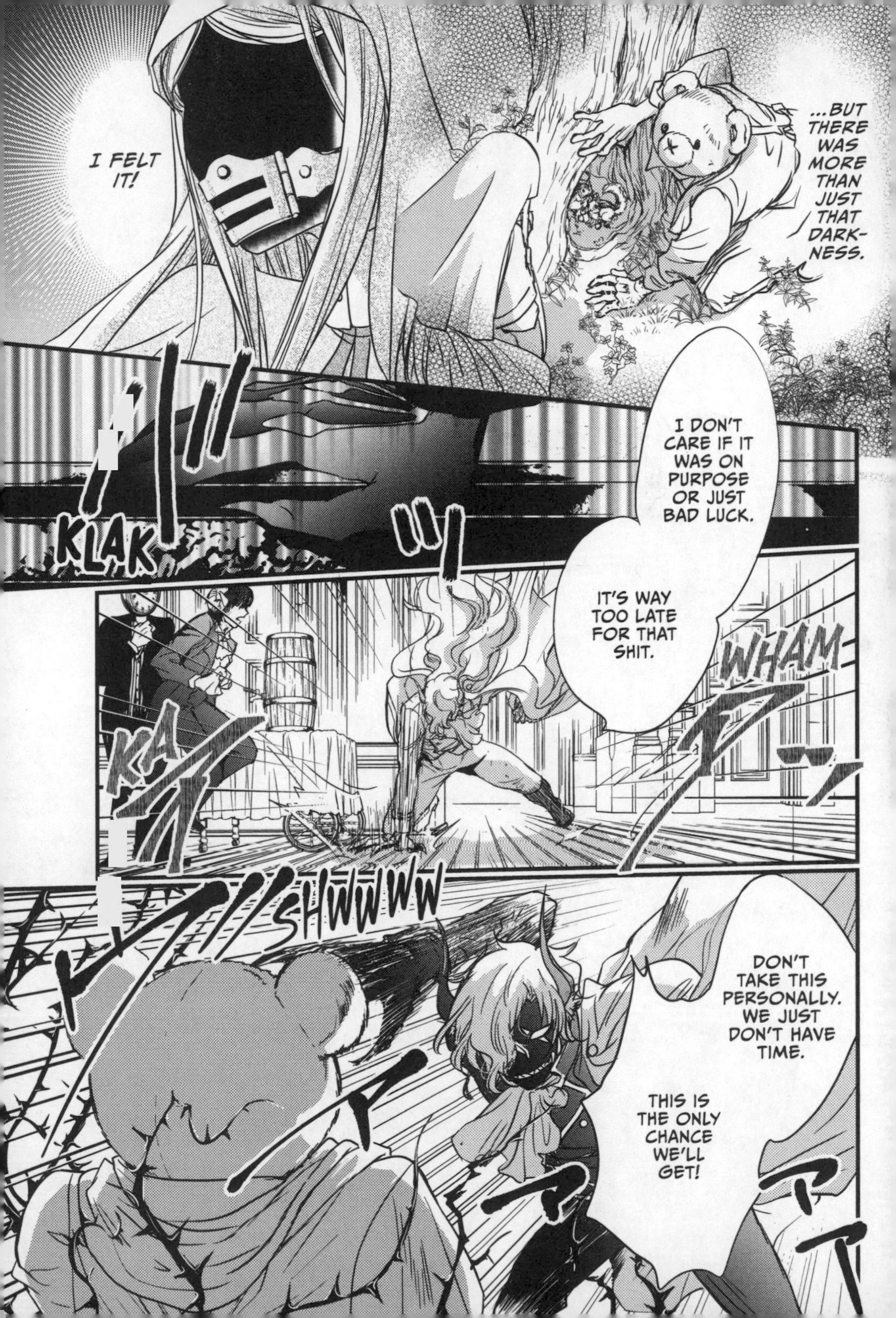
...BUT THERE WAS MORE THAN JUST THAT DARKNESS.
I FELT IT!
I DON'T CARE IF IT WAS ON PURPOSE OR JUST BAD LUCK.
KLAK
IT'S WAY TOO LATE FOR THAT SHIT.
WHAM
KA
DON'T TAKE THIS PERSONALLY. WE JUST DON'T HAVE TIME.
THIS IS THE ONLY CHANCE WE'LL GET!
SHWWWW

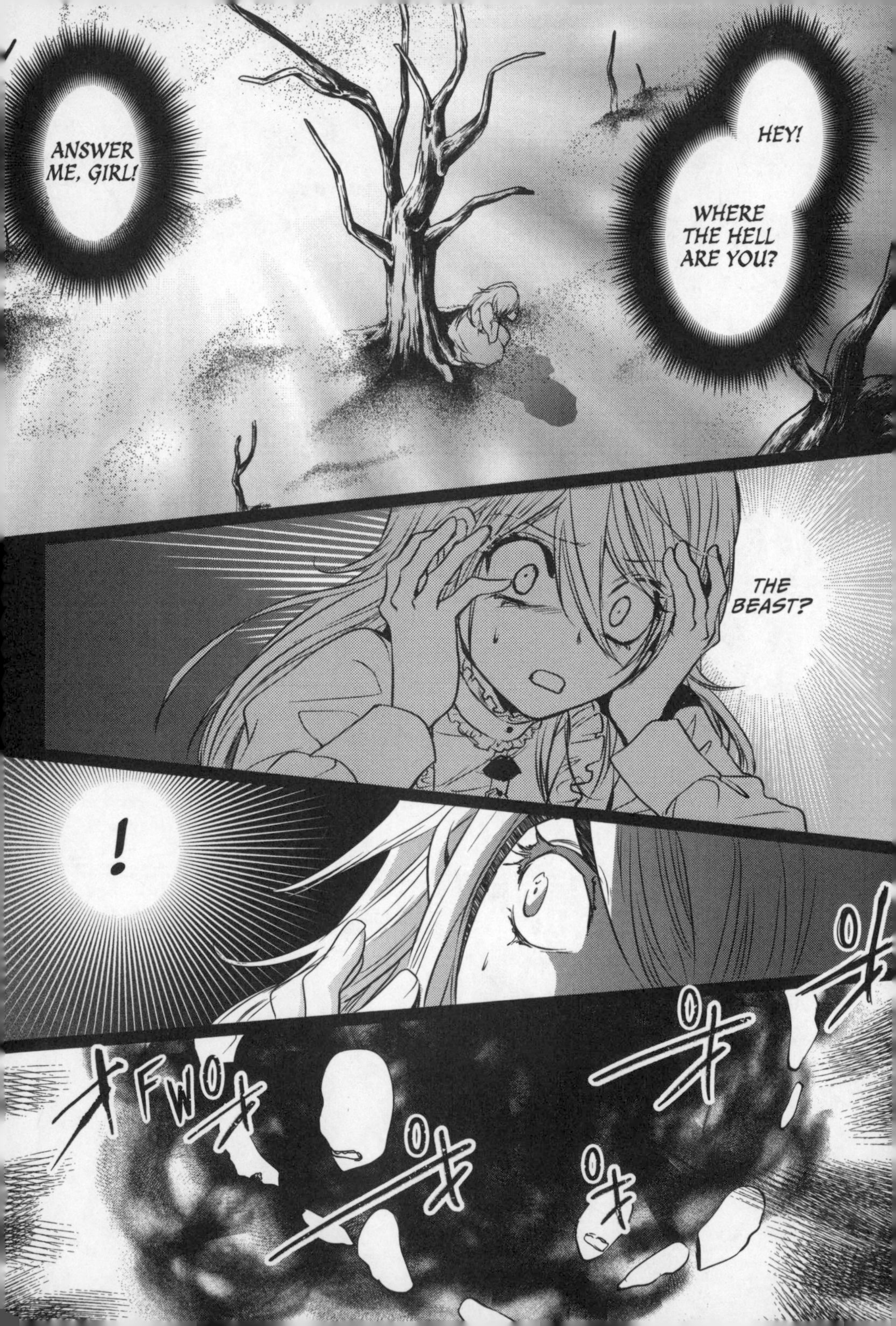
HEY!
WHERE THE HELL ARE YOU?
ANSWER ME, GIRL!
THE BEAST?
!
FWOOOOO

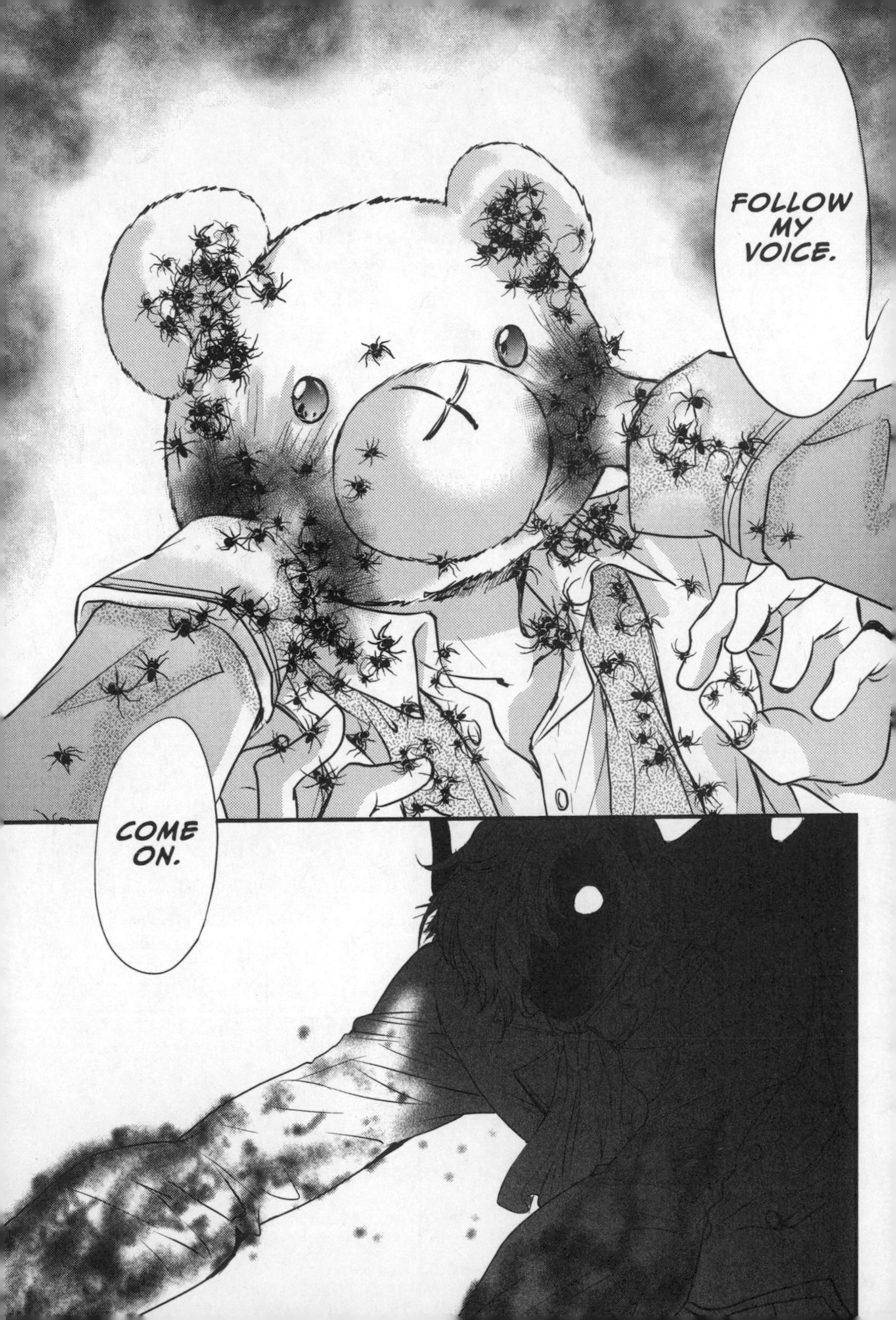
FOLLOW MY VOICE.
COME ON.

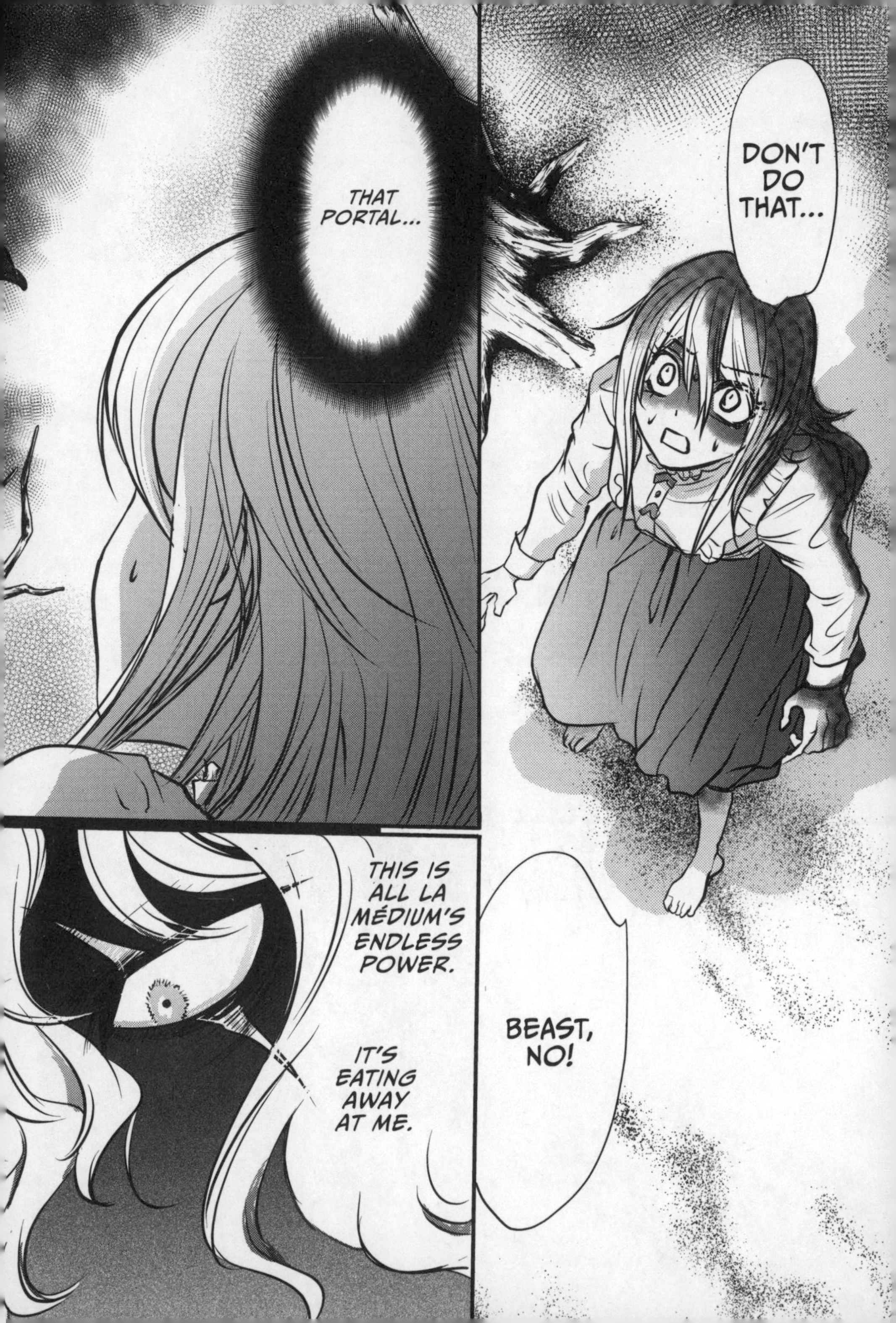
DON'T DO THAT...
BEAST, NO!
THAT PORTAL...
THIS IS ALL LA MÉDIUM'S ENDLESS POWER.
IT'S EATING AWAY AT ME.

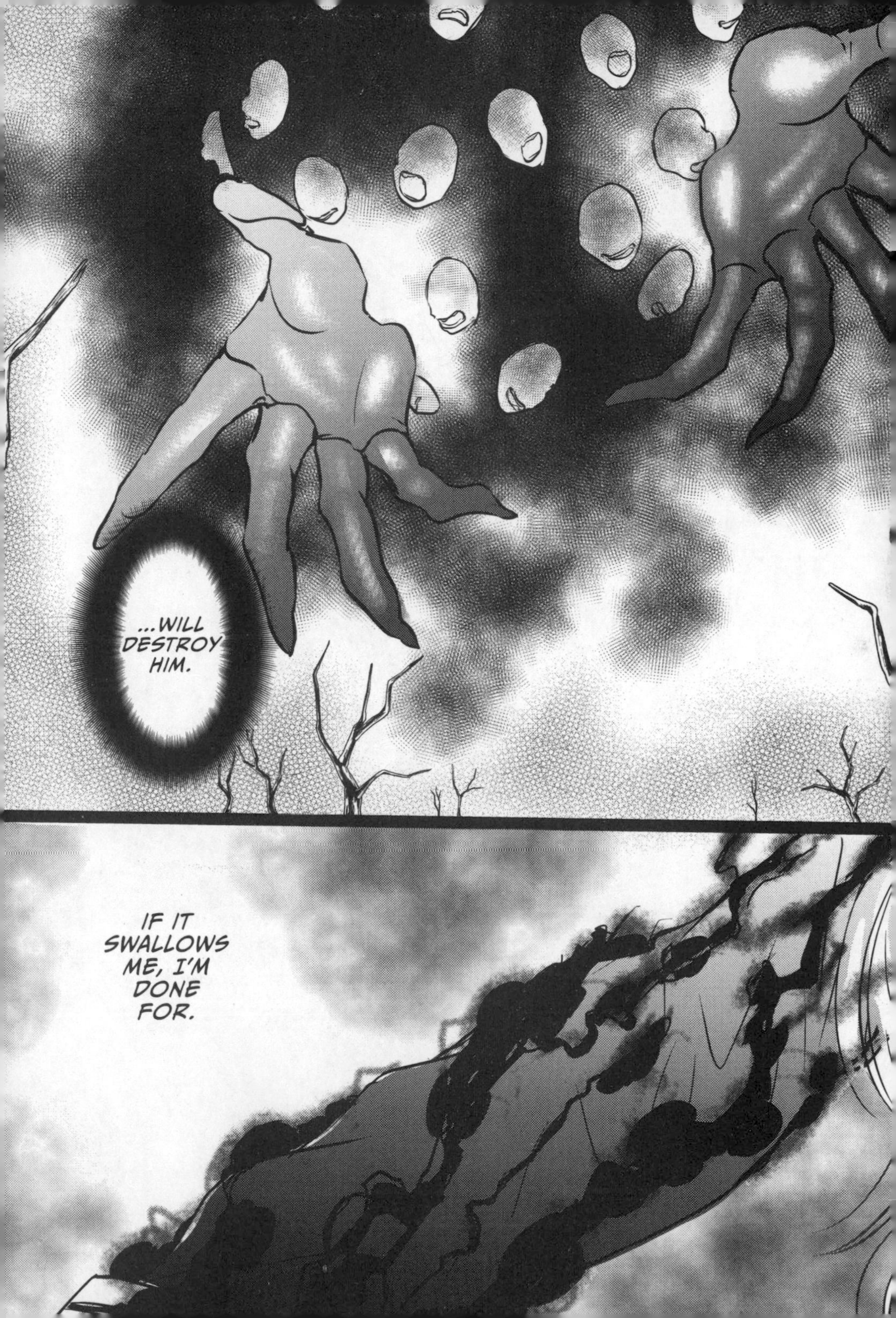
...WILL DESTROY HIM.
IF IT SWALLOWS ME, I'M DONE FOR.

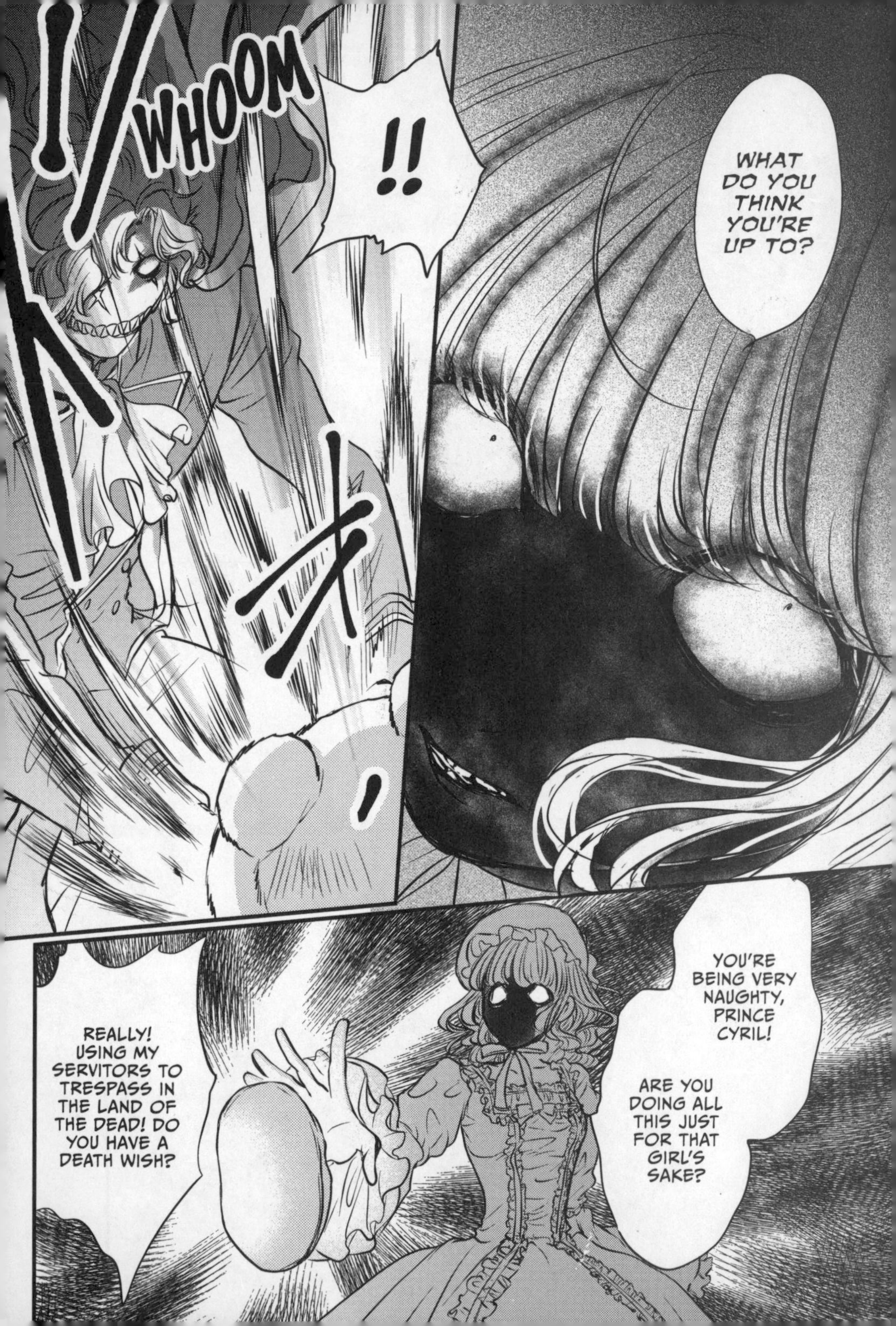
WHAT DO YOU THINK YOU'RE UP TO?
!!
WHOOM
YOU'RE BEING VERY NAUGHTY, PRINCE CYRIL!
ARE YOU DOING ALL THIS JUST FOR THAT GIRL'S SAKE?
REALLY! USING MY SERVITORS TO TRESPASS IN THE LAND OF THE DEAD! DO YOU HAVE A DEATH WISH?

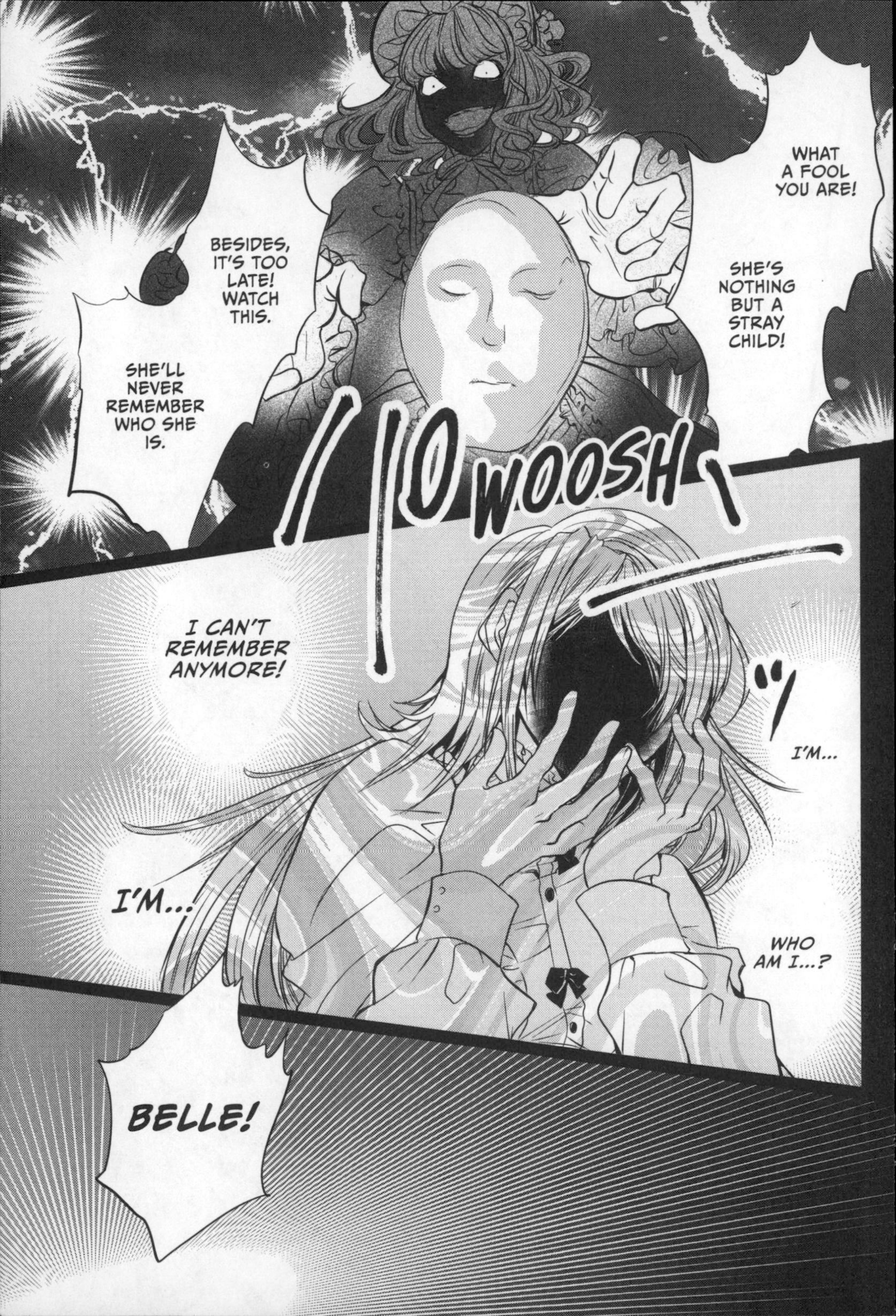
WHAT A FOOL YOU ARE!
SHE'S NOTHING BUT A STRAY CHILD!
BESIDES, IT'S TOO LATE! WATCH THIS.
SHE'LL NEVER REMEMBER WHO SHE IS.
WOOSH
I'M...
WHO AM I...?
I CAN'T REMEMBER ANYMORE!
I'M...
BELLE!

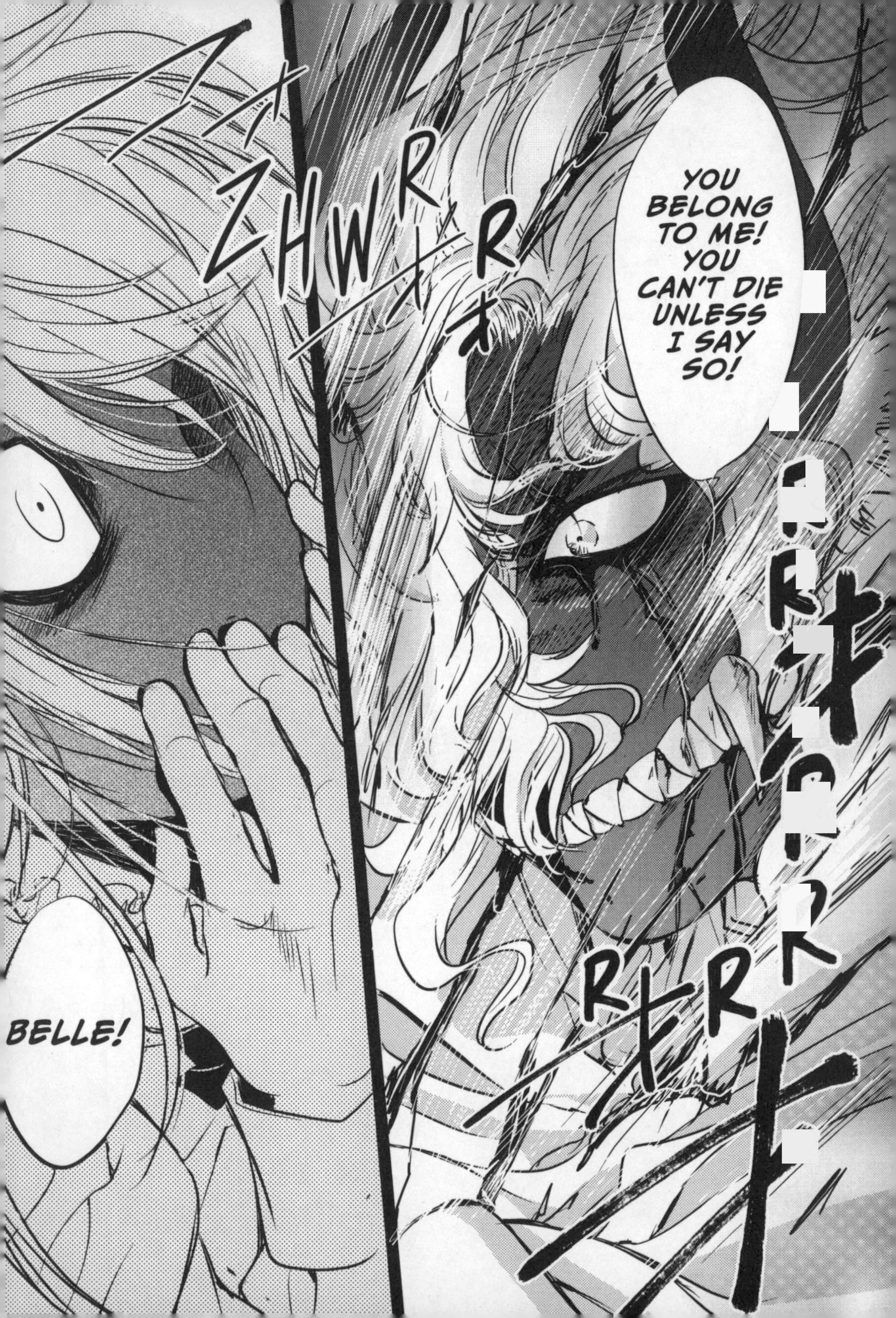
YOU BELONG TO ME! YOU CAN'T DIE UNLESS I SAY SO!
ZHWRR
BELLE!

LA BELLE ET LA BÊTE

DU PARADIS PERDU

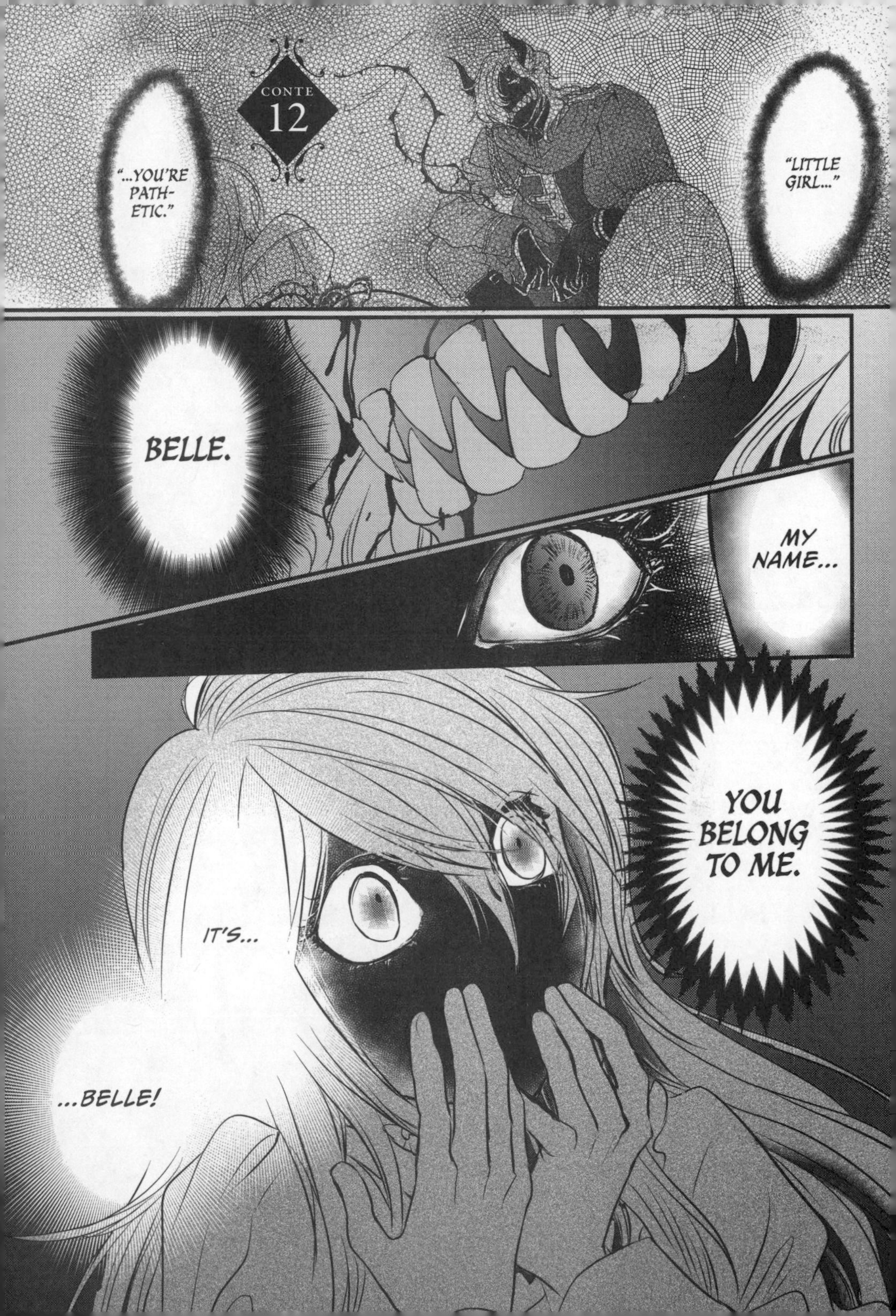
CONTE 12
"LITTLE GIRL..."
"...YOU'RE PATHETIC."
BELLE.
MY NAME...
YOU BELONG TO ME.
IT'S...
...BELLE!

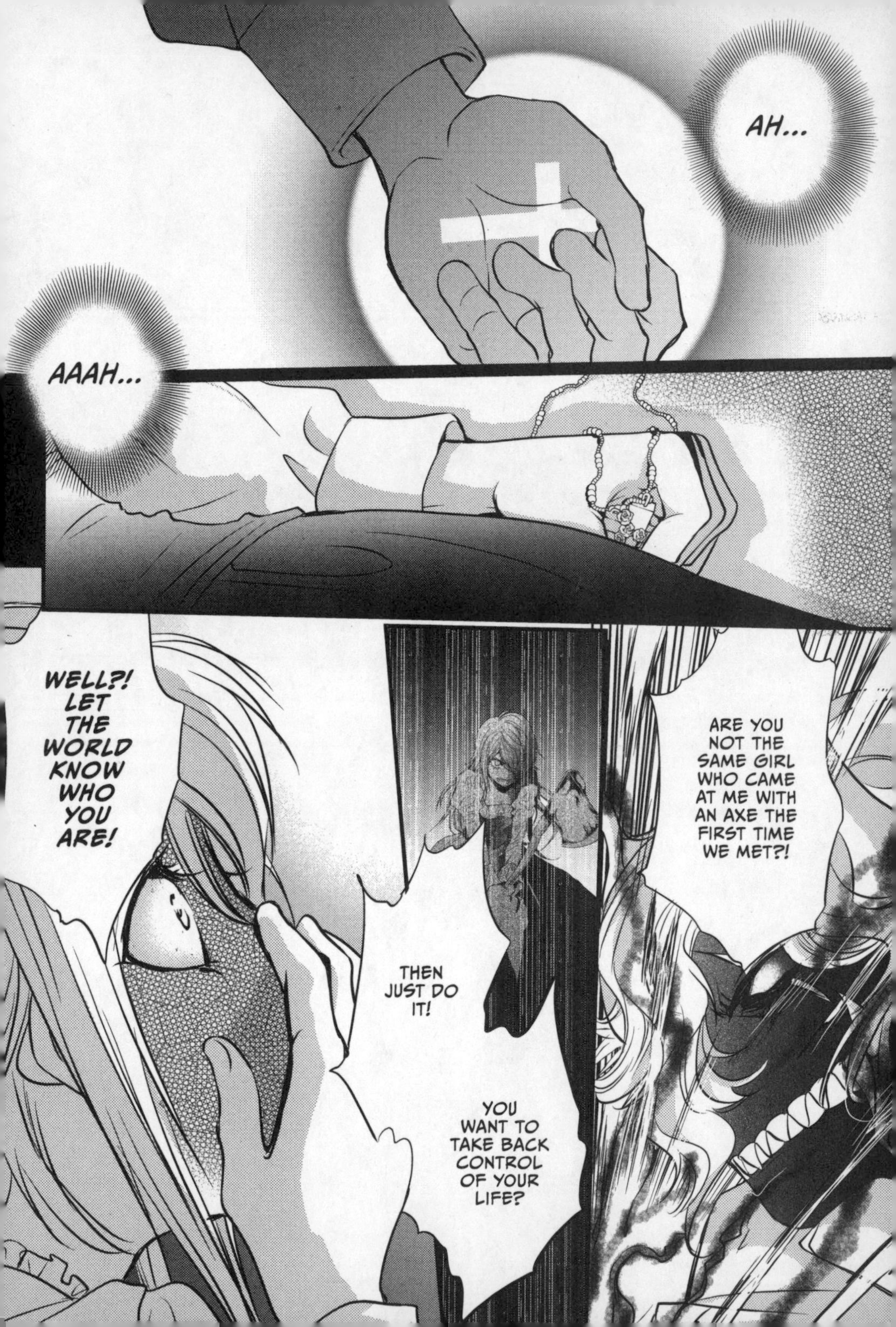
AH...
AAAH...
ARE YOU NOT THE SAME GIRL WHO CAME AT ME WITH AN AXE THE FIRST TIME WE MET?!
YOU WANT TO TAKE BACK CONTROL OF YOUR LIFE?
THEN JUST DO IT!
WELL?! LET THE WORLD KNOW WHO YOU ARE!

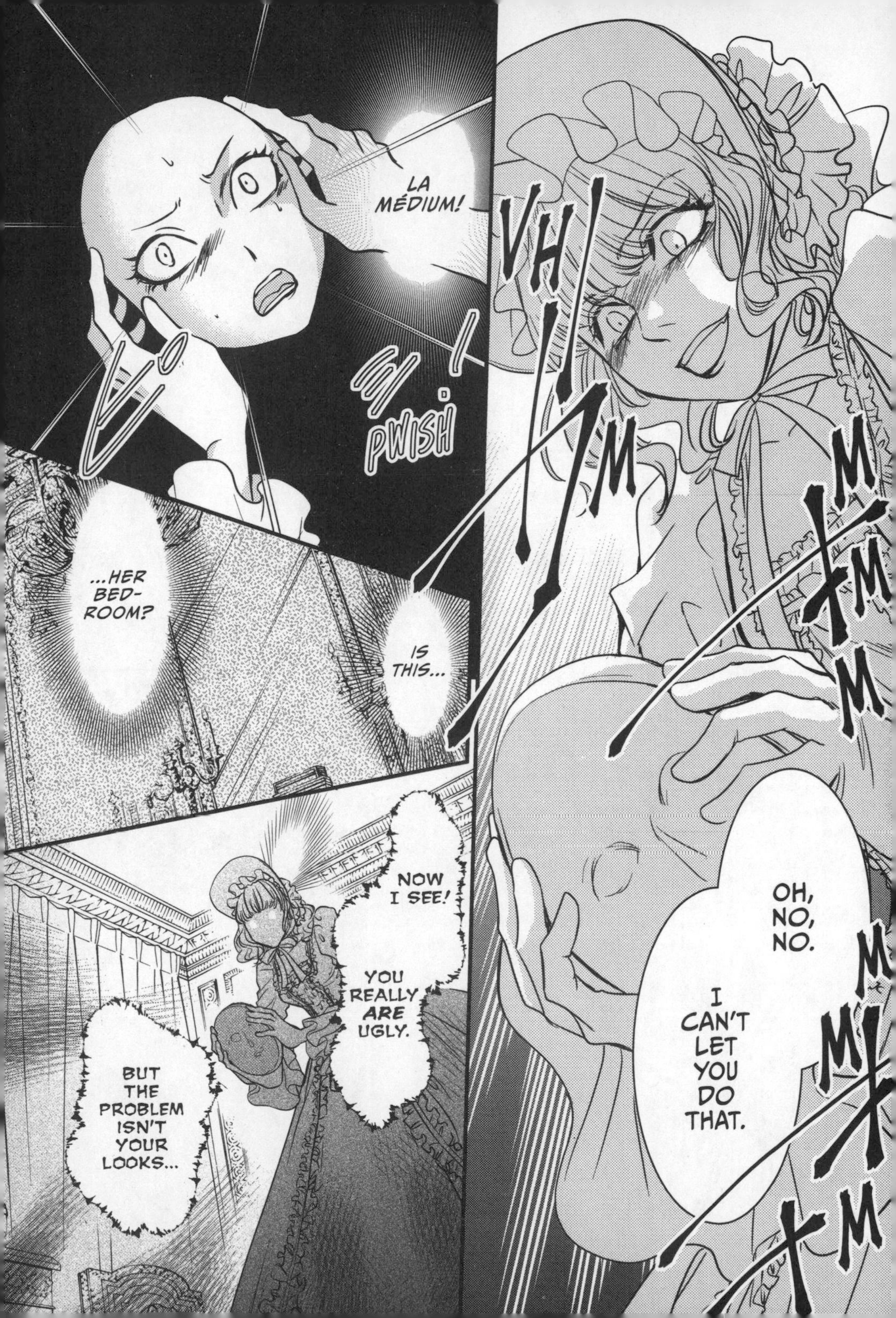
VHMM
MMMM
OH, NO, NO.
I CAN'T LET YOU DO THAT.
MMMM
LA MÉDIUM!
PWISH
IS THIS...
...HER BEDROOM?
NOW I SEE!
YOU REALLY ARE UGLY.
BUT THE PROBLEM ISN'T YOUR LOOKS...

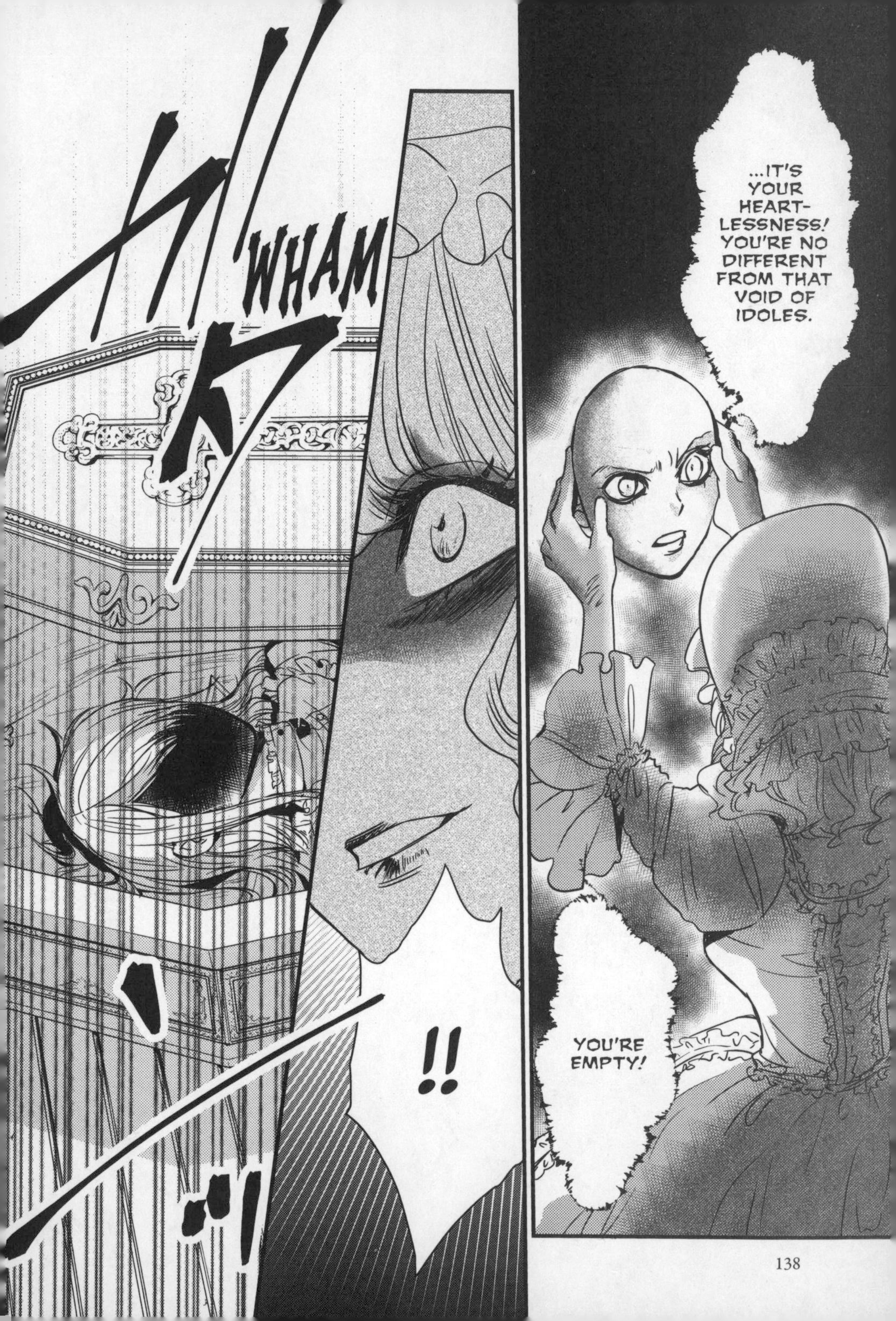
...IT'S YOUR HEART-LESSNESS! YOU'RE NO DIFFERENT FROM THAT VOID OF IDOLES.
YOU'RE EMPTY!
!!
WHAM
!

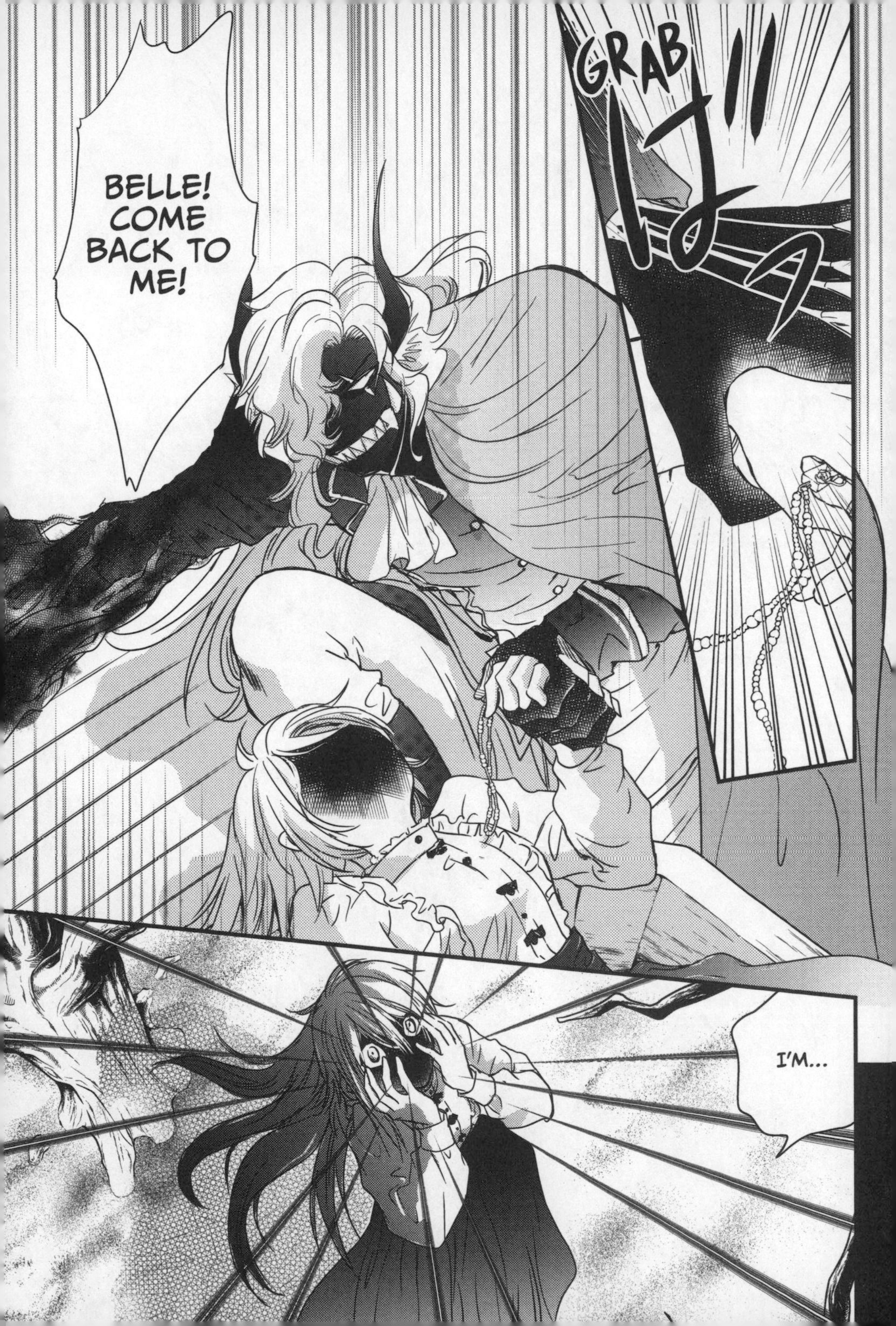
GRAB
BELLE! COME BACK TO ME!
I'M...

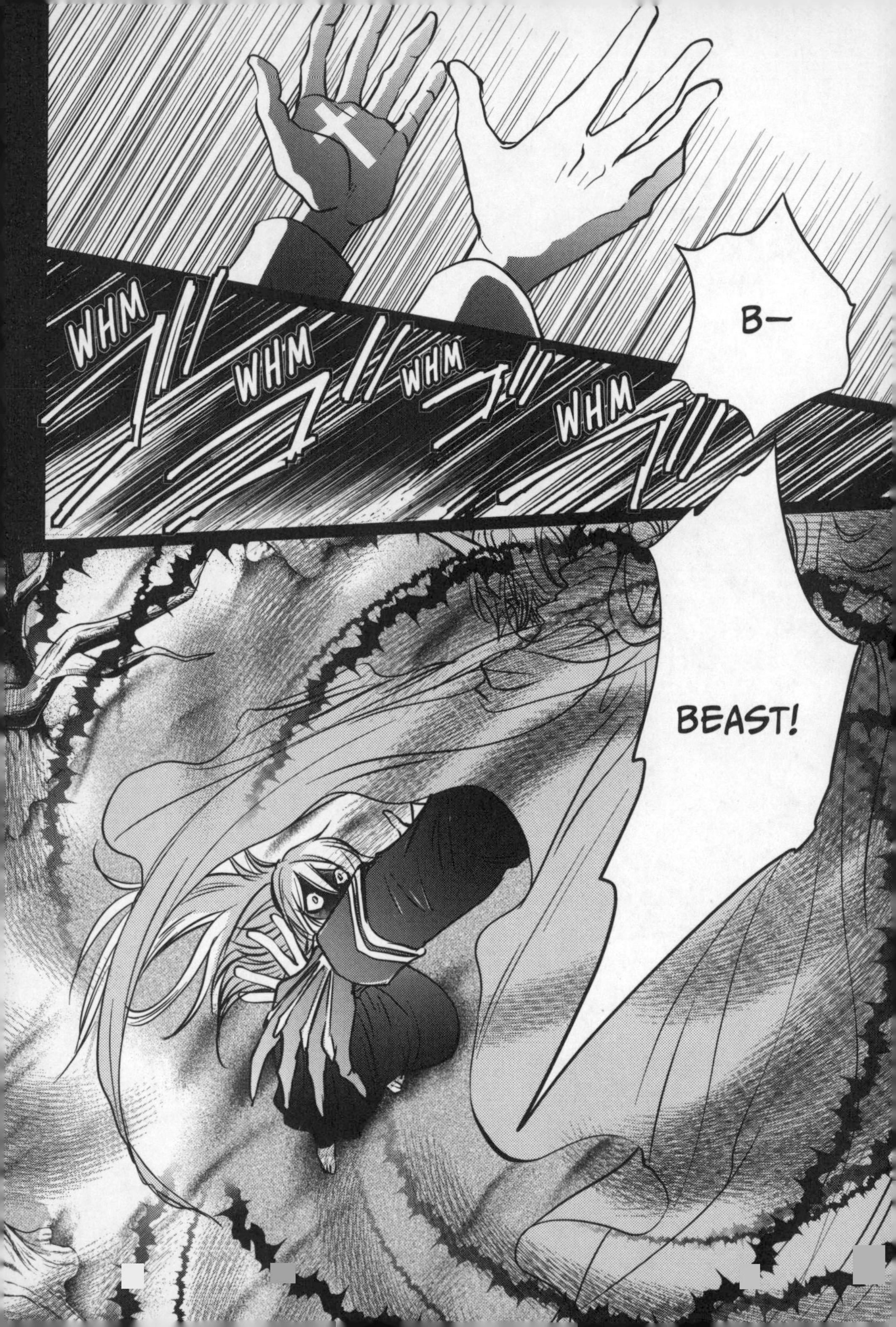
B—
WHM
WHM
WHM
WHM
BEAST!

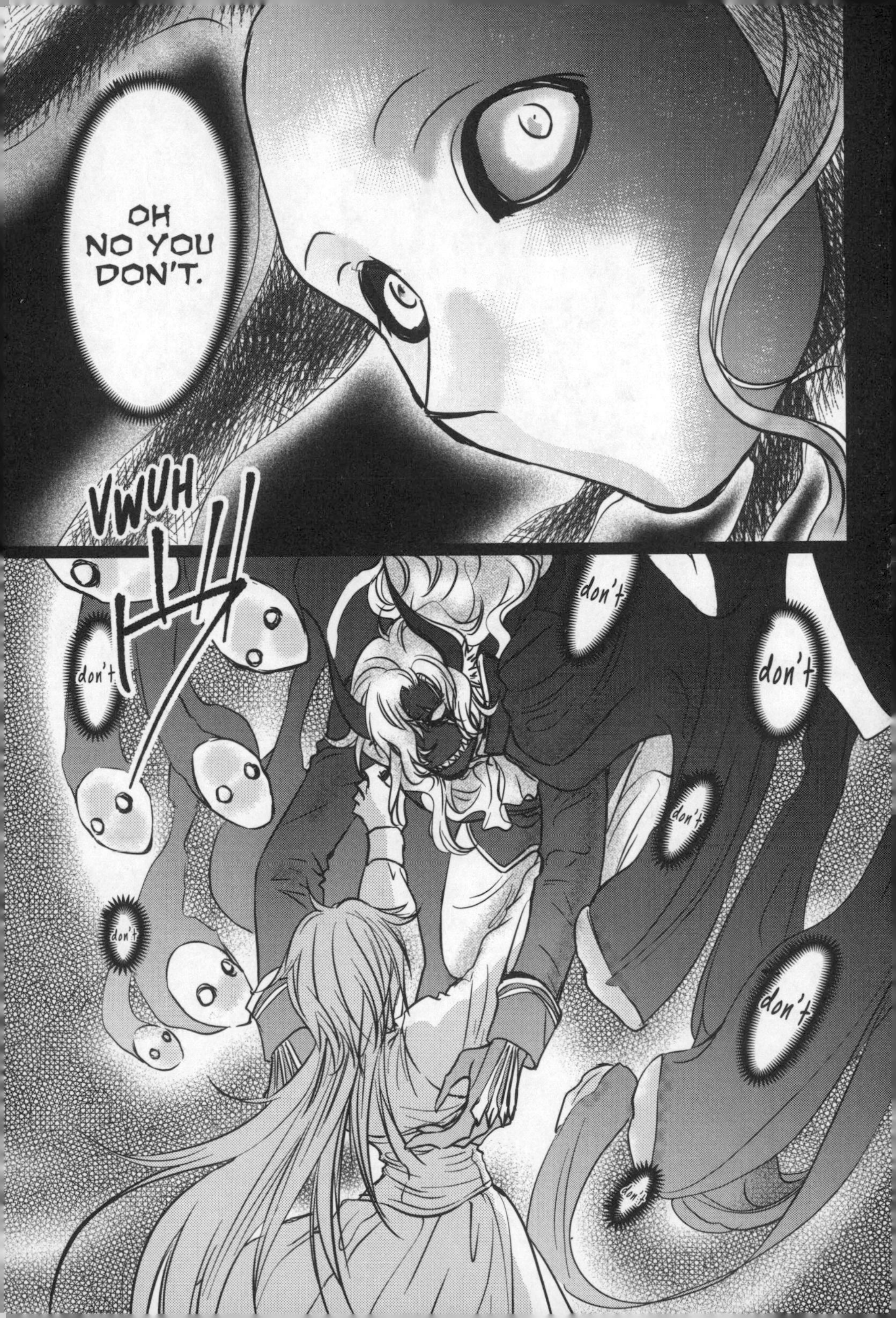
OH NO YOU DON'T.
VWUH
don't
don't
don't
don't
don't
don't
don't

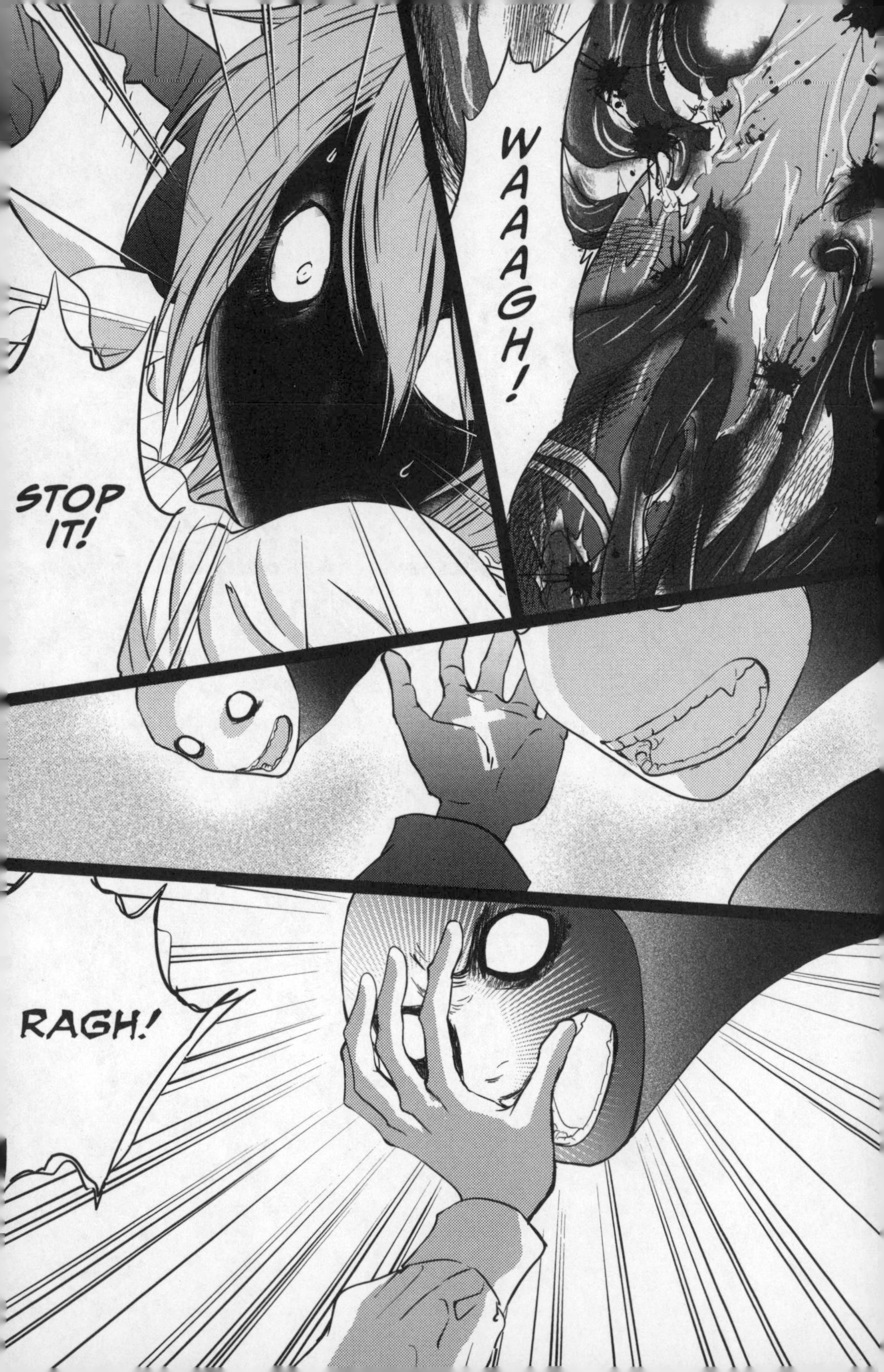
WAAAAGH!
STOP IT!
RAGH!

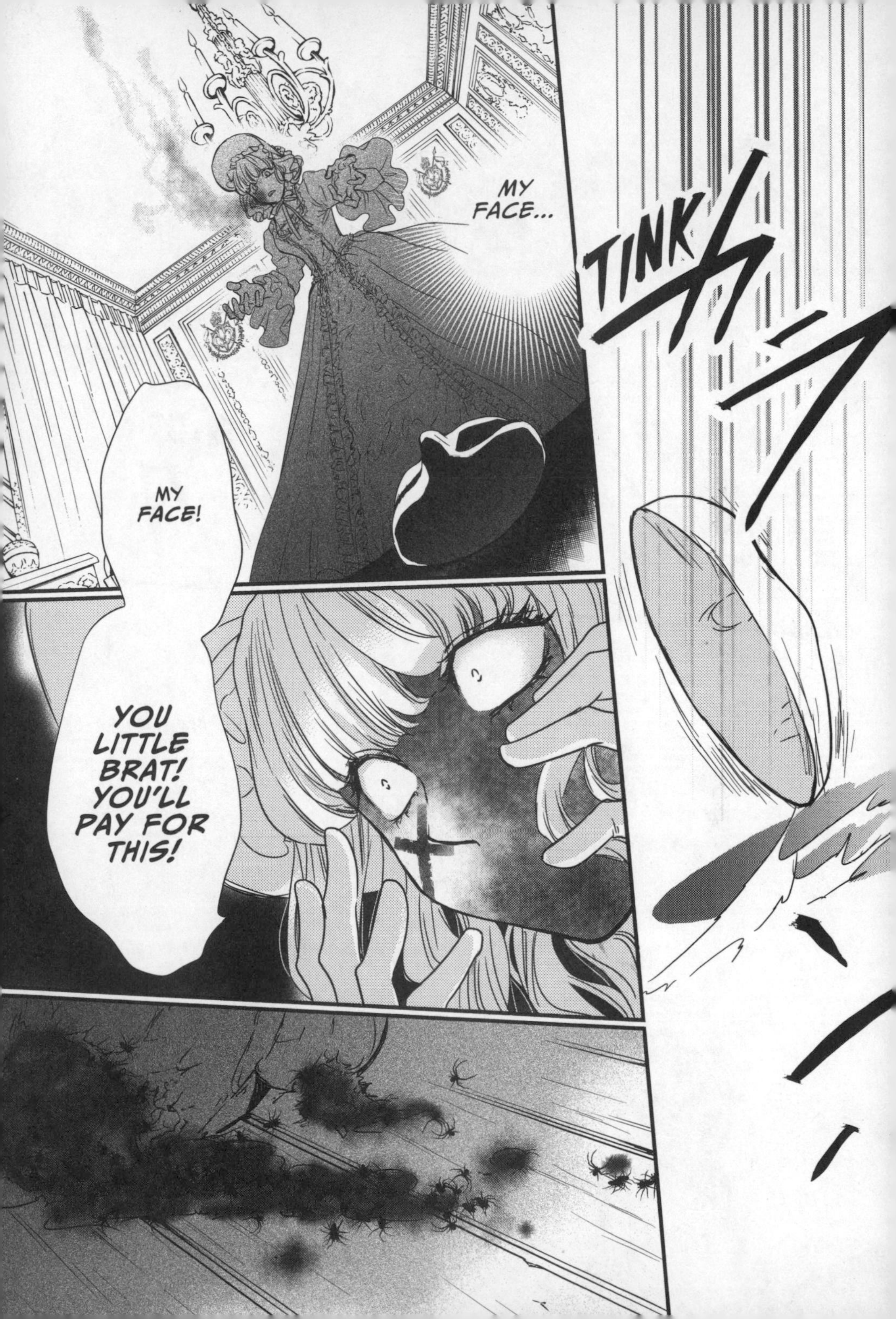
TINK
MY FACE...
MY FACE!
YOU LITTLE BRAT! YOU'LL PAY FOR THIS!

！

ポ DRIP
タ.

BEAST!

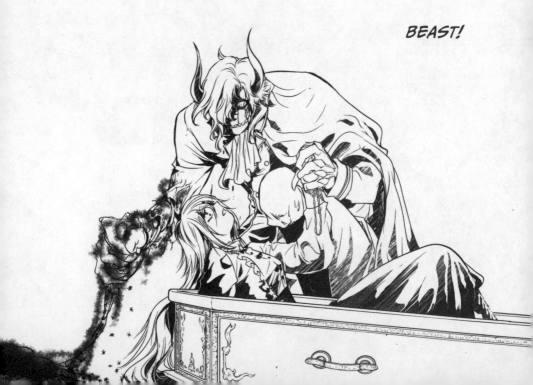

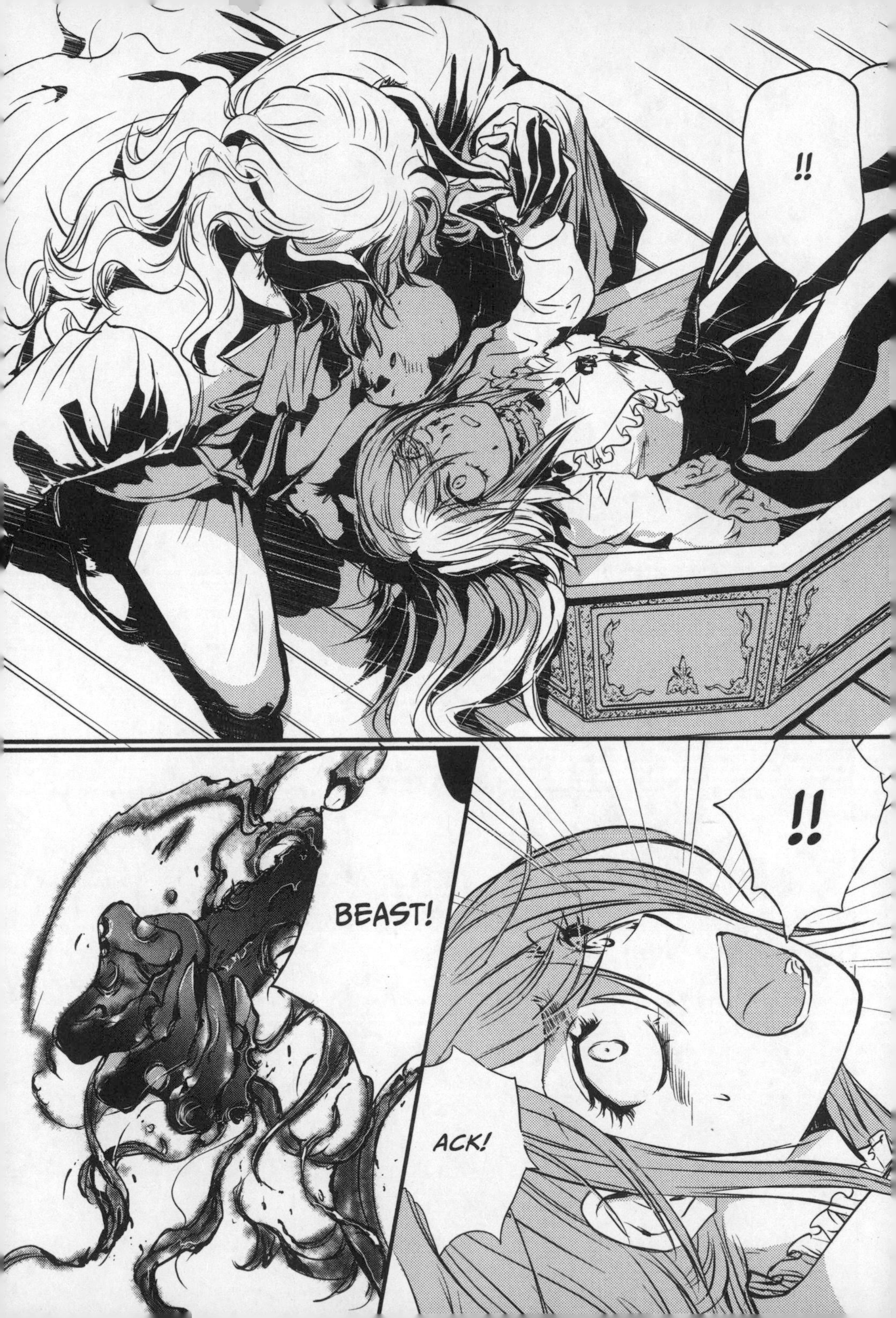
!!
!!
ACK!
BEAST!

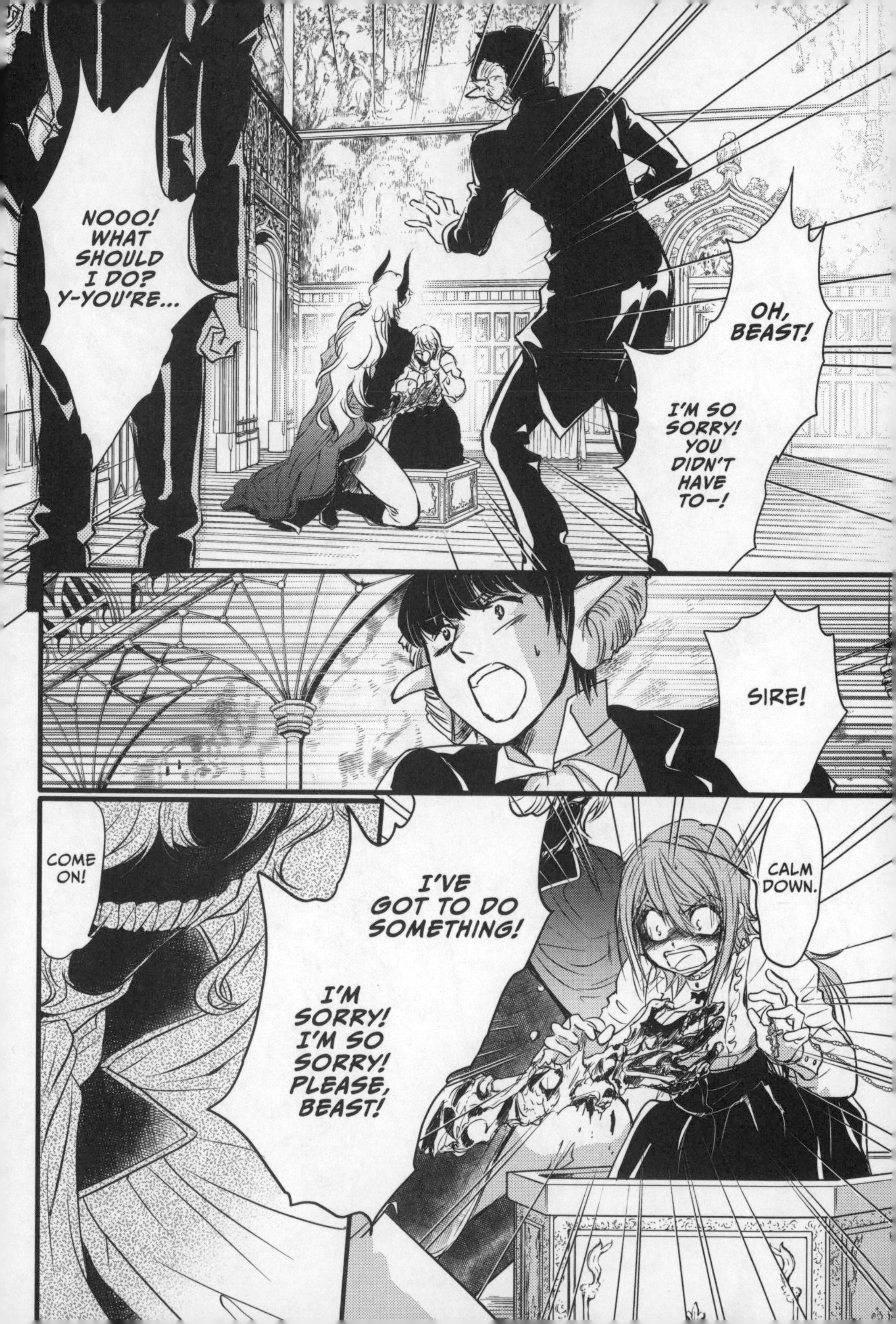
OH, BEAST!
I'M SO SORRY! YOU DIDN'T HAVE TO—!
NOOO! WHAT SHOULD I DO? Y-YOU'RE...
SIRE!
CALM DOWN.
I'VE GOT TO DO SOMETHING!
I'M SORRY! I'M SO SORRY! PLEASE, BEAST!
COME ON!

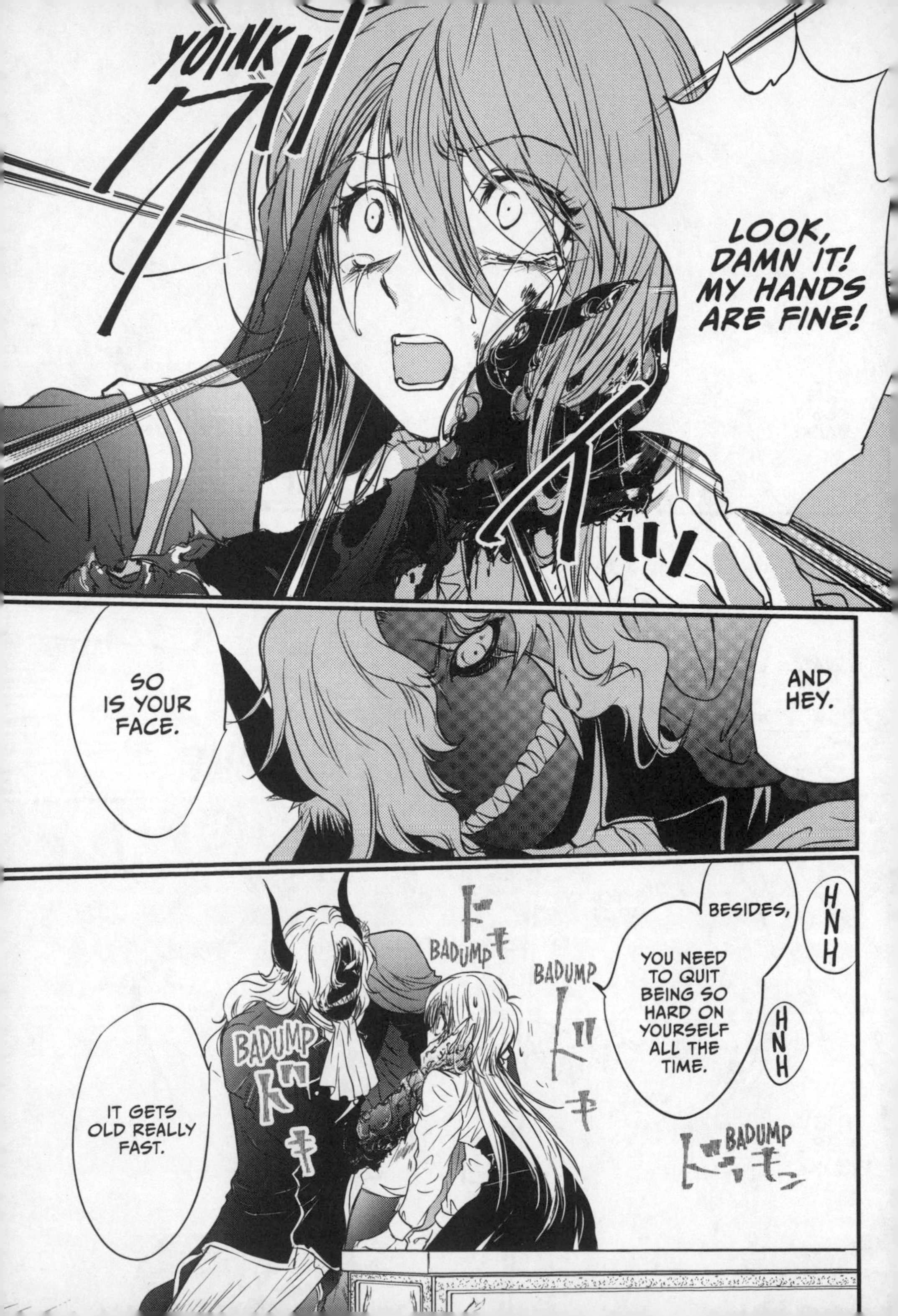
YOINK
LOOK, DAMN IT! MY HANDS ARE FINE!
AND HEY.
SO IS YOUR FACE.
HNH
HNH
BESIDES,
YOU NEED TO QUIT BEING SO HARD ON YOURSELF ALL THE TIME.
BADUMP
BADUMP
BADUMP
BADUMP
IT GETS OLD REALLY FAST.

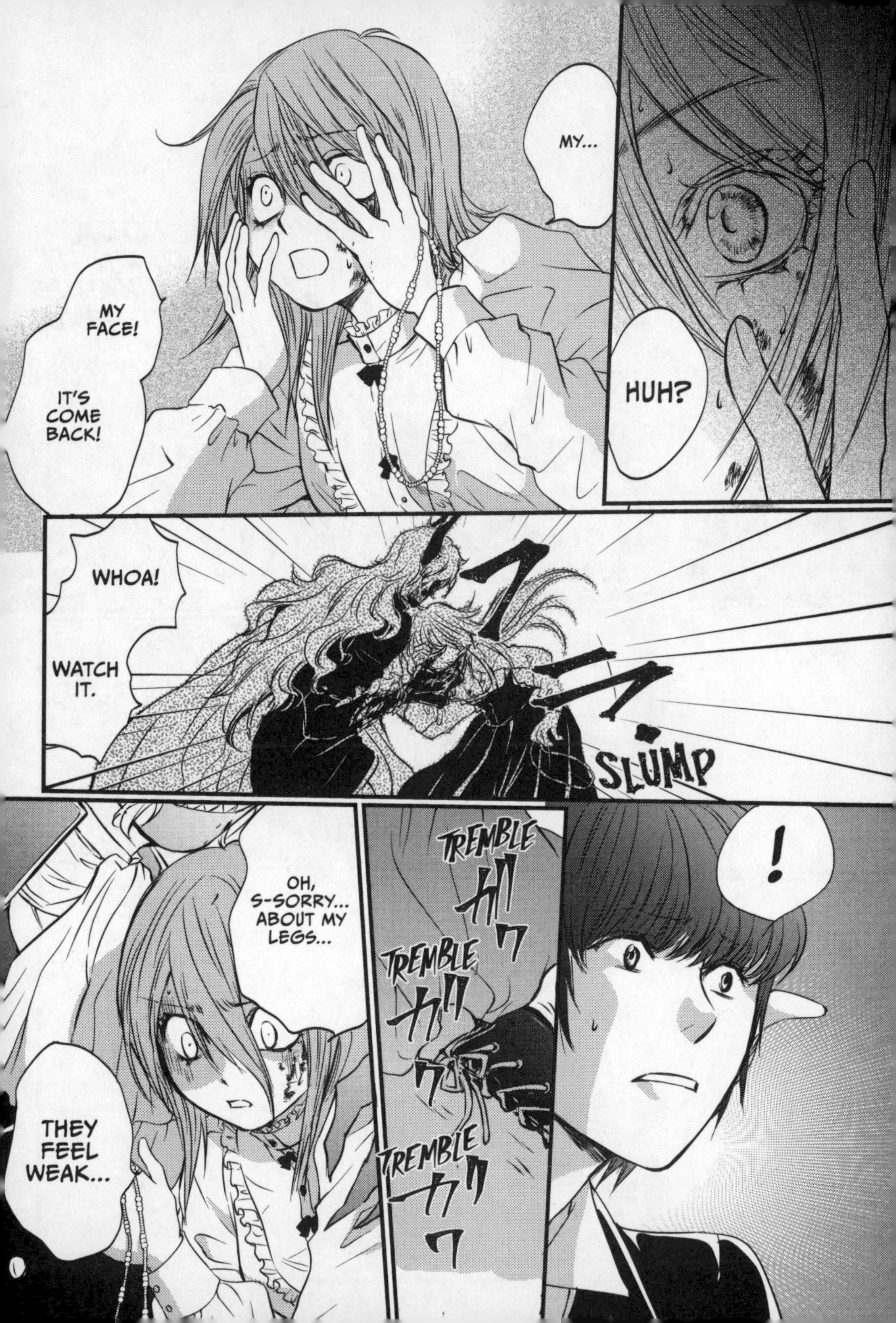
HUH?
MY...
MY FACE!
IT'S COME BACK!
WHOA!
WATCH IT.
SLUMP
!
TREMBLE
TREMBLE
TREMBLE
OH, S-SORRY... ABOUT MY LEGS...
THEY FEEL WEAK...

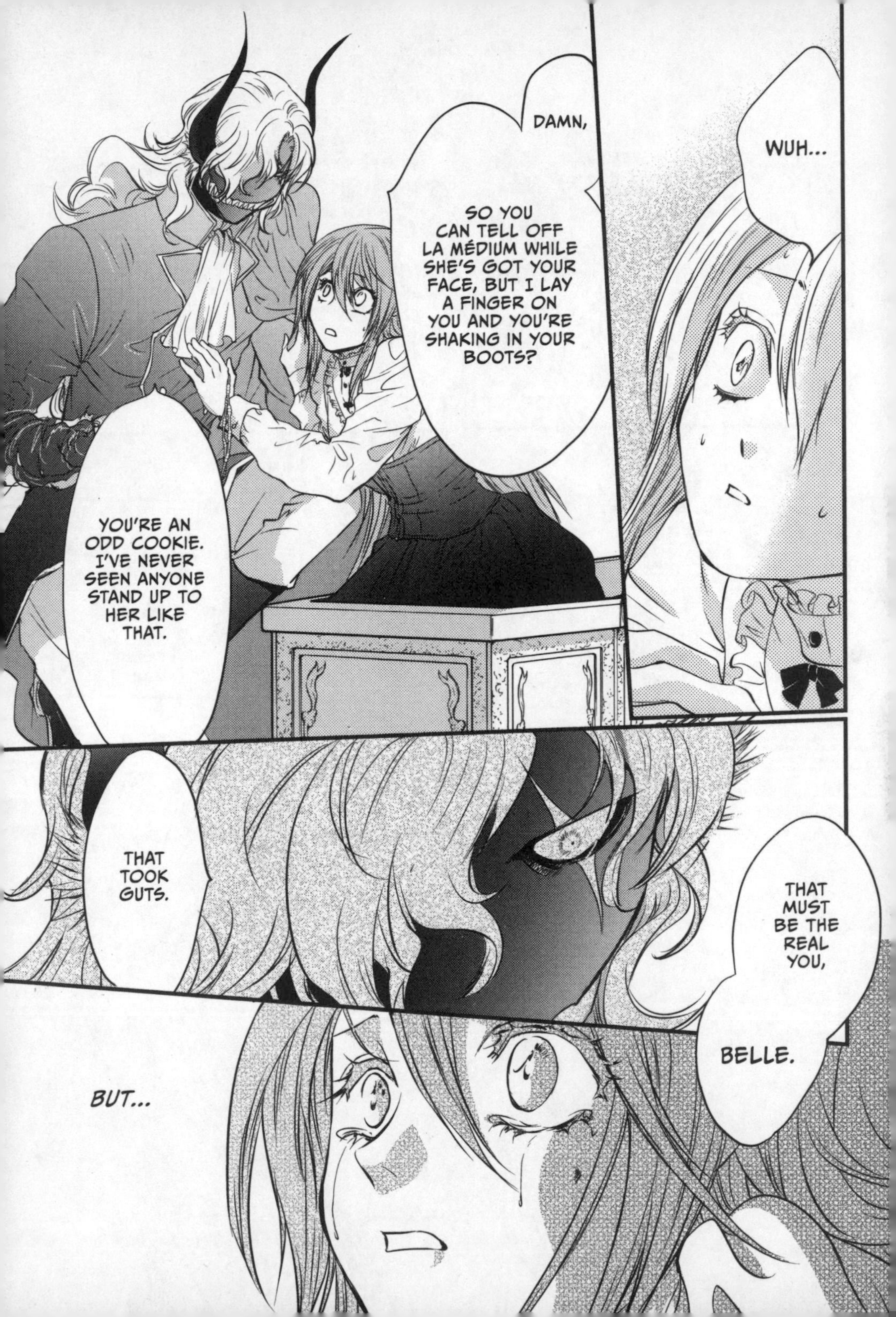
WUH...
DAMN,
SO YOU CAN TELL OFF LA MÉDIUM WHILE SHE'S GOT YOUR FACE, BUT I LAY A FINGER ON YOU AND YOU'RE SHAKING IN YOUR BOOTS?
YOU'RE AN ODD COOKIE. I'VE NEVER SEEN ANYONE STAND UP TO HER LIKE THAT.
THAT TOOK GUTS.
THAT MUST BE THE REAL YOU,
BELLE.
BUT...

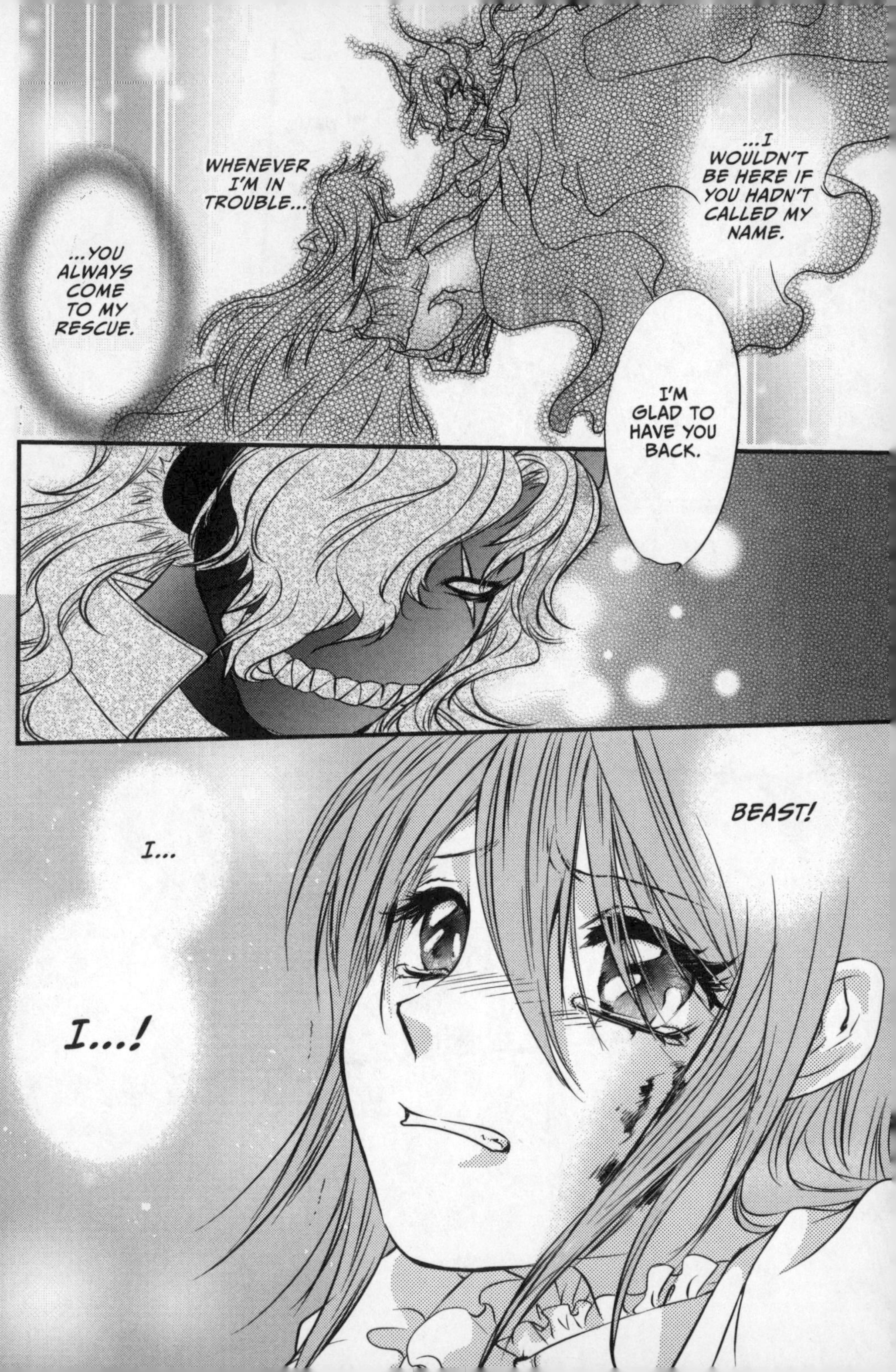
...I WOULDN'T BE HERE IF YOU HADN'T CALLED MY NAME.
WHENEVER I'M IN TROUBLE...
...YOU ALWAYS COME TO MY RESCUE.
I'M GLAD TO HAVE YOU BACK.
BEAST!
I...
I...!

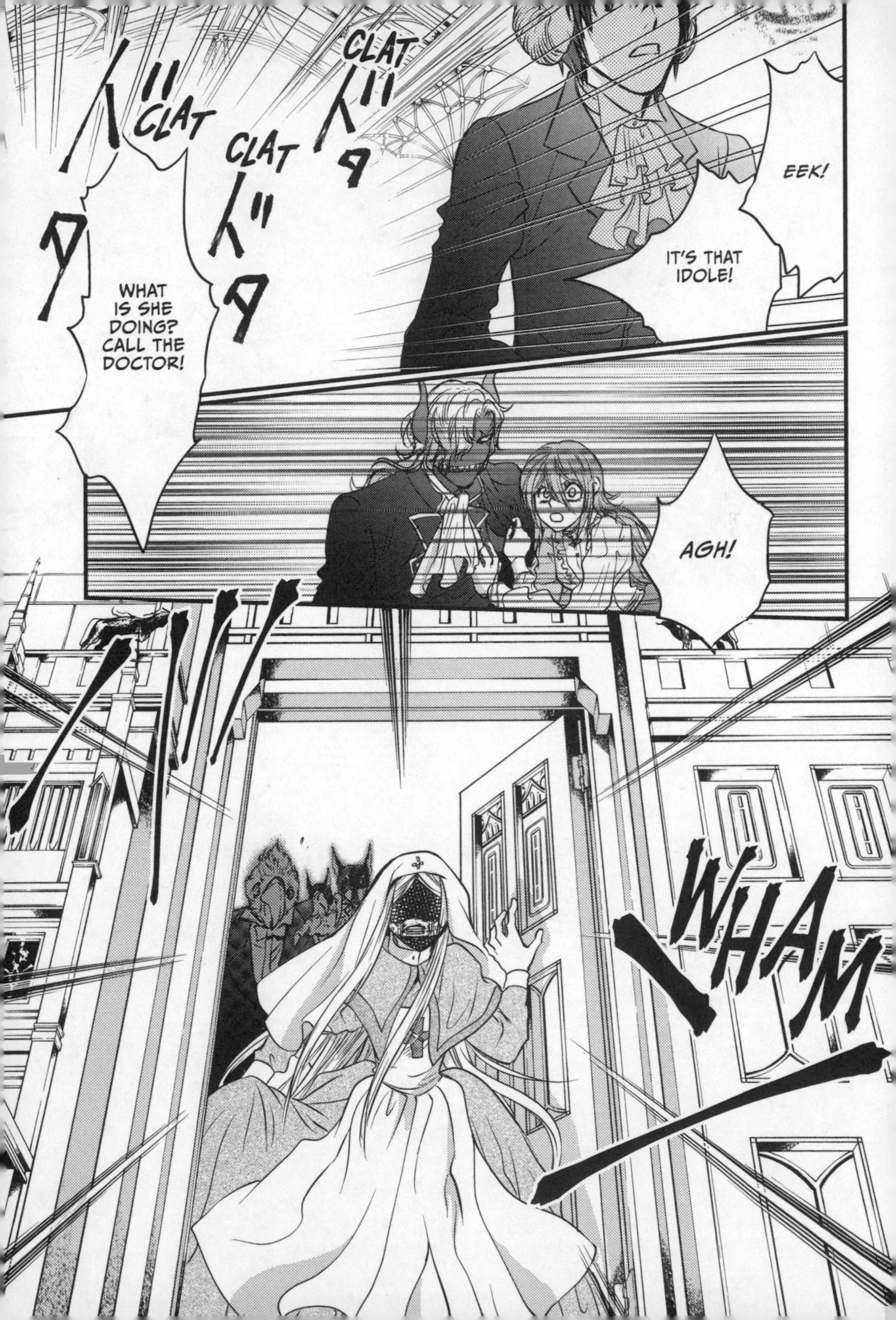
EEK!
IT'S THAT IDOLE!
CLAT
CLAT
CLAT
WHAT IS SHE DOING? CALL THE DOCTOR!
AGH!
WHAM

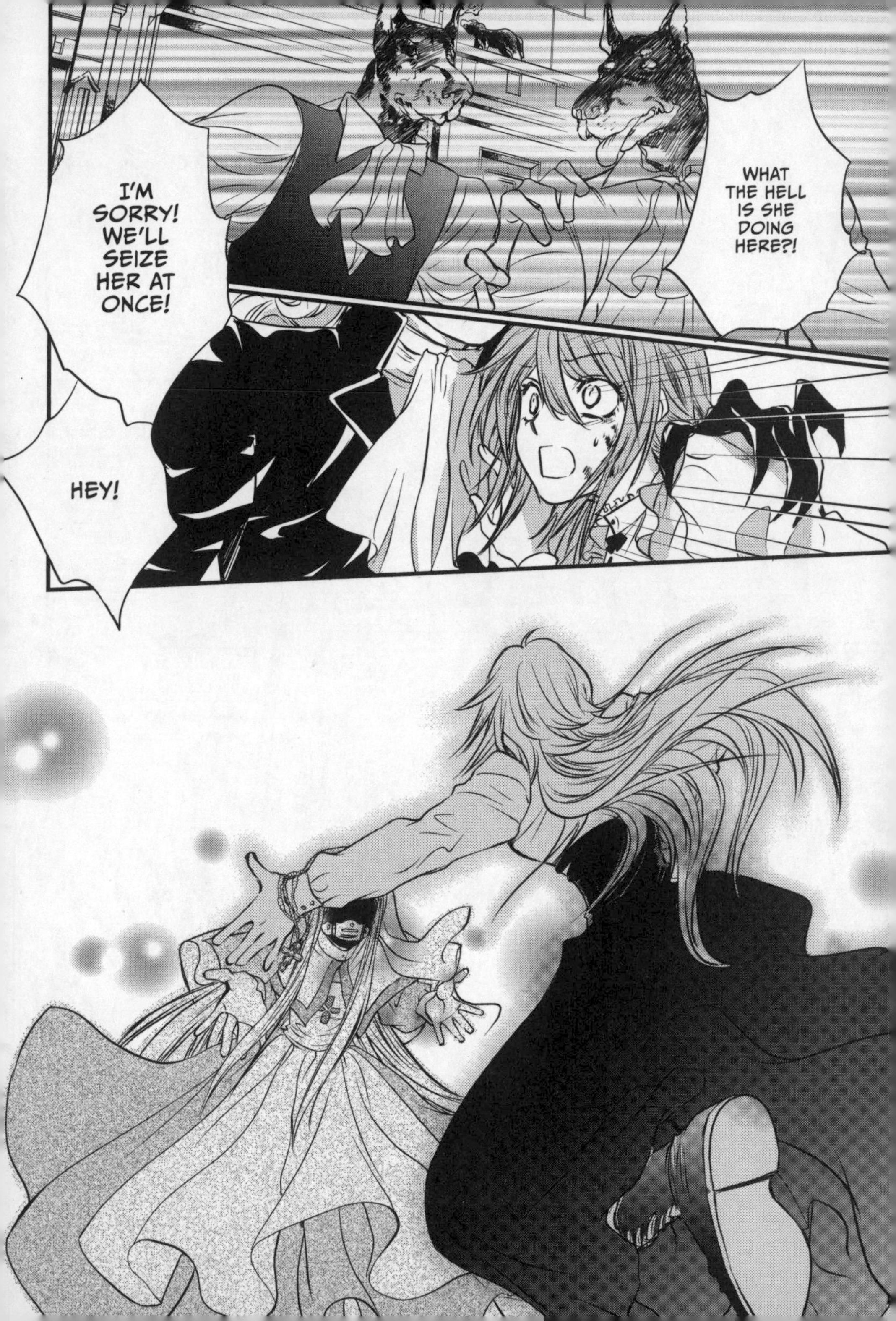
WHAT THE HELL IS SHE DOING HERE?!
I'M SORRY! WE'LL SEIZE HER AT ONCE!
HEY!

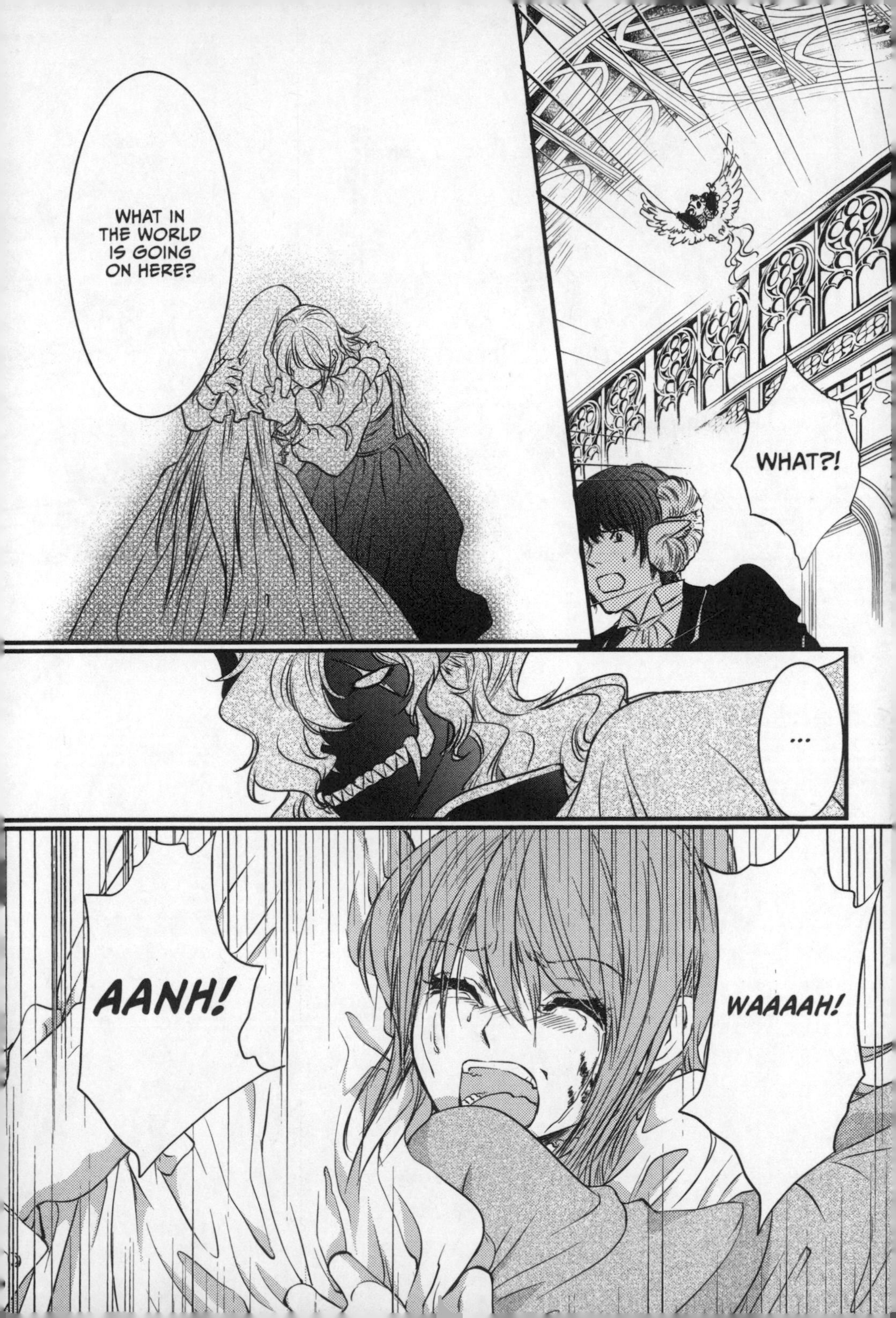
WHAT?!
WHAT IN THE WORLD IS GOING ON HERE?
...
WAAAAH!
AANH!

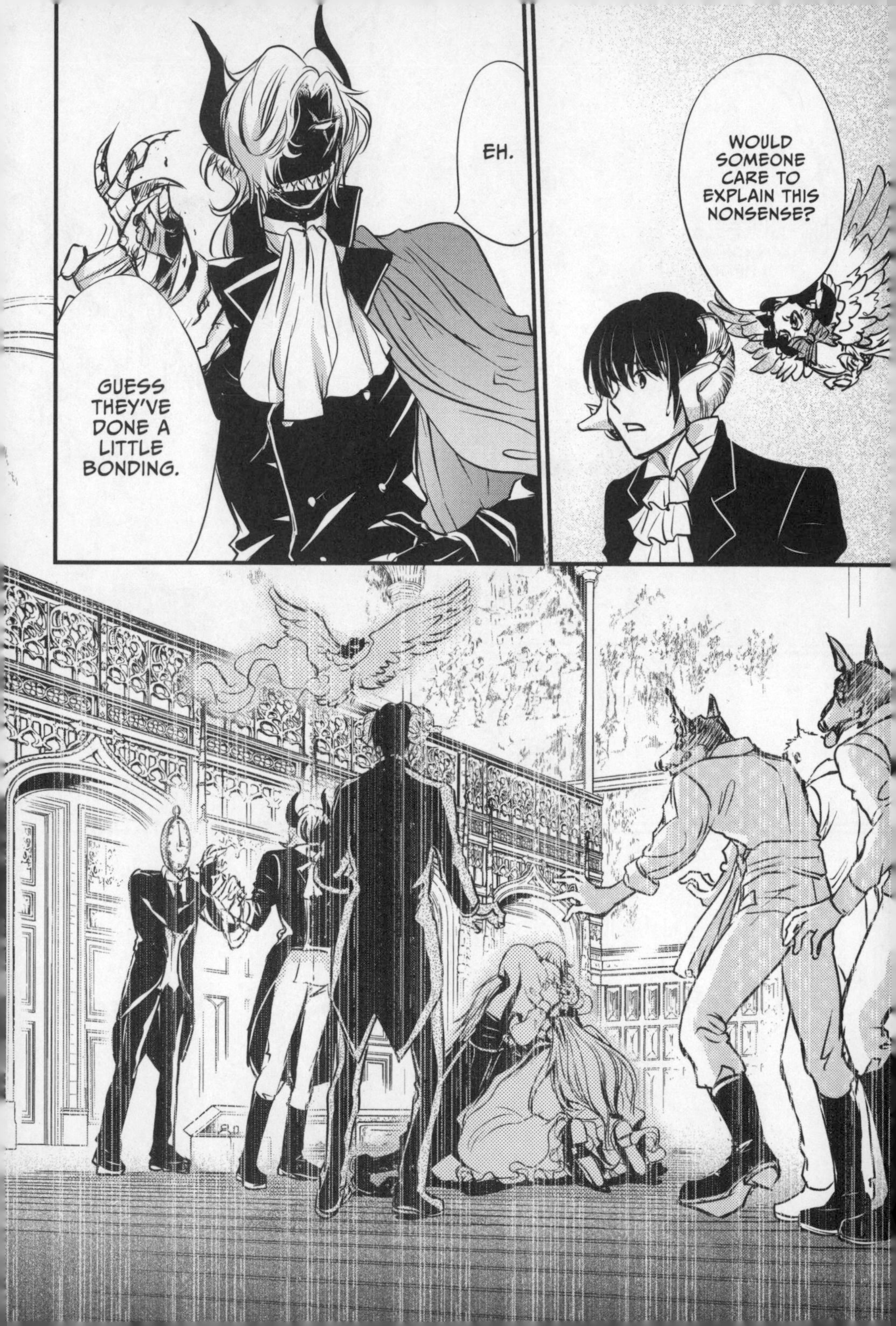
WOULD SOMEONE CARE TO EXPLAIN THIS NONSENSE?
EH.
GUESS THEY'VE DONE A LITTLE BONDING.

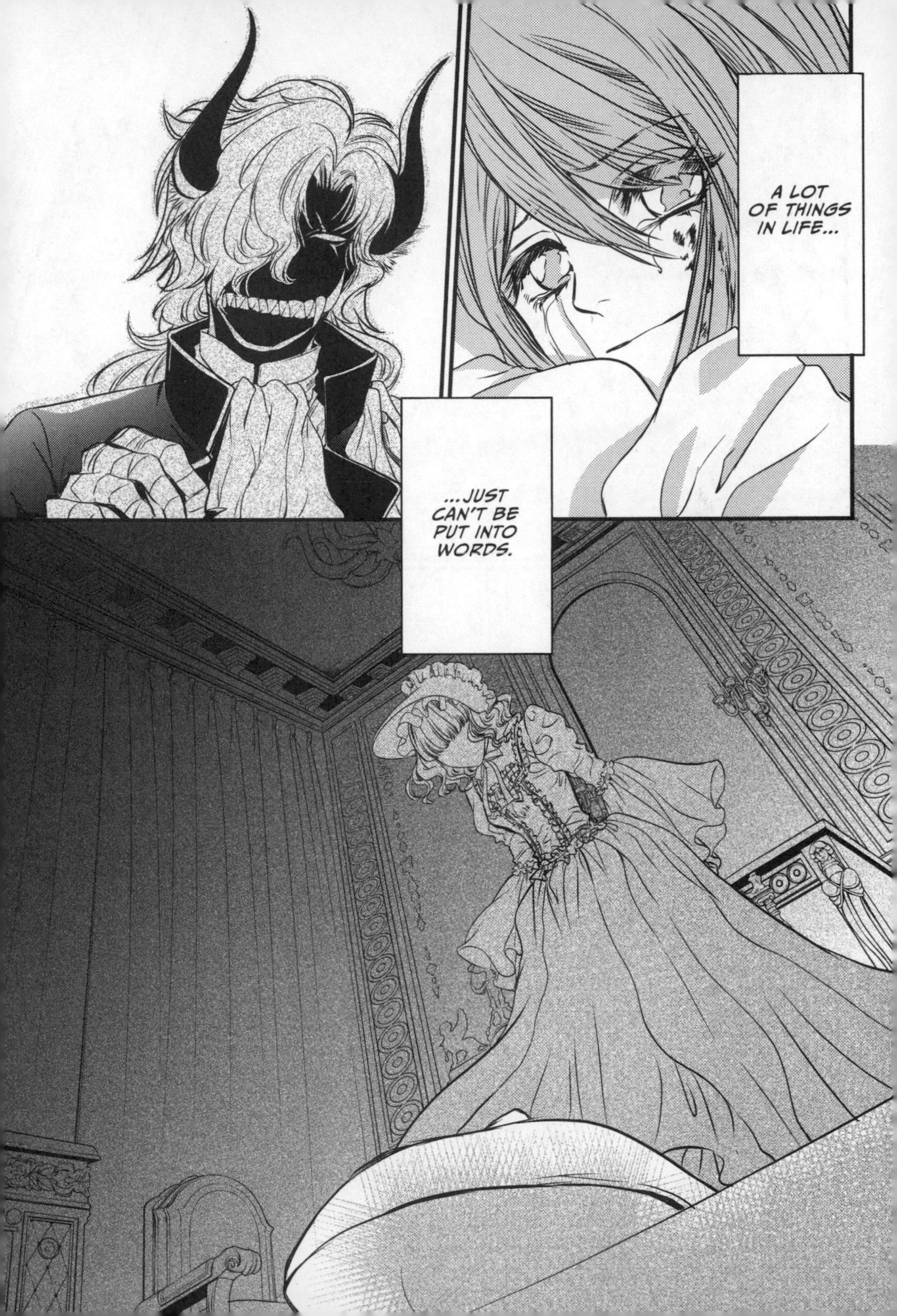
A LOT OF THINGS IN LIFE...
...JUST CAN'T BE PUT INTO WORDS.

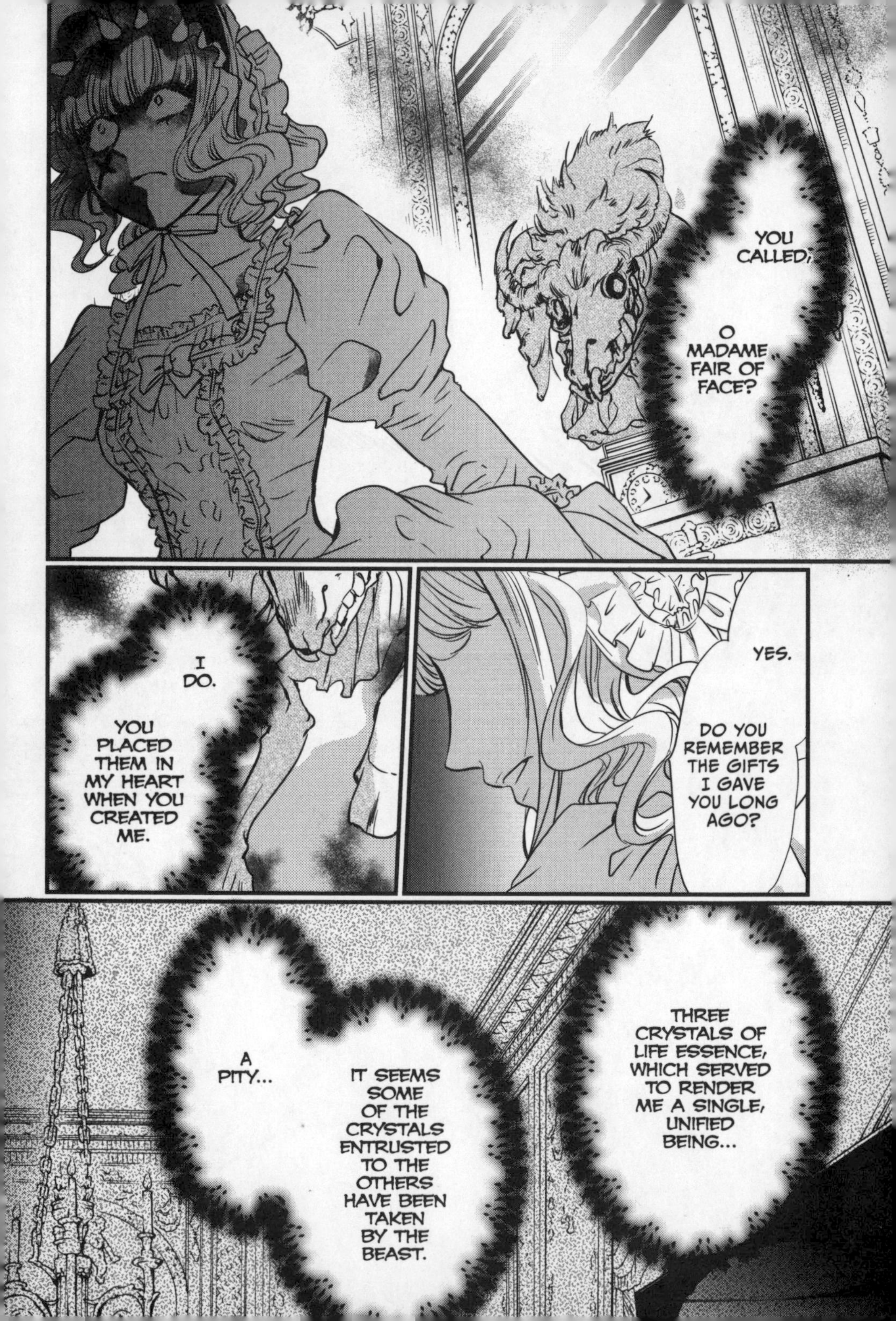
YOU CALLED,
O MADAME FAIR OF FACE?
YES.
DO YOU REMEMBER THE GIFTS I GAVE YOU LONG AGO?
I DO.
YOU PLACED THEM IN MY HEART WHEN YOU CREATED ME.
THREE CRYSTALS OF LIFE ESSENCE, WHICH SERVED TO RENDER ME A SINGLE, UNIFIED BEING...
A PITY...
IT SEEMS SOME OF THE CRYSTALS ENTRUSTED TO THE OTHERS HAVE BEEN TAKEN BY THE BEAST.

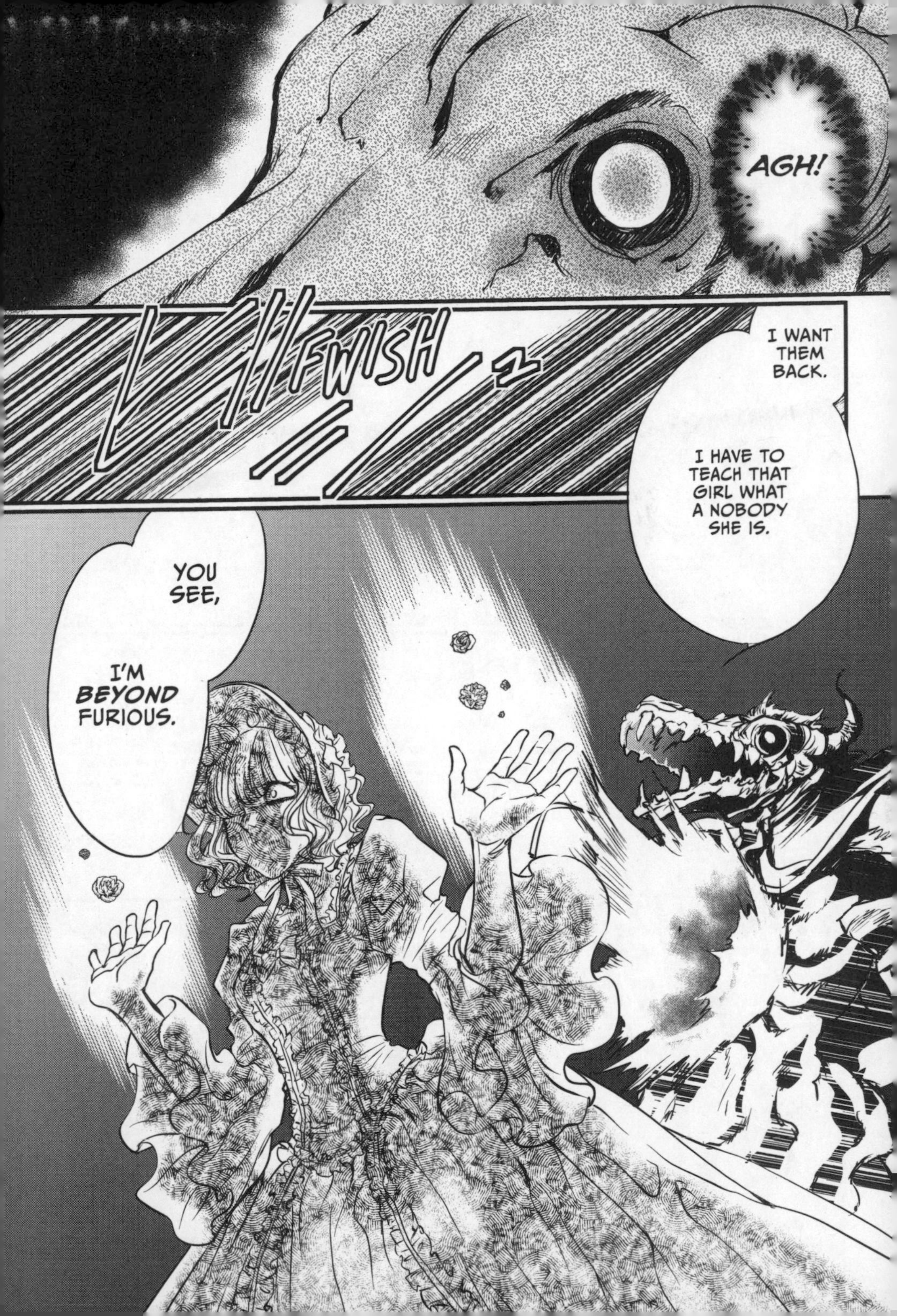
AGH!
FWISH
I WANT THEM BACK.
I HAVE TO TEACH THAT GIRL WHAT A NOBODY SHE IS.
YOU SEE,
I'M *BEYOND* FURIOUS.

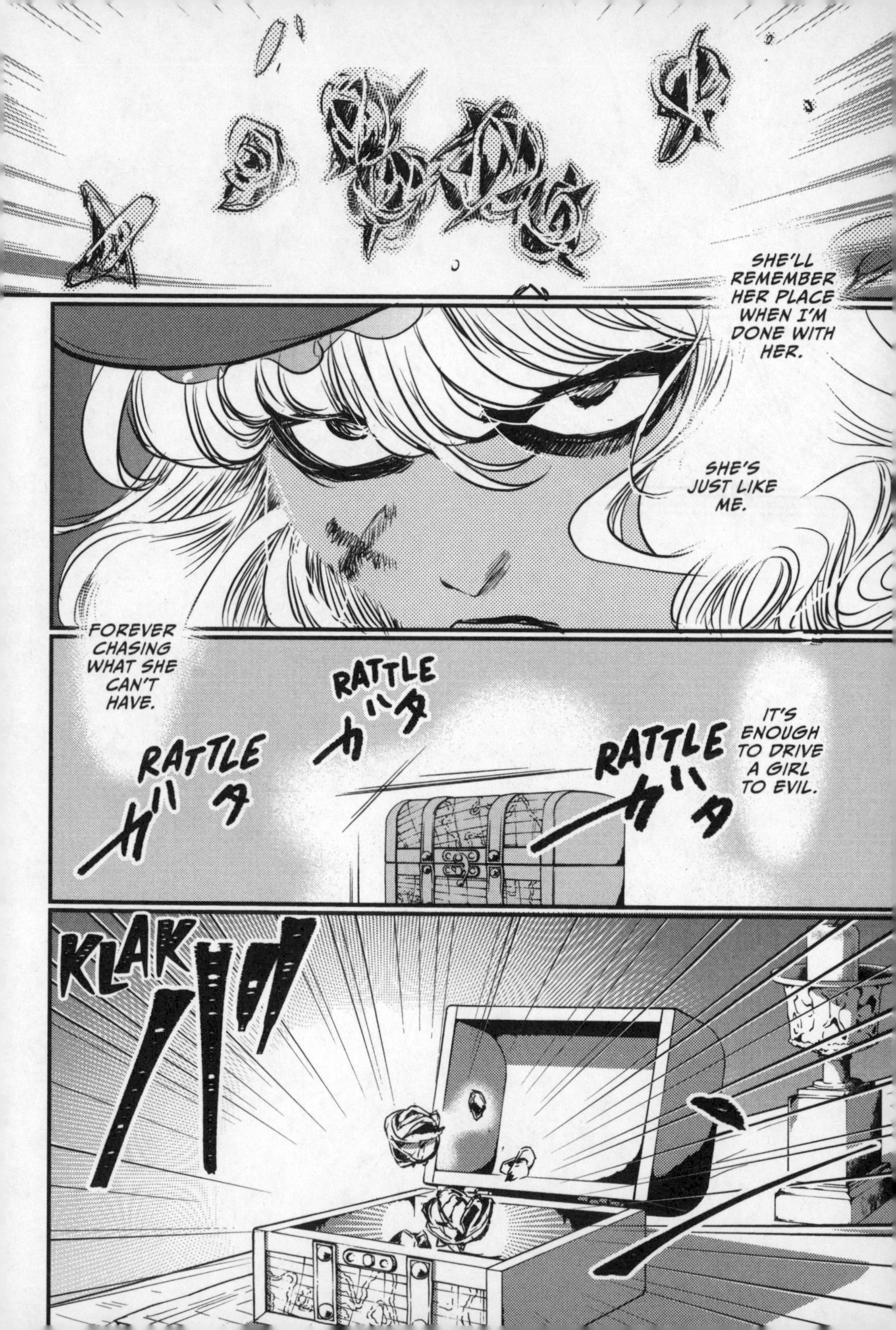
SHE'LL REMEMBER HER PLACE WHEN I'M DONE WITH HER.
SHE'S JUST LIKE ME.
FOREVER CHASING WHAT SHE CAN'T HAVE.
RATTLE
RATTLE
RATTLE
IT'S ENOUGH TO DRIVE A GIRL TO EVIL.
KLAK

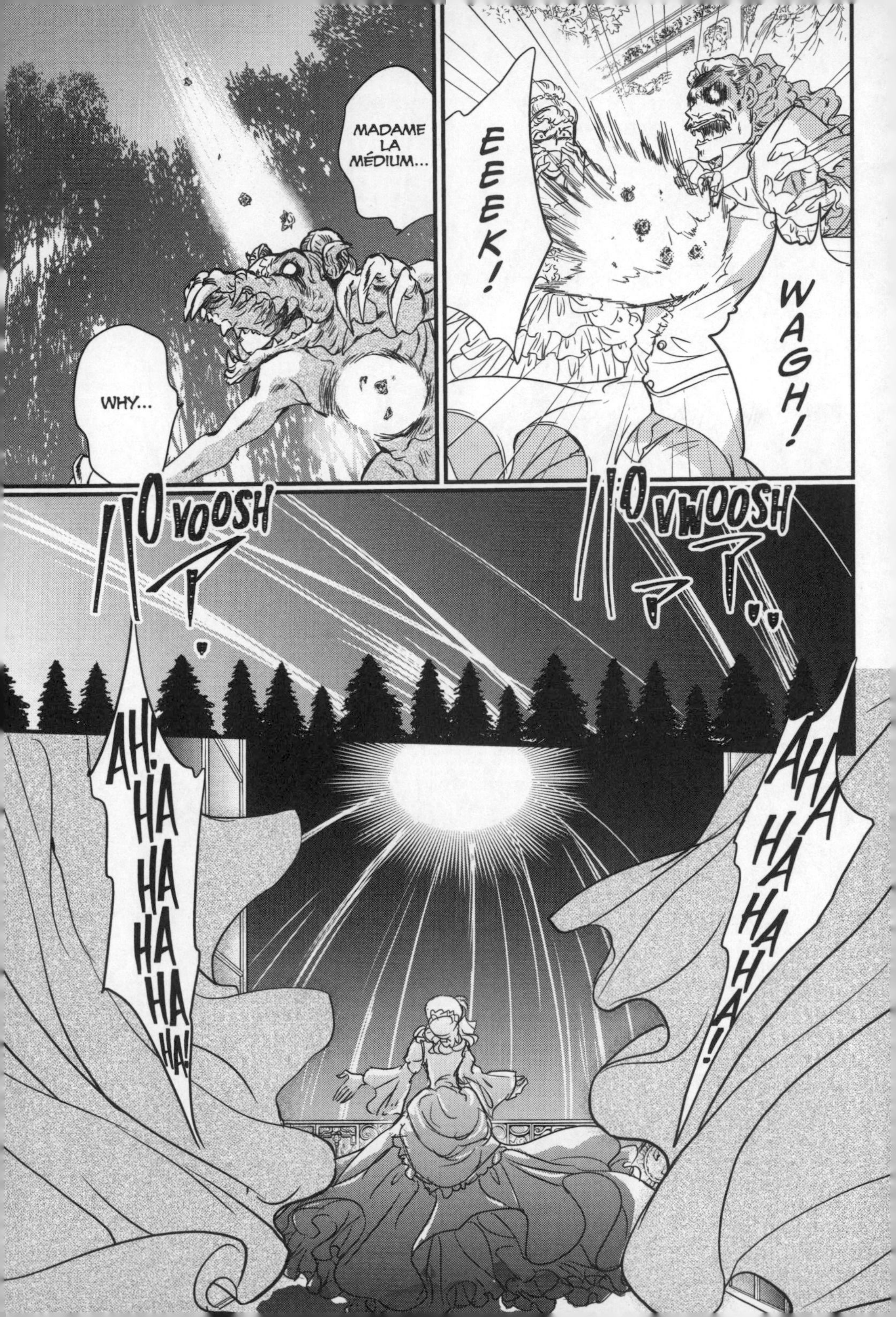
EEEK!
WAGH!
MADAME LA MÉDIUM...
WHY...
VWOOSH
VOOSH
AHAHAHAHAHAHA!
AH! HAHAHAHAHAHAHA!

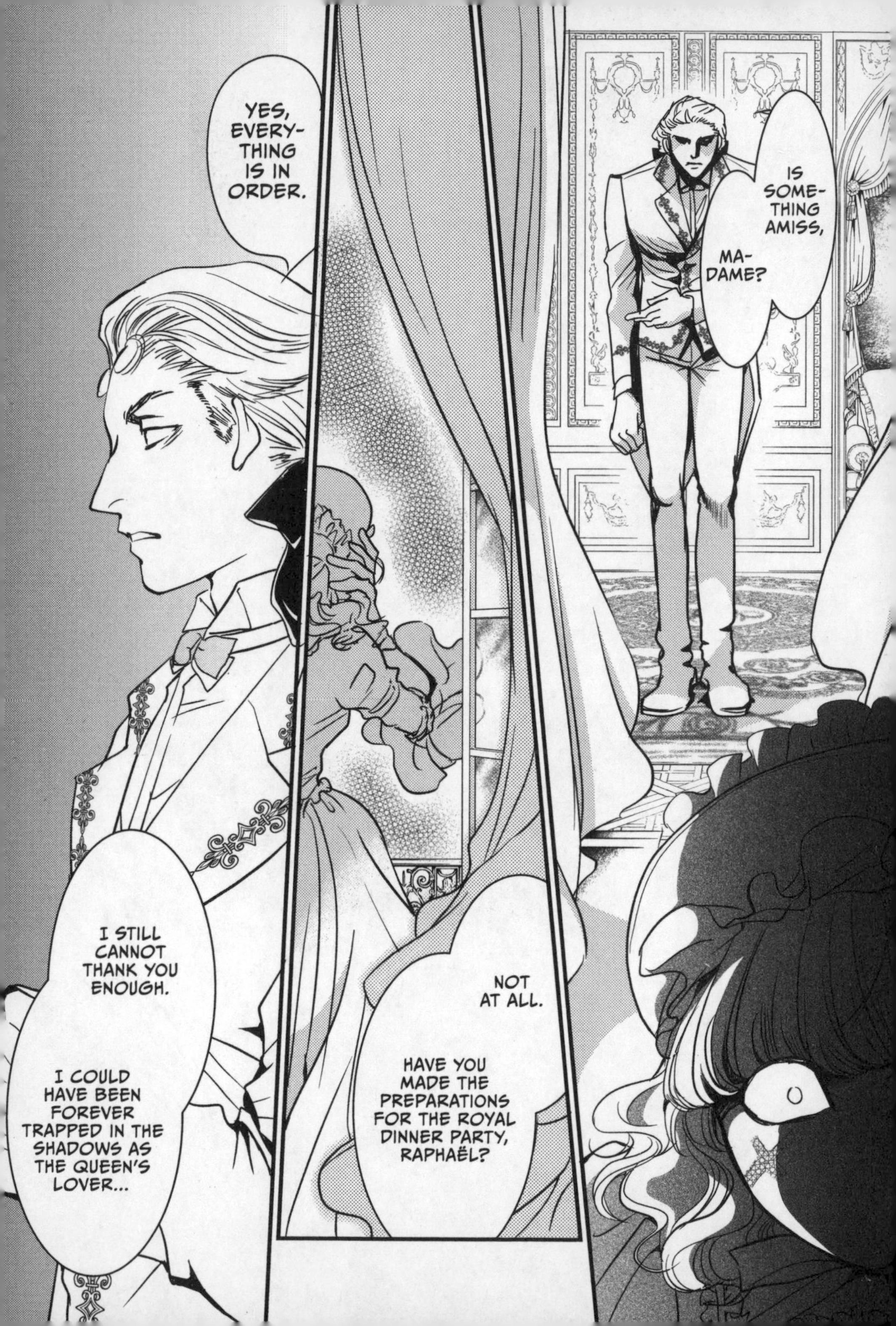
IS SOMETHING AMISS, MADAME?
NOT AT ALL.
HAVE YOU MADE THE PREPARATIONS FOR THE ROYAL DINNER PARTY, RAPHAËL?
YES, EVERYTHING IS IN ORDER.
I STILL CANNOT THANK YOU ENOUGH.
I COULD HAVE BEEN FOREVER TRAPPED IN THE SHADOWS AS THE QUEEN'S LOVER...

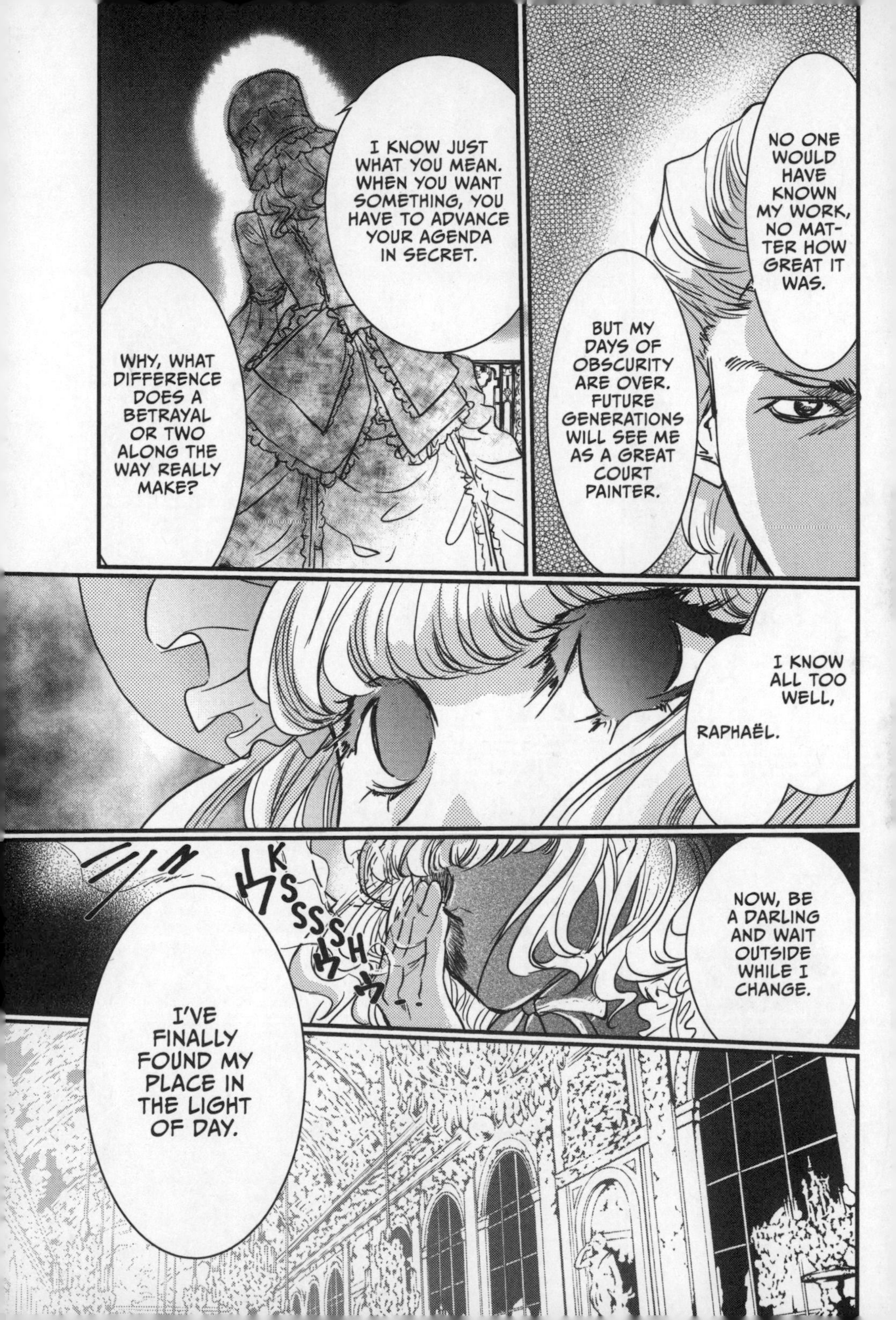
NO ONE WOULD HAVE KNOWN MY WORK, NO MAT-TER HOW GREAT IT WAS.
BUT MY DAYS OF OBSCURITY ARE OVER. FUTURE GENERATIONS WILL SEE ME AS A GREAT COURT PAINTER.
I KNOW JUST WHAT YOU MEAN. WHEN YOU WANT SOMETHING, YOU HAVE TO ADVANCE YOUR AGENDA IN SECRET.
WHY, WHAT DIFFERENCE DOES A BETRAYAL OR TWO ALONG THE WAY REALLY MAKE?
I KNOW ALL TOO WELL,
RAPHAËL.
NOW, BE A DARLING AND WAIT OUTSIDE WHILE I CHANGE.
KSSSSH
I'VE FINALLY FOUND MY PLACE IN THE LIGHT OF DAY.

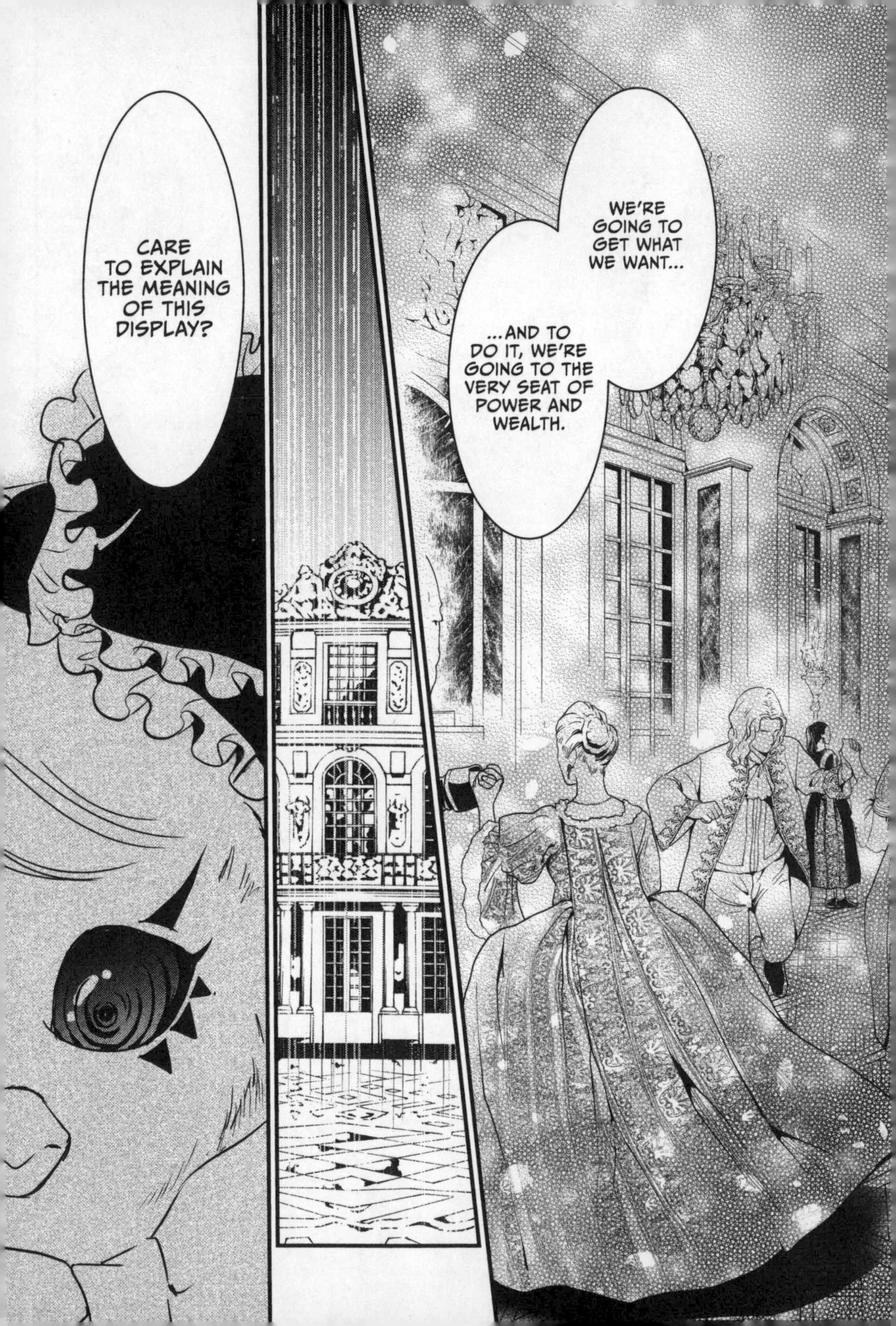
WE'RE GOING TO GET WHAT WE WANT...
...AND TO DO IT, WE'RE GOING TO THE VERY SEAT OF POWER AND WEALTH.
CARE TO EXPLAIN THE MEANING OF THIS DISPLAY?

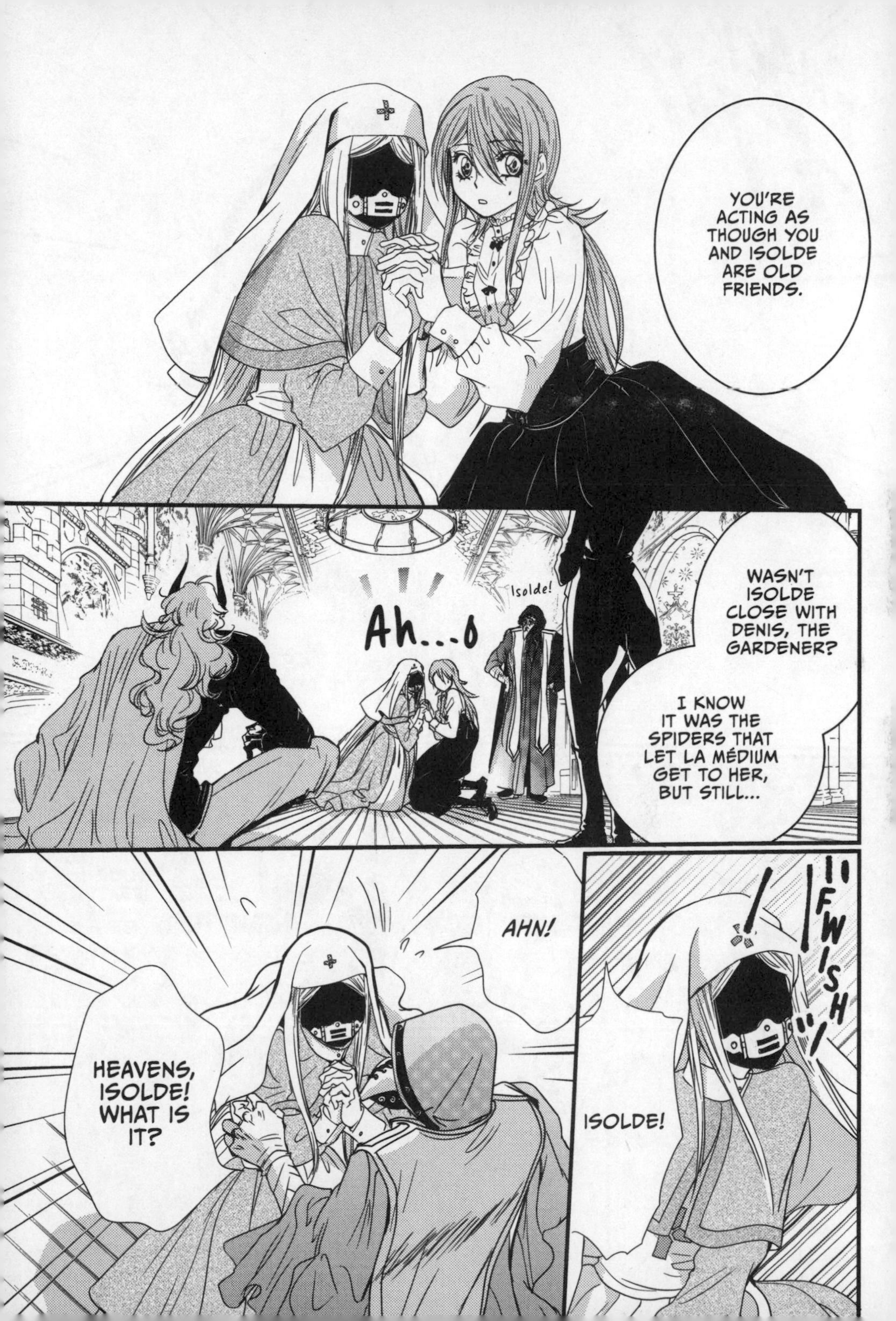
YOU'RE ACTING AS THOUGH YOU AND ISOLDE ARE OLD FRIENDS.
WASN'T ISOLDE CLOSE WITH DENIS, THE GARDENER?
I KNOW IT WAS THE SPIDERS THAT LET LA MÉDIUM GET TO HER, BUT STILL...
Isolde!
Ah...♪
FWISH
ISOLDE!
AHN!
HEAVENS, ISOLDE! WHAT IS IT?

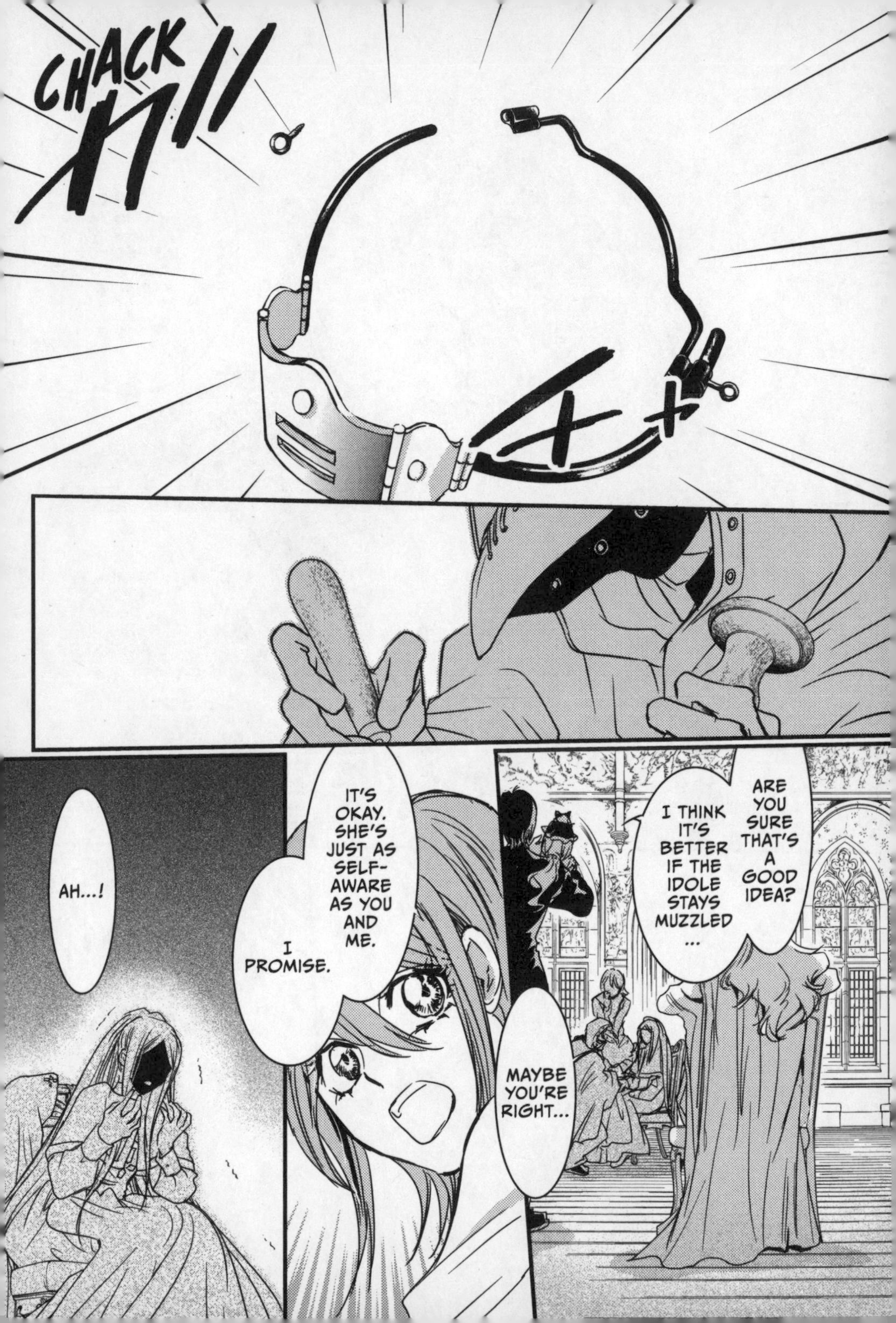
CHACK
ARE YOU SURE THAT'S A GOOD IDEA?
I THINK IT'S BETTER IF THE IDOLE STAYS MUZZLED ...
IT'S OKAY. SHE'S JUST AS SELF-AWARE AS YOU AND ME.
I PROMISE.
MAYBE YOU'RE RIGHT...
AH...!

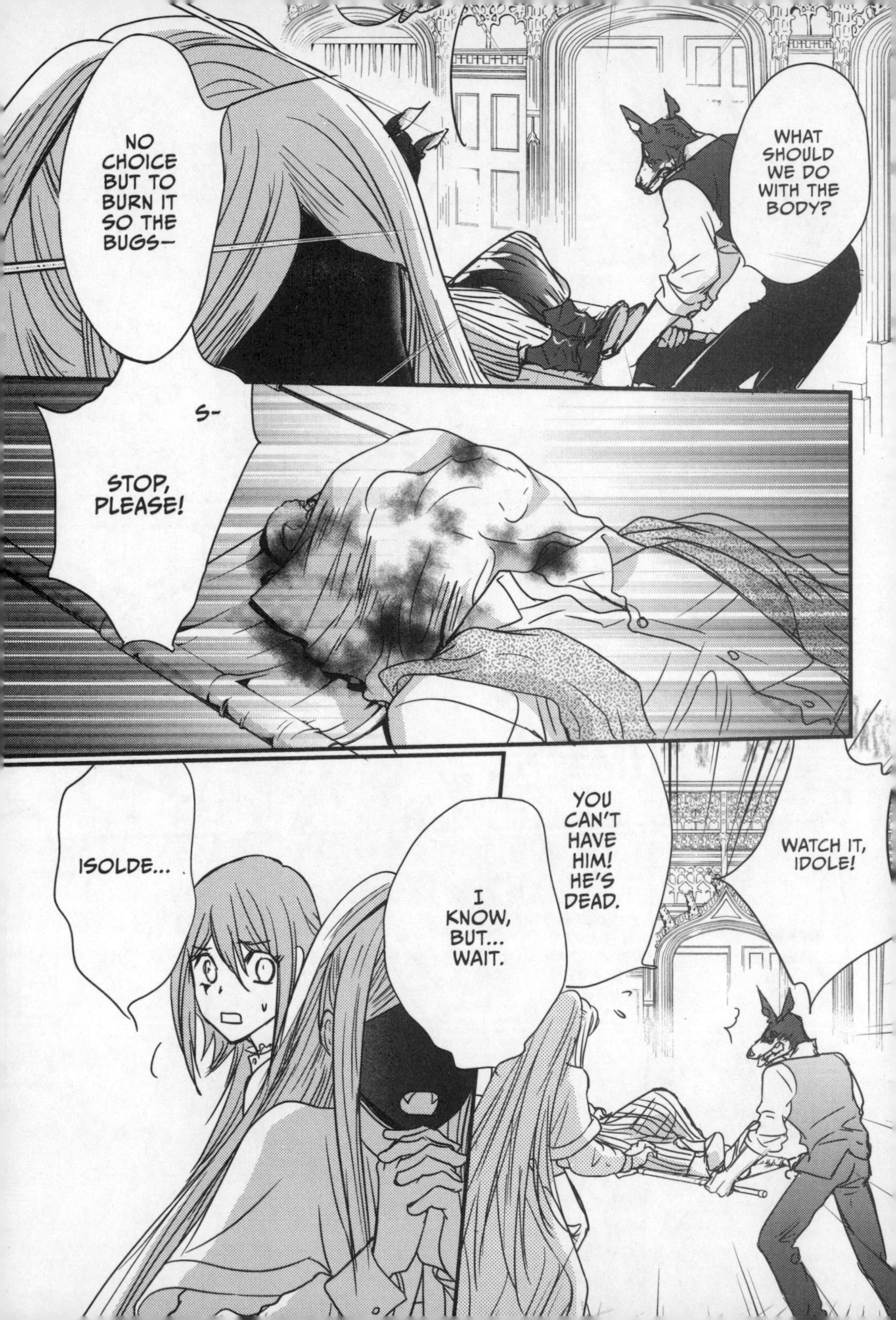
WHAT SHOULD WE DO WITH THE BODY?
NO CHOICE BUT TO BURN IT SO THE BUGS—
S-
STOP, PLEASE!
WATCH IT, IDOLE!
YOU CAN'T HAVE HIM! HE'S DEAD.
I KNOW, BUT... WAIT.
ISOLDE...

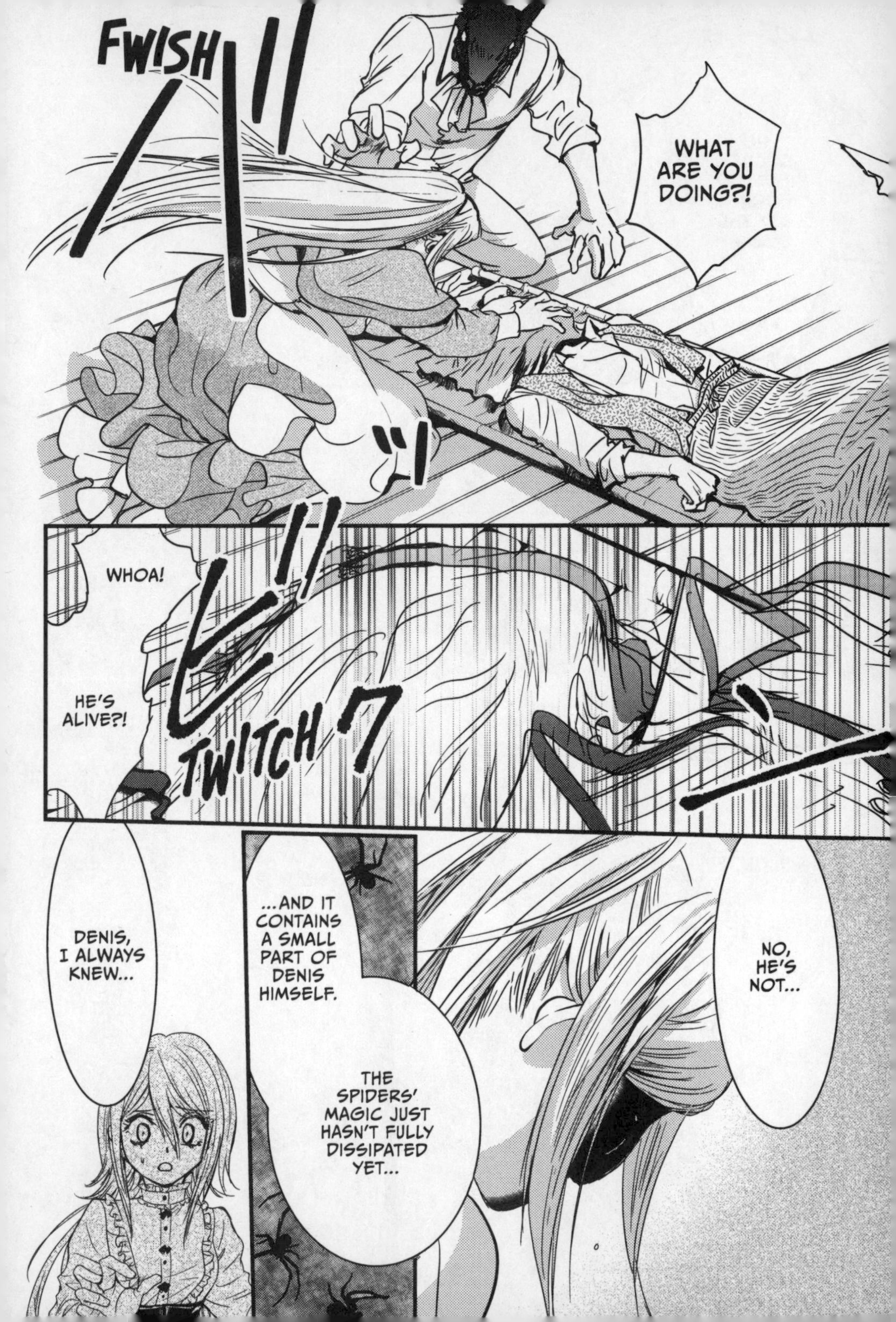
WHAT ARE YOU DOING?!
FWISH
TWITCH
WHOA!
HE'S ALIVE?!
NO, HE'S NOT...
THE SPIDERS' MAGIC JUST HASN'T FULLY DISSIPATED YET...
...AND IT CONTAINS A SMALL PART OF DENIS HIMSELF.
DENIS, I ALWAYS KNEW...

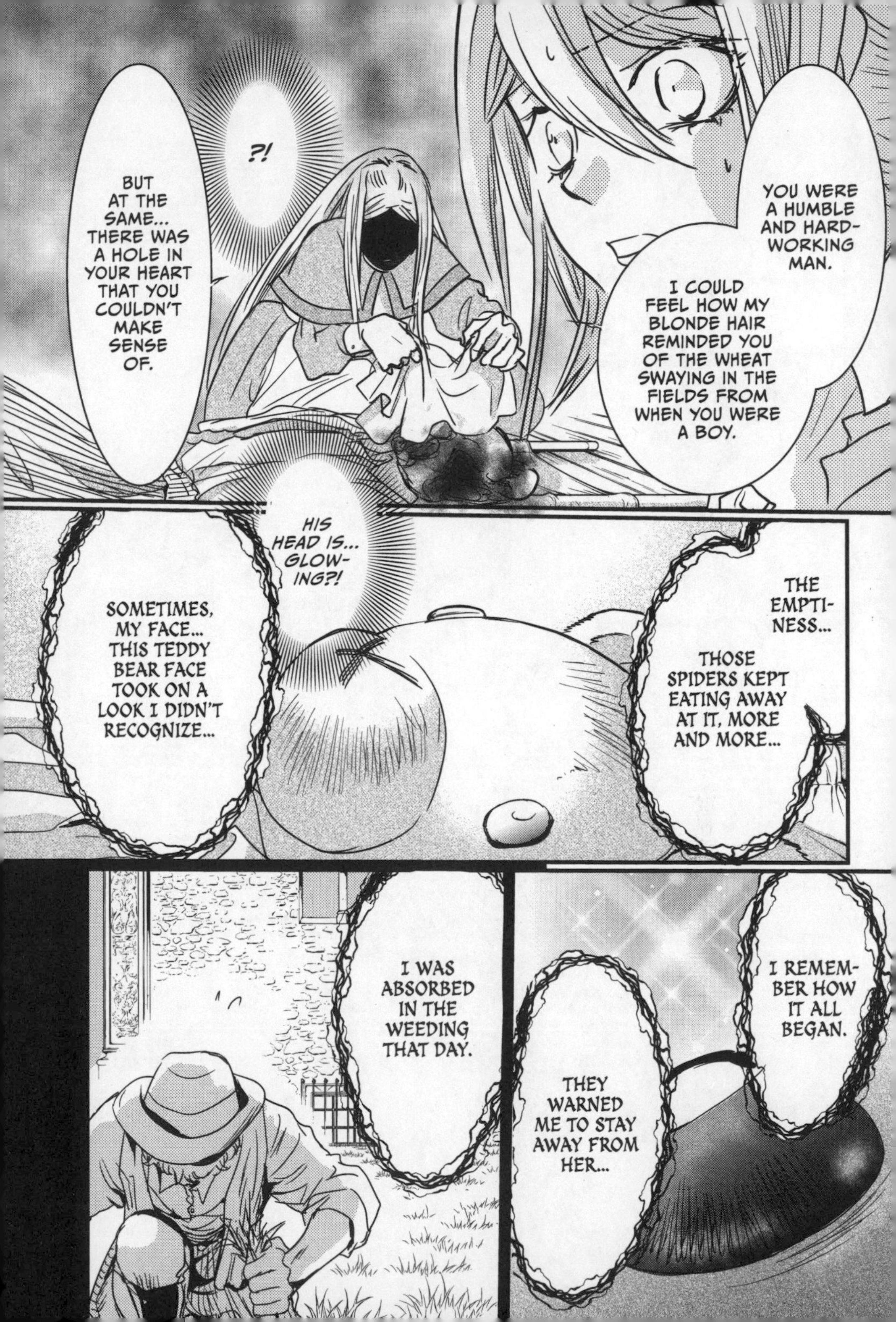
YOU WERE A HUMBLE AND HARD-WORKING MAN.
I COULD FEEL HOW MY BLONDE HAIR REMINDED YOU OF THE WHEAT SWAYING IN THE FIELDS FROM WHEN YOU WERE A BOY.
?!
BUT AT THE SAME... THERE WAS A HOLE IN YOUR HEART THAT YOU COULDN'T MAKE SENSE OF.
THE EMPTINESS...
THOSE SPIDERS KEPT EATING AWAY AT IT, MORE AND MORE...
HIS HEAD IS... GLOWING?!
SOMETIMES, MY FACE... THIS TEDDY BEAR FACE TOOK ON A LOOK I DIDN'T RECOGNIZE...
I REMEMBER HOW IT ALL BEGAN.
THEY WARNED ME TO STAY AWAY FROM HER...
I WAS ABSORBED IN THE WEEDING THAT DAY.

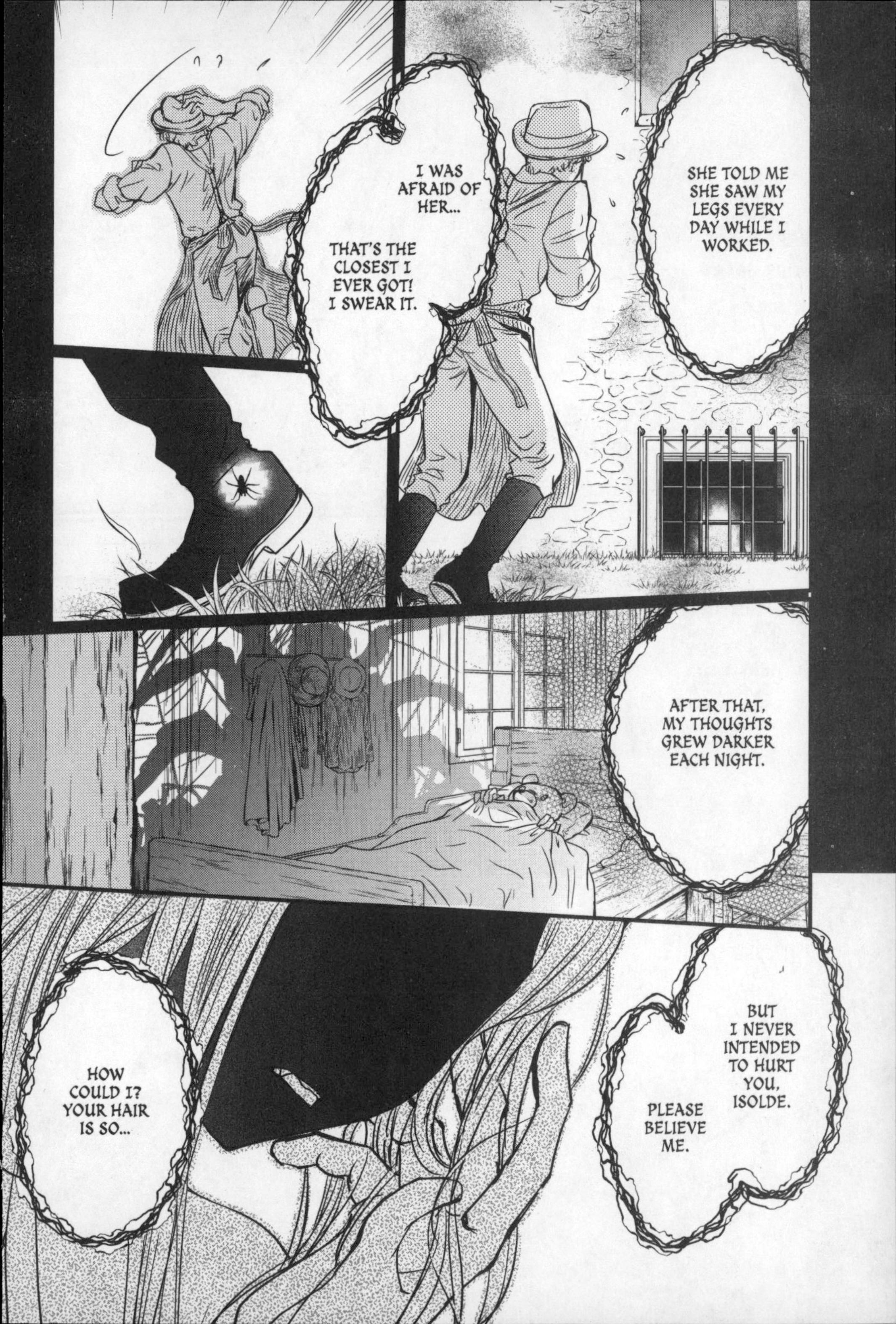
SHE TOLD ME SHE SAW MY LEGS EVERY DAY WHILE I WORKED.
I WAS AFRAID OF HER...
THAT'S THE CLOSEST I EVER GOT! I SWEAR IT.
AFTER THAT, MY THOUGHTS GREW DARKER EACH NIGHT.
BUT I NEVER INTENDED TO HURT YOU, ISOLDE.
PLEASE BELIEVE ME.
HOW COULD I? YOUR HAIR IS SO...

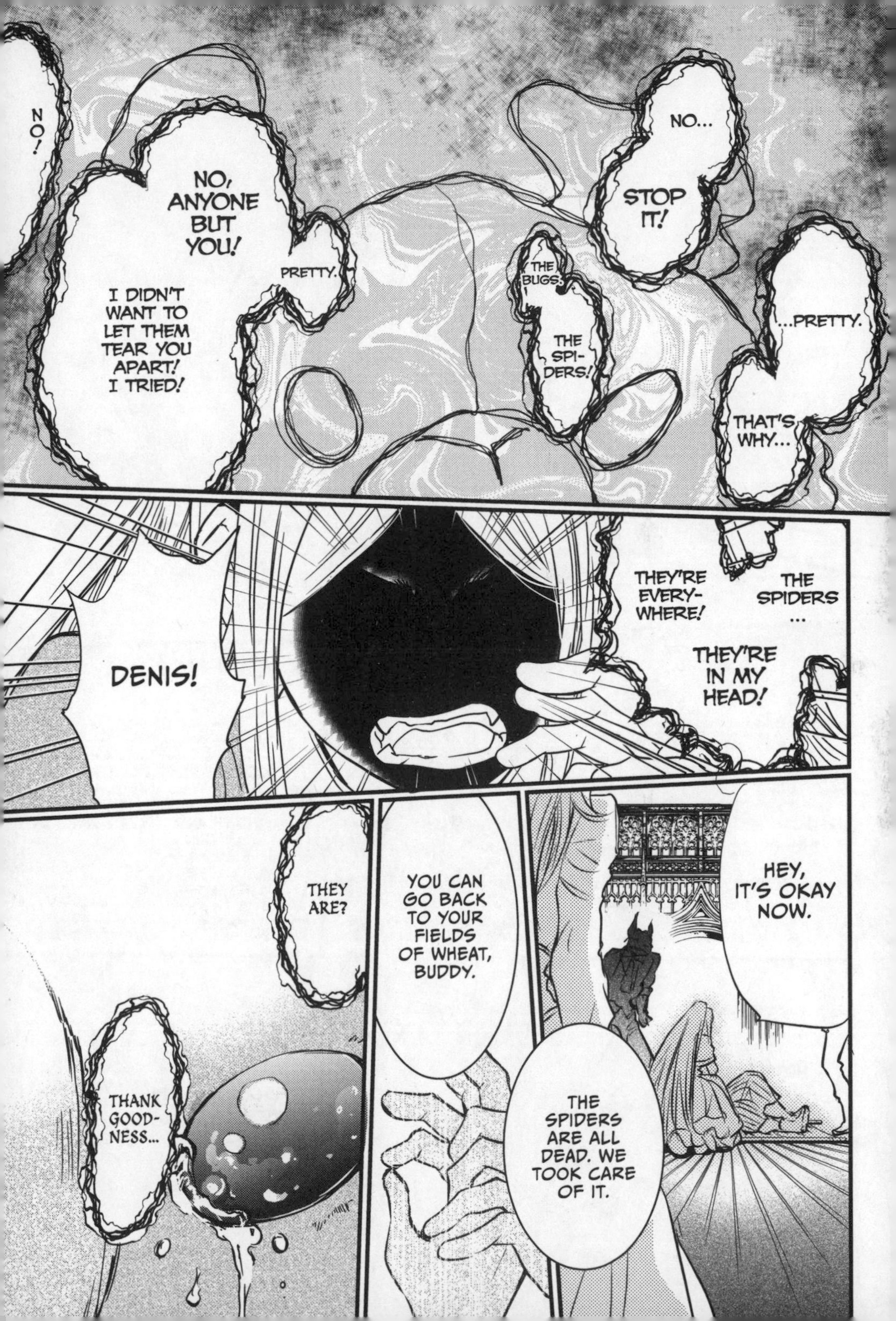
NO...
STOP IT!
...PRETTY.
THAT'S WHY...
THE BUGS.
THE SPIDERS!
PRETTY.
NO, ANYONE BUT YOU!
I DIDN'T WANT TO LET THEM TEAR YOU APART! I TRIED!
NO!
THE SPIDERS...
THEY'RE EVERYWHERE!
THEY'RE IN MY HEAD!
DENIS!
HEY, IT'S OKAY NOW.
THE SPIDERS ARE ALL DEAD. WE TOOK CARE OF IT.
YOU CAN GO BACK TO YOUR FIELDS OF WHEAT, BUDDY.
THEY ARE?
THANK GOODNESS...

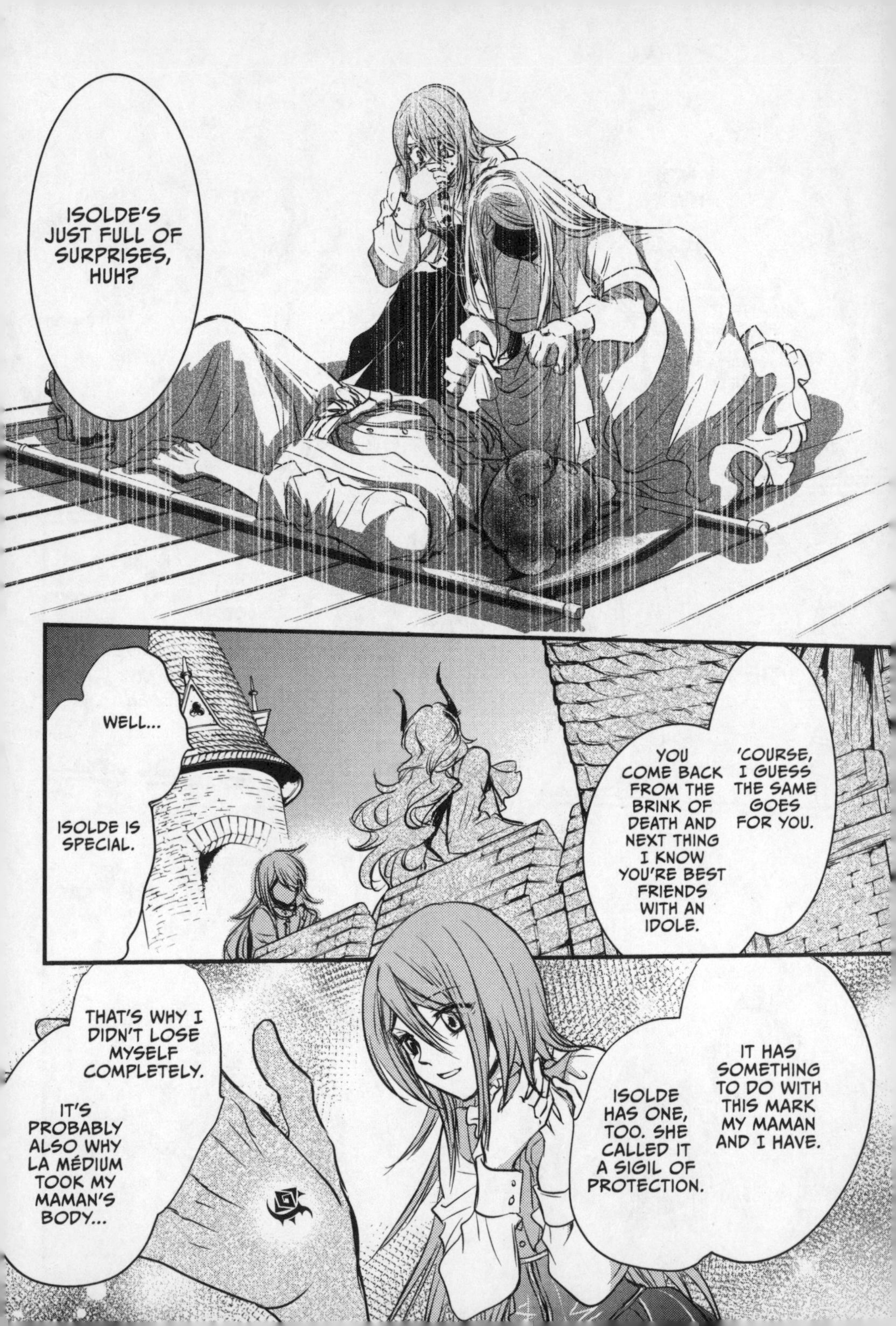
ISOLDE'S JUST FULL OF SURPRISES, HUH?
'COURSE, I GUESS THE SAME GOES FOR YOU.
YOU COME BACK FROM THE BRINK OF DEATH AND NEXT THING I KNOW YOU'RE BEST FRIENDS WITH AN IDOLE.
WELL...
ISOLDE IS SPECIAL.
IT HAS SOMETHING TO DO WITH THIS MARK MY MAMAN AND I HAVE.
ISOLDE HAS ONE, TOO. SHE CALLED IT A SIGIL OF PROTECTION.
THAT'S WHY I DIDN'T LOSE MYSELF COMPLETELY.
IT'S PROBABLY ALSO WHY LA MÉDIUM TOOK MY MAMAN'S BODY...

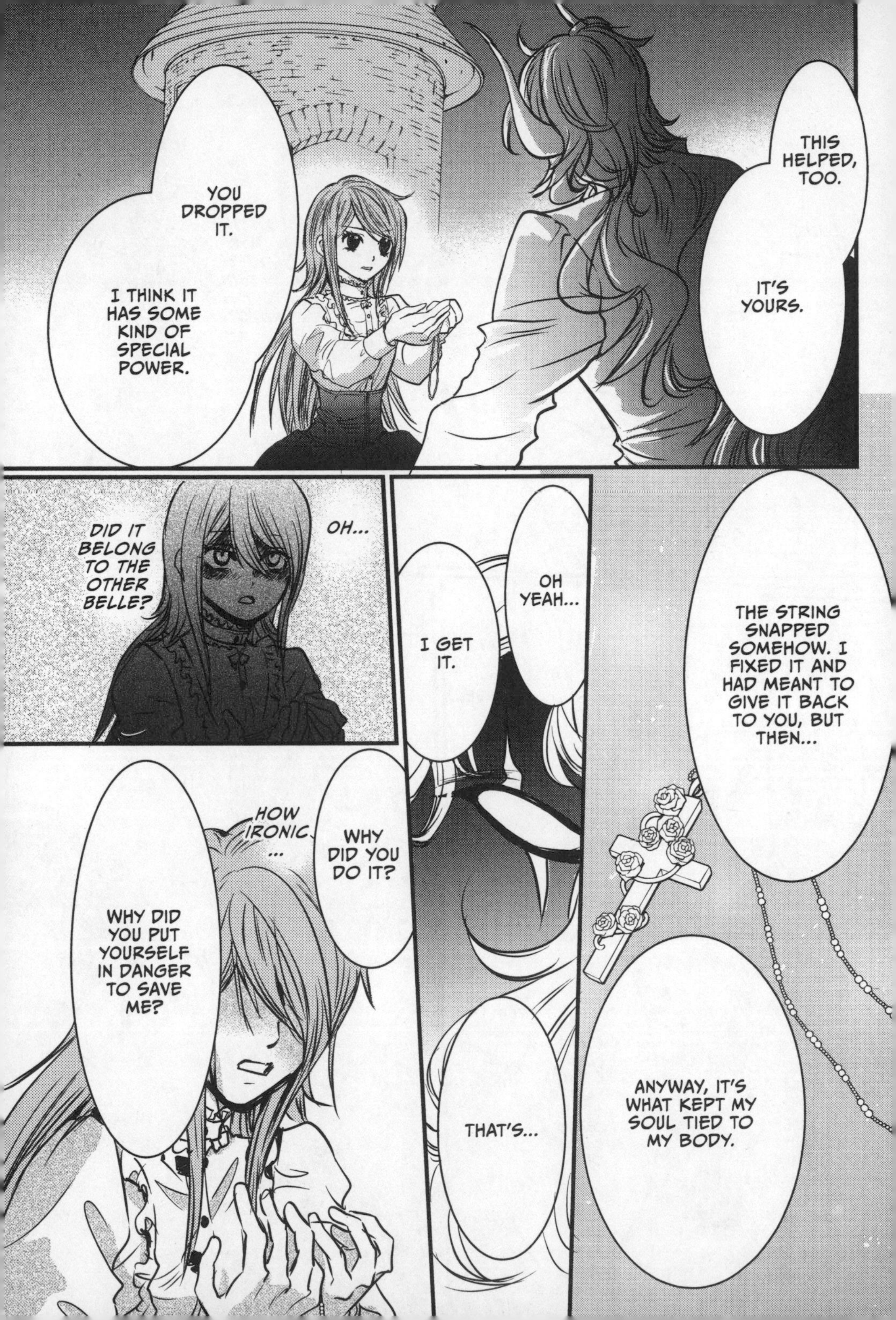
THIS HELPED, TOO.
IT'S YOURS.
YOU DROPPED IT.
I THINK IT HAS SOME KIND OF SPECIAL POWER.
THE STRING SNAPPED SOMEHOW. I FIXED IT AND HAD MEANT TO GIVE IT BACK TO YOU, BUT THEN...
ANYWAY, IT'S WHAT KEPT MY SOUL TIED TO MY BODY.
OH YEAH...
I GET IT.
THAT'S...
OH...
DID IT BELONG TO THE OTHER BELLE?
WHY DID YOU DO IT?
HOW IRONIC...
WHY DID YOU PUT YOURSELF IN DANGER TO SAVE ME?

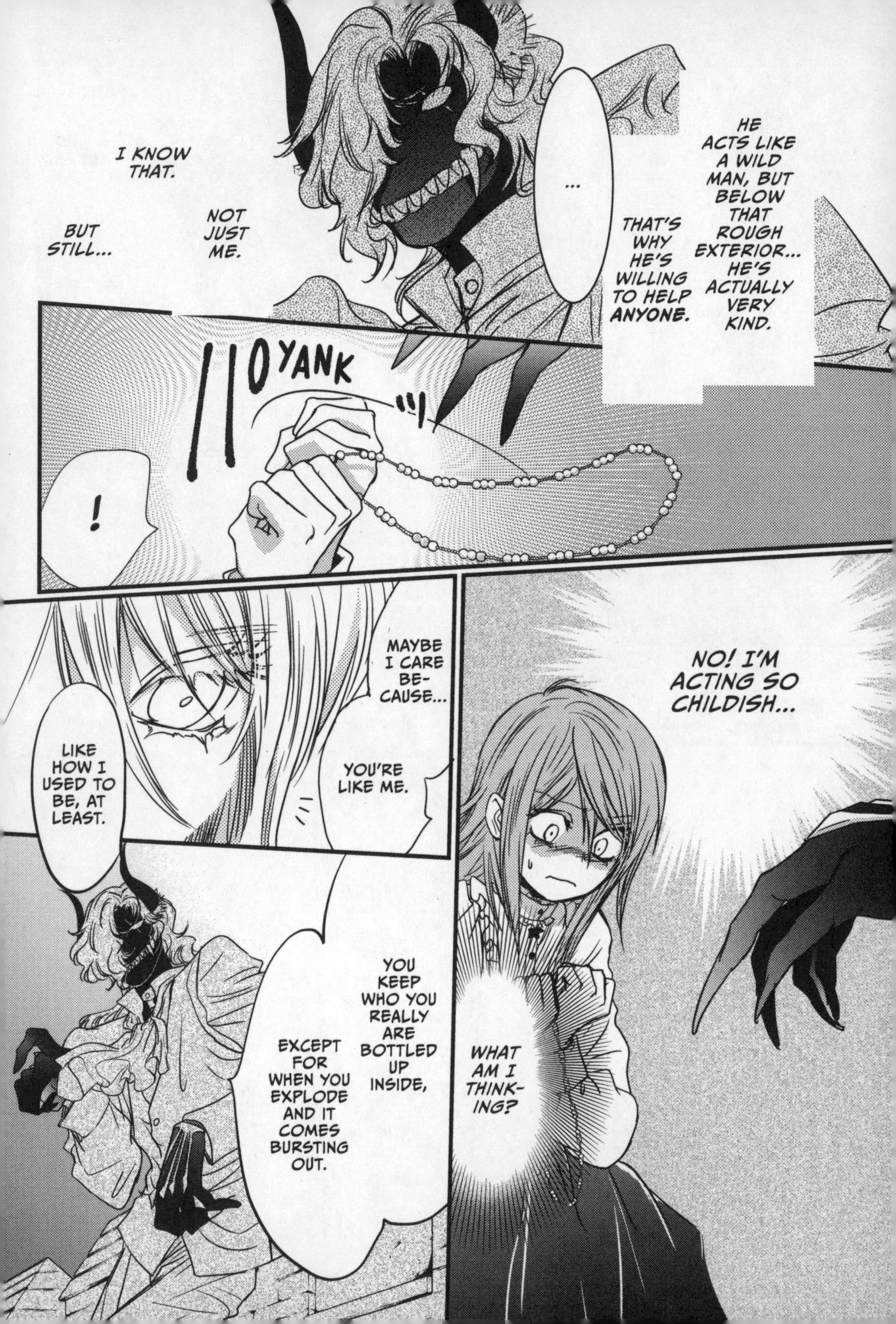
HE ACTS LIKE A WILD MAN, BUT BELOW THAT ROUGH EXTERIOR... HE'S ACTUALLY VERY KIND.
THAT'S WHY HE'S WILLING TO HELP ANYONE.
...
NOT JUST ME.
I KNOW THAT.
BUT STILL...
YANK
!
NO! I'M ACTING SO CHILDISH...
WHAT AM I THINK-ING?
MAYBE I CARE BE-CAUSE...
YOU'RE LIKE ME.
LIKE HOW I USED TO BE, AT LEAST.
YOU KEEP WHO YOU REALLY ARE BOTTLED UP INSIDE,
EXCEPT FOR WHEN YOU EXPLODE AND IT COMES BURSTING OUT.

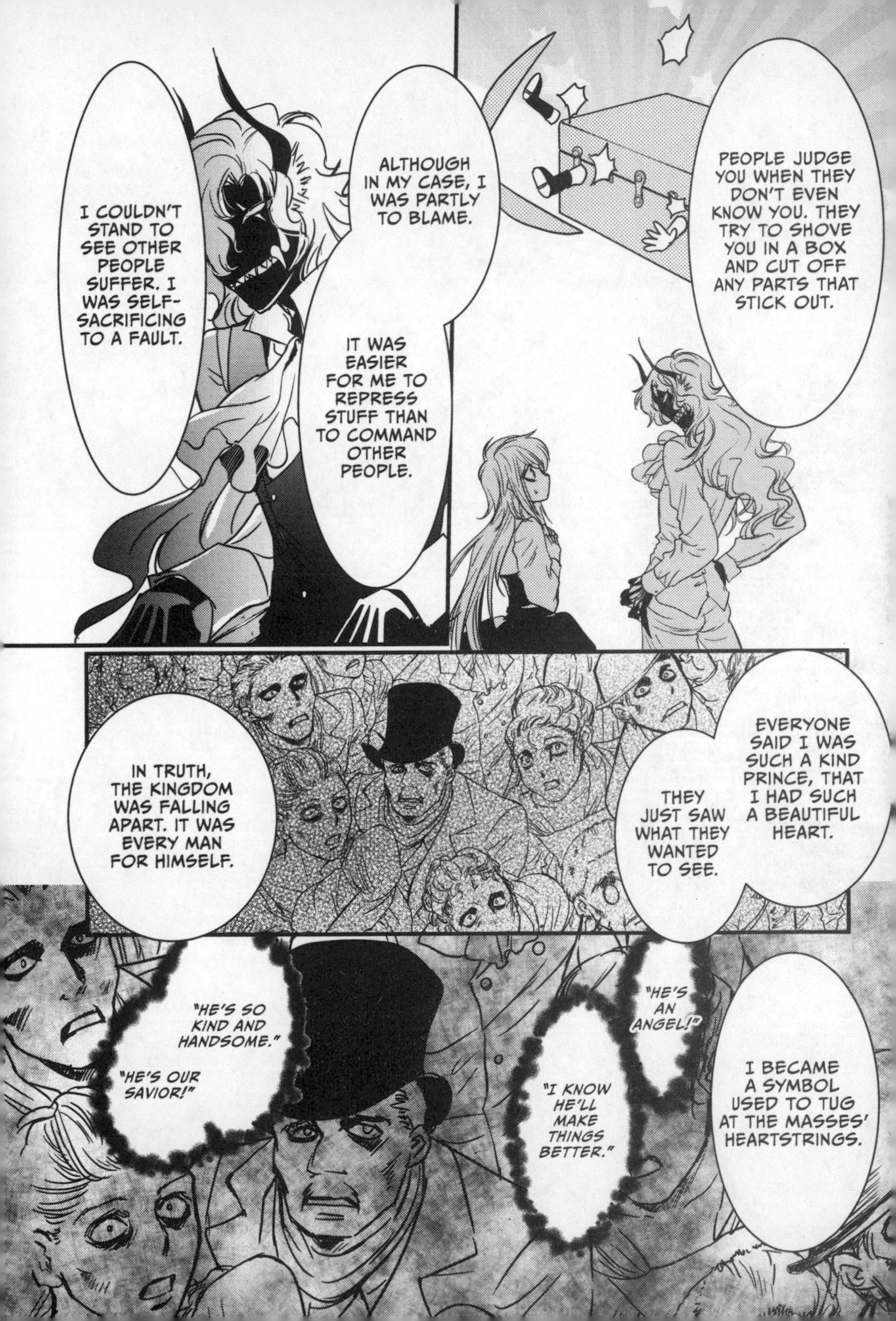
PEOPLE JUDGE YOU WHEN THEY DON'T EVEN KNOW YOU. THEY TRY TO SHOVE YOU IN A BOX AND CUT OFF ANY PARTS THAT STICK OUT.
ALTHOUGH IN MY CASE, I WAS PARTLY TO BLAME.
IT WAS EASIER FOR ME TO REPRESS STUFF THAN TO COMMAND OTHER PEOPLE.
I COULDN'T STAND TO SEE OTHER PEOPLE SUFFER. I WAS SELF-SACRIFICING TO A FAULT.
EVERYONE SAID I WAS SUCH A KIND PRINCE, THAT I HAD SUCH A BEAUTIFUL HEART.
THEY JUST SAW WHAT THEY WANTED TO SEE.
IN TRUTH, THE KINGDOM WAS FALLING APART. IT WAS EVERY MAN FOR HIMSELF.
I BECAME A SYMBOL USED TO TUG AT THE MASSES' HEARTSTRINGS.
"HE'S AN ANGEL!"
"I KNOW HE'LL MAKE THINGS BETTER."
"HE'S SO KIND AND HANDSOME."
"HE'S OUR SAVIOR!"

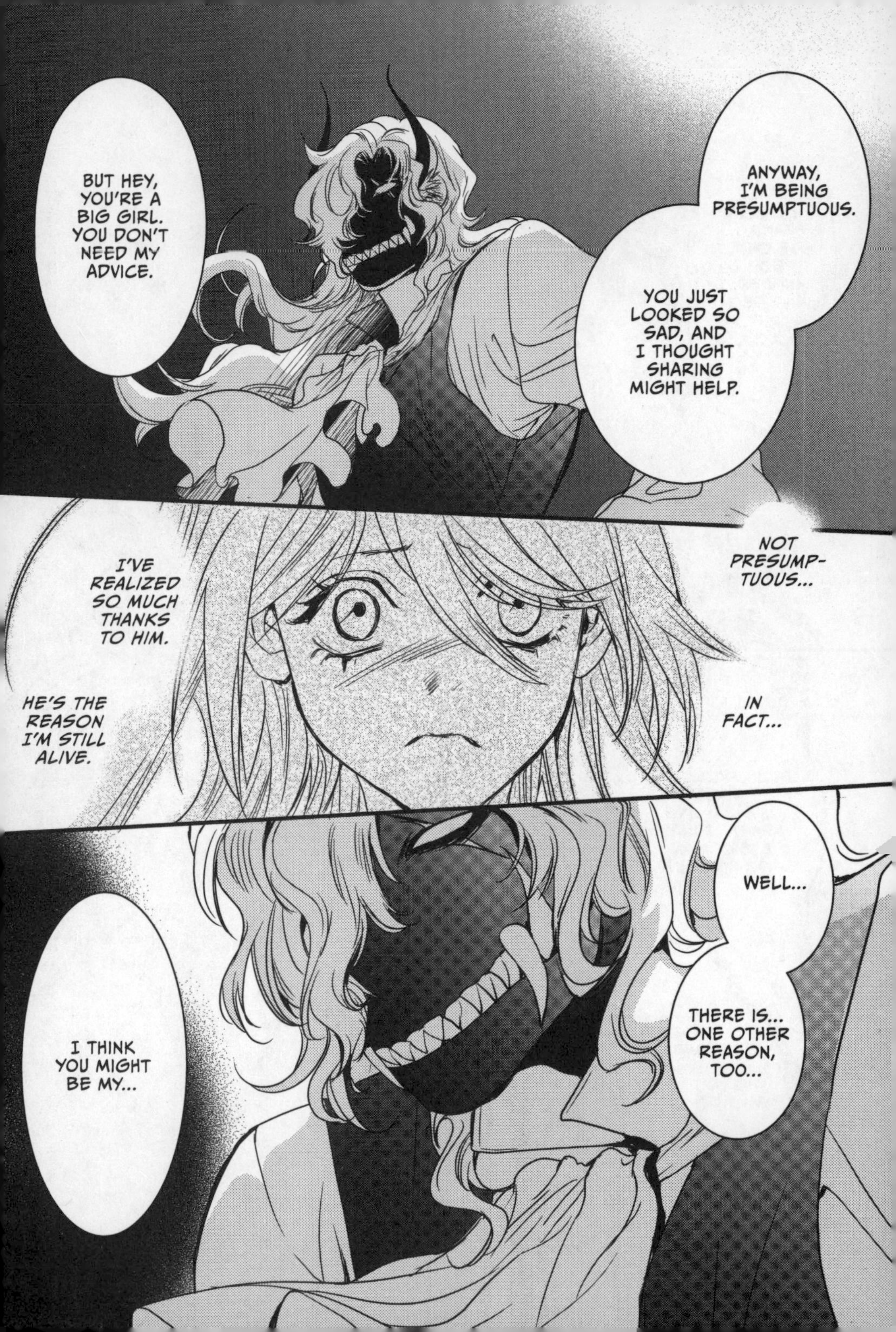
ANYWAY, I'M BEING PRESUMPTUOUS.
YOU JUST LOOKED SO SAD, AND I THOUGHT SHARING MIGHT HELP.
BUT HEY, YOU'RE A BIG GIRL. YOU DON'T NEED MY ADVICE.
NOT PRESUMPTUOUS...
IN FACT...
I'VE REALIZED SO MUCH THANKS TO HIM.
HE'S THE REASON I'M STILL ALIVE.
WELL...
THERE IS... ONE OTHER REASON, TOO...
I THINK YOU MIGHT BE MY...

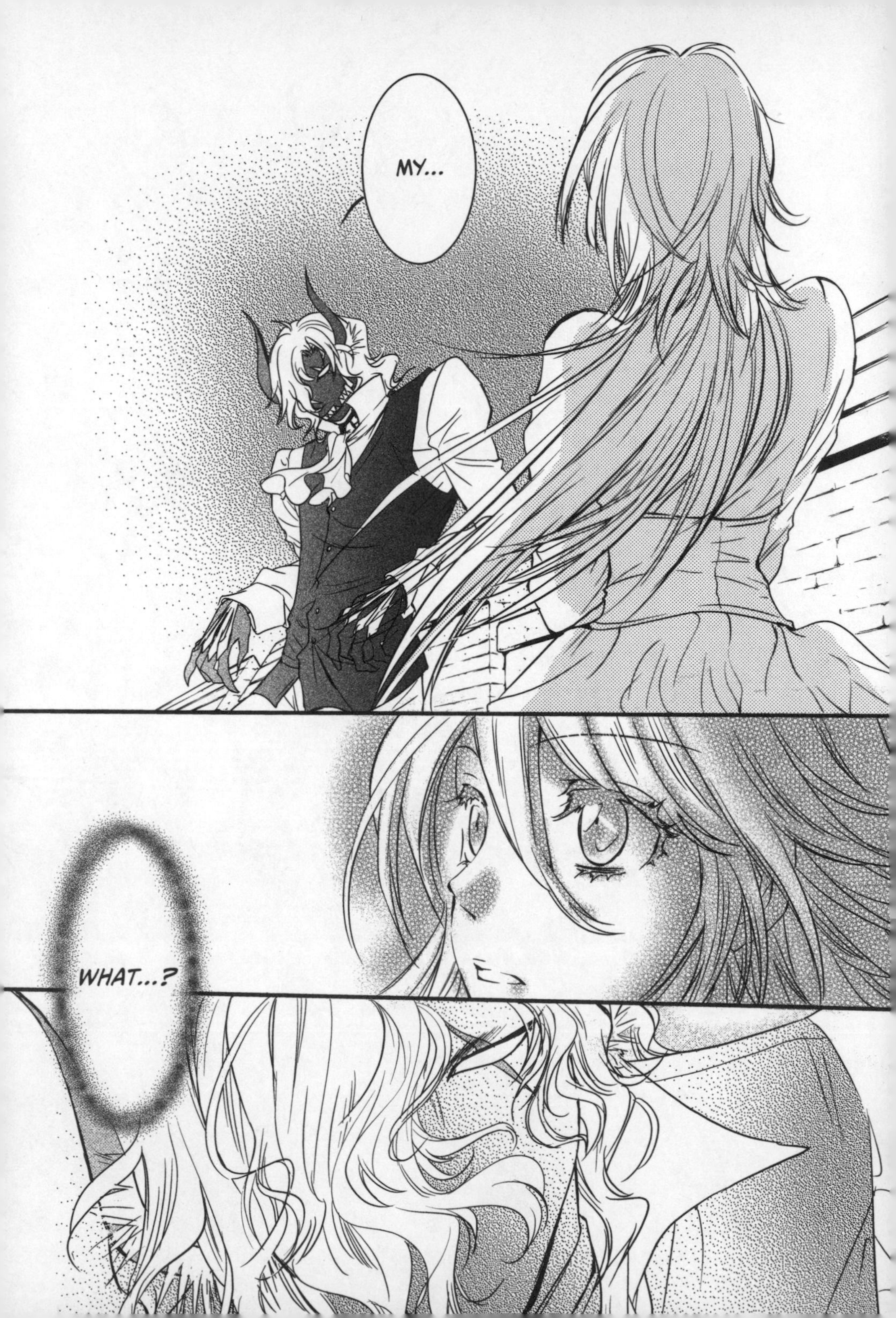
MY...
WHAT...?

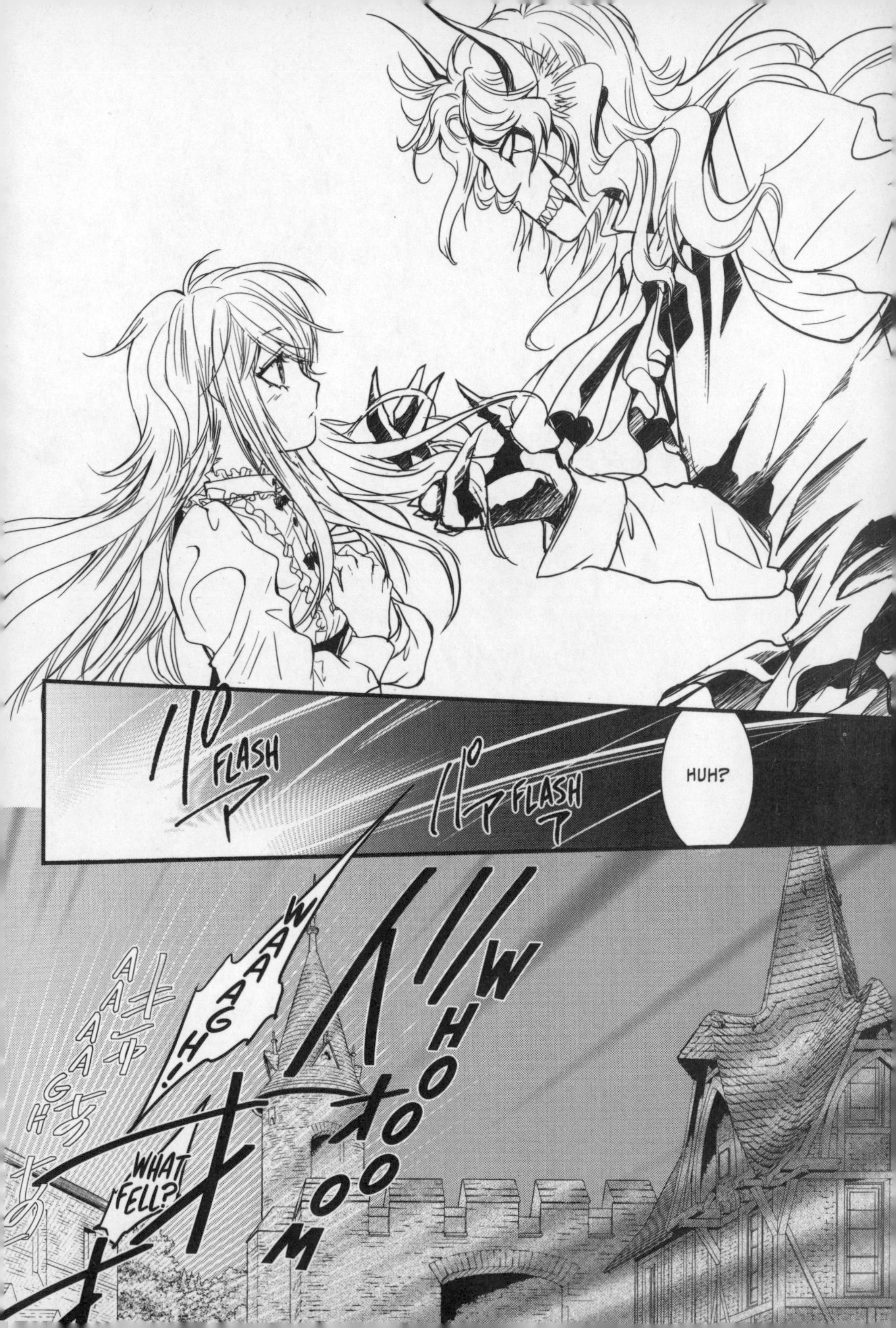
HUH?
FLASH
FLASH
WHOOOOOM
WHAT FELL?
WAAAGH!
AAAAAGH

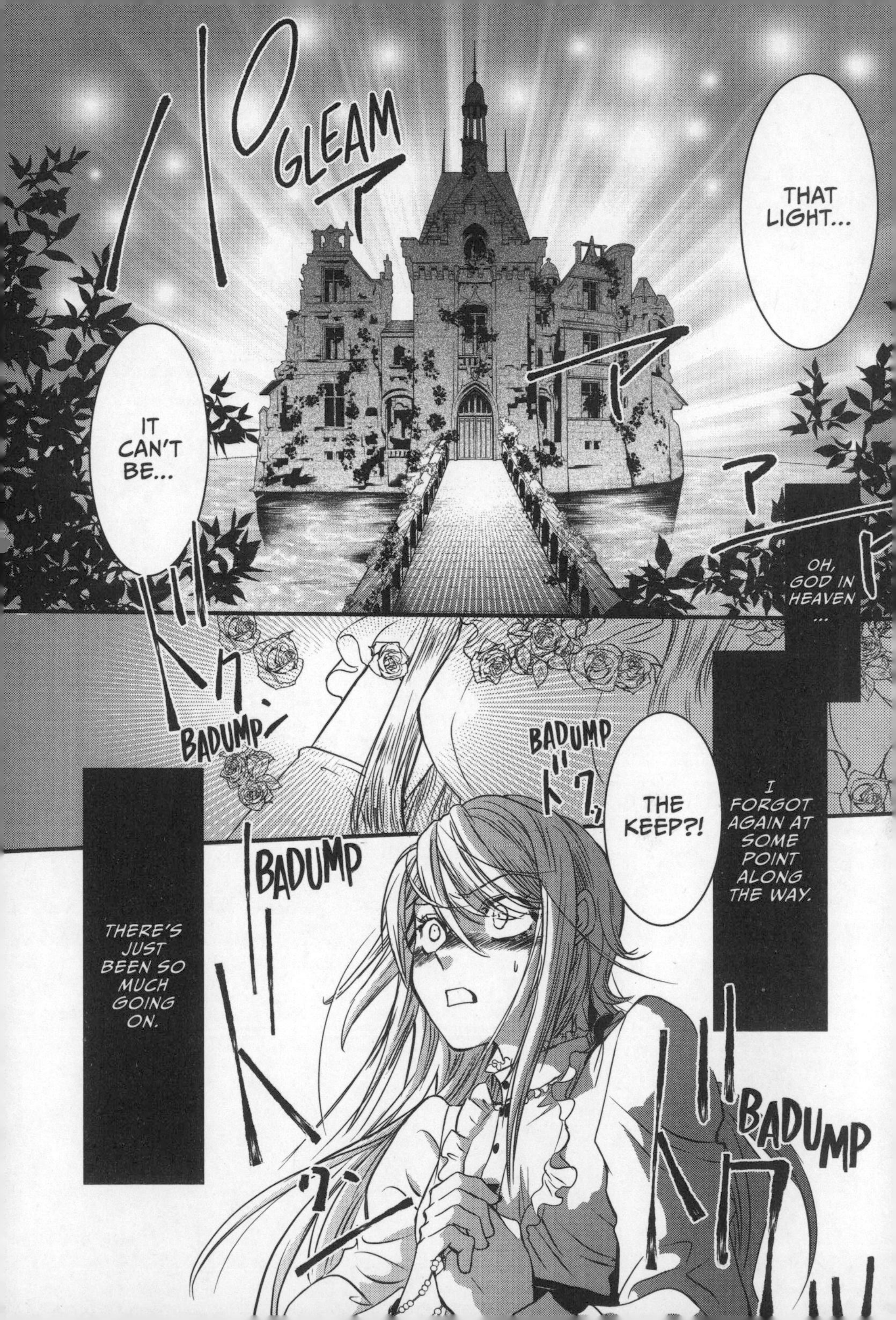
THAT LIGHT...
GLEAM
IT CAN'T BE...
OH, GOD IN HEAVEN ...
I FORGOT AGAIN AT SOME POINT ALONG THE WAY.
BADUMP
BADUMP
THE KEEP?!
BADUMP
BADUMP
THERE'S JUST BEEN SO MUCH GOING ON.

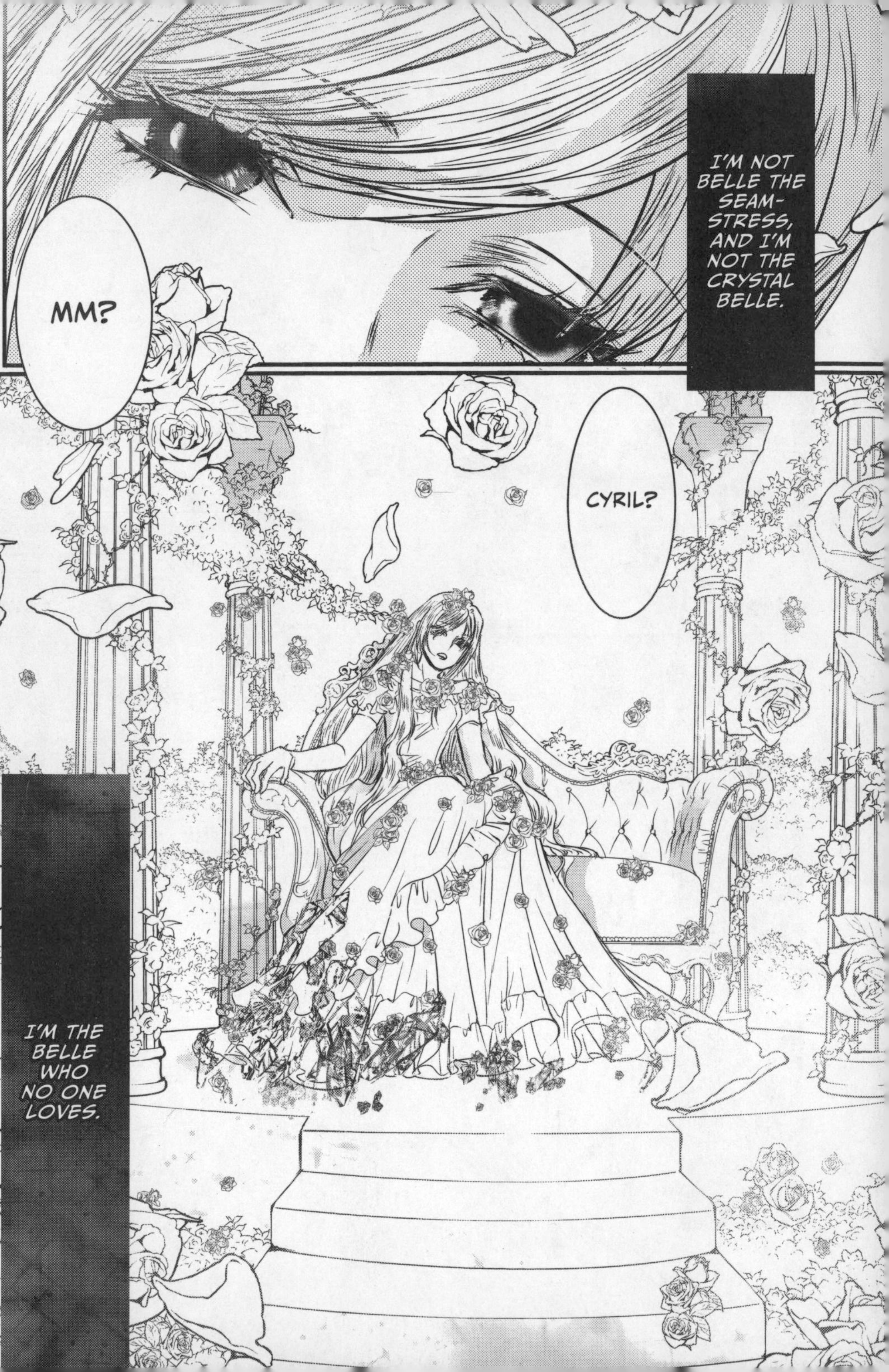
I'M NOT BELLE THE SEAM-STRESS, AND I'M NOT THE CRYSTAL BELLE.
MM?
CYRIL?
I'M THE BELLE WHO NO ONE LOVES.

TO BE CONTINUED...

LA BELLE ET LA BÊTE

DU PARADIS PERDU

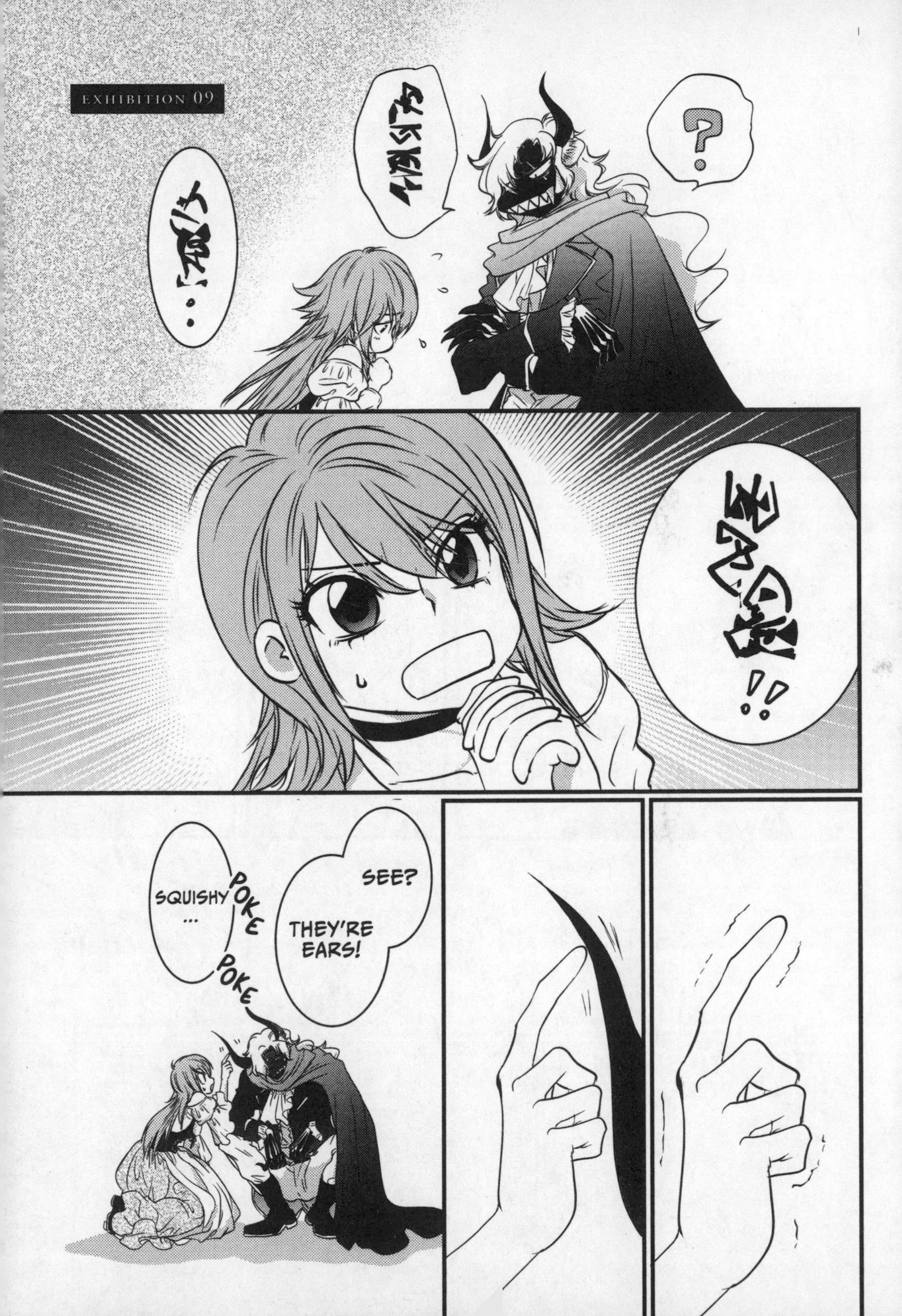
?
SEE?
THEY'RE EARS!
POKE
POKE
SQUISHY
...

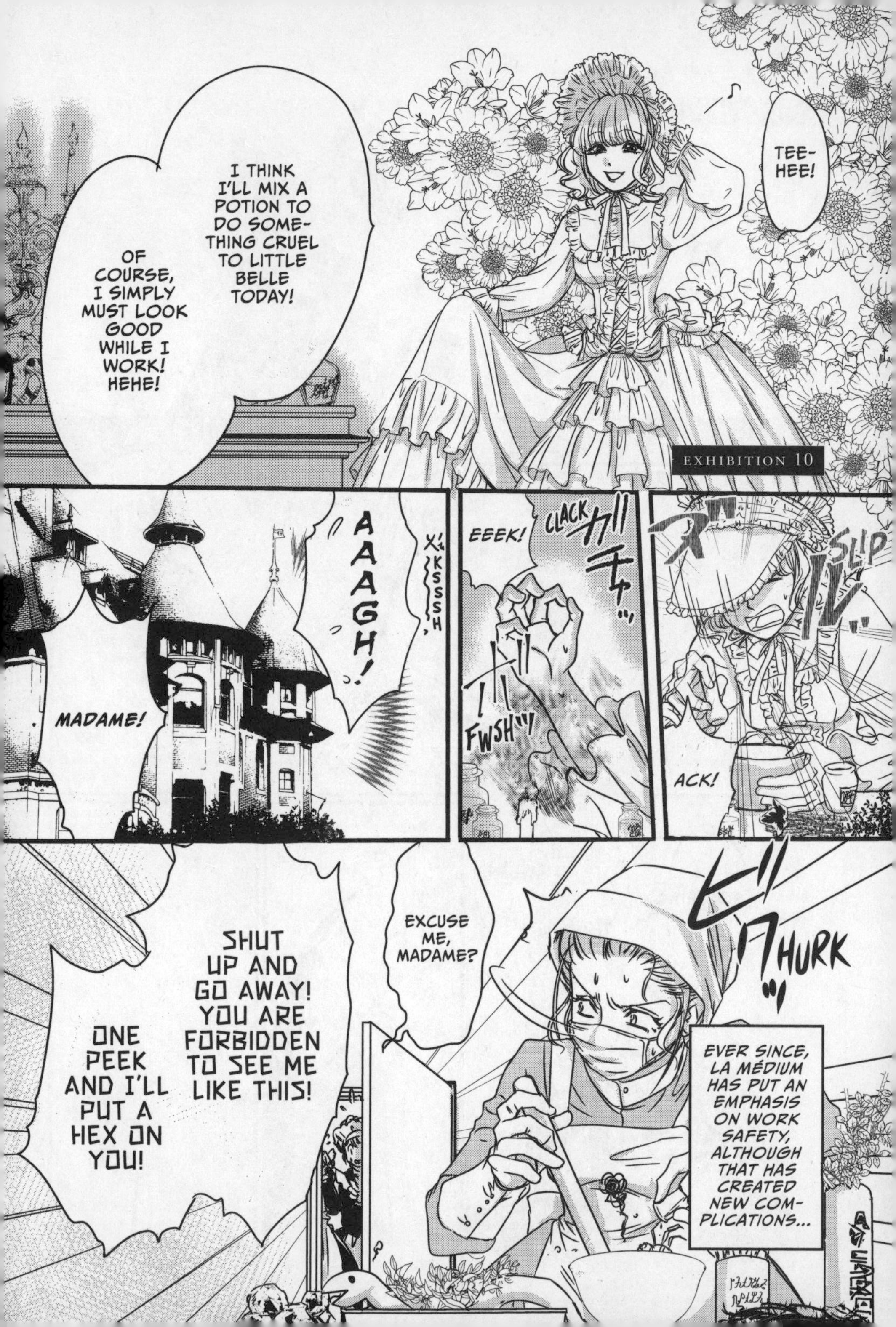
EXHIBITION 10
TEE-HEE!
I THINK I'LL MIX A POTION TO DO SOME-THING CRUEL TO LITTLE BELLE TODAY!
OF COURSE, I SIMPLY MUST LOOK GOOD WHILE I WORK! HEHE!
SLIP
ACK!
CLACK
EEEK!
FWSH
KSSSH
AAAGH!
MADAME!
HURK
EXCUSE ME, MADAME?
SHUT UP AND GO AWAY! YOU ARE FORBIDDEN TO SEE ME LIKE THIS!
ONE PEEK AND I'LL PUT A HEX ON YOU!
EVER SINCE, LA MÉDIUM HAS PUT AN EMPHASIS ON WORK SAFETY, ALTHOUGH THAT HAS CREATED NEW COM-PLICATIONS...

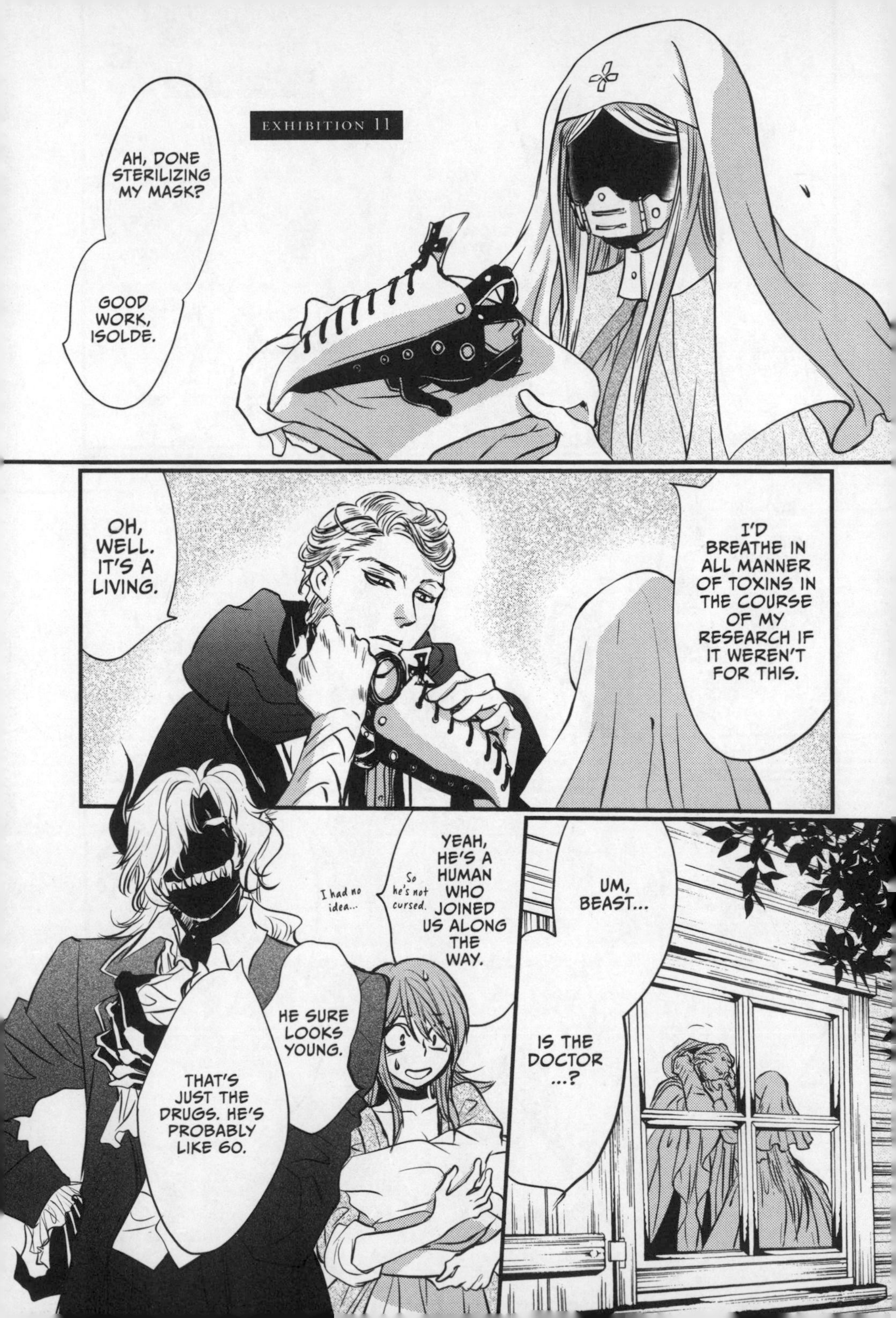
EXHIBITION 11
AH, DONE STERILIZING MY MASK?
GOOD WORK, ISOLDE.
I'D BREATHE IN ALL MANNER OF TOXINS IN THE COURSE OF MY RESEARCH IF IT WEREN'T FOR THIS.
OH, WELL. IT'S A LIVING.
UM, BEAST...
IS THE DOCTOR ...?
YEAH, HE'S A HUMAN WHO JOINED US ALONG THE WAY.
So he's not cursed.
I had no idea...
HE SURE LOOKS YOUNG.
THAT'S JUST THE DRUGS. HE'S PROBABLY LIKE 60.

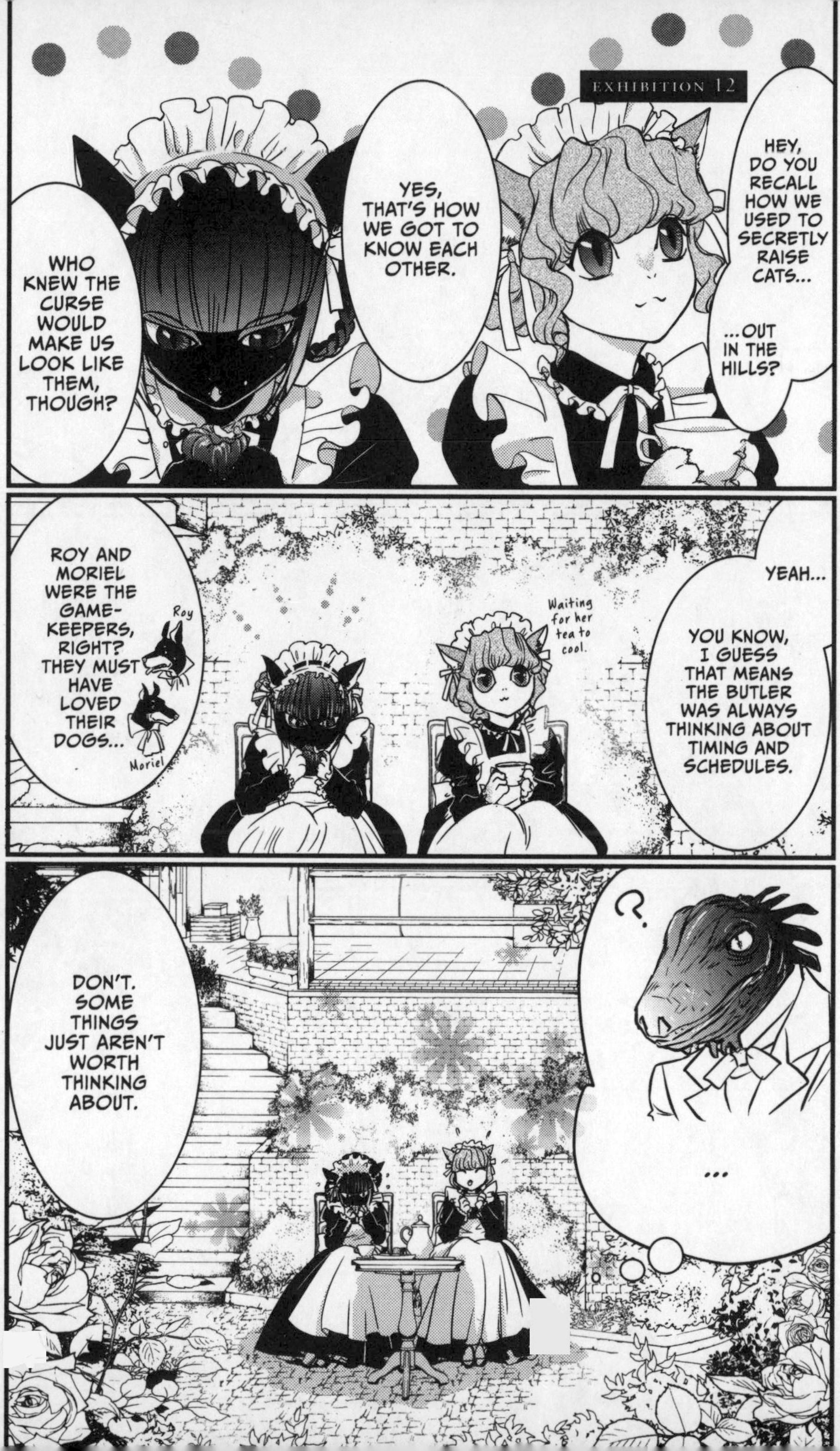
HEY, DO YOU RECALL HOW WE USED TO SECRETLY RAISE CATS...
...OUT IN THE HILLS?
YES, THAT'S HOW WE GOT TO KNOW EACH OTHER.
WHO KNEW THE CURSE WOULD MAKE US LOOK LIKE THEM, THOUGH?
YEAH...
YOU KNOW, I GUESS THAT MEANS THE BUTLER WAS ALWAYS THINKING ABOUT TIMING AND SCHEDULES.
Waiting for her tea to cool.
ROY AND MORIEL WERE THE GAME-KEEPERS, RIGHT? THEY MUST HAVE LOVED THEIR DOGS...
Roy
Moriel
?
...
DON'T. SOME THINGS JUST AREN'T WORTH THINKING ABOUT.

ISOLDE
(FORMER NAME UNKNOWN)

SINCE SHE'S THE DOCTOR'S ASSISTANT, SHE WEARS A NURSE'S OUTFIT. THAT'S WHY SHE WEARS A VEIL. SHE'S NOT A NUN.

SHE HAD TO WEAR A MUZZLE FOR THE COMFORT OF THOSE AROUND HER.

SHE HAS ENVIABLY SOFT, STRAIGHT, BLONDE HAIR.

AREN'T HER PROMINENT CANINES CUTE?

I CAN'T BELIEVE HOW I TREATED HER. I WAS SO FULL OF MYSELF...

Dummy!

I WAS AFRAID OF HER BECAUSE SHE'S AN IDOLE, BUT IT TURNS OUT SHE'S FRIENDLY AND KIND.

...

Mmf mmf...

Thanks for reading all the way to volume three!
Sometimes people complain about the lack of romance in this series, but I think it's gotten pretty drippy at this point...
I'm looking forward to doing the rest! lol
See you next time!

KAORI YUKI
twitter:@angelaid
(Japanese only)

In the next volume...

At last, she awakens...

...the beloved Belle.

CYRIL?
OH, CYRIL! I LOVE YOU MORE THAN ANYONE.
I NEVER WANT US TO BE APART AGAIN!

COMING SOON!

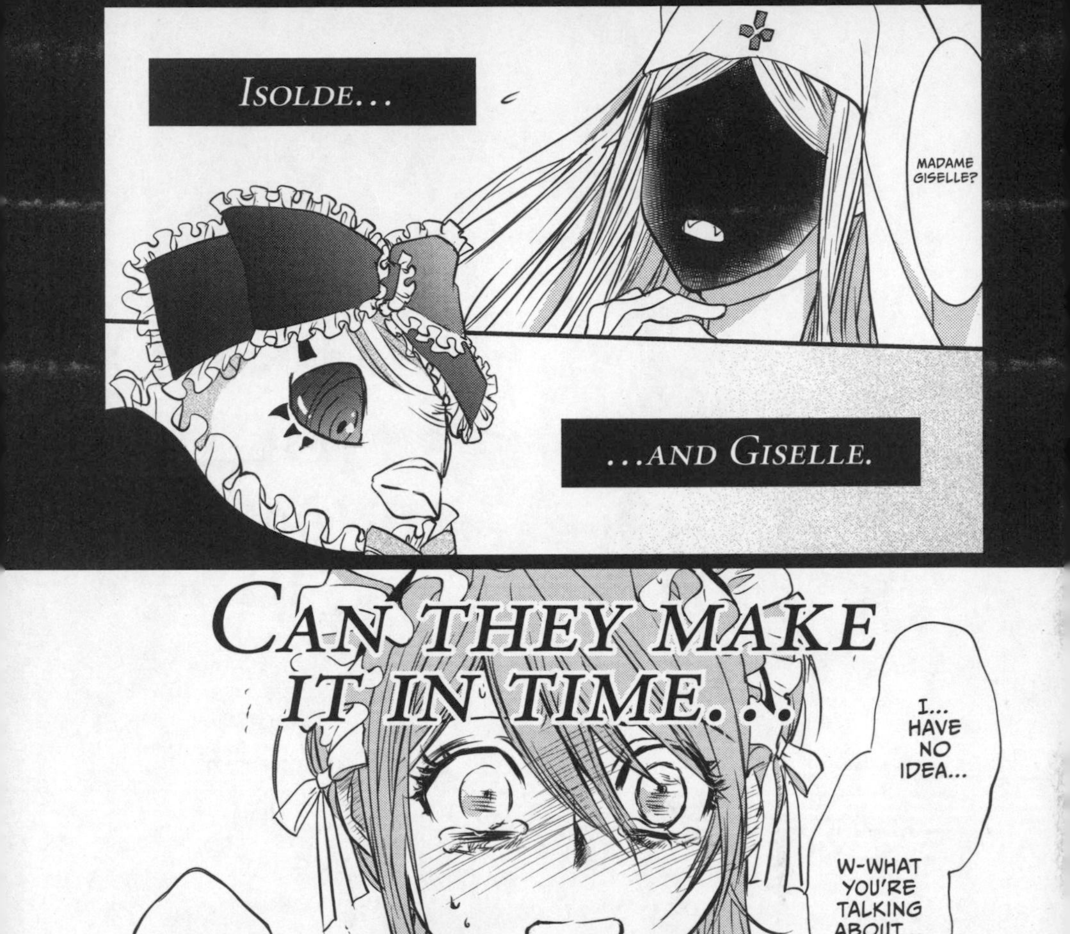
MADAME GISELLE?
ISOLDE...
...AND GISELLE.
CAN THEY MAKE IT IN TIME...
I... HAVE NO IDEA...
W-WHAT YOU'RE TALKING ABOUT...
I'D N-NEVER EVEN DREAM OF SUCH A THING...
...TO SAVE BELLE?

BEAUTY AND THE BEAST OF PARADISE LOST 4

Knight of the Ice ©Yayoi Ogawa/Kodansha Ltd.

SKATING THRILLS AND ICY CHILLS WITH THIS NEW TINGLY ROMANCE SERIES!

A rom-com on ice, perfect for fans of *Princess Jellyfish* and *Wotakoi*. Kokoro is the talk of the figure-skating world, winning trophies and hearts. But little do they know... he's actually a huge nerd! From the beloved creator of *You're My Pet* (*Tramps Like Us*).

Chitose is a serious young woman, working for the health magazine *SASSO*. Or at least, she would be, if she wasn't constantly getting distracted by her childhood friend, international figure skating star Kokoro Kijinami! In the public eye and on the ice, Kokoro is a gallant, flawless knight, but behind his glittery costumes and breathtaking spins lies a secret: He's actually a hopelessly romantic otaku, who can only land his quad jumps when Chitose is on hand to recite a spell from his favorite magical girl anime!

PERFECT WORLD

Rie Aruga

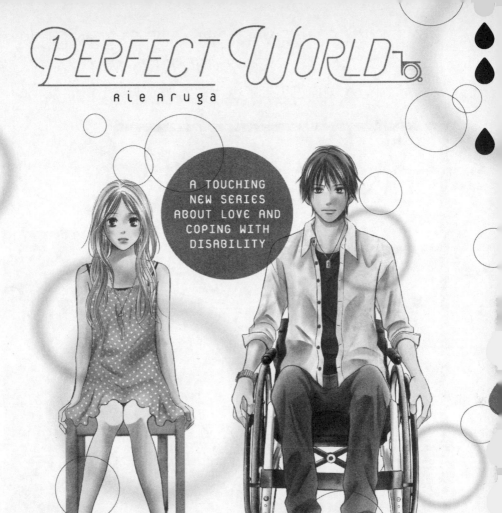

A TOUCHING NEW SERIES ABOUT LOVE AND COPING WITH DISABILITY

An office party reunites Tsugumi with her high school crush Itsuki. He's realized his dream of becoming an architect, but along the way, he experienced a spinal injury that put him in a wheelchair. Now Tsugumi's rekindled feelings will butt up against prejudices she never considered — and Itsuki will have to decide if he's ready to let someone into his heart...

"Depicts with great delicacy and courage the difficulties some with disabilities experience getting involved in romantic relationships... Rie Aruga refuses to romanticize, pushing her heroine to face the reality of disability. She invites her readers to the same tasks of empathy, knowledge and recognition."
—Slate.fr

"An important entry [in manga romance]... The emotional core of both plot and characters indicates thoughtfulness... [Aruga's] research is readily apparent in the text and artwork, making this feel like a real story."
—Anime News Network

KC KODANSHA COMICS

A SMART, NEW ROMANTIC COMEDY FOR FANS OF *SHORTCAKE CAKE* AND *TERRACE HOUSE*!

A romance manga starring high school girl Meeko, who learns to live on her own in a boarding house whose living room is home to the odd (but handsome) Matsunaga-san. She begins to adjust to her new life away from her parents, but Meeko soon learns that no matter how far away from home she is, she's still a young girl at heart — especially when she finds herself falling for Matsunaga-san.

Something's Wrong With Us

NATSUMI ANDO

The dark, psychological, sexy shojo series readers have been waiting for!

A spine-chilling and steamy romance between a Japanese sweets maker and the man who framed her mother for murder!

Following in her mother's footsteps, Nao became a traditional Japanese sweets maker, and with unparalleled artistry and a bright attitude, she gets an offer to work at a world-class confectionary company. But when she meets the young, handsome owner, she recognizes his cold stare...

KC
KODANSHA COMICS

A Kodansha Comics Trade Paperback Original
Beauty and the Beast of Paradise Lost 3 copyright © 2020 Kaori Yuki
English translation copyright © 2021 Kaori Yuki

All rights reserved.

Published in the United States by Kodansha Comics, an imprint of
Kodansha USA Publishing, LLC, New York.

Publication rights for this English edition arranged through
Kodansha Ltd., Tokyo.

First published in Japan in 2020 by Kodansha Ltd., Tokyo
as *Rakuen no bijo to yaju*, volume 3.

ISBN 978-1-64651-294-2

Printed in the United States of America.

www.kodansha.us

1st Printing
Translation: Rose Padgett
Lettering: Phil Christie
Editing: Vanessa Tenazas
Kodansha Comics edition cover design by Phil Balsman

Publisher: Kiichiro Sugawara

Director of publishing services: Ben Applegate
Associate director of publishing operations: Stephen Pakula
Publishing services managing editors: Alanna Ruse, Madison Salters
Production managers: Emi Lotto, Angela Zurlo
Logo and character art ©Kodansha USA Publishing, LLC